PECULIAR
INSTITUTION

PECULIAR INSTITUTION

America's Death Penalty

in an Age of Abolition

DAVID GARLAND

THE BELKNAP PRESS OF HARVARD UNIVERSITY PRESS
Cambridge, Massachusetts
2010

Library of Congress Cataloging-in-Publication Data

Garland, David.
Peculiar institution : America's death penalty in an age of abolition / David Garland.
p.   cm.
Includes bibliographical references and index.
ISBN 978-0-674-05723-4 (alk. paper)
1. Capital punishment—United States—History.   2. Discrimination in capital
punishment—United States—History.   3. Decentralization in government—United
States—History.   4. Power (Social sciences)—United States—History.   I. Title.
HV8699.U5.G36   2010
364.660973—dc22   2010019967

For Anne, Kasia, and Amy

Contents

PECULIAR
INSTITUTION

Prologue

The Exemplary Execution

The following report appeared on Thursday, October 26, 2006, in the pages of an American newspaper:

Killer of 5 Florida Students Is Executed

Gainesville, Fla., Oct. 25—*The serial killer who gruesomely murdered five college students here in 1990 was put to death on Wednesday by lethal injection, and relatives of his victims said afterward that they could finally feel the beginnings of relief.*

Danny H. Rolling, 52, was pronounced dead at 6:13 P.M. at Florida State Prison in Starke, about 30 miles northeast of Gainesville. Witnesses said he stared toward them and sang a hymn-type song just before the drugs were administered.

"Maybe now that we don't have this on us," said Dianna Hoyt, the stepmother of one victim, "we can try and relax and live with the memories we have of our children and be at peace."

Mr. Rolling was 36 when he arrived in Gainesville shortly before the fall semester began at the University of Florida, a drifter with a criminal past who pitched a tent in some woods near campus. He followed two freshman roommates, Sonja Larson, 18, and Christina Powell, 17, to their off-campus apartment, raped Miss Powell, repeatedly stabbed both women with a hunting knife and mutilated their bodies.

The police discovered them on Aug. 26, after Miss Powell's parents re-

ported that their daughter was not answering her door or phone. Later
that night, the police found Christa Hoyt, 18, dead in her off-campus du-
plex. Mr. Rolling had raped and stabbed her, severed her head and placed
it on a shelf.

The next day, Tracy Paules and Manuel Taboada, both 23, were discovered stabbed to death in their apartment, not far from where the other
killings took place. Mr. Rolling attacked Mr. Taboada, a former high
school football player, as he slept, then killed Miss Paules. . . .

Gainesville, a small city of pretty homes and live oaks, was crippled
with dread. The campus shut down for a week and many of the 34,000
students scrambled home, some never to return. Others bought baseball
bats and Mace, put triple locks on their doors or slept in shifts. . . .

[I]n January 1991, the police discovered Mr. Rolling in a county jail
south of Gainesville, awaiting trial in a supermarket robbery. He initially
denied committing the murders, but DNA tests ultimately showed he was
responsible. He pleaded guilty on the eve of his trial in 1994, telling the
judge, "There are some things that you just can't run from."

Mr. Rolling was also believed guilty of three slayings in his hometown,
Shreveport, La., but was never tried for those crimes. He attributed his
behavior to abuse by his father, a police officer, and to an evil alter ego.

In prison, he drew disturbing pictures and wrote a graphic book, "The
Making of a Serial Killer," with a woman who was his fiancée for a time.
For his last meal, he asked for lobster tail and butterfly shrimp, prison of-
ficials said.

Across the road from the prison, dozens of onlookers gathered into
groups for and against the death penalty. It was perhaps the largest turn-
out for an execution here since that of Ted Bundy, who was put to death
at Florida State Prison in 1989 after being suspected of murdering more
than 30 young women across the nation. . . .

Mr. Rolling was the third death row inmate executed here in recent
weeks, and like the others he had filed a late appeal claiming that the lethal injection procedure was so painful as to be unconstitutional.

But Bill Cervone, the state attorney for the Eighth Judicial Circuit and
a witness to the execution, said Mr. Rolling's death did not seem punishing enough.

"To watch his death in such an antiseptic and clinical environment con-
vinces me that the punishment does not fit that crime," Mr. Cervone said.
"We are, however, a society of laws, and the law governed what we carried out this evening."

Laurie Lahey, the sister of Tracy Paules, said she had been reluctant to
witness Mr. Rolling's death but felt exhilarated afterward.

"Once everything quiets down, I'll think about Tracy and I'll be sad,"
she said. "But right now, he's gone. He's gone."

This is a capital case report, a real-life death penalty story, written by Abby Goodnough for the *New York Times*. Danny Rolling's case may not be typical of death penalty cases in contemporary America—outside of media reports, mundane robbery-murders are more common than macabre serial killings—but it is, in a certain respect, exemplary.

Capital cases most often make national news nowadays because they raise claims of innocence, inadequate assistance of counsel, or racial injustices; because DNA exonerates the accused; because execution methods are challenged as "cruel and unusual"; or because botched executions and their aftermaths result in public outrage. When capital punishment features in the news today, it is often as a "broken system," an institution subject to challenge and rebuke. The Rolling case appears, in contrast, as a striking example of the death penalty being "properly" imposed and "properly" carried out as punishment for murderous acts of breathtaking horror and wickedness. To read the *Times* report is to get a sense of what the death penalty is, at least officially, supposed to be. Florida Governor Jeb Bush said of Rolling, "He is the poster child . . . of why there should be a death penalty."[1] We might think of Rolling's execution, in turn, as a poster image of the modern American death penalty, imposed and administered as the law and the authorities intended.

A violent career criminal turned notorious serial killer ("the Gainesville Ripper"), convicted of horrendous capital crimes (multiple counts of murder, rape, torture, mutilation, and necrophilia) after due process of law (Rolling was represented by "the state's outstanding public defender"; his guilty plea was backed by a confession and DNA; his multiple appeals were duly heard and turned down), is provided a last meal ("lobster tail and butterfly shrimp") and gently put to death by lethal injection ("He relaxed, went to sleep, did not feel anything"), while grieving family members express exhilaration and relief and officials talk of what "a society of laws" requires.[2]

Unmarred by suspicions of race discrimination (like most American serial killers, Rolling was white); untouched by claims of actual innocence, inadequate assistance of counsel, or disproportionality; and unspoiled by any hitch in the execution protocol, Rolling's case gives us a glimpse of the death penalty at its most legitimate, its most unproblematic, and, if the reports are to be believed—about his eve-of-death confession to other murders, about the feelings of relief experienced by the victims' families, and about its cleansing effect on the local community—at its most effective.[3]

But if the Rolling case is exemplary, in its way, it is certainly not unproblematic. No death penalty case today ever is.

On October 4, 2006, a few days after Governor Bush signed the execution warrant, Rolling's attorneys filed a motion claiming that their client had been denied access to relevant records, that the lethal injection protocol was unconstitutional, and that newly discovered evidence demonstrated that his execution would constitute cruel and unusual punishment. These claims were summarily denied by the Florida district court and, on appeal, by the Florida Supreme Court. On Wednesday, October 25, the U.S. Supreme Court voted seven to two not to grant a stay of execution pending an appeal challenging the method of execution. (The same challenge would eventually be taken up by the Supreme Court the following year, leading to lengthy reprieves for dozens of other inmates facing execution.) On the day before Rolling's execution, the National Coalition to Abolish the Death Penalty distributed the following press release:

Do Not Execute Danny Rolling

Danny Rolling is set to be executed by the state of Florida on October 25. In late August 1990, Rolling went on a killing spree in Gainesville. Rolling broke into three apartments in the area belonging to five college students, whom he went on to assault and kill. The victims were Christina Powell, Sonja Larson, Christa Hoyt, Manuel Taboada, and Tracy Paules.

While these crimes are heinous and inexcusable, the death penalty is not the right choice for Danny Rolling. Rolling grew up in a dysfunctional household with an abusive father. Furthermore, he suffered from emotional and psychological problems, as noted in one appellate judge's opinion at his sentencing. Rolling pleaded guilty in his 1994 trial, where it was established that at the time of his crimes, he had the emotional maturity of a 15-year-old and that he suffered from extreme emotional disturbance.

During his trial, Rolling and his defense team tried to get a change of venue for the trial, which was denied. His story had been sensationalized by the media, so that he could not have received a fair trial where jury members had no bias about the crimes. Furthermore, several pieces of evidence, including statements made without counsel present and items gathered without a warrant from Rolling's place of residence were allowed in the trial.

Rolling expresses remorse for his crimes, as demonstrated by his confession and eventual guilty plea. His family has a history of mental illness, and his father's abuse influenced his mental instability. Rolling's emo-

*tional state, as well as several errors in his trial, prove that justice will not
come to him in the form of capital punishment.*

Please send appeals to Gov. Jeb Bush on behalf of Danny Rolling.

These appeals by Rolling's attorneys and supporters focused not on his
crime or his guilt but on his person and his punishment. What others had
seen as wickedness and evil they saw as evidence of mental illness and a
damaged personality. Whereas others viewed the death penalty as a just
and fitting punishment, they saw it as an undeserved, legally unsound, and
deeply immoral act.

In America today, a defendant can plead guilty to multiple heinous murders, have his conviction survive years of appellate review and federal
court scrutiny, and even confess to further murders, but his death sentence
will still be regarded by many as unjust and inappropriate. Questions will
be raised about procedural injustice, about mitigation and mental illness,
and about numerous other issues that might put the sentence in doubt.
And, always, behind these challenges, and in the background of every capital case, are the devout objections that the death penalty evokes: "Justice
will not come . . . in the form of capital punishment." Even in its best-case,
"poster-image" examples, America's death penalty is a deeply troubled institution.

If the Rolling story is a best-case illustration for the institution of capital
punishment, the *New York Times* article is also exemplary in its way. The
reports of executions carried by today's newspapers exhibit a definite generic format, and the *Times* story is a model of the genre. All the usual elements are there: disturbing descriptions of the crime and its impact; emotional statements from the victims' kin; the offender's criminal history; the
years of legal struggles and the last-minute appeals; homely details of the
final meal; eyewitness accounts of the execution and the condemned's last
words; interviews with supporters and protesters outside the prison; formal statements from officials. And they all add up to form a satisfying narrative of an evil offender being brought to justice, accorded his legal rights,
then executed with maximum humanity.

In the public telling of Rolling's story, the October 2006 *Times* article
presents the concluding chapter of a tale that had begun decades before,
in 1990, with the initial reports of the Gainesville murders. That narrative continued, in local and national news, with dramatic accounts of
Rolling's arrest, trial, and conviction, followed by more sporadic reports
of postconviction proceedings and Rolling's exploits on death row. Viewed
in the overall arc of its unfolding, this dramatic narrative has the form of a

morality play in two acts—Act I: the crime and the criminal's conviction; Act II: the punishment and its ultimate execution—of which the *Times* report presents the concluding scene and epilogue.

Rolling's case is altogether singular in terms of its characters, events, and the twists and turns of its narrative, which is what makes it fresh and compelling as a news story. But the plot of the play, the *dramatis personae* involved, and the moral issues at stake are all too familiar, being repeated time after time in a standard performance that is well known to its audience and has a special place in contemporary American culture. In Rolling's case, as in all the others, the morality play performed for the watching public begins with reports of a violent murder and ends in eyewitness accounts of a judicial execution. The dramatic relation between these paired killings—the murder and the execution—draws the audience in, ensuring popular interest, emotional involvement, and continuing engagement with the story. As the sociologist Emile Durkheim long ago observed, news of atrocious crimes provokes passionate outrage, generates collective excitement, and produces powerful narratives that concentrate public sentiment and give it force and focus. Capital cases—cases in which the death penalty is invoked—double this dramatic effect. The story of the initial killing is intensified by the promise of another, more righteous killing that will settle accounts, express collective anger, and move the public audience cathartically from outrage to relief. That the terrifying mystery of death lies at the heart of these dramas serves only to deepen their emotional impact and extend their metaphoric appeal.

Evidence of this excitement and emotional involvement becomes more apparent if we turn to the stories carried by newspapers less sober than the *Times*. In the breathless reports of the tabloid press, much space is devoted to lurid descriptions of Rolling's crimes: "Rolling posed his mutilated victims in sexually provocative positions and kept body parts as trophies"; "Christa's lifeless head was found sitting on a bookshelf in the bedroom, and her body was propped, sitting up on her bed"—and to expressing community views about his sentence: "I'm an eye-for-an-eye person . . . I think he's getting off so easy it's sickening."[4]

Rolling's deeds and Rolling's death were also put into cultural circulation by other media: TV, film, and the Internet. If we examine these words and images we see dramatic excitement shade into prurient interest and morbid fascination, and the narrative style shift from sober tragedy to sensational entertainment. Rolling wrote and published a book while on death row, in collaboration with a woman to whom he became engaged while in prison. Several books were written by others about him. Several

Hollywood films and TV dramas were produced, depicting his serial killer exploits and his eventual execution. And, inevitably, the publicity about the Rolling case triggered a fresh round of the public debate about the legitimacy of the death penalty.[5] Rolling's story, like each new version of the old morality play, serves as an occasion for the airing of opposing views and the ritualized back and forth of death penalty discourse.

The *New York Times* story, then, is not just a factual report of a case. It is the specific enactment of a generic cultural form. In America today, capital cases are more than legal and political events: they are significant cultural performances as well.

The aim of this book is not to challenge the legitimacy of American capital punishment or to show the death penalty being botched, unfairly imposed, or unjustly administered. Rather, it is to describe and explain the peculiar institution of American capital punishment in all its complex, controversial detail and to explore its relationship to the society that sustains it. To pursue this aim faithfully requires a measure of detachment—a suspension of judgment in the interests of clear-eyed description and objective analysis. To understand the emotive, contested field that today's death penalty has become, we need to put aside partisan argument (to the extent that this is possible) and strive to understand the passions and interests of both sides of the debate, together with the values and attitudes that underlie them.

I have begun with the "official" version of the institution, a story of the death penalty "properly" applied, to show that this conception is as much a part of the institution as the miscarried cases and botched procedures that so often undermine it. I have quoted from the *Times* report to make clear that the practice of capital punishment in America today is as much about discourse as it is about death, and as much about cultural politics as about the punishment of crime. When considering the death penalty, we must conjure an image of the *contemporary* American practice—a lethal injection administered after many years of legal process—for theorists of capital punishment are all too prone to think of the death penalty as if it were still violently executed on a scaffold before a watching crowd.

This heinous case allows the moral and emotional aspects of capital punishment to be rendered a little more complex than they sometimes are when we think about the injustice, or racism, or exonerations associated with the contemporary institution. To understand today's American death penalty—which, despite the French proverb, is not to forgive it—we must try to see its moral power, its emotional appeal, its claim to be doing justice. We must strive to see in it what its supporters claim to see and not dwell exclusively on its injustices and pathologies. As sociologists have long been taught, to explain a practice we must first appreciate what it means for the actors involved.

So the conviction and execution of Danny Rolling are presented here not as a moral tale but as an aid to thinking. In Rolling's disturbing story and its *denouement* we catch a glimpse of a peculiar institution that operates today in America and nowhere else in the Western world. Understanding that institution, and the society that maintains it, is what this book sets out to do.

ONE

A Peculiar Institution

Every people, the proverb has it, loves its own form of violence.
CLIFFORD GEERTZ, *THE INTERPRETATION OF CULTURES,* 1973

As a Philadelphia journalist observed in 1812, "So much has been writ-ten and said on the subject of capital punishments that it seems al-most like presumptive vanity to pursue the topic any further."[1] Yet after two and a half centuries of moral debate and four decades of constitu-tional argument, the one thing that seems indisputable is that the death penalty produces an endless stream of discourse. Our bookstore shelves and law library stacks groan under the weight of writing provoked by this institution, and still the ink continues to flow. The rate at which we put of-fenders to death may have declined over the last few centuries, but there has been no let up in the practice of talking and writing about it. In twenty-first-century America, capital punishment remains a perennial sub-ject of commentary and debate.

Perhaps all this talk should not surprise us. After all, the institution of capital punishment raises profound moral questions and possesses more than its share of controversial characteristics. As one scholar of criminal law noted, "Only someone who is morally obtuse could fail to perceive how charged the issue of capital punishment is with questions of funda-mental value."[2] And it is no doubt true that the death penalty poses, in the starkest form, a deliberate choice between life and death in situations where killing is neither necessary nor unavoidable. Perhaps we ought not to find it strange that it prompts so much discussion.

Perhaps. But bear in mind that American society does not always respond to moral problems by making them topics of prolix discourse and debate. The moral attention of Americans is highly selective. As a society, the United States does not spill so much ink over each individual fatality in war, or each life cut short by poverty, though these deaths are often "unnecessary" and "avoidable," and those who die are certainly no more deserving of their fate than convicted killers. Yet if a murder suspect is capitally charged or a convicted murderer is sentenced to death, Americans somehow contrive to make this headline news, an occasion for a flurry of commentaries, and a rehearsal of all the familiar arguments for and against the institution.

Or compare the endless talk about capital punishment with the relative silence with which American public discourse (and Supreme Court case law) passes over extraordinarily severe prison sentences and the mass imprisonment they produce, even though incarceration affects tens of millions of individuals and families in the United States while death sentences are imposed on fewer than 120 offenders each year. Whatever else capital punishment does or does not do, it certainly functions as an incitement to talk.

The subject of capital punishment seems to invite, even to compel, the repetitive restatement of arguments and counterarguments that are all too familiar. For centuries now, it has given rise to a set-piece debate that contrasts the New Testament with the Old, Enlightenment with Tradition, humanity with justice, and restraint with retribution. There is very little in today's debates that would not be familiar to those who addressed the issue 200 years ago, as a glance at the writings of Cesare Beccaria, Jeremy Bentham, or Benjamin Rush will quickly reveal. And although the emergence of constitutional challenges in the 1960s produced some novel legal arguments—about arbitrary application, "evolving standards of decency," and the unreliability of a sanction that is so rarely used—even these propositions now seem commonplace.[3]

Yet the recent history of capital punishment has taken a surprising turn that raises a whole new set of questions. Increasingly over the last thirty years, the issue of American capital punishment has taken on a new character and urgency. The familiar moral-political debate continues, of course, with the same arguments being traded back and forth. But recent developments have produced a new challenge for analysis: the need to make sense of the peculiar institution that has emerged in the United States since the 1970s. What was once a familiar moral debate has been reborn as a sociological and historical problem: how to explain the peculiarities of America's twenty-first-century death penalty?

The contemporary American death penalty is, in several respects, a peculiar institution. At the start of the twenty-first century, the federal government and dozens of states continue to use capital punishment at a time when all other Western nations have decisively abandoned it. The "age of abolition"—as we might name the recent decades when abolitionism became standard throughout the West—has made America an anomaly, the last remaining holdout in a historical period that has seen the Western nations embrace abolitionism as a human rights issue and a mark of civilization. Yet paradoxically, several American states abolished capital punishment long before the European nations, and one of them—Michigan—has been continuously abolitionist since 1846, making it a world leader in the abolitionist cause.[4] Indeed, for the 200 years between the 1770s and the 1970s, America was in lockstep with the other Western nations as they gradually withdrew from the scaffold and disavowed the executioner. Why did America suddenly diverge from the long-term reform trajectory in which it had played such a leading role?[5]

America today practices capital punishment in a peculiar form that is difficult to understand or to justify even for its committed supporters. American legislators continue to pass capital punishment statutes, American courts continue to sentence murderers to death, and on forty or fifty occasions each year, mostly in the Southern states, executions are authorized and convicted offenders are put to death. This is what people mean when they say America is a "retentionist" nation where capital punishment still exists. But most of the thirty-five states with the death penalty rarely carry out their threat to put capital murderers to death, and the vast majority of convicted killers end up serving a life-long prison sentence. Wherever capital proceedings are undertaken, the process is skirted round with procedural, evidentiary, and appellate rules that are much more elaborate than in noncapital cases. And even in the rare instance when a death sentence is imposed—which occurs in less than 1 percent of homicides—the majority of these death sentences are never executed because the sentence is overturned, the prisoner is exonerated, or the authorities refrain from setting an execution date.[6] The primary cause of death for capitally convicted murderers is not judicial execution: it is "natural causes."

Capital punishment in America today is a story of a legal norm combined with its widespread evasion. The law stipulates that convicted capital murderers may be put to death. In practice, most capital murderers are not put to death, and those who are eventually executed go to their deaths after a very long process of legal contestation and uncertainty. The overall picture looks less like the simple "retention" of capital punishment and more like an extreme form of institutional ambivalence, expressed in a uniquely cumbersome and conflicted set of arrangements. As a federal judge put it in 1995, "[W]e have the worst of all worlds. We have capital punishment, and the enormously expensive machinery to support it, but we don't really have the death penalty."[7]

Another peculiar aspect of the American death penalty is that it continues to operate in a racialized manner, disproportionately targeting black offenders whose victims were white. Before the case of *Furman v Georgia* (1972), in which the Supreme Court ruled that arbitrary imposition of the death penalty constituted cruel and unusual punishment, racial bias was more extensive and more blatant, involving "race-of-defendant" discrimination. (Black defendants were more likely, other things being equal, to be sentenced to death than were white defendants.) Since *Furman,* discrimination has become more subtle—chiefly involving "race of victim"—but it has continued nevertheless.[8] As Thomas Laqueur observes, "capital punishment in the United States subsists—inescapably—in a miasma of race."[9] This generally acknowledged fact evokes widespread criticism and has prompted many commentators to view contemporary capital punishment as a continuation of the nation's history of racial violence and lynching.

One hundred years ago, the formerly slave-owning Southern states of America attracted worldwide criticism as the locus of hundreds of spectacular public lynchings and burnings at the stake. At these notorious events, crowds of white townspeople looked on as lynch mobs tortured and burned black men and women accused of heinous crimes. Following the lynching, the dismembered black body would be displayed for all to see, and picture postcards would be mailed to friends and relatives as mementoes of the occasion.[10] Today these same Southern states are once more attracting international criticism, this time for their practice of executing offenders, a disproportionate number of whom are African American and have been sentenced to death without the benefit of adequate legal representation. In the minds of many people, today's death penalty—which is more than ever before an institution of the Southern states—carries clear traces of racial lynching and is inextricably linked to the "peculiar institution" of slavery that lies at the root of this blood-stained history.[11] As one observer remarked, "When we think about the death penalty, we think . . . of black victims and white mobs, of black defendants and white juries, of slave codes and public hangings."[12]

But these relationships between past and present are more easily sensed than specified. The vague understanding that there is a connection between nineteenth-century lynchings and twenty-first-century capital punishment has trouble coming to terms with the following facts. Whereas lynchings operated outside state law, as acts of summary justice, today's executions proceed within a legal framework, involving lengthy trials, multiple appeals, and many years of postconviction process. Whereas spectacle lynchings were designed to maximize ceremonial display, physical pain, and bodily degradation, today's executions are conducted out of sight of the crowd, according to a protocol that aims to avoid physical suffering, leave the prisoner's body unmarked, and prohibit the circulation of photographic images. Whereas lynching was, after the Civil War, concentrated in the Southern states, capital punishment laws operate today in thirty-five states, spread across much of the country. (It is the *execution* of these laws, not the laws themselves, that is heavily concentrated in the South.) And whereas Southern lynch mobs targeted blacks, it is nevertheless true that most of those executed today are in fact white, albeit poor, badly represented whites. The evidence of race discrimination in capital punishment today mostly concerns the more subtle race-of-victim discrimination, rather than the crude race-of-defendant bias.[13] If there are continuities linking today's death penalty with the popular justice and racial violence of the past—and such continuities seem undeniable—there are also crucial differences that make the nexus between communal lynching and capital punishment less straightforward than is commonly understood.

The American death penalty is *peculiar* insofar as it is the only capital punishment system still in use in the West. It is *peculiar* insofar as the forms through which it is now enacted seem ambivalent and poorly adapted to the stated purposes of criminal justice. And it is *peculiar* insofar as it seems, somehow, to be connected to the South's "peculiar institution" of slavery and its legacy of racial violence, though the precise relationship is by no means clear.[14] Explaining these peculiarities requires a comparative historical analysis, a close study of institutional and cultural forms, and a detailed investigation of the legal legacy of lynching.

The Capital Punishment Complex

To understand today's death penalty we have to think in new ways about an institution that we appear to know all too well. To do so requires us to step outside that institution and view capital punishment from a distance. Instead of engaging with the institution, as everyone feels compelled (and surprisingly competent) to do, the social science strategy is to disengage, to avoid taking positions *within* the field of debate and instead to chart how the institution—and its debates—appear when viewed from the outside.

From this perspective we can regard capital punishment not as a moral dilemma to be addressed or a policy issue to be resolved but as a social fact to be explained. And we can focus less on the death penalty as a matter of principle and more on the complex field of institutional arrangements, social practices, and cultural forms through which American death penalties are actually administered. The object of study thus ceases to be "the death penalty" as such and becomes instead the "capital punishment complex"—the totality of discursive and nondiscursive practices through which capital punishment is enacted, represented, and experienced in American criminal justice and in American society.

At the start of the twenty-first century, the death penalty remains popular with a majority of Americans and a matter of serious moral commitment for many. But it is also opposed by a substantial minority, making it deeply controversial, within the United States as well as abroad. In penological terms, it is a minor institution, directly affecting a minuscule percentage of criminal cases. But in the public domain it remains highly visible, a subject on which everyone has an opinion. And though its constitutional validity is affirmed by the highest court in the land, its administration closely regulated by law, and its execution undertaken by state officials in a professional, bureaucratic manner, it is nevertheless enveloped in an unmistakable aura of transgression, anxiety, and embarrassment—particularly among those who actually carry out the practice. (In many states outside the South, executions occur only when death row inmates abandon their appeals and "volunteer" to be put to death.) For all these reasons, it is a rich subject for cultural analysis, especially when cultural analysis is understood as a way to get at questions of power and social relations.

Sociology strives for finely detailed description rather than for ethical critique or moral assessment. Its first concern (though not necessarily its final one) is to understand what is really going on, to learn to see things from the point of view of the participants and the social world they occupy, rather than to impose the judgments of the writer and his or her community. So rather than engage in the legal and normative debates that swirl around the death penalty, this approach regards these debates as an intrinsic part of the institution and analyzes them accordingly.

Public engagement with capital punishment—critiques, apologias, exposés, expressed attitudes for and against, opinion polls, and so on—is normally a matter of taking sides, joining the debate, playing the game. Moral criticism and defense, legal arguments for and against, political campaigns for abolition and against abolition, together with the extensive commentary that always accompanies these contests, are not incidental to the institution of capital punishment: they are intrinsic elements of the social fact that needs to be explained. Discourse may sometimes seem insubstantial and unimportant, especially when measured against the physicality of putting a person to death. But words, ideas, and images are real forces in the social field and need to be understood as such. If human beings are deliberately put to death by the state in a liberal-democratic society, it is always because certain words, ideas, and images have made this possible. These "forces in the practice of power" form part of the institution that needs to be explained.[15]

Viewing the clashing values and arguments of the death penalty debate as integral parts of the object of study rather than as opposing sides between which one has to choose brings certain features more clearly into view. From this vantage point we more readily notice the repetitive nature of death penalty discourse and the excess of talk that characterizes the capital punishment complex. We notice the curious fact that many of the practices deemed "cruel and unusual" by critics are nevertheless remarkably "civilized" in form—lethal injection is a good case in point. Viewing matters in a more detached, historical way, we notice many unacknowledged continuities that link America's death penalty history to that of other Western nations—as we will see, America was long regarded as typical rather than exceptional in this respect. This approach also reveals the historical ironies that connect capital punishment not just to America's most shameful legacies (slavery, lynching, racial violence) but also to its most cherished values (democracy, localism, individual responsibility). Finally, a social science approach makes more apparent the positive uses of capital punishment, the opportunities it offers not just for professional success or political mobilization but also for profit, for cultural consumption, and for certain pleasures such as vengeance, *schadenfreude,* and the vicarious enjoyment of the death of demonized others—uses that are rarely part of today's public discussions but are vital to the institution's contemporary existence. There is plenty of evidence to support each of these observations, but they remain largely unremarked in contemporary debates because they fit poorly with the two moral viewpoints that dominate discussion and structure the field of death penalty debate.

The perspective pursued here develops a detailed description of death penalty practices and an explanatory account of their sources, uses, and meanings. In place of moral and legal argument, it provides historical and sociological analysis. Instead of discussing capital punishment in general it analyzes American capital punishment in particular. And rather than argue for the institution's reform or its retention, it describes exactly how it came to be retained and reformed in its present form. What is offered here, in short, is neither apology nor critique but a sociological history of an institution that forms a puzzling part of our present.

According to Michel Foucault, a "history of the present" focuses on an aspect of our contemporary world that has become somehow problematic, incoherent, or unintelligible.[16] Using historical materials and "genealogical" analysis, such an inquiry seeks to show how the capital punishment complex came to exist in its present form. It seeks to uncover historical processes and political conflicts that are now obscured beneath the day-to-day practices of the institution. In producing such an account, and reconnecting the institution with the values, interests, and power relations out of which it emerged, a history of the present may change our perception of what that institution is and how, in fact, it functions. Paradoxically, then, a historical inquiry that strives to be detached and objective may nevertheless transform our evaluations of the contemporary institution—not by converting others to the writer's viewpoint but by altering the perceived character of the phenomenon in question.

A sociological look at punishment uses the study of society to understand punishment, but it also uses punishment to understand society. Running alongside the primary inquiry about capital punishment is a related inquiry about American society, an inquiry that seeks, however tentatively, to use the peculiar institution of capital punishment as a window onto American culture and social relations. By attending to the ways in which legal, political, and cultural actors have engaged with the death penalty and shaped it into its current form, we catch some glimpses of how America is put together, how it deals with its chronic disagreements, and how it coheres in the face of conflict and contradiction. This is a "law and society" project that works in both directions—studying a social context to better understand a legal institution, but also using a legal institution to better understand a society.

To frame matters this way—to suppose that the death penalty is somehow revealing about America—is not to assume that American culture is especially punitive or bloodthirsty. Capital punishment has been a feature of every nation and is still practiced in most of the world's societies, even in a few developed, democratic ones such as Japan and India. There is no need to posit a more-than-usually punitive culture to explain a practice that continues to hold popular appeal for the publics of virtually every nation.

Large-scale developmental processes have shaped the history of capital punishment throughout the Western world, but every nation nevertheless engages with capital punishment in its own distinctive way. Broad historical processes have transformed the death penalty in similar directions all across the West, but if we look closely, the governmental structures, political struggles, and cultural dynamics of each individual nation (and often of regions *within* nations) are what shape the particular form of capital punishment that exists in a specific place at a specific time. In analyzing the institution up close, paying regard to its distinctive forms and its multiple meanings, we get a tangible sense of the society and history that produced it as well as of the political and cultural fields in which it is deployed.

The American death penalty has, for the best part of two centuries, been the terrain of continuous political, cultural, moral, and legal struggle. The peculiar institution that has emerged out of these struggles bears clear traces of the interests, values, and processes out of which it has been constructed. By observing the American death penalty up close, we can identify some of the major struggles that have shaped modern America and some of the fault lines that define its social landscape, as well as the diverse localities and regional cultures that compose this complex nation. And by observing it from a distance—placing capital punishment's American history in the broader comparative context of its Western history as a whole—we can trace the ways in which this nation both is and is not similar to the other nations that compose the Western world.

Against Conventional Wisdom

The conventional wisdom that shapes the way we think about the death penalty consists of a set of received ideas generated, in large part, from the debate that surrounds the institution. These ideas are rarely plain wrong or totally unfounded, but they are mostly half-truths that are partial in their perceptions and partisan in their judgments. Let us look at these familiar ideas more closely, using a critique of their misperceptions to move toward a more appropriate analytical perspective:

Today's death penalty is a vestige of a former age, an anachronistic holdover from a previous era. Contemporary capital punishment is often characterized as an archaic institution that inexplicably survives in a modern environment to which it is fundamentally ill suited and from which it will soon become extinct. Supreme Court Justice John Paul Stevens refers to it as "more and more anachronistic." Charles Black calls it a "vestigial cruelty." Hugo Bedau says that "the death penalty may at last be generally recognized for the anachronism it is—a vestigial survivor from an earlier era." Sunil Dutta supposes it to be "no less than a vestige of medievalism," and says that "when it comes to capital punishment we are still mired in the Dark Ages." And Thorsten Sellin long ago concluded that it is "an archaic custom of primitive origin." This death-penalty-as-dinosaur conception is spelled out explicitly by the cultural historian Thomas Laqueur: "The death penalty as it is carried into practice today is like an endangered species brought back from the brink of extinction, a creature from an earlier age making its way in a very different time from when it ruled the earth."[17]

Important truths are contained within this recurring characterization. Capital punishment is indeed a long-standing practice that has been rendered problematic by the evolving social structures and cultural commitments of modern liberal-democratic states. The death penalty was more widely used, less contested, and more fully integrated in earlier times and in less developed societies. The American institution has persisted for decades after it disappeared elsewhere in the Western world, and this survival is to some extent a matter of contingent historical events.

These are valid insights, but what is misleading here is the idea that the institution lacks a contemporary habitat and support system, and is maladapted to its current environment. This assumption prompts us to think about the death penalty in a manner in which we never would think about other contemporary institutions—that is, by means of models and exemplars drawn from a much earlier historical period. The dominant theoretical account—largely derived from the work of Michel Foucault—views today's death penalty as a contradiction: an archaic, sovereign punishment surviving in a modern welfare state, the ancient power to kill mixed up with the modern politics of life. When sociologists discuss capital punishment in contemporary America, the accounts they typically invoke—those of Foucault, Durkheim, Gatrell, or Hay—are based on the workings of capital punishment in eighteenth-century Europe and not on the distinctive practices of twenty-first-century America. For this standard account, the death penalty is a practice standing out of time, a poorly adapted institution without roots in contemporary forms of life.

A corrective to this standard account is the more valid picture of an institution that has been remade and effectively adapted to its late–modern American environment. Most of its forms and arrangements are of recent origin and have been crafted to fit the culture and sensibilities of the present. Far from being an atavistic survival, doomed to disappear, American capital punishment has adapted in order to survive. The adoption of lethal injections to replace more openly violent and painful execution methods is a case in point, as is the recent abolition of capital punishment for juvenile and mentally deficient offenders. And in that process of adaptation, the death penalty has developed new forms, new functions, and new social meanings—few of which are well captured by the standard account.

We need to think about capital punishment not as a lumbering dinosaur with an ancient physiology but instead as a mobile assemblage of practices, discourses, rituals, and representations that has evolved over time in response to the demands of the social environment and the pressure of competing forces. Doing so reminds us that capital punishment has a history that shapes its forms as well as its uses. And it obliges us to take account of its contemporary incarnation—the institutional arrangements, legal procedures, discursive figures, and dramatic forms that actually exist today.

The arrangements through which American capital punishment is currently enacted undermine the death penalty's objectives. Today's death penalty serves no identifiable function and accomplishes nothing. It is, in the usual phrase, "merely symbolic." This familiar claim was put precisely by the sociologist Thorsten Sellin when he said that, "as now used, capital punishment performs none of the utilitarian functions claimed by its supporters, nor can it ever be made to serve such functions." The historian Gary Wills says the same thing when he describes how the death penalty has ceased to be a vital instrument of state power and penal justice and has become, instead, a hollowed-out shell, devoid of positive meaning and social purpose. Wills lists more than a dozen functions traditionally associated with the death penalty—a grim catalogue of utilities he takes from Nietzsche—before going on to show that most of these purposes are no longer credible in contemporary Western society, and that the American institution is so constructed as to undermine those few objectives (such as deterrence and retribution) that continue to make sense.[18]

Wills's points are well taken, and it is easy to show that the criminal justice functions of deterrence and retribution are poorly served by present-day arrangements.[19] But it would be a mistake to end the analysis there. Capital punishment's forms and functions have always been in motion, adapting to the various social environments in which the institution has been deployed. What we now think of as its "core" criminal justice functions (above all, crime control) were once peripheral, just as the forms we assume to be traditional (elaborate public ceremonies, for example) were once new and innovative. We would thus do better to assume that today's system does in fact serve specific functions, even if these are not the ones historians lead us to expect. Instead of rushing to judge the death penalty dysfunctional, we should take the trouble to look for its positive uses and functions, even when these are not officially declared or acknowledged.

We ought to consider the possibility that today's capital punishment is organized and oriented differently from its predecessors—that it is a different social form, not a degenerate one. Instead of supposing that this is a traditional institution that is now rarely used because it serves no purpose, we ought to ask whether its new forms and modes of deployment actually meet specific needs and serve specific functions in today's society. We need a positive theory of what the late-modern death penalty is and does.

The related charge that the death penalty is now "mere symbolism," "illusion," or "gesture" is one that recurs over and over again in the literature, made by frustrated death penalty supporters as well as by abolitionist opponents.[20] The implicit claim that underlies these charges is that because capital punishment appears to lack an instrumental crime-control rationale it must therefore be a mere symbol lacking in substance. But this argument misunderstands the nature of symbolic communication as well as the effectiveness of modern death penalty discourse. The idea that "symbolic" is necessarily "noninstrumental" relies on a distinction that makes little sense when penal rituals routinely use symbols of condemnation as instruments of marking, degradation, and control. Worse, this misleading distinction prevents users of the term from following through with a positive analysis of important issues—such as the specific meanings being symbolically communicated; the rhetorical means by which they are being communicated; the audience to whom they are directed; and the effects that these communications produce. To understand the forms and functions of the death penalty today, we have to take communication seriously. We have to regard symbolic measures as effective actions, not as empty gestures or mere talk.

Today's death penalty is an instance of American Exceptionalism: an exception to the international norm that is explained by the fact that America, its history, its people, and its culture are constituted differently from other nations and driven by different dynamics. When commentators try to explain why America retains capital punishment in the context of comprehensive abolition in other Western nations, a popular notion quickly comes to mind. The conventional way they think about this question is to pose a simple opposition between abolition and retention—"the West" (or, more often, "Europe") has abolished the death penalty, while America has retained it—and then to suggest an explanation that accounts for this stark contrast. The trouble is that if the phenomenon to be explained is presented as a simple, binary contrast, the explanations that come to mind tend also to be simplified, binary ones: "Americans" are punitive and "Europeans" are not. Americans are Puritan, or vigilante, or racist, or individualistic, and Europeans are not. These, of course, are the preferred simplicities of the system's critics. But supporters have simplicities of their own:

for them, the explanation is that America is truly democratic and Europe is not, or that Americans continue to be God-fearing while Europeans have lost their faith.[21]

Such oppositions are misleading, quite apart from the dubious explanations that they propose. By aggregating "America" and "Europe," they collapse important internal distinctions, for example, between states such as Michigan, Wisconsin, or Rhode Island, which have been abolitionist since the mid-nineteenth century, and others such as Texas, Oklahoma, or Virginia, which still regularly put offenders to death. Likewise, they fail to distinguish between European nations such as Portugal, which first abolished capital punishment for ordinary crimes in 1867, and others such as France and Britain, which did not repeal their death penalty laws until more than a century later.[22]

The opposition between American retention and European abolition also collapses historical time, relying on a snapshot comparison at a particular moment that may be misleading. In 1972, for example, the U.S. Supreme Court ruled all existing capital statutes unconstitutional while the French authorities decapitated Claude Buffet and Roger Bontems in the courtyard of the Santé Prison.[23] Or consider that "abolition" usually occurs, when it does, not as the abrupt cessation of an unquestioned policy of routine executions but instead as the final stage of a long-term historical process in which the death penalty is incrementally restricted and restrained and displaced by other sanctions such as banishment, galley slavery, transportation, or life imprisonment.[24]

Major historical change usually takes the form of a process rather than an event. It is therefore a mistake to juxtapose "abolition" and "retention"—a binary opposition better suited to moral argument than to historical analysis. This too-stark dichotomy prompts us to think of the American institution as the *opposite* of Western abolition, as if America is altogether unrestrained in its use of the death penalty, like the Stuart monarchs of seventeenth-century Britain or Nazi Germany's criminal courts. But if we view the American system of capital punishment historically and comparatively, on a continuum of death penalty practices that ranges from the most spectacular, widespread, and intense to the most restricted, reformed, and restrained, then it seems clear that the contemporary United States is much closer to the minimalist pole than to the maximalist pole.[25]

American jurisdictions still permit the death penalty, and this is, of course, a significant moral and political fact that properly commands our attention and shapes our debates. But the actual execution of this penalty is comparatively infrequent; its use is subject to close regulation and restraint; and its existence is a matter of legal and political controversy. Such facts ought not to be ignored. Taken together, the point of view of the present and the rhetoric of popular debate are powerful influences, and they push us to regard the U.S. situation as diametrically opposed to that of Europe. But a more historical perspective suggests that, in many important respects, the two continents are not so far apart. If we visualize the full range of death penalty practices as a line of continuous variation, we would picture the European nations (and other Western countries such as Canada, Australia, and New Zealand) as having gradually moved to the minimalist end of the continuum and then finally stepped off altogether, while the United States hovers close to that same end.

These comparative and historical points do not aim to make America's death penalty disappear or to deny its distinctiveness. In the Western world, contemporary America is clearly an outlier in terms of the death penalty as well as other aspects of penal policy. Other Western nations, most notably the United Kingdom, share much of the punitive trajectory and culture of control that emerged in late twentieth-century America, but no other Western nation exhibits the harsh sentencing tariffs, mass imprisonment, or capital punishment that now characterize the United States.[26] So America is different from other Western nations in important respects, and a central aim of current research is to explain these differences, not deny their existence. That there are differences is not at issue. The question is, how best to frame an inquiry that can explain them?

Talk of American Exceptionalism usefully reminds us of the need for a comparative perspective and of the distinctive institutional structures and cultures of which the American polity consists. It reminds us that Americans often think of themselves as "exceptional" and care little for international opinion. But in their conventional usage, notions of "American Exceptionalism" can be unhelpful, particularly when the explanations they offer rely on undifferentiated, ahistorical conceptions of "American culture" or the "American condition."[27] America is not a single place for penological purposes, any more than is "Europe" or "the West." There are major regional and state-level differences within the United States (including differences among the thirty-five so-called death penalty states) which make talk of "American" capital punishment somewhat misleading. Until recently there were also major differences between the capital punishment practices of the European nations, though the fact that all of them are now abolitionist has obliterated these contrasts. Like Tolstoy's families, abolitionist nations all seem alike, but every death penalty nation is retentionist in its own way. The European Union's contemporary abolitionism hides a variety of different histories. Each of the European nations was previously retentionist, and each deployed the death penalty using distinctive national forms in a context of specific local meanings.

In comparative terms, there is no all-encompassing international standard against which the United States is an "exception," no single norm from which America deviates. Nor is there a constant difference between America and other Western nations that persists through time. If the comparisons were made in the 1830s or 1840s (when the mildness of American punishments impressed European visitors such as Charles Dickens and Alexis de Tocqueville); or in the early 1940s (when American executions began a sharp decline and Nazi Germany moved toward "assembly line" executions); or even in the mid-1970s (at which point the United States had gone nearly ten years without a single execution), the ratios would look quite different.[28] Instead of a constant contrast, the historical record shows commonalities and differences, generic developments and distinctive variants. America is in historical motion, as are each of the European nations with which it is being compared, and its relationship to them varies over time, growing now closer, now further apart.

American Exceptionalism is a theory developed to explain a long-term, widespread, and persistent phenomenon—classically, the weakness of the American labor movement and socialist parties—by reference to structural and cultural features of the American nation that are also long-term and persistent.[29] An analytical framework of that kind cannot plausibly be applied to a phenomenon (America's retention of the death penalty following abolition in all other Western nations) that is less than forty years old, is unevenly distributed across the nation's states and regions, and may yet prove to be transient rather than persistent over the long term.

If we replace the conventional dichotomy (capital punishment retained and capital punishment abolished) with a more refined sense of variation along a continuum, then the causal picture alters accordingly. Instead of supposing that qualitatively different effects must have qualitatively different causes, we can think in terms of general causal processes producing varied outcomes in different settings and circumstances. We might then hypothesize that the reasons for death penalty abolition in Europe are much the same as those for death penalty reform in the United States—except that America's anti–death penalty movement, the social forces that propelled it, and the political processes that gave it legal expression were somehow weakened, countered, or constrained in their operation, particularly in the final stages of the movement toward abolition. Instead of thinking in conventional terms of an "exceptional" history and all that this entails, we ought to think of America as a specific variant within a general set: an outlier on some dimensions, in the central tendency on others, but not different in kind. This approach leads away from myopic talk about "exceptions" toward more detailed and more nuanced historical comparisons.

Capital punishment is an exercise of sovereign state power, a top-down display of might, imposed by an all-powerful state authority that monopolizes violence and reserves to itself the power to kill. This final piece of conventional wisdom is the tendency to think about today's American death penalty using a model designed to describe the capital punishments of absolutist states in early-modern Europe. The explanation for this misleading habit of thought lies in the enormous influence exerted by the work of the French philosopher and historian Michel Foucault, whose writings have become a central reference point in academic discussions of the power to punish.[30]

Foucault's unforgettable account of Robert Damiens's execution in 1757 presents a searing image of capital punishment—an archetype that has shaped much thinking about the subject ever since. Here is the passage with which Foucault opens *Discipline and Punish*:

> On 2 March 1757 Damiens the regicide was condemned to "make the *amende honorable* before the main door of the Church of Paris," where he was to be "taken and conveyed in a cart, wearing nothing but a shirt, holding a torch of burning wax weighing more than two pounds"; then, "in the said cart, to the Place de Greve where, on a scaffold that will be erected there, the flesh will be torn from his breasts, arms, thighs and calves with red-hot pincers, his right hand, holding the knife with which he committed the said parricide, burnt with sulphur, and, on those places where the flesh will be torn away, poured molten lead, boiling oil, burning resin, wax and sulphur melted together and then his body drawn and quartered by four horses and his limbs and body consumed by fire, reduced to ashes and his ashes drawn to the winds."[31]

Many readers will know this passage. It is fixed in the theoretical imagination and has shaped much of our thinking about capital punishment in the thirty-odd years since it was first published. If there is a standard account of the meaning and purposes of capital punishment, then this is it.

In his painstaking analysis of Damiens's destruction, Foucault theorizes capital punishment as a ritual of "sovereign state power," a public ceremony in which state actors utilize spectacular violence to display the force and majesty of the sovereign's power. Capital punishment is a means used by the sovereign to create submission, obedience, and social order: a demonstrative act that asserts a monopoly claim over violence in a specific territory. As Foucault explains, "The public execution . . . has a juridico-political function. It is a ceremonial by which a momentarily injured sovereignty is reconstituted. It restores that sovereignty by manifesting it at its most spectacular. The public execution, however hasty and everyday, belongs to a whole series of great rituals in which power is eclipsed and restored."[32]

In this account, the sovereign state is the principal actor in a theater of cruelty. It is the unmoved mover, provoked by the insult of the criminal's offense, but obedient to no one outside of itself. "The people" have merely an auxiliary part in this drama, as onlookers and consumers. They may be supporters, but they are in no way essential to the process. As Foucault puts it, "The vengeance of the people was called upon to become an unobtrusive part of the vengeance of the sovereign. Not that it was in any way fundamental, or that the king had to express in his own way the people's revenge; it was rather that the people had to bring its assistance to the king."[33]

Foucault's account of capital punishment and its political meaning is embedded in a definite political milieu—a predemocratic absolutist monarchy that has little in common with contemporary America. But such is the power of his thought that this conception is frequently viewed as a general theory, applicable to capital punishment wherever it exists.[34] Whenever the death penalty is discussed, especially in academic settings, Foucault's analyses are there in the background, shaping conversations and conceptualizations. The result, in relation to American capital punishment at least, is a serious misunderstanding.

It is certainly true that capital punishment in twenty-first-century America is a state-administered process, conducted in accordance with state and federal law, and carried out by state functionaries. The authority of state law and the force of state power are what guarantee the sanction and render it valid. In that formal-legal sense, the American practice fits the Foucaultian model. But in more substantive respects, Foucault's "sovereign state" model does not fit well at all with American practices and institutions.[35] The American death penalty is never a straightforward assertion of untrammeled sovereign power—there is no such power in the United States. The process of producing an execution in America is always conflicted, with competing authorities pressing against one another. Sovereignty is not "expressed" in these processes, it is asserted, contested, and divided, and there is no single sovereign state that expresses its imperious will. In contrast to Foucault's Eurocentric conception, the American state is a divided, pluralistic entity. In terms of the death penalty, the American state is a self-effacing one, preferring to disappear into the concepts of "the people" and "the law" rather than execute offenders in its own name.

In enacting and administering the death penalty, American state officials point to the jury, the victims, the public, the electorate, *the people,* as the real principals of the action. They represent themselves as the servants of the people, doing the voters' bidding, taking care to observe the due process of law, dutifully carrying out a democratic legal mandate. As the U.S. government declared in 2000, "[W]e believe that in democratic societies the criminal justice system—including the punishment for the most serious and aggravated crimes—should reflect the will of the people freely expressed and appropriately implemented through their elected representatives."[36]

Let me be clear: Foucault is correct to insist that sovereignty and capital punishment are related. For centuries a deep historical association existed between the claim of sovereignty and the power to impose a penalty of death—an association that dates from the formation of the first nation states. And today, in situations where sovereignty is in question, the death penalty can still function as a demonstrative marker of sovereign power.[37] But most liberal democratic governments nowadays have no need of death penalties to demonstrate their autonomy and sovereign command, which suggests that the association is now contingent rather than essential, largely historical rather than contemporary.

If the Foucaultian account misleads when it depicts sovereignty and death as essential corollaries, it also misleads, in the American context, when it characterizes "sovereignty" as an unreconstructed, absolutist phenomenon. Foucault's account leads us to think about sovereignty as a given rather than as an ongoing contest, to associate it with the imperious state and not with its constituent elements and subdivisions (the people, subnational "states," local counties), and to suggest that wherever sovereignty exists, the death penalty must, too.

In modern America, it is a mistake to view capital punishment as a relationship between a sovereign state and a disobedient subject. If we think of capital punishment as an exercise of sovereign state power, we lose any sense of the political processes and popular forces that drive American decision-making at the various levels of local, state, and federal government. We lose sight of the political arrangements that reflect group conflicts and racial hierarchies. And we neglect the energy, the passions, the values, and the pleasures that popular culture injects into the politics of capital punishment. Foucault's account gives us no sense of any of this. To follow this conventional academic wisdom is to move away from most of the important action.

Foucault's framework is instructive in reminding us that the imposition of the death penalty is always, at its core, an exercise of power—and in insisting, more generally, that punishment is "a complex social function" that produces positive effects.[38] But its uneasy relationship with the American case—where the state was never so singular, so sovereign, or so differentiated from the people as it was in eighteenth-century France—makes it unsuitable in the U.S. context. For an understanding of the American case, we need a different way of approaching capital punishment, its use, and its historical development, one in which power is more contested, legal authority less secure, and "the voice of the people" more prominently represented.[39]

We have seen how Foucault's analysis began with the image of Robert Damiens being put to death in the Paris square in 1757. Let us see how a rather different conception might be constructed, moving from a more distinctively American point of departure: not a grand state ceremony but an act of local "popular justice," conducted not in Paris, the capital of France, but in Paris, a small town in Texas.

The Lynching of Henry Smith

An eyewitness account of the lynching of Henry Smith was published in the *New York Times* on February 2, 1893. The lynching had taken place the day before in Paris, Texas. Smith, a black man and former slave, was alleged to have sexually assaulted and murdered a four-year-old white child, the daughter of a local police officer:

Paris, Texas, Feb 1.—*Henry Smith, the negro assailant of four-year-old Myrtle Vance, has expiated, in part, his crime by death at the stake. Ever since the perpetration of his crime this city and the entire surrounding country has been in a frenzy of excitement. When the news came last night that he had been captured, that he had been identified by B. B. Sturgeon, James T. Hicks, and many others of the Paris searching party, the city was joyful over the apprehension of the brute.*

Hundreds of people poured into the city from the adjoining country, and the word passed from lip to lip that the punishment should fit the crime, and that death by fire was the penalty that Smith should pay for the most atrocious murder and outrage in Texas history. Curious and sympathizing alike came on trains and wagons, on horse and foot, to see what was to be done. Whisky shops were closed, and unruly mobs were dispersed. Schools were dismissed by a proclamation from the Mayor, and every thing was done in a business-like manner. Officers saw the futility of checking the passions of the mob, so the law was laid aside, and the citi-

zens took into their own hands the law and burned the prisoner at the stake.

The story of the crime is as follows: On Thursday last Henry Smith, a burly negro, picked up little Myrtle Vance, aged three and a half years, near her father's residence, and, giving her candy to allay her fears, carried her through the central portion of the city to Gibson's pasture, just within the corporate limits. . . .

Arriving at the pasture he first assaulted the babe, and then, taking a little leg in either hand, he literally tore her asunder. He covered the body with leaves and brush, and lay down and slept through the night by the side of his victim. . . .

Upon being questioned, he denied everything. He was kept under heavy guard at Hope last night and later confessed to the crime. This morning he was brought through Texarkana, where 5,000 people awaited the train. Speeches were made by prominent Paris citizens, who asked that the prisoner be not molested by Texarkana people, but that the guard be allowed to deliver him up to the outraged and indignant citizens of Paris. Along the road the forces gathered strength from the various towns, the people crowding upon the platforms and on top of coaches, anxious to see the lynching and the negro who was soon to be delivered to an infuriated mob.

Arriving here at 12 o'clock, the train was met by a surging mass of humanity 10,000 strong. The negro was placed upon a carnival float in mockery of a king upon his throne, and, followed by the immense crowd, was escorted through the city so that all might see. The line of march was up Main Street to the square, down Clarksville Street to Church Street, thence to the open prairie, about three hundred yards from the Texas and Pacific depot. Here Smith was placed upon a scaffold six feet square and ten feet high, securely bound, within the view of all beholders. Here the victim was tortured for fifty minutes by red-hot irons being thrust against his quivering body. Commencing at the foot, the brands were placed against him inch by inch until they were thrust against his face. Then, being apparently dead, kerosene was poured over him, cottonseed hulls placed beneath him, and he was set on fire. Curiosity seekers have carried away already what was left after the memorable event, even to pieces of charcoal.

The negro for a long time after starting on the journey to Paris did not realize his plight. At last, when he was told that he must die by torture, he begged for protection. He was willing to be shot and wanted Marshal Shanklin of Paris to do it. Scarcely had the train reached Paris when his torture began. His clothes were torn off and scattered to the crowd, peo-

ple catching the shreds and putting them away as mementos. The child's
father, her brother, and two uncles then gathered about the Negro as he
lay fastened to the torture platform and thrust hot irons into his quivering
flesh. Every groan from the fiend, every contortion of his body was
cheered by the crowd. . . .

The men of the Vance family having wreaked vengeance, the crowd set
at the fire. The negro rolled and wriggled and tossed out of the mass only
to be pushed back by the people nearest him. He tossed out again, and
was roped and pulled back. Hundreds of people turned away, but the vast
crowd still looked calmly on. People were there from Dallas, Fort Worth,
Sherman, Dennison, Bonham, Texarkana, Fort Smith, Ark. And a party of
fifteen came from Hempstead County, Ark., where he was captured.
When the news was flashed over the wire at every town, anvils boomed
forth the announcement.[40]

The public lynching of Henry Smith, appalling as it was, was by no means
a unique event. Between three and four hundred spectacle lynchings of this
kind took place in the South between 1890 and 1940, along with several
thousand other lynchings that proceeded with less cruelty, smaller crowds,
and little ceremony.[41] These lynchings were not summary killings undertaken for want of a functioning criminal justice system. Public torture
lynchings were a preferred alternative to "official" justice rather than a
necessary substitute for it. All the "crimes"—they were, of course, merely
alleged crimes—that were punished this way were inter-racial atrocities.
They were, in every case, crimes that would have been subject to the death
penalty had the accused been tried and convicted within the official state
process. But for Southern mobs, regular hangings were too good for these
"offenders," regular justice too respectful and too dignified.[42] By reviving
the ancient penalties—of torture, burning, dismemberment, and display—
the lynchers created an aggravated form of capital punishment, more terrible than official justice, and more nearly proportionate to the outrage they
sought to express.

Nor was this a "traditional" or long-standing practice. The public torture lynching was invented at the turn of the twentieth century to communicate impassioned sentiments that could no longer be expressed in the official idiom of the criminal law, and to inflict a level of suffering that had
long since been officially disavowed. The penal excess of these lynchings
was not an accidental effect of a crowd getting carried away—it was at the
very core of the event's penal purpose and political meaning. This characteristic, together with several other elements of these complex events, provide valuable points of departure for thinking about today's death penalty.

As the *New York Times* report shows, these lynchings were enjoyed as good days out, as entertainments—both by the crowds who were there and by readers of the newspaper reports that later appeared. The report describes a "frenzy of excitement," a surging crowd that was alternately "curious," "sympathetic," and "joyful" as it watched the "infuriated" mob do its work. Here we see what Emile Durkheim might describe as a "collective effervescence" provoked by the prospect of the reckoning: an unabashed pleasure in punishment and its associated festivities.

These spectacle lynchings were open, public, communicative events—and the modern media were immediately drawn to them. Newspaper reports like the one above appeared all across the country, carrying photographs as well as eyewitness accounts. They were what we would now call "media events," putting death into discourse, circulating images of dead black bodies, exploiting the tremendous entertainment potential that these lethal dramas possessed. Professional photographers set up shop at the scene and did a brisk business selling photo-souvenirs. Picture postcards, showing black-and-white images of the lynchings and their victims, were purchased by locals and kept as mementoes or else sent to friends and relatives who had missed out on the excitement.[43] On the reverse side of cards featuring photographs of lynching victims and watching crowds were messages such as the following:

> Well John—This is a token of a great day we had in Dallas, March 3rd [1910], a Negro was hung for an assault on a three year old girl. I saw this on my noon hour. I was very much in the bunch. You can see the Negro hanging on a telephone pole.

> This is the Barbecue we had last night my picture is to the left with a cross over it Your son Joe.

> This was made in the court yard, In Center, Texas, he is a 16 year old Black boy, He killed Earl's Grandma, She was Florence's mother. Give this to Bud. From Aunt Myrtle.[44]

These lynchings gave a prominent role to the white victim of the alleged crime and to his or her kin and supporters—a role defined by the customary rules of honor and revenge. The "men of the Vance family" were allowed to "wreak vengeance." The right to exact vengeance also belonged to the local community where the crime occurred. The Texarkana people were asked to exercise restraint and deliver the prisoner "unmolested" to the proper parties. The offense involved remained essentially personal, a private wrong to be directly and locally avenged, not a legal violation to be impersonally sanctioned by state officials elsewhere.

At the same time, the object of punishment, Henry Smith, was perceived by the crowd as a "brute," a "fiend," the perpetrator of an inhuman atrocity against an innocent white child. His alleged acts, his inferior status as a black man, and the sympathetic, well-connected good character of his victim converged to put him outside the law, beyond its protection. His punishment was dictated not by the legal code—"the law was laid aside"—but by the collective passions his act had aroused. His fate was determined not by the rule of law but by the will of the people. Far from regarding him as a citizen and a legal subject, the mob granted Smith neither personhood nor human dignity. His humanity having been denied, he became a body to be destroyed, flesh to be tormented, a living screen onto which the crowd's furious power might be projected. Smith's broken body was displayed—at the event and in the photographic images that circulated subsequently—as a trophy and a warning.

The atrocious, inter-racial crimes that these public lynchings sought to avenge—like the rape and murder of Myrtle Vance—provided important occasions for political mobilization. They helped forge alliances: between "race radicals"—who sought to undo the civil rights granted to blacks by Reconstruction—and lower-class Southern whites and, elsewhere, between Northern blacks and civil rights activists. They created ideological associations, forging a link between black males and violent crime; between community justice and the right to kill. They legitimated racial violence by representing it as criminal punishment. They empowered some groups *vis-à-vis* others within the white community. They generated political opportunities—not just for white against black but for white against white.[45]

In these lynchings there is no strong state asserting its power, but rather a group of local people defying it. Such defiance could occur precisely because local law officials were not subject to the controlling power of their state's government, let alone of the federal government in Washington. The Paris lynching is a story not of state sovereignty *affirmed* but rather of state sovereignty *contested*—by "the people," the mob, the county—in the name of popular justice and white supremacy. Throughout the early decades of the twentieth century, federal and state authorities struggled in vain to gain control of a power to punish that local Southern communities arrogated to themselves. Even as late as the 1960s, federal and state control sometimes remained tenuous.

By their actions, and in the subsequent statements of their apologists, the lynch mobs made clear their insistence that these particular "criminals" and these specific "crimes" should be accorded harsher treatment than the criminal law allowed. The state's official criminal justice was deemed too lenient, too slow, too uncertain, and altogether too respectful of the "criminal" and his so-called rights. As a recent historian of lynching observes:

> Whites who collectively murdered African Americans . . . in the late nineteenth and early twentieth centuries not only made a statement about racial hierarchy but also a statement about law. Law was too capricious, too unpredictable, too formal, too abstract, and too concerned with process and at least the procedures of fairness to regulate the crucial social distinctions of the color line . . . the criminal justice system, in its maddening variability could not be entrusted with the sacred responsibility of performatively reenacting white supremacy when it was challenged.[46]

The spectacle lynching was not an official ceremony but a popular carnival—a "lynching bee," a "negro barbecue." It took place not in the centers of national power but in the rural counties of the South far from the seat of federal or state government. Its mode was not rule-bound legal process but passionate, popular expression. These lynchings were explicitly violent and self-consciously uncivilized. The mob insisted on punishments—torture, burning, dismemberment, and display—that were widely regarded outside the South as anachronistic and barbaric, the better to maximize terror and degradation. They defiled and dismembered the human body in defiance of a modern humanist culture that regarded it as sacrosanct. And of course they were openly and unashamedly racist: utterly rejecting the law's commitment to equality and affirming local norms of caste superiority. That they scandalized liberal opinion elsewhere was an important part of the event's local appeal.

Lynching and Capital Punishment

Conventional wisdom views the death penalty as an exercise of sovereign state power and conjures up Foucaultian images of Damiens on the scaffold. But when it comes to American capital punishment, it is more appropriate to think in terms of local popular justice and remember Henry Smith's fate at the hands of the Texas lynch mob. The historical image of the lynch mob sheds light on contemporary capital punishment in a number of important respects. The savage, carnivalesque character of the public lynching displays some of the passions and pleasures that the punishment of hated enemies can evoke—passions that are now buried beneath the "civilized" restraint with which the death penalty is publicly discussed and administered. Lynch mob behavior conveys disturbing truths about the potential for raw violence that resides in American race relations and traditions of popular justice. Reflecting on these events also reminds us that, as late as the mid-twentieth century, American federal and state authorities were far from sovereign in their command of violence and their capacity to do justice. Like capital punishment today, these lynchings were occasions for many kinds of action and display—most notably dominance, defiance, contempt, and degradation—and worked as symbolic vehicles for transactions unfolding on many different levels. But above all, this historic legacy is instructive because the specter of these lynchings has long haunted the American legal system and played a crucial role in shaping the reinvented death penalty that emerged at the end of the twentieth century.

Public lynchings also prompt us to think about the entertainment aspects of lethal punishments and the communicative action that these events generate—important aspects of the capital punishment complex that are too often neglected. Here the lynching postcards are particularly revealing. These brief letters suggest the pleasure of narrating such events and the possibility of using transgressive narratives of this kind as tokens of solidarity to bond with like-minded others. The postcards, photographs, and newspaper reports generated by the lynchings were ways of putting death into discourse, circulating images of the killing, and thus extending the event over time and space. The very different reactions that these communications produced—among Southern whites, Southern blacks, and Northern liberals—help us keep in mind that practices such as lynchings and executions are always unruly public texts with which different groups of people engage and whose meanings are caught up in power struggles and cultural conflicts.

Henry Smith's destruction reminds us of the raw power of the American mob and the furious demands of "popular justice" that emerge when local majority sentiment is outraged by crime, empowered by normative codes, and untrammeled by legal restraint. The self-righteous power of "the people," emboldened by ideologies of popular democracy and myths of self-rule, is an incendiary force in American politics that is less actively mobilized in European nations, at least outside of warfare or revolutionary situations. And popular justice is one of the key forms of its expression. The image of a lynching also reminds us of an important respect in which America's penal history diverges from the developmental pattern of the other Western nations and from the process of "civilization" that characterized it—a divergence embodied in popular practices that were on the margins of the law, were regional, and, though they were short-lived, were nevertheless symptomatic. To a greater or lesser degree, these same characteristics remain part of the institutional and social fabric of the American polity—long-term structural features that made lynchings possible a century ago and make capital punishment more likely today.

Should we infer from these observations that capital punishment in contemporary America is, in fact, some kind of lynching? A "modern lynching" perhaps? Or a "legal lynching"?[47] Not at all: quite the contrary, in fact. If we think about the distinctive forms of contemporary American capital punishment in relation to the lynching model, we discover that these forms, taken together, embody a strikingly precise mirror image of those we see in the lynchings.

Today's capital punishment process is administered by state officials and regulated by federal law. It provides the defendant with multiple opportunities to contest the court's finding and to appeal his sentence, taking considerable trouble to uphold his rights and ensure the observance of due process and proper procedure. Executions, if they actually occur, take place not in the local town square but instead at a great distance from the crime, both in time and in space. Execution methods are avowedly "nonviolent," designed to minimize bodily injury and degradation. Bureaucratic protocols dictate a dispassionate administrative routine with crowds, ceremony, and cruelty reduced to a minimum. If lynching is "the very essence" of open, full-throated, retributive violence, as George Herbert Mead suggested, then the modern American death penalty is, in some key respects, its essential opposite: a punishment overlaid with ambivalence, anxiety, and embarrassment, striving hard to appear lawful and nonviolent.[48]

Viewed alongside the lynching, today's death penalty suggests a radical inversion of form, a mirror image, a reformed present that vehemently rejects its past. This negative symmetry is so striking that we must suppose that the contemporary American death penalty has, in important respects, been *designed* to be an antilynching—and that is precisely the hypothesis that will be pursued here. The American archetype of a lynching will guide our analysis of the social meaning of today's death penalty as we explore the historical and political processes that forged such remarkably close, inverted symmetries between these two institutions.

Despite extensive, ongoing efforts by the federal courts to ensure that the American death penalty does not resemble a lynching, has none of the appearance of a lynching, and is not understood to be a lynching, many of the same social and political dynamics that produced lynchings in the early twentieth century continue to produce death penalties now. In other words, the relationship between these peculiar American institutions is more complex than it initially appears. What at first sight seems to be a stark and simple contrast, a mirror image, turns out, on closer inspection, to have underlying continuities and connections. For all the inversion of form, the social forces and political processes that enabled lynchings, mobilized lynch mobs, and made lynchings useful for political actors have somehow persisted and continue to structure the modern death penalty's deployment and utility.

Contemporary capital punishment continues to have many substantive features in common with those lynchings that it does its best to disavow.[49] It continues, where executions are concerned, to be concentrated in the South. It continues to be driven by local politics and populist politicians. It continues to be imposed by leaders and lay people claiming to represent the local community. It continues to give a special place to victims' kin. It continues disproportionately to target poorly represented blacks, convicted of atrocious crimes against white victims.[50] The passions aroused by heinous crimes, together with racial hatreds and caste distinctions, still provide much of its energy.[51] Its supporters still insist that regular punishment is too good for the perpetrators of atrocities and that only death can sufficiently mark the enormity of their crimes. It continues to produce false accusations and racialized outcomes. It continues to provide drama and casual pleasure for masses of curious onlookers. Finally, the collective killing of hated criminals (or merely the assertion of the right to do so) remains one of the ways in which groups of people express their autonomy, invoke their traditional values, and assert their local identity.

Considered in formal terms, today's death penalty may be a mirror image of a public torture lynching—an inverse institution, a disavowal, calculated to resist and deny any such association. But if we look beyond forms and consider the practice substantively, many of the same social forces that once prompted lynchings nowadays prompt capital punishment; many of the same social functions performed by lynchings then are performed by capital punishment now; and many of the same political structures that permitted lynchings at the start of the twentieth century enable capital punishment at the start of the twenty-first.

The image of the lynching offers a powerful tool with which to think about this question comparatively and historically. It trains our attention on the question of governmental power in the United States, bringing into focus the weakness of the American state and the fragmented character of governmental authority. It points us to the ways in which the right to kill and the assertion of sovereignty are bound up with regional conflicts and power structures, as well as with questions of justice and the constitution of penal authority. It points to the tradition of popular, communal justice and the cultural expectation—still strong in some American regions—that local people will be allowed to shape how justice is done. It shows how group conflicts—between black and white, rich and poor, conservative and liberal, Northerner and Southerner—can be played out around the scaffold and over the body of the condemned.

In all these ways the lynching model prompts us to focus on the structural conditions that enable collective violence—the limits of state power, incomplete pacification, popular sovereignty, and the power of local actors—as well as the situational ones, including group relations, racial divisions, levels of violence, and despised low-status outsiders accused of atrocious crimes against higher-status victims, that mobilize and direct it.

Local Power and Abolition

The archetypal Southern lynching scene will serve to orient this study of American capital punishment and its peculiar characteristics. But what if we had used a different image, a different starting point? Would the analysis have turned out very differently, thereby raising questions about the approach suggested here? Let us test that proposition by considering a very different point of departure—namely, the path-breaking abolition that occurred in Michigan in the middle of the nineteenth century—to see how that might have reoriented the investigation.

In 1846, a small group of reformers in the Michigan legislature succeeded, after several attempts, in passing a law abolishing capital punishment for ordinary crimes. The 1846 Act retained the death penalty for treason against the state, but in the 164 years since then, no death sentences have been imposed and no state executions have taken place. The last execution prior to the reform occurred in 1830, and the reformers argued that the death penalty had long been a "dead letter," quite inessential for crime control—though they took the precaution of stipulating solitary confinement for life with hard labor as the punishment for anyone convicted of murder.[52] Michigan, at that time, had comparatively low levels of crime, no black slave population, and no sharp racial or class divisions giving rise to insecurity on the part of the dominant groups.

A legislative committee report of 1844 stated that capital punishment was illiberal ("a usurped power of government"), bad for the wealth of the state ("to punish an offender with death destroys . . . both his life and his usefulness"), uncivilized, and inhumane.[53] It also stressed the "fallibility" of the punishment ("innocent men have been convicted, sentenced and executed"); in fact, it appears that the reform may have been triggered by a case in neighboring Canada in which the authorities executed an innocent man in error.[54] The senator who introduced the bill, Daniel Quakenbass, had himself presided over the execution of an innocent person while serving as a sheriff in New York.

The 1844 report stated that "public opinion is against the infliction of the penalty of death," but there is reason to doubt the basis of that claim.[55] The committee had no survey evidence, nor had the issue been put to the electorate, and in 1850, when considering whether to write a death penalty prohibition into the state constitution, legislators objected that "a large proportion of the people of the state are in direct hostility to the principle," so its inclusion would "array a hostile feeling against the constitution itself."[56] It seems, in fact, that the 1846 abolition was the work of a small group of liberal reformers, drawn from Puritan Yankee New England backgrounds, sympathetic to the antislavery and antigallows causes, suspicious of state power, and unmoved by the arguments for retention put to them by ministers of religion who opposed abolition.[57] ("Your committee do not consider the abolition of capital punishment as a theological question. They see no necessity or propriety in making it a matter of scriptural controversy.") The reformers—acting in the relative openness of the state's early stage of political development—took advantage of Michigan's autonomous police power and its independence from the control imperatives of the larger nation to press home their reform agenda. Having taken up the mantle of pioneering reformers ("the eyes of the people of the Union are upon us to see whether we will sustain the advance we have made"), the abolitionists resisted all subsequent attempts to undo their historic act, even as the state's demographics changed and homicide rates rose.[58] A prohibition on capital punishment was eventually written into the state constitution in 1963.

Michigan's pioneering abolitionism—soon followed by that of Wisconsin and Rhode Island—placed America, or at least its Northern states, in the vanguard of the world's abolitionist movement.[59] The event's status, to its admirers, is that of a noble, progressive undertaking, altogether different from the regressive barbarism suggested by the public torture lynching. An account oriented by the Michigan experience would come at the American death penalty from a very different angle and might seem to give rise to a very different analysis.

But on closer examination, we see that the Southern lynching and the Michigan abolition do not lead to two entirely different and incompatible analyses. On the contrary: they suggest a consistent causal account that points to the importance of certain structural features shared by all American states, and to the role of situational processes in determining how these structural properties are played out in social action and events. The most important structural features of the Michigan case—the state's relative autonomy from the national state, the local control of the power to punish, the political dominance of small groups—are in fact shared by the Southern lynching, even if the situational features (group relations, racial demographics, violence rates, symbolic associations of the death penalty) are altogether different. Both stories are versions of an American narrative: not a grand narrative of abolition or retention, nobility or barbarism, but a detailed story of local democratic politics in all its varieties.

The American public is not a lynch mob, nor is it more than usually punitive, or racist, or given to vigilante justice. But the American polity devolves decision-making about punishment (and much else) to the local level, thereby empowering local political actors in ways that have had major consequences for the history of the death penalty. The effect of this devolution depends on local political structures and relations; on the orientation of local elites and their capacity to exert leadership; on group and race relations; on homicide and violence levels; on events and contingencies. The Michigan example shows how the empowerment of local actors could produce a politics of liberal reform giving rise to a pioneering abolition. The lynching example shows the opposite. The vanguard abolitions of capital punishment that characterized America then, and the laggard survivals that characterize it now, may be explained within one and the same framework.

TWO

The American Way
of Death

For us, what the Americans are doing is completely
incomprehensible.

HENRI LECLERC, PRESIDENT OF THE LIGUE DES
DROITS DE L'HOMME, 2000

Widespread puzzlement surrounds the death penalty in America today. Henri LeClerc, the president of the Human Rights League in
Paris, was speaking on behalf of European abolitionists when he expressed
disbelief at America's continued use of the death penalty, but his sense of
incomprehension could also describe much of the critical literature on the
other side of the Atlantic. If commentators abroad wonder why America
retains capital punishment when other nations have abandoned it, commentators at home—whether supporters or opponents—wonder why the
current system is so painfully slow, so prone to error, and so ill adapted to
its ostensible purposes. As a prominent supporter of capital punishment
remarked, "Whatever purposes the death penalty is said to serve—deterrence, retribution, assuaging the pain suffered by victims' families—these
purposes are not served by the system as it now operates."[1]

Why, for example, do states take such trouble to enact death penalty
laws when they mostly fail to enforce them? (Or, as a *New York Post* columnist exclaimed, "Please tell me why in bloody hell we have a so-called
death penalty on the books if we never use it?"[2]) Why, when death sentences are imposed at trial, are they so seldom subsequently executed? And
why, if the aim is to produce deterrence or retribution or victim satisfaction, are executions held in private, often decades after the crime, with
such a minimum of display and so much concern to ensure that the condemned feels no pain?

No less puzzling than the institutional forms of today's death penalty are its cultural status and political meaning. Why so much talk about a punishment so infrequently used? Why would the people of a liberal nation, famously suspicious of state power, grant states the right to kill? Why is the country's most government-phobic region also the most execution-prone?

These puzzles prompt us to focus not just on the big fact of capital punishment's survival but also on the more finely grained questions of its institutional forms, cultural status, and political meanings. They push us beyond broad-gauge comparisons between "retentionist" and "abolitionist" nations to more detailed investigations of capital punishment's contemporary forms and meanings, probing the histories out of which they emerged, the dramas through which they are performed, and the discourses in which they are represented. They move us to consider capital punishment not as an abstract issue but as a set of practices through which America's death penalty is enacted and experienced. And they suggest that any study of capital punishment ought to include not just legal and administrative arrangements but also the social practices that engage with the institution and connect it with America's circuits of political exchange and cultural consumption. Instead of regarding capital punishment simply as a penal measure we need to view it as a complex institution with legal, political, and cultural dimensions.

The Law and Practice of Capital Punishment

Capital punishment is always enacted in and through specific legal and administrative arrangements that determine why, where, how, and which persons will be put to death. Such arrangements have varied enormously in different historical periods, from one society to another, and in the American case, from one region, state, or county to the next.

In the contemporary era—the period from 1976 to the present—capital punishment arrangements have differed greatly from state to state, existing sometimes as no more than a law on the books, sometimes as a sentencing practice, and sometimes as a full-fledged practice of death sentences followed by executions. The state of New Hampshire had the law on the books for decades after 1976 but imposed no death sentences and carried out no executions; states like Kansas impose sentences but have not carried out an execution since the 1960s; states like California impose many death sentences but execute very few of them; and states like Texas or Oklahoma or Virginia have the law, impose sentences, and carry

Death penalty states (35)

State	Executions since 1976 (1,193)	Death row inmates (3,279)
Northeast		
Connecticut	1	10
New Hampshire*	0	1
Pennsylvania	3	225
South		
Alabama	44	200
Arkansas	27	43
Delaware	14	19
Florida	68	403
Georgia	46	108
Kentucky	3	36
Louisiana	28	84
Maryland	5	5
Mississippi	10	60
Missouri	67	52
North Carolina	43	169
Oklahoma	91	86
South Carolina	42	63
Tennessee	6	92
Texas	449	342
Virginia	105	16
West		
Arizona	23	129
California	13	690
Colorado	1	3
Idaho	1	18
Nevada	12	78
Oregon	2	33
Washington	4	9
Wyoming	1	1
Midwest		
Illinois	12	15
Indiana	20	17
Kansas*	0	10
Montana	3	2
Nebraska	3	11
Ohio	34	176
South Dakota	1	3
Utah	6	10
U.S. government	3	58
U.S. military*	0	8

Source: Death Penalty Information Center, January 31, 2010.
* No executions since 1976.

Abolitionist states (15 plus District of Columbia)

State	Date of abolition
Northeast	
Maine	1887
Massachusetts*	1984
Michigan	1846
New Jersey	2007
New York*	2004
Rhode Island	1984
Vermont	1964
South	
District of Columbia	1981
West Virginia	1965
West	
Alaska	1957
Hawaii	1957
New Mexico**	2009
Midwest	
Iowa	1965
Minnesota	1911
North Dakota	1973
Wisconsin	1853

Source: Death Penalty Information Center, January 31, 2010.

* Abolished by judicial decision.

** Statute effective July 1, 2009, but two people left on death row as statute not retroactive.

out frequent executions.[3] Then there are the fifteen states (and the District of Columbia) in which capital punishment does not exist as a legally available sanction. In short, remarkable variation exists *within* the United States in terms of capital punishment law and practice.

Of the thirty-five states in which the death penalty is a legal punishment, roughly one-third—Colorado, Connecticut, Idaho, Kansas, New Hampshire, South Dakota, and Wyoming (and the U.S. military)—make minimal use of the sanction, having few capital trials, small death row populations, and few or no executions. Another third—California, Illinois, Indiana, Kentucky, Maryland, Mississippi, Montana, Nebraska, Nevada, Ohio, Oregon, Pennsylvania, Tennessee, Utah, and Washington (and the U.S. government)—use the death penalty at the trial level and have large death row populations but make more limited use of executions. The final third—Alabama, Arizona, Arkansas, Delaware, Florida, Georgia, Louisiana, Missouri, North Carolina, Oklahoma, South Carolina, Texas, and Virginia—regularly impose death sentences and carry out executions.[4]

This pattern is distinctive and revealing. As a comparative matter, subnational variation of this kind is highly unusual. Outside the United States, few modern nations contain local jurisdictions in which capital punishment is lawfully executed alongside others where it is prohibited.[5] And although some writers proceed as if capital punishment only really exists when it is carried through to an executed death sentence and talk of "*de facto* abolition," the continued existence of unexecuted laws and sentences—and the political energy invested in maintaining and extending them—suggests that even death penalty practices that stop short of death have political meaning and social uses.

The different varieties of American capital punishment map onto a definite geography. Abolitionist states are concentrated in the Northern tier of the country (especially the Northeastern and North Central region), mixed states in the middle tier (the mid-Atlantic and Midwestern regions), and execution states are heavily concentrated in the South. In the period since the Supreme Court revalidated capital punishment in 1976, Southern states have carried out about 83 percent of all American executions, with the state of Texas accounting for more than one-third of the 1,193 executions that have taken place. This North/South disparity is even more pronounced considering that as many as 40 percent of non-Southern executions have been of "volunteers"—that is, of death row inmates who have given up their appeals process and encouraged state authorities to put them to death. The proportion of "volunteers" in the South is much lower, at 8 percent.[6]

These geographical patterns have changed over time with the distribution of executions becoming much more skewed between North and South in the late twentieth century. In sharp contrast to the contemporary period, between 1930 and 1964 the Northern states of Ohio, Pennsylvania, and New York were consistently among the country's top nine executing states. The increasing "Southernness" of the death penalty—at least in terms of executions—is a relatively new phenomenon that needs to be explained.

Today's capital punishment process is overlaid by a web of rules and procedures that is more complex and elaborate than that of any other area of criminal law. A dense skein of substantive rules and procedural requirements regulates every stage of the capital trial from jury selection to sentence choice, as well as the complicated process of appeal and post-conviction review that each capital case undergoes.[7]

If a convicted murderer is to be put to death, the imposition of a death sentence is only the beginning of a long, involved process. In the wake of a capital conviction the case must proceed on direct appeal to the state courts—sometimes to an intermediate court of appeals as well as to the

The appeal process

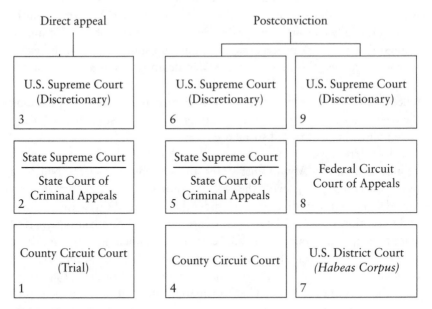

Source: Bryan Stevenson.

state supreme court. Thereafter, several further obstacles must be surmounted before an execution can occur. The case will await the resolution of legal challenges in state postconviction proceedings; then the resolution of challenges in federal court via federal *habeas corpus* review; then the decision of the state authority (usually the governor) in any clemency proceedings; and finally the setting of an execution date, which is usually done by the state's supreme court or the governor.[8] Of these obstacles, the most complex and time-consuming are the appeals and federal *habeas* challenges. Capital cases typically go through nine stages of direct appeal, postconviction appeal, and federal *habeas* review as the case makes its way up and down and back and forth between the state and federal court hierarchies.

Given these procedural possibilities, a good defense lawyer with sufficient resources can keep his client alive for many years. Take the case of Robert Alton Harris, who was sentenced to death on March 9, 1979, for the murder of two teenage boys and executed more than thirteen years later by the state of California. In the years between sentence and execution, Harris first exercised his federal constitutional right to lodge a direct appeal to the supreme court of California. When that failed, he petitioned the U.S. Supreme Court to hear his appeal, again without success. He then lodged two unsuccessful *habeas corpus* petitions in the California state system, followed by a federal *habeas* petition that was unsuccessful in the federal district court, successful in the Ninth Circuit Federal Court of Appeals, and ultimately denied by the U.S. Supreme Court.[9] Next he launched a second federal *habeas* petition, which was filed in 1982 and finally denied in 1988; a further effort to reverse the denial, which was also denied; and a third federal petition that was filed on March 26, 1990. This petition persuaded a federal court to stop Harris's scheduled execution on April 3, 1990, but the court subsequently voted to deny Harris's claim. Thereafter, Harris's lawyers lodged a series of increasingly desperate petitions to the federal courts, until eventually the U.S. Supreme Court brought the saga to an end on April 21, 1992, on which date Harris was executed.[10]

In the period since *Furman v Georgia* in 1972, this lengthy and elaborate legal process has become a central feature of American capital punishment. Long years of slow-moving appeals and rulings are often followed by a frantic time crunch at the very end as the case moves toward its execution date. Defense lawyers file flurries of last-minute petitions and applications for stays of execution, which federal and Supreme Court justices have to decide, sometimes convening middle-of-the-night conferences to do so. By the 1980s, the Supreme Court had appointed a "death clerk" whose job it is to handle last-minute filings and coordinate with any local execution team about to carry out a sentence.[11]

Significant consequences flow from these labyrinthine legal processes, the most obvious being the temporal extension of death sentences. The legal process ensures that years and sometimes decades go by before the sentence of the court is finally executed, during which time the case travels from state court to federal court and back again in search of review. In 2007, the average time elapsed between sentencing and execution was just over twelve years.[12] Several executions have occurred after more than twenty years, and some prisoners currently have been awaiting their execution for more than three decades. In this process the punishment of death is suspended and effectively transformed into something else—a decades-long incarceration during which the prisoner awaits a final decision as to execution or reprieve.

Such delays do not just undermine the death penalty's deterrent effect; they also spoil its capacity for satisfying retribution. As one legal scholar put it, "Even a five or six year delay in killing is enough to gut the meaning of revenge. The man you wanted to kill was the abusive robber, high on crack, who pistol-whipped and shot two customers at a Seven-Eleven store in 1984. Instead, in 1990, the state electrocutes a balding, religious, model prisoner in a neat blue-denim uniform."[13] Sometimes, in the process, a death row inmate will become an object of sympathy for those who oppose capital punishment, redefining the convicted murderer as the victim of a cruel and unusual system.

The legal process and its inherent delays have also led to the expansion and consolidation of the modern institution of "death row"—that special form of imprisonment whereby thousands of condemned prisoners spend many years in solitary confinement awaiting the outcome of appeals and hearings that will decide whether they live or die. Imprisonment on death row—lengthy confinement under sentence of death, in a special enclosure, subject to greater than usual deprivation—is an administrative arrangement with no specific legal authority, but it has become the punishment experienced by thousands of convicted capital offenders.[14]

Although America's lengthy waiting periods are not unique, they contrast sharply with earlier practices. Before the 1960s, the average time that American inmates spent awaiting execution was much shorter than it is today—measured in weeks and months rather than in years and decades—and death row populations were much smaller.[15] At the start of 2010, more than 3,000 prisoners were being held in "death rows" and "condemned units" around the country.

Doctrinal and procedural complexity also increase the importance—and the relative scarcity—of competent death penalty lawyering. As Federal Court of Appeals Judge Alex Kozinski comments, "The jurisprudence of death is so complex, so esoteric, so harrowing, this is the one area where there aren't nearly enough lawyers willing and able to handle the current cases." Most states with the death penalty tightly restrict expenditure on counsel for indigent capital defendants, with the result that "inadequate assistance of counsel" has become a central basis for contesting death sentences. Except in rare cases in which a defendant can afford experienced trial counsel—and such people, as Supreme Court Justice Ruth Ginsburg notes, "do not get the death penalty"—defendants mostly rely on the *pro bono* services of appellate litigators who typically become involved only when cases near an execution date.[16]

The existence of complex laws together with the involvement of motivated, competent appellate counsel (in those cases where such counsel do become involved) ensures that a very high proportion of all capital sentences are reversed prior to execution: as many as 66 percent, according to the leading study. As Justice John Paul Stevens remarked, "The reversible error in capital trials is staggering." "Exonerations" (whereby condemned individuals are found to be innocent and are released from custody) have also become a recurring feature of the system; indeed, since 1973, more than 130 people have been exonerated and freed from death row, more than a dozen of them on the basis of DNA evidence.[17]

These reversals and exonerations are, like every aspect of the system, subject to competing interpretations. For critics, they are proof that the system is dangerously fallible, that inappropriate death sentences are often imposed and that innocent individuals may have been put to death. For supporters, they have a different significance: "Reversal of an erroneous conviction on appeal or on habeas, or the pardoning of an innocent condemnee through executive clemency, demonstrates not the failure of the system but its success."[18] But even for supporters, such a high rate of error is difficult to justify.

As a consequence of all this, completed death sentences are relatively rare. Since executions resumed in 1977, the highest number carried out in any one year was 98, which was the national total for 1999. In subsequent years, annual figures have trended downward, with an average of around 60, this, in a nation where more than 14,000 murders occur every year.

The lengthy legal process ensures that each capital case is expensive, whether or not it results in execution. In New York between 1995 and 2005, the state spent $170 million on capital prosecutions, none of which produced an executed death sentence. According to an Urban Institute study, the state of Maryland has spent $187 million on capital cases since 1976, which averages out to $37.2 million for each of the five executions that the state has carried out. Even in a high-volume execution state such as Texas, the costs of a capital case are reported to be twice as high as the total costs of a case resulting in life imprisonment. These figures do not reflect the costs of the time that corporate litigators devoted *pro bono,* an amount that often reaches hundreds of thousands of dollars per case (not including the cost of corporate litigation fees forgone), nor do they include the cost of the extensive docket time taken up by capital cases in state and federal courts.[19]

The legal process put in place since *Furman v Georgia* in 1972 has brought with it many costs and difficulties. The question is, how did such a system emerge and why have its problems been allowed to persist?

In the great majority of cases, the decision to mount a capital indictment is made not by professional, nonpartisan civil servants but by elected county prosecutors whose discretionary decisions are largely unsupervised by state or federal authorities.[20] The decision to bring death penalty charges—like the decision to accept a plea or to press for a death sentence following conviction—is a choice rather than a legal requirement. That choice is subject to whatever subjective prejudices, political incentives, and situational pressures are brought to bear, including the expressed wishes of the murder victim's family. And it is made by individual prosecutors, 97 percent of whom are white, though the racial composition of most death penalty states is much more mixed, and a majority of murder defendants are people of color.[21]

For the most part, the state judges who preside over trials and hear appeals are, like the elected prosecutors, "politicians who must run for office." Judicial elections take place in thirty-one out of thirty-five death penalty states, and judges have sometimes been deselected because their capital appeals decisions were out of line with the views of their constituents. In states where judges were until recently empowered to override jury sentences, elected judges typically used this power to impose death rather than life. In Alabama the death-to-life ratio of these judicial overrides was ten to one. The exception was Delaware, where judges are not subject to election; in that state judicial decisions more often benefited the defense.[22]

State governors also make death penalty decisions in the context of electoral competition, and the views of gubernatorial candidates on capital punishment have sometimes played a prominent role in electoral contests—for example, when George Pataki defeated New York Governor Mario Cuomo in 1994. The political salience of the issue goes a long way toward explaining why governors more often authorize executions in election years than in nonelection years, and why the power to grant mercy is rarely exercised except by governors who are no longer running for office.[23]

This tight connection between legal decision-making and local politics produces regional disparity and an obvious risk of bias in capital cases.[24] The local ties and electoral accountability of criminal justice decision-makers can also give the American process a raw, emotive character, since an aroused community is more directly involved and legal decisions are more responsive to its promptings. Politicization and localization of this kind are unknown in other Western democracies. European judges and prosecutors are typically tenured civil servants not directly accountable to voters. And the political officials who used to exercise the power to grant clemency in European nations were high-ranking officials in the national government—the British home secretary, the French president, the German chancellor—who were less susceptible to local opinion. In the United States, by contrast, all politics are local. How, we might ask, did a modern nation state permit the power to kill to become a matter of local politics?

Although locally elected officials make key decisions in the capital punishment process, the most important of these decisions is made not by the community's officials but by twelve of its lay members. The choice to impose a death sentence—which is quite separate from the decision to convict the defendant of capital murder—is made in America today not by a judge, or even by application of a legal rule, but by a jury of lay people who exercise a discretionary and unreviewable sentencing power.[25]

If the idea of the jury as the capital sentencing authority has come to seem natural in the American context—if Americans "believe instinctively" that the jury is best suited to this task—it is worth noting that, except in a very few states, jury sentencing occurs in no other area of American criminal law. Nor does it exist in most other countries.[26] When the idea of jury sentencing was tentatively raised by the Royal Commission on Capital Punishment in Britain in the 1950s, it was roundly condemned by the press as well as by members of both houses of Parliament. Why, the *Times* editors asked, should a "random group" of "chance-met people," "ordinary people who know nothing," be regarded as competent or reliable? Moreover, why ought a group of lay people be made to shoulder this "dread obligation"?[27]

Only in the last few years has jury sentencing become an essential feature of American capital proceedings. Until recently, a few states retained the judge as the sentencing authority or allowed the judge to override the jury's decision, but recent Supreme Court cases have made jury sentencing a constitutional requirement of capital cases. Before they may settle on a death sentence, juries in most states are instructed that they must find that the murder of which the offender was convicted was accompanied by at least one statutorily specified aggravating factor—for example, the murder was especially heinous, atrocious, cruel, or depraved, or was committed in the course of another felony, such as robbery, kidnapping, or rape.[28] Having made this finding, they are then required to "weigh" aggravating factors against any mitigation (such as mental or emotional distress, or previous good character) adduced by the defense, and to decide, on balance, whether a death sentence is appropriate. Given the absence of any controls beyond this "weighing" requirement, the jury has a virtually untrammeled power to choose between life and death. As Justice Stevens observed, "in the final analysis, capital punishment rests not on a legal but an ethical judgment—an assessment of . . . the 'moral guilt' of the defendant."[29] As with Roman emperors, the fateful choice between thumbs up or down is theirs and theirs alone.

Given this decision-making power, the composition of juries and the views of individual jurors become crucial determinants of sentencing outcomes. If capital punishment is justified because it "expresses the community's moral sensibility"—and the Supreme Court has identified that as the fundamental rationale for today's institution—then it follows that "a representative cross-section of the community must be given the responsibility for making that decision."[30] As a consequence, attorneys have a long history of challenging state practices of jury selection, many of them concerned with racialized selection processes, peremptory challenges to members of ethnic minorities, and the "death qualification" of jurors—a selection process that excludes those who have principled objections (or "scruples") about capital punishment.[31] Questions of who exactly constitutes "the people" or "represents the community" are contentious matters of local politics and federal law.

Following the Supreme Court's 1991 decision in *Payne v Tennessee,* it became constitutionally permissible for victims' relatives to present "victim-impact statements" to the jury. The practice, which is established in most death penalty states, is part of the penalty phase, that is, the adversarial sentencing trial that takes place after the jury has rendered a guilty verdict in a capital trial.[32] This reinsertion of the victim's supporters into the sentencing process has been criticized for increasing the emotional temperature of an already highly charged process and exerting additional pressure on the jury to return a death sentence.

Together with the prosecutor's practice of consulting the victim's relatives about the decision to bring a capital indictment, and recent attempts by some officials to represent capital punishment as a form of "closure" for relatives of murder victims, the victim-impact statement is the product of the new victim-centered politics that dominated crime policy in the 1990s. Islamic jurisdictions allow victims' relatives to choose an offender's punishment and sometimes to participate in its administration, as did the revenge cultures of medieval Iceland and the lynching practices of the Jim Crow South.[33] But the involvement of victims' kin in capital sentencing is a new and distinctive phenomenon in the American context, with no equivalent in U.S. capital punishment proceedings prior to 1991 nor, indeed, in the capital processes of other common law nations.[34]

The 1960s litigation that eventually produced the *Furman v Georgia* decision in 1972 was initially brought to challenge the racism and lynchlike practices that characterized the death penalty in some regions before the federal courts' intervention. *Furman's* historic decision deemed such practices to be a violation of constitutional rights and invalidated every one of the nation's capital statutes to bring these practices to an end. In *Gregg v Georgia* (1976) and its companion cases, the Court upheld a new set of capital statutes because it found that the states had resolved these problems. In subsequent decades, the Court has emphasized the importance of due process safeguards to ensure that death sentences are not imposed summarily, arbitrarily, or on the basis of race. In the contemporary capital process, then, race discrimination is strictly prohibited and all capital defendants are entitled to due process and effective assistance of legal counsel.

It is surprising, therefore, to discover that racially disparate outcomes, summary trials, and ineffective assistance of counsel in capital cases are routine features of the contemporary, post-*Furman* death penalty process. Even more surprising is that these facts are widely known and officially recognized—with organizations such as the U.S. General Accounting Office and the American Bar Association publishing widely cited reports acknowledging these problems.[35]

Decades after *Furman,* research still consistently shows that race (above all, the race of the victim), social class, and the quality of legal counsel are the chief factors that structure outcomes, with the result that poorly represented blacks convicted of atrocious crimes against white victims are the group most likely to be sentenced to death.[36] These findings show that the racial hierarchy that the Yale law professor Charles Black identified in 1982 still operates today. That hierarchy is, in a "steep descending order of death sentence probability," ranked as follows: "(1) Black kills white (2) White kills white (3) Black kills black (4) White kills black," a pattern that is strongly suggestive of racial attitudes that value the human worth of whites above that of blacks. When critics today describe the death penalty processes of various states, with more or less exaggeration, as "legal lynchings," these are the characteristics they have in mind.[37]

These phenomena are all too familiar, but they are surprising nevertheless. That these discriminatory patterns should persist, despite decades of federal law reform intended to end arbitrary decision-making and to ensure equal due process and protection of law, is certainly a scandal. But it is also a puzzle that needs to be explained.

The Cultural Contradictions of Capital Punishment

The death penalty is delivered by a legal process, but it is also a cultural performance. It is enacted by means of legal and administrative arrangements but also through dramatic forms and cultural figures. And if the legal forms determine capital punishment's application and constitutional validity, the cultural forms shape its broader social meanings, its popular authority, and its emotional appeal.[38] In accounting for the authority of the capital punishment system, neither one is more nor less important. As the sociologist John Lofland notes, "The world is ruled perhaps as much by the dramaturgic encasement of actions as by the actions encased."[39]

Historically, the dramatic character of the death penalty has always been most apparent at the moment of execution. The traditional death ritual of the condemned man, with its elaborate procession, staging, ceremonial, and speeches, was a cultural event *par excellence,* shaped by social and religious beliefs as well as by the exigencies of bringing about the death of a living, breathing person. That performative moment is organized very differently today.

American executions no longer take place in the public square as in previous centuries, nor in the jail yard, as with the hangings of more recent times. They occur instead in a specialized enclosure—a death chamber—inside a state or federal prison, largely hidden from the public gaze. The protocols of today's low-visibility executions owe less to the conventions of dramatic ritual than to the principles of management science.

Commentators often talk of today's execution as a "ritual," but that description is misleading. Properly speaking, a ritual is a formal social practice that is standardized, repetitive, and conducted in a symbolic fashion. In today's execution process, communicative, symbolic, and ceremonial elements have been reduced to a minimum. Theatrical staging has largely been abandoned, and in its place is a more technical sensibility. Instead of performing a ritual, today's execution officials approach their task in an instrumental manner. Speed and effectiveness are the key concerns rather than signaling or display. What gets performed is nonperformance.[40]

This sensibility is also apparent in the execution method that has become the new American standard. The lethal injection, the execution technique used today by all the states, is the fifth execution method to be used in rapid succession in the United States. Since 1976, states have made use of firing squads, hanging, electric chairs, and gas chambers before settling on the lethal injection as the technology of choice. All the modern methods of execution have been represented by their proponents as painless, humane, and instantaneous. But the lethal injection—which kills by means of the intravenous injection of poisons ("execution medications") into the body of the condemned while he or she lies strapped to a gurney—takes this one stage further, modeling the execution as a medical procedure.[41] Here the projected sensibility is a therapeutic one, with the death chamber redesigned as a hospital ward and the infamous figure of the hangman replaced by paramedics and nurses. According to Federal Circuit Judge Stephen Reinhardt, this medicalization is now seen as a requirement of the Constitution, which obliges states to "eliminate the degrading, brutal, and violent aspects of an execution" and to put in their place "a scientifically developed and approved method of terminating life through appropriate medical procedures in a neutral, medical environment."[42]

The result is a strange hybrid. The tools of modern medicine (the gurney, the syringe, the IV, the sedatives, the paramedics) are merged with the ancient act of putting a person to death to create a procedure that makes little reference to the retributive, condemnatory nature of the sentence being carried out. As death penalty proponent Robert Blecker complains, "The final scene in the execution chamber too nearly resembles the final scene at hospices. . . . Doctors should not be involved with lethal injection. How we kill the people we hate should never resemble easing excruciating pain for those we love."[43] One Texas journalist, who has witnessed more executions than any other, remarks, "The act is very clinical, almost anticlimactic."[44]

Whereas the execution itself is now medicalized, the process through which it is undertaken is thoroughly bureaucratized. Every stage of the procedure is precisely specified in advance and then logged and recorded as the process unfolds. As the execution protocol of the Federal Bureau of Prisons states: "The log will reflect . . . the time each of the following events occurs: The condemned individual removed from Inmate Holding Cell; The condemned individual strapped to gurney; Last statement by condemned individual; Reading of Judgment and Commitment Order by Warden; Signal by Executioner(s) that lethal substances have been administered; Determination of condemned individual's death through the EKG readout by designated qualified person," and so on.[45]

The primary aims of today's execution arrangements, which are by no means always realized, are to minimize the sights, sounds, and smells of suffering and to carry out the court's death sentence in a manner that is professional, efficient, and humane. As a spokesman for the Arkansas Department of Corrections told the *New York Times,* "The people that are involved in this are very concerned that what they do is proper, done professionally, and with decorum. They want this to go well."[46] The same priorities are apparent in the execution protocol of the Federal Bureau of Prisons: "It is the policy of the BOP that the execution of a person sentenced to death under Federal law by a court of competent authority and jurisdiction be carried out in an efficient and humane manner."

Today's executions place a premium on speed and no-nonsense efficiency. They are viewed not by a crowd or an audience but by authorized "witnesses"—typically about a dozen people including state officials, journalists, and relatives of the condemned and his or her victim—who see nothing at all of the execution process until a curtain is pulled back to reveal the prisoner, prone on a gurney, intravenous lines already inserted, ready to die.[47] Federal authorities require execution witnesses to sign an agreement "not to photograph or make any other visual or audio recording of the execution" and threaten arrest and prosecution for any persons who "violate prohibitions against filming, taping, broadcasting, or otherwise electronically documenting the death of the condemned individual."[48] In the aftermath of the event, officials issue brief, pro-forma statements that supply the press with much of the copy for the reports they will publish. The story is extended only if something goes wrong. Otherwise there is a minimum of publicity and all of it controlled.

A journalist's comments following the execution of Timothy McVeigh, America's most notorious mass murderer, give a sense of this new standard:

> Timothy McVeigh died yesterday with the whole world watching, but few actually seeing. Eight television networks broadcast reports about his execution live from Terre Haute, Ind., though none came within a mile of it . . . Barred by prison officials from being anywhere near the death chamber, most reporters relayed what news they could from a nearby media encampment . . . In all, the tone of what was the most widely covered execution in history was downbeat, restrained, almost funereal.[49]

Today's authorities do what they can to de-dramatize executions, carefully avoiding the sensational or the spectacular: "The point is to make what you see as uneventful as possible," as a spokesman for Florida's Department of Corrections put it. But this aim is often subverted by the drama inherent in the act of putting a man to death, however much we dress it up as something else. As the Louisiana director of executions admits, "Like it or not, you are putting on a show."[50]

If we pause to reflect on the execution, it quickly becomes apparent that we have here another instance of a peculiar institution. Americans have become used to this arrangement, only occasionally protesting that the event ought to be more public. But for all its familiarity, the low-visibility character of executions is surprising because it would seem to undermine the institution's avowed purposes of deterrence and retribution. As Jeremy Bentham put it, "A real punishment, which is not an apparent punishment, is lost to the public."[51] If the motivating idea is to deter potential offenders or to express public sentiment, we would expect the punishment to be given maximum publicity, not the reverse.

But all this hush and secrecy is also surprising because it is completely at odds with the proliferation of discussion and excitement that characterizes all the earlier stages of the capital process.[52] It seems paradoxical that in a capital punishment process that generates public energy, excitement, and conversation at every stage leading up to the execution, the actual execution itself should be designed to do the opposite. Why is it that at the very last moment, when the much-proclaimed sentence is about to be carried out, the official strategy suddenly shifts to one of concealment and containment?

This arrangement also seems oddly out of place in our televised, mass-mediated society, where the dominant urge is to reveal backstage behavior, to show images, to render things transparent. The logic of today's open, democratic, confessional culture is to give access, to let the cameras in, to reveal backstage conduct, to maximize transparency, accountability, and inside knowledge. Voyeurism is nurtured and catered to, not sternly denied. In an age when most mysteries of state have been exposed, when we know who has slept in the Lincoln bedroom and what sexual activities took place in the Oval Office, state executions have become *arcana imperii*, state secrets to which the public must be denied access. Despite the intense public interest in capital punishment and the prolix nature of death penalty discourse, despite its potential for sensational mass media impact, the contemporary execution takes place behind closed doors, hidden away from television cameras and the public eye. It is a "forbidden spectacle," a "dirty little secret."[53]

Executions were once occasions on which rulers communicated to subjects about the larger political and cosmic forces at work in state justice. Today's officials represent the execution, in symbolic terms, as a nonevent: as merely the dutiful execution of a court order by bureaucrats. Instead of a ceremony in which power is sacralized, we have a procedure in which power is made minimally visible, its character coded as the inevitable unfolding of legal mandates and bureaucratic processes. Whereas executions once loudly proclaimed the sovereign state's might, they now present a silent tableau in which prison employees carry out the law's command in accordance with the will of the people. An event that once expressed the grandeur of a sovereign state now represents that state as nothing other than a law-abiding servant of the people.

Although executions continue to evoke elements of the sacred, the religious, and the transcendental in the minds of some onlookers—and images of state power, communal vengeance, and racial violence in others—such considerations form no part of the authorities' intent. The most striking aspect of today's execution protocol is, in fact, the opposite: the extent to which it has become an instrumental process, devoid of staged drama or deliberate symbolic communication. If the execution contains larger meanings today it is because others insist on projecting them onto the event and interpreting it accordingly.

AMERICAN capital punishment throws a long cultural shadow, producing an extent of political, cultural, and legal engagement that seems quite out of proportion to the institution's actual use or penological importance.

Whereas discussion of the pros and cons of other criminal punishments is mostly restricted to experts, the American death penalty is a perennial subject of political and public concern. Far from a technical issue of criminal justice, capital punishment has come to be tangled up in dense webs of political and cultural associations connecting the death penalty to all sorts of issues, many of which seem quite remote from the punishment of criminals or the control of crime.

Death penalty discourse also exhibits some curious contradictions. The prolix public conversation generated by capital punishment today seems strange in a culture that usually shies away from talking of death. Why, we might ask, does the death penalty excite so much interest, release so much energy, and find so much resonance?

The death penalty is justified today, by the Supreme Court among others, as an expression of retributive community sentiment that demands an appropriately punitive response to the most serious crimes. Capital punishment is intended to express harsh condemnation and to deliver fitting retribution—both of which are morally respectable responses to serious crime. But powerful unwritten rules govern how such sentiments may be respectably voiced and represented. In particular, there is a strict prohibition on the expression of vengeful emotion and on any suggestion of pleasure in contemplating the death of capital offenders. Assemblyman Eric Vitaliano acknowledged these norms when, after presenting his capital punishment bill to the New York State Assembly, he immediately declared, "You haven't heard vengeance from me!"[54] So, too, did Solicitor General Robert Bork when he insisted in his pleadings in *Gregg v Georgia* that retribution is a "vital social function" but quickly added that such retribution must be "stripped of its vindictiveness."[55]

This prohibition on vengefulness allows an exception for the family and friends of murder victims, who are generally permitted, even expected, to express such sentiments. But the victim exception is one that proves the rule. The public functionaries who legislate and administer America's capital punishment system are obliged to avoid any suggestion that their actions are motivated by vengeful impulses. As one commentator puts it, "We are willing to kill murderers, but we do not want anyone to derive satisfaction from doing it."[56]

We see these same norms articulated in official discourse about capital punishment, in which a dispassionate retribution is embraced but vengeful sentiments are emphatically denied and disavowed.[57] Likewise, many legislators, prosecutors, judges, and prison officials take care to discuss the issue in solemn tones, carefully distinguishing dutiful, dispassionate retribution from pleasurable, passionate revenge, referring to the death penalty as

a necessary evil, and protesting repeatedly that they take no personal pleasure in the act. Here is a sampling of commentary:

> A New York state legislator, in the act of passing a capital statute: "I don't get
> any pleasure out of the death penalty and never have."[58]

> A state attorney general, announcing an execution: "Even though justice was
> served, the State takes no joy in fulfilling its obligation"; and, following an-
> other execution: "there is no joy in taking the life of another human being."[59]

> A prison warden, addressing an inmate about to be put to death: "I take no
> pleasure in carrying out this duty, son."[60]

> Members of an execution team, describing their work: "no one enjoys putting
> a man to death"; "We're not a bunch of redneck backwoods hicks killing peo-
> ple. I don't look forward to [executions]."[61]

> State governors, stressing that their support for the institution does not
> amount to inappropriate enthusiasm: "It's a necessity, but an unpleasant ne-
> cessity"; "capital punishment is never pleasant to contemplate"; "some
> crimes deserve it, but that doesn't mean I like it."[62]

> A pro-death–penalty activist, commenting on the resumption of executions
> following a moratorium: "I'm not shouting with glee, but I think that the gas
> chamber is going to be busy."[63]

We can accept these denials as authentic and made in good faith. But the
need of so many officials to deny that they enjoy state killing seems curious. After all, insisting that there is no pleasure to be had in imposing capital punishment is not an obvious response to the situation. Officials in
hospitals and at funerals feel no need to assure their audiences that the
deaths at which they officiate bring them no pleasure. Nor do soldiers in
warfare. But many legislators who enact capital punishment statutes, wardens who oversee executions, victims who view them, judges who uphold
them, and supporters who welcome them all make a point of doing so.
They seem, in short, embarrassed, as if caught in a transgression.

Prohibitive norms and linguistic taboos exist only where there is a continuing need to repress and restrain. If vengefulness and bloodlust had
disappeared altogether, contemporary culture would not expend energy
repressing them. Indeed, newspaper reports, congressional records, and
legal opinions often reveal instances when the prohibitions of propriety
and proper speech have to struggle with an undercurrent of vindictive,
vengeful sentiment that pulls in a different direction. So when the *New
York Post* greets the imposition of a death sentence with the headline, "Fry
Baby!" the journalist is connecting to primitive, aggressive sentiments that

gleefully flout the official rules of decency and decorum. And when Florida's attorney general reacts to news of a botched electrocution—the inmate's face mask had burst into flames and the smell of burnt flesh filled the witness room—by commenting, "People who wish to commit murder, they better not do it in the state of Florida because we may have a problem with our electric chair," he too is violating the rules of solemn restraint, while giving a knowing nod to voters who have no qualms about killing killers.[64] If we look beyond the prison where the execution occurs to the parking lot where locals stage carnival celebrations of the event, the persistence of vengeful pleasures can hardly be in doubt:

> *Glee, outrage, hatred:* A cheer went up from the more than 200 people waiting in the early morning cold. They were carrying signs expressing glee, outrage or hatred for Bundy—"Bundy BBQ," "Burn Bundy Burn," "Roast in Peace" and "Hey Ted, This Buzz is For You."[65]

> *High fives and cigars:* One of the Neal brothers shouted to the heavens as he left the witness chamber. "Alleluia!" . . . Ronnie, Raymond and Darryl Neal were less subdued after watching the execution of the man who confessed to killing [their] sister Ramona. They high-fived and puffed cigars as reporters converged on them outside Florida State Prison.[66]

Official representations of the execution are solemn and subdued, taking care to stress humanity and minimize suffering. That is the official line, the declarative norm. But there is a subterranean current, a sentiment of righteous revenge and punitive pleasure that continues to flow beneath the surface. America's halls of justice and legislative assemblies may protest that vengeance, sadism, and *shadenfreude* have no place in death penalty discourse. But the crowds in the parking lot tell a different story.

A similar disconnect affects the ambience surrounding executions. The enormity of taking a human life, even in societies that are far from liberal or humane, has usually ensured that executions evoke an air of respectful solemnity and awe—even if unruly hanging-day crowds sometimes disrupt this atmosphere.[67] But in America today the execution is often marked by a different emotional tone—one of embarrassment, anxiety, and even guilt. Far from being self-confident, assertive, and assured of the righteousness of their actions, those who carry out executions find the imposition of this legal sentence problematic in a way that other punishments are not. Critics argue that too many people are sent to prison and that conditions of confinement are often inhumane, but the state can nevertheless deploy imprisonment in a positive, confident manner. Not so the death penalty. Even for the worst offenders, the imposition of a death penalty always evokes ambivalence and anxiety.

The executioner has always been an infamous figure, but at least in some parts of America today, the whole process has the feel of dirty work, tainting not just the executioners but everyone else as well. Death work is surrounded by euphemisms. Few people in public life speak out with unbridled enthusiasm on its behalf, and it is rare to hear suggestions that we need many more death sentences or many more executions.[68] In today's debates there is no equivalent of the famous eighteenth-century pamphlet "Hanging Not Punishment Enough." There are certainly sections of the public who confidently hold that capital punishment for murderers is simply the right thing, or the traditional thing, and that's an end of it. But the institution's more elite supporters—the politicians, the judges, the op ed writers—represent capital punishment as a tragic necessity, an unpleasant duty that we must be prepared to carry out, however distasteful it may be. There is an awkwardness, an anxiety, and sometimes a palpable embarrassment of the kind that arises when a moral rule is broken or a taboo violated. "Botched" executions have always been problematic, as have executions of sympathetic individuals. But even when today's executions are properly administered and involve prisoners who are universally detested, they often have an air of shamefulness—particularly in Northern states, where executions are rare events and often involve "volunteers" such as Connecticut's Michael Ross in 2005.

Michael Bruce Ross had been convicted of the rape and murder of eight women and was sentenced to death in 1987.[69] On January 26, 2005, after eighteen years on death row and three attempts at suicide, Ross abandoned his appeals, fired his attorneys, and requested that his death sentence be executed. Ross's insistent request caused consternation among officials and the Northeastern legal community. His defense attorney resisted, claiming that Ross was mentally incompetent to waive his appeals, but subsequently acceded to his request. A federal district judge then threatened to disbar Ross's attorney for acceding to his client's wish to abandon his appeals. "We're not in this profession to help people get killed," he is reported to have said. After a postponement of three months, during which a new attorney was appointed by the court to ensure that Ross's mental state was fully examined, Ross was eventually executed on May 13. That day, Connecticut Governor Jodi Rell, a supporter of the death penalty, said, "Today is a day no one truly looked forward to," describing the lead-up to the event as "a protracted ordeal for the entire state." This is not how executions were regarded in their early-modern heyday. Nor is it how they are typically regarded in the more execution-prone Southern states, where fifteen executions were carried out in the three-month period that Ross was made to wait. But for certain parts of the country, and for certain of the groups involved, the meaning of the death penalty is caught up in a web of conflicts and ambivalence.

This ambivalence is apparent in the statements of judges who express discomfort at being a part of law's "machinery of death." Think of Justice Blackmun (who coined that phrase) describing the "agonies of the spirit" he suffered when dealing with capital cases, or the lengthy confessionals of Ninth Circuit Court of Appeal Judges John T. Noonan and Stephen Reinhardt, or the frustration and rage sometimes expressed by Justices Rehnquist and Scalia when the question of capital punishment is addressed. As James Liebman has documented, capital case opinions display an unusually frequent use of double negatives, expressions of anger, passionate dissents, personalization, inflexibility, defensiveness, over-rationalization, efforts at detachment, and the later expression of regrets.[70]

These difficulties are most pronounced at the point of execution and least apparent at the earlier stages of the process. The awkwardness intensifies as we come closer to the actual killing. American officials continue to enact, evoke, and impose the death penalty in an emphatic, confident tone, but when it comes to taking the life of a living, breathing human being their confidence slips. The result is that executions often seem on the verge of violating propriety and decency. The all-important sense of decorum at these events is fragile and easily breached—by a nose bleed, trouble finding a vein, an inmate too heavy to be hanged, or an aged inmate who has to be wheeled into the death chamber in a wheelchair.

The furtive, behind-the-curtain nature of the execution preliminaries, the suppression of communication, the contorted speech, the air of embarrassment and anxiety—all these suggest an institution that is peculiarly troubled and problematic. The case for the death penalty may seem uncontestable to unapologetic traditionalists and unabashed retributivists. But the practice of capital punishment in America today places officials and their supporters in a cultural contradiction, obliging them to behave in ways that are at once lawful and transgressive. It traps them in the uncomfortable space between the cultural norms of liberal humanism and the legal practice of putting offenders to death.

Narratives and Metaphors

Capital punishment must make sense in the culture in which it operates. It has to be made intelligible, legitimate, and, if possible, compelling. This task is accomplished through narrative. Cultural actors—which is to say officials, activists, commentators, journalists, and artists—tell stories

about the death penalty that give it sense and meaning, invoking metaphors and associations that anchor it in familiar cultural scripts and established forms of authority. Since these narratives are always controversial
and contested, its supporters connect it to positive values, institutions, and
outcomes, while its critics make it a part of different stories that reveal its
problems and its corrosive qualities.

These stories, repeated over time and given the imprimatur of courts
and state officials, shape perception, accord significance, and fix associations. By invoking certain metaphors and symbols, and by offering a
ready-made structure for discussion and debate, these narrative frames
shape thinking and help form attitudes. They prompt people to think of
the death penalty in this way rather than that, to adopt one perspective
rather than another, to make particular associations and inferences rather
than others that would be equally possible. They are, in short, a rhetoric of
motives.[71]

The active creation and reproduction of these frames is always a politically consequential act. It is no surprise then, that state officials and their
supporters take care to present the death penalty using frames that maximize its legitimacy and appeal, while critics do their best to challenge such
reasoning, dispute its rationales, and subvert its meanings.

In the abundant discourse that surrounds today's death penalty, five basic metaphors supply the institution with its dominant meanings. These
are the metaphors of rules, of war, of order and balance, of healing, and of
the people's will. Each of these metaphors is challenged by critics who propose counternarratives with which to frame the practice. But taken together, these five frameworks structure much of what gets said about the
institution in the mainstream media and the political process. If capital
punishment is a public text, these are the narratives that give that text its
standard meanings.

The metaphor of rules frames the death penalty as a constitutionally approved undertaking, a matter of legal determinations rather than personal
decisions, an outcome of painstaking procedural safeguards that amount
to "super due process." It is capital punishment represented as law.

In today's newspaper reports, law reviews, court decisions, and statements by officials, the American death penalty is represented first and foremost as a lawful procedure, validated by the Constitution, regulated by
rules, and supervised by the courts. Capital punishment as law is the dominant frame in America today, and the Constitution is used by both supporters and opponents to supply chapter-and-verse textual support for
their claims in much the same way that Scripture was deployed in earlier
centuries.[72]

Litigation campaigns and Supreme Court cases from the 1960s to the present have ensured that the metaphor of rules sets the terms in which the issue is presented to the American public. All the talk about constitutional rights, procedural proprieties, legal appeals, *habeas* hearings, and court-ordered stays of execution—dutifully reported by the news media—has a definite cultural effect. Long before he is put to death, the capital defendant is made over as the judicial subject *par excellence*.[73] An illustrative example is a public statement by President George W. Bush following the execution of Timothy McVeigh in 2001: "Due process ruled. The case was proved. The verdict was calmly reached. And the rights of the accused were protected and observed to the full and to the end. Under the laws of our country, the matter is concluded."[74]

The "capital punishment is law" frame is attacked head on by the institution's opponents. For much of the last thirty years, the central challenge to the death penalty in America has been that it is, in fact, *not* lawful. Critics charge that it is, on the contrary, arbitrarily, cruelly, or unequally imposed in ways that violate the Eighth and Fourteenth Amendments. The counternarrative of capital punishment's opponents depicts an institution driven by arbitrariness, racism, and collective emotion. Law professor Robert Weisberg turns the official frame on its head by arguing that the metaphor of rules propounded by the Supreme Court is just that—a metaphor—and that the most important decisions in the capital process (made by prosecutors, jurors, and governors) are discretionary, subjective, and not liable to external review. To the metaphor "capital punishment as the rule of law" the critics respond "capital punishment as a legal lynching."[75]

A second metaphor depicts the death penalty as a weapon of self-defense in a war on crime; a lethal response needed to deter or incapacitate the enemy while raising our side's morale; an effective means of fighting back against armed criminals who are dangerous or monstrous individuals impervious to lesser punishments: a vital protection for an endangered public.

The negativity of the death penalty presents a problem for liberal states in welfare-oriented societies. How can governments, committed to promoting "life, liberty, and the pursuit of happiness," legitimately put citizens to death? One answer is to represent capital punishment not as the imposition of death but as the saving of lives—a paradox that becomes more plausible if we assume that the death penalty can operate as a deterrent to dissuade potential murderers. This was the argument presented recently by the legal academics Cass Sunstein and Adrian Vermeule, who argued that utilitarian considerations should persuade liberals that the death penalty is morally sound if research into deterrence showed that capital punishment would reduce future lives lost. (The authors acknowledged that such an empirical claim is highly controversial.) This same framework was more unconditionally invoked by Texas Governor George W. Bush when he insisted, "When the death penalty is administered in a . . . sure and fair way, it will save lives. It will save lives." His brother, Governor Jeb Bush of Florida, argued much the same: "Floridians believe in the death penalty because they know it saves innocent lives." So did Republican Governor George Pataki, as he signed New York state's 1995 Death Penalty Act: "I know that by restoring the death penalty we have saved lives."[76]

The metaphor of a war on crime has been prominent in American political discourse since at least the 1960s and was especially prominent in the early 1990s, when homicide rates and public fear of crime reached historic highs.[77] This frame depicts capital punishment not as a policy choice but as a necessary act of public self-defense. As Vice President George H. W. Bush put it, "I say that some crimes are so heinous, so outrageous, so brutal that the death penalty is warranted. . . . If this is a war, then let's treat it like a war." And when New York Governor George Pataki signed the death penalty into law in 1995, he described it not as a punishment but as a defensive weapon in the war on crime: "I must and do appreciate my duty: to provide the maximum possible protection to all persons in New York . . . from vicious and ruthless acts of murder."[78] Once the argument is framed in this way, it becomes possible to ask of any politician or public official, "Whose side are you on? The public's or the murderer's?" A policy position on the death penalty is thereby transformed into a litmus test of one's concern about public welfare, even of one's patriotism.

The war metaphor makes its way into the courts as well. In their pursuit of a capital sentence, prosecutors identify the defendant as a public enemy, enlist the jurors in the war effort, and encourage them to do their civic duty: "I say to you we're in a war again in this country, except it's not a foreign nation, it's against the criminal element in this country. [The defendant, William Brooks, is a] member of the criminal element, and he's our enemy."[79]

In other cases the defendant is depicted not as an enemy but as a monster. And if the war metaphor is designed to evoke fear, the monstrosity trope aims to evoke horror and repulsion. Here is Federal Judge Alex Kozinski, depicting the monstrous evils against which the death penalty is directed:

Take for example Jacob Dougan, who brutally murdered an eighteen-year-old boy and then sent a tape to the boy's mother bragging about the crime.

Dougan told the victim's mother, "He was stabbed in the back, in the chest, and the stomach, it was beautiful. You should have seen it. I enjoyed every minute of it. I loved watching blood gush from his eyes." Other examples abound: Robert Alton Harris, who abducted two young boys from a McDonald's, and after shooting them down in cold blood calmly finished off the burgers they had been eating and laughed about how the bullets had dismembered them; Thomas Schiro, who drugged, raped, beat and ultimately strangled a woman, then mutilated and sexually assaulted her corpse; and there are many more. . . . John Wayne Gacy, Juan Corona, Theodore Frank, Ted Bundy, Charles Manson . . . Jeffery Dahmer . . .[80]

Faced with these grotesque atrocities—and such graphic depictions are a standard feature of pro-death discourse—jurors or members of the public are likely to recoil in horror and incomprehension. They are also more likely to embrace capital punishment as a necessary bulwark of public safety, as well as a proper retributive response to appalling acts of wickedness.

Death penalty opponents challenge this framework in several ways. They argue that life imprisonment without parole provides equally effective protection; that the war metaphor mischaracterizes the relationship between a state and its law-breaking citizens; and that even the most heinous offenders are potentially redeemable human beings not reducible to their worst acts. Their counternarrative is that the death penalty is a weapon of *choice,* not of necessity, imposed not against monsters or enemies but against individuals—often mentally damaged individuals—who are fellow human beings.

A third metaphor—that of order and balance—depicts the death penalty as morally appropriate, as just desert, as a repayment in kind. It is the restoration of order following the disruption of a murderous act, a balancing response to a horrific crime. The death of the murderer is construed as a necessary means to reestablish equilibrium; a way of honoring a dishonored victim; a vindication of violated rights. This is capital punishment as retributive justice.

This framework, with its metaphors of weighing, balancing, and proportionality, or of reckoning and equivalence, represents the death penalty as a moral counterweight to the wrong of murder. The scales of justice—but also the community's retributive passions—demand a life for a life, the ultimate punishment for the ultimate crime. What is important here is not so much the moral demand for retributive punishment, since this could be satisfied by severe punishment of a nonlethal kind, such as the sentences of life imprisonment with which other Western nations punish murderers. What is important, rather, is payment in kind, the equivalent exchange of death for death. Once again, capital punishment is represented not as a choice but as a duty. It is a necessary expression of community outrage, a correct and essential response, a morally required avengement. As Justice Potter Stewart put it, there are "crimes so gross, so heinous, so cold-blooded that anything short of death seems inadequate."[81]

When prosecutors press jurors to bring in a sentence of death, or explain a capital sentence to the viewing public, they rarely describe it as a deterrent or as incapacitation. They present it as a moral imperative. As Alabama Attorney General Troy King declared to the jury judging Westley Harris, "This case cried out for a sanction commensurate with the wickedness and brutality of his actions, and the penalty of death is the only just and proper answer to the evil Harris unleashed on August 26, 2002."[82]

Politicians also represent the issue as a matter of justice, a solemn duty rather than a political choice or policy preference. According to Governor Jeb Bush of Florida, "The citizens of Florida have decided that the death penalty is an appropriate form of justice for those who have committed the most heinous crimes against innocent victims."[83] His brother, President George W. Bush, following the execution of Timothy McVeigh, solemnly proclaimed, "The victims of the Oklahoma City bombing have been given not vengeance, but justice. . . . Today every living person who was hurt by the evil done in Oklahoma City can rest in the knowledge that there has been a reckoning."[84]

Unlike the utilitarian rationales for capital punishment (deterrence, denunciation, incapacitation, and so on), which are open to empirical challenge or admit of alternative means to the same end, the claims of retributive justice are absolute.[85] This may explain why retributive justice is now the major justification offered by the institution's supporters. Scott Turow, who served on an Illinois state commission on capital punishment, observes that this was the central rationale that featured in the language of the system's supporters: "Sometimes a crime is so horrible that killing its perpetrator is the only correct response." In the insistent rhetoric of this perspective, the community is *obliged,* the murder *demands,* duty *must be done.* Like the metaphor of war and patriotic duty, the moral obligation to do justice is one that binds us and may not be shirked because the prospect of killing an offender is an unpleasant one. This sense of obligation is vividly expressed by Judge Alex Kozinski, who says that he hears "the tortured voices of the victims crying out to me for vindication." The felt need to respond to this cry and let haunting spirits finally find peace is why, "despite the qualms, despite the queasiness," Kozinski believes "that society is entitled to take the life of those who have shown utter contempt for the lives of others."[86]

There is, in this understanding of capital punishment, a clear echo of the traditional rules of vengeance, a definite sense that the death penalty is a way to honor the deceased and recognize the worth and status of his or her kin. Wherever this understanding prevails, a failure to demand death can be taken to mean that the worth of the deceased is being undervalued, his or her memory slighted.

Critics respond that morality demands no such thing: that nothing is gained by further killing; that there are other, more appropriate ways of doing justice, the most important being life imprisonment. The counternarrative here is forward-looking and redemptive. It strives to depict backward-looking, payment-in-kind retribution as little more than mindless vengeance.

A more surprising means of representing the death penalty is the metaphor of healing. This frame depicts the death penalty as a way of restoring a community's well-being and providing psychological closure for traumatized victims. The same metaphor shapes our perception of the execution as a medical procedure. The lethal injection protocol's evocations of medical solicitude and humane concern suggest that we respect the person of the condemned even as we put him to death. Capital punishment, this frame would have us believe, is humane treatment.

The old idea of murder as moral pollution points in the same direction. If murder is a bloodstain on the community, the killer's death can be viewed as a cathartic act of cleansing, a way of ridding the community of moral contamination and restoring social health. David Gelernter's statement that "a deliberate murder embodies evil so terrible that it defiles the community" contains precisely this idea.[87] These metaphors of cleansing, restoration, and cure represent the death penalty as promoting social health. They use the imagery of the welfare state to justify an act that might otherwise seem to have no place in liberal government. This inversion is especially important when it comes to the execution itself, where the contradiction between the state's politics of life and its punishment of death is at its most intense, and where the practice has greatest need of legitimation.

The metaphor of healing also shapes recent attempts to justify capital punishment by reference to its therapeutic effects for relatives of the victim. As Texas Attorney General John Cornyn remarked after the execution of Gary Graham, "Graham's victims and their families have had to live with the consequences of his crimes. It is now time for them to have the closure and the justice our system provides." Attorney General John Ashcroft had the same therapeutic goals in mind when he authorized a closed-circuit telecast that allowed victims and victims' families to witness the execution of Timothy McVeigh. In Ashcroft's words, witnessing the execution was intended to "help them meet their need to close this chapter in their lives."[88] As McVeigh's attorney noted, "We have made killing a part of the healing process."[89]

Capital punishment's opponents regard this way of framing the issue as an appalling misrepresentation. Deliberately killing a healthy person who represents no immediate danger to others is, they insist, a travesty of the medical vocation and a violation of the Hippocratic Oath. They point to the American Medical Association's refusal to allow its members to take any part in executions; to the amateurish, unsafe fashion in which lethal injections are sometimes administered; and to the possibility that the current protocol entails unseen pain and suffering on the part of the condemned. They present the death penalty not as humane treatment but as human sacrifice.

Finally, we have the recurring metaphor of the people's will. Here the death penalty is depicted as a vital expression of local community sentiment, as moral outrage authentically expressed, as collective choice and community justice. Death sentences express the will of the people dutifully carried out by their lawful representatives. This is capital punishment represented as democracy in action.

In the United States there are few claims more powerful than that of the democratic will. A social practice that can claim the support of a popular majority avails itself of an authority that is hard to challenge, whatever criticisms can be made of the way the practice is carried out. Until quite recently, death penalty supporters justified the practice by reference to the benefits it brought, the purposes it served, and the traditional justice it expressed. Today, when these benefits and purposes are more often in doubt, and when other nations have turned away from that tradition, we see a new emphasis on the institution's democratic credentials and its popular support. Courts point to opinion polls, legislators point to electorates, prosecutors point to communities, and appellate judges point to jury decisions, each time as evidence that the death penalty, whatever its practical shortcomings, represents the will of the people. As a Texas prosecutor put it, "No prosecutor gives the death penalty, only people do."[90]

When President George W. Bush addressed a foreign press corps, defending America's retention against European criticism, he talked not about the death penalty's effectiveness or utility but instead about its democratic credentials: "The death penalty is the will of the people in the United States." The same justification is heard in every state legislature where capital legislation is considered. As a New York state assemblyman put it in 1995, "You know what the bottom line is here, ladies and gentlemen? The people of New York want the death penalty, and it's about time we gave them the death penalty."[91]

The same political rationale is offered by Texas officials, who explain that the state's remarkably high volume of death penalty indictments simply reflects "the will of the people in a democratic society." They respond to critics by invoking "the people" and "the voters" as the higher authority behind their acts. "The people of Harris County believe in the death penalty," according to a prosecutor in the nation's leading capital punishment county, "and those same people employ the district attorney and his staff. All these people in New York say something is wrong with Harris County and its prosecutors. We're rabid and zealous, they say. Those folks need to come down here and listen to these voters."[92]

Notice that "the voters" to whom the Texas prosecutor refers for her death-dispensing authority are not the voters of the United States, nor even those of the state electorate of Texas, but the voters of Harris County. America allocates penal law-making powers to the fifty states, but decisions about the enforcement of these laws are made at a lower level still—by county prosecutors who are accountable to county voters.

Most arguments for the death penalty come with ready-made counter-arguments, but in the United States it is difficult to challenge an argument grounded in the will of the people—especially when the issue is a matter of morality and political preference. Some death penalty opponents—such as Supreme Court Justices William Brennan and Thurgood Marshall and the Legal Defense Fund litigators who brought suit in the *Furman* case—have tried to claim the people's authority for *their* cause, arguing that opinion polls, jury decisions, and enforcement patterns (at least in the 1960s) indicated that the American people did not truly support capital punishment.[93] Others argue that majority preferences ought not to be allowed to trample individual rights, that popular opinion is superficial and based on misunderstandings, and that community sentiment is too volatile to be allowed to control such momentous matters. But the obvious counternarrative, that popular judgment is untrustworthy in these matters and ought to give way to more educated, expert opinion—a position that we might call "the European view"—is virtually unavailable. Such a view would be deemed elitist and un-American, contemptuous of the populist democratic sentiment at the core of American culture.

THESE, then, are the institutional forms, cultural figures, and narrative frames that characterize the capital punishment system in the United States today—the American way of death. None of the institutional arrangements is "irrational" or "senseless," as critics allege, but nor do any of them appear well adapted to their ostensible purposes. None of the cultural forms is incoherent or unintelligible, but they are sometimes odd or contradictory in important respects. None of the narrative frames that legitimate capital punishment is especially novel, though it seems revealing that America's death penalty is increasingly represented not as an instrumental policy but as an expressive act of local people's will.

In thinking about these distinctive forms we should begin from the premise that none of them is accidental nor arbitrary. They emerged out of a specific history in the context of definite power relations and institutional constraints. America's capital punishment arrangements correspond to specific social structures and cultural sensibilities. They crystallize the balances of power and contending interests that define the social field in which they exist.[94] Like any social fact, today's capital punishment complex bears witness to the social organization, cultural patterns, and conflicting interests of the people who produced it.

■ THREE ■

Historical Modes
of Capital Punishment

(1) Auto da fe (2) Beating with clubs (3) Beheading: Decapitation
(4) Blowing from cannon (5) Boiling (6) Breaking on the wheel (7)
Burning (8) Burying alive (9) Crucifixion (10) Decimation (11) Dichotomy (12) Dismemberment (13) Drowning (14) Exposure to
wild beasts etc. (15) Flaying alive (16) Flogging: Knout (17) Garrote (18) Guillotine (19) Hanging (20) Hari kari (21) Impalement
(22) Iron Maiden (23) Peine Forte et Dure (24) Poisoning (25)
Pounding in mortar (26) Precipitation (27) Pressing to death (28)
Rack (29) Running the gauntlet (30) Shooting (31) Stabbing (32)
Stoning (33) Strangling (34) Suffocation.

LIST OF EXECUTION METHODS COMPILED BY THE NEW YORK STATE
COMMISSION TO INVESTIGATE AND REPORT THE MOST HUMANE
AND PRACTICAL METHODS OF CARRYING INTO EFFECT
THE SENTENCE OF DEATH, 1888

Capital punishment has been practiced in most known societies over
the course of human history. In modern liberal democracies, however,
the legitimacy and effectiveness of the institution have increasingly come
into question. In these nations, with their commitment to limiting state violence, promoting social welfare, and respecting human dignity, the death
penalty exists, if at all, in tension with important institutions and cultural
commitments. Where not altogether abolished, it is now used much less
often and in forms that are increasingly restrained and refined.

This transformation is remarkable. The death penalty once formed an
elementary particle of governmental power in every nation state. Today
the practice is widely regarded as shameful and is prohibited throughout
most of the Western world. What happened?

The death penalty can be defined as a practice whereby a properly constituted public authority puts to death a convicted offender in punishment
for crime. It is thus distinct from unauthorized forms of killing, such as revenge killing or murder or lynching, and from nonpenal forms of state kill-

ing, whether legal (human sacrifice, killing in war, and so on) or illegal (political killings, summary executions). Stripped to its essence, it involves nothing more elaborate than putting law-breakers to death—an undertaking that has obvious utility for group authorities and is readily available without need of elaborate technology, know-how, or social arrangements. These characteristics, together with its capacity to terrorize anyone who fears death, explain why for millennia the death penalty was close to a cultural universal.[1]

In the early-modern period, newly emergent state authorities took up the death penalty and accorded it a central role in the task of state building. Elaborate public ceremonies, horrifying execution techniques, and ritual proclamations were developed as so many means to this end. By the mid-nineteenth century, in a context of increasingly well established and rationalized states, capital punishment's primary purpose had altered, so that what had once been an instrument of rule, essential to state security, became an instrument of penal policy, focused on the narrower goals of rendering justice and controlling crime.

As its functions changed, so too did its forms. The death penalty came to be formatted as a penal sanction rather than as a political spectacle. Its focus came to center on criminal rather than political offenses. Its executions came to be more swiftly administered, not in the political space of the town square but in the penal space of the jail yard. By the late twentieth century, in the very different context of the modern liberal-democratic welfare state, capital punishment had ceased to be a central plank in the apparatus of crime control and had become increasingly rare and controversial. By century's end, it had been abolished by all the developed nations of the West except for the United States, and by many non-Western nations besides.[2]

This long-term process of transformation should not be mistaken for moral and political progress. The decline of the death penalty did not necessarily signal the diminution of punishment or the end of state violence, even in Western democracies. Nor was it the story of "civilization" taking hold of capital punishment, though some of the civilizing processes highlighted by the sociologist Norbert Elias certainly played a part.[3] Nor, finally, was it a narrative of the death penalty's continual decline. At the dawn of the modern period, between the fifteenth and seventeenth centuries, the use, display, and intensity of the death penalty increased exponentially as it became a central weapon in the armory of newly formed states struggling to establish sovereign power. And at various moments in the nineteenth and twentieth centuries, several European nations that had earlier reduced their reliance on the death penalty or abolished it altogether returned to the practice with a vengeance, whether in response to political instability or in pursuit of totalitarian power.[4]

There was no natural process at work in these transformations, no inexorable law that dictated the course of historical events. But a discernible pattern emerged nonetheless because, for the most part, modern Western history has been shaped by the forces of state formation and rationalization, liberalization and democratization, "civilization" and humanization. And these political and cultural processes have had definite consequences for the shape and survival of the death penalty.

The history of the death penalty is a world-historic one, and no general theory can explain every outcome in every locality. But it is possible to outline the general pattern of change in Western nations and to develop an explanatory account of how social developments transformed the institution.[5] The long-term movement toward a more restrained, refined, and reduced death penalty occurred for reasons that are quite intelligible. State authorities strove to deploy the death penalty more effectively and to ensure its continuing legitimacy despite changing contexts of use. The political forces of liberalism worked to limit state power and to establish legal protections for individuals. Democrats struggled to equalize punishment and extend liberal protections to all social groups. Cultural elites, disturbed by the sight of raw violence and unruly mobs, sought to civilize the institution, while antigallows reformers of all stripes—variously motivated by religious faith, fellow feeling, or humanitarian sentiment—campaigned to reduce the suffering of convicted offenders and uphold their right to life.

The historical situations in which these social processes were translated into specific reforms were often recurring ones (shifts between political regimes; the installation of left-wing governments; responses to scandals; attempts to repair malfunctioning processes; and so on), and the individuals translating them into action were typically state officials, responding to a changed political climate, to criticism, or to control problems. The final stage of complete, nationwide abolition was typically a top-down reform legislated by a political elite in the face of popular opposition or indifference.

These reforms occurred when large-scale processes of change connected with the specific concerns of well-placed actors. They failed to occur when the processes were hindered by political instability, high rates of criminal violence, public insecurity, or effective political resistance. Only by understanding these causal forces and the situations in which they typically play out will we be in a position to explain the survival of the death penalty in the United States and the peculiar form that it now takes.

Abolition is now the Western norm, but for most of human history the death penalty was what anthropologists call a "cultural universal," forming an element of every organized society.[6] Even today, following a wave of abolition in the late twentieth century, more than one hundred nations still retain capital punishment in some form, and the vast majority of the world's population still lives under its threat.[7] The age of abolition is a decidedly Western phenomenon.

These facts should hardly surprise us. If we set aside contemporary moral qualms and political objections to its use, it is easy to see why capital punishment has been so widespread. "Death is . . . of all dreadful things the most dreadful," Samuel Johnson remarked, "an evil beyond which nothing can be threatened."[8] As a political weapon and a penal instrument, the death penalty has an irresistible power. Putting political enemies, serious wrongdoers, and dangerous individuals to death is an obvious, effective, and efficient way for authorities to eliminate the threat that such individuals represent. Imposing a death penalty on law-breakers permits the punishing authority to proclaim its power, impress onlookers, and denounce the proscribed conduct, while simultaneously exacting revenge, undoing pollution, restoring social order, and sending a warning to would-be offenders. This very useful practice, "rife with utilitarian purposes of every kind," requires little in the way of technology or know-how and can be inflicted by states that have no apparatus of prisons and penitentiaries.[9] As a punishment, death has elemental force and meaning.

Nor has this self-evident efficacy diminished in the contemporary period. If swiftly applied, frequently utilized, and imposed with the requisite amount of pain and publicity—as it still is in places such as China, Iran, Singapore, Sudan, and Saudi Arabia—the death penalty retains much of its power as a penal and political instrument. If anything, its potential is enhanced as these societies become more developed, more affluent, and more inclined to value human life.

Viewed in long-term comparative perspective, penalties of death are the norm, not the exception. The phenomenon that stands most in need of explanation is not America's retention of capital punishment but rather the ongoing transformation that has occurred in every Western nation, America included.

The pattern of change transforming the Western death penalty is neither continuous nor even, nor does it proceed without reversals. But there is a discernible pattern that is widespread and recurrent, and which exhibits the overall direction of a structured, developmental change. As the historian Richard Evans puts it:

> [W]hat strikes the observer . . . is the fact that similar changes in penal practice happened virtually everywhere at roughly the same epoch. In almost all major European states, the eighteenth and nineteenth centuries saw a diminu-

tion of public punishment, the abolition of torture, the banishing of the more baroque cruelties from the scene of the scaffold, and the decisive phase in the rise of imprisonment. Everywhere, the middle of the nineteenth century saw the ending of public executions, or at least their restriction to a small number of spectators and the stripping away of the most elaborate embellishments of public ritual associated with them . . . Right across Europe, the same period saw the culmination of a long-heralded crisis in the legitimacy of capital punishment.[10]

Like any historical process, this development has definite causes and conditions of existence—it does not just happen. If these causes and conditions are absent, as they were in many non-Western nations, the changes in the death penalty discussed here will not occur. If these causes cease to operate, the process does, too: the pattern of change has altered and reversed in the past and it can do so again in the future. Nor is there anything mysterious about it; we can trace the implications and effects of identifiable causes of change. Finally, although there is a discernible pattern of concurrent development across national boundaries in the West over long periods of time, each nation's developmental path has been distinctive in certain respects. Instead of thinking of a general history with America as a deviant exception we should think in terms of a transnational developmental pattern composed of distinct but converging national histories within which America can be included.

We can distinguish three eras of capital punishment in the West since the middle ages: the "early modern," the "modern," and the "late modern." In each of these eras, capital punishment operated differently, exhibiting a distinctive modality with its own forms and functions. Each modality is associated with a different historical period and social organization, and each one is loosely associated with a distinctive state form (the early-modern absolutist state, the nineteenth-century liberal state, the late twentieth-century liberal-democratic welfare state). The first two periods (the early modern and the modern) are sharply differentiated in most respects, whereas the third (the late modern) is a variant of the second, though it is sufficiently distinct to warrant separate classification.[11]

In the first two periods, capital punishment was an important social practice, though its structural position changed, as did its forms and functions, as it shifted from an early-modern to a modern mode. In the third period—which might be termed the "late modernity" of the last decades of the twentieth century and the first decades of the twenty-first—we see the decline and marginalization of capital punishment as a social institution and its rapid disappearance from most Western legal codes.[12] Where it survives—as it does in the United States—the institution's forms and functions have been further altered, its use more attenuated, and its place in so-cial organization more controversial.

The Early-Modern Mode

The emergence of the modern political entity known as "the state" was a long-term process that developed at different rates in different regions. In England, state formation was apparent as early as the twelfth century; elsewhere, in Italy and Germany, for example, unified national states emerged much later. The period from 1400 to 1700 is the crucial era in which this process took place. By the end of that period, a European system of sovereign states had emerged, the existence of which was explicitly recognized in the 1648 Peace of Westphalia.

A crucial element of state formation was the effort of nascent political authorities to exert a monopoly of power over territory they now claimed as their own. This historic struggle to impose sovereign rule gave a new prominence and intensity to capital punishment. Before the emergence of the state, the death penalty appears to have been carried out without elaborate ceremony. Discussing the late-medieval evidence from Germany, Evans says, "Illustrations of executions in the fourteenth and fifteenth centuries show them as casual and unceremonial affairs, with a handful of people standing informally around while the hangman does his work." Referring to England, James Sharpe writes that there "is little evidence that any elaborate ceremonial attended the execution of felons in the later middle ages." Keith Otterbein's ethnographic survey also suggests that executions in prestate societies were mostly carried out in secret or without fanfare.[13]

The emergence of sovereign states altered these older practices in several respects. The punishment of death became the prerogative of state authorities who asserted their monopoly over legitimate violence and prohibited traditional practices of private vendetta and vengeance. Death penalties came to be imposed and administered under the auspices of the royal courts, imparting a greater degree of rule-governed formality and legal rationality. And the execution of these penalties became more public, more elaborately ceremonial, and more violent, as the new states sought to use shock-and-awe tactics to impress the populace and strike fear in the hearts of enemies.[14] Though we sometimes describe cruel punishments as "medieval," it was in fact the emergence of despotic states in the late-medieval and early-modern period that transformed these events into elaborate spectacles of suffering. Not Europe's medieval lords but the absolutist rulers who replaced them gave capital punishment its greatest cruelty, intensity, and display.

In the states of early-modern Europe—many but not all of which were absolutist in form—the death penalty operated within a distinctive political and penological context.[15] Politically, the state was usually weak and unstable. It lacked any powerful infrastructure of control or any settled claim on the allegiance of its subjects. It faced the threat of rebellion by internal enemies or war waged by hostile neighboring states. In terms of criminal justice, early-modern states were similarly weak, lacking any well-developed, police force or prison system. Moreover, their capacity to communicate was limited, with few means other than public, dramatic displays with which to assert their claims to authority. Consequently, as Esther Cohen notes, "Government power was often displayed in visual theatrical form: solemn royal or urban processions, festivals, and most commonly, the execution of criminals."[16]

Against this background the death penalty became a vital instrument of state rule and developed its distinctive early-modern character. Later, as governmental capacities increased and a differentiated penal infrastructure was built, the death penalty's all-purpose utility began to diminish. Other sanctions—banishment, transportation to the colonies, galley slavery, forced labor on public works projects, and above all, imprisonment—arose to take its place.

The imposition of the death penalty is first and foremost an exercise of power, wherever, whenever, and however it occurs. Any account of its development must focus, therefore, on the fundamental question of power: its dispersion and concentration; its claims to authority and the rules for its legitimate exercise; its developing techniques and their relation to social organization; and finally, its expression through symbols and cultural performance.

Death sentences had a variety of uses in the early-modern period, among them the maintenance of order, the rendering of justice, and the reinforcement of social hierarchies. But whatever other purposes the institution might have served, at the core of the death penalty's meaning was the assertion, preservation, and protection of the authority of the state.[17] Even the great liberal abolitionist Cesare Beccaria recognized the necessity of the death penalty when the stability of the early-modern state was in jeopardy:

> The death of a citizen cannot be *necessary* except in one case. When, though deprived of his liberty he has such power and connections as may endanger the security of the nation; when his existence may produce a dangerous revo-

lution in the established form of government. But even in this case, it can only be necessary when a nation is on the verge of recovering or losing its liberty; or in times of absolute anarchy, when the disorders themselves hold the place of laws.[18]

The elaborate cruelty and display with which the early-modern authorities put enemies to death on the scaffold were driven less by a passion for punishment than by the practical need to demonstrate sovereignty to skeptics.[19]

The early phases of state formation brought a new importance to capital punishment as aspiring rulers shifted their efforts from military conquest to internal pacification and the establishment of order. Rulers staged the death penalty as a military ceremony intended to terrorize enemies and impress onlookers with spectacular displays of ritualized violence.[20] Especially in the absolutist state, the execution became a structural support in the edifice of state power and a necessary concomitant of social order. As Joseph de Maistre put it, "all grandeur, all power, all subordination rests on the executioner: he is the horror and the bond of human association. Remove this incomprehensible agent from the world and at every moment order gives way to chaos, thrones topple, and society disappears. God, who has created sovereignty, has also made punishments."[21]

If the spectacular execution was the product of early-modern state formation, its political utility ensured its continuing use by states keen to project an appearance of political strength. Richard Evans shows how the regimes that emerged in continental Europe toward the end of the seventeenth century relied on capital punishment to communicate their political claims:

> In the world of Absolutism, punishment had to be seen as coming directly from the state itself, through concrete physical actions undertaken by the state's servant, the executioner, on the body of the offender. The full execution ritual, with its elaborate procession and ceremonial procedures at the scaffold, was a phenomenon of the late seventeenth and eighteenth centuries, and crowds attending it were a consequence of the state's increasing tendency to orchestrate such occasions. . . . Absolutism, from the great patrimonies of Austria and Prussia, Saxony and Bavaria, down to the petty principalities and city-states that littered Central Europe in this period, demanded that sovereignty be asserted with pomp and circumstance.[22]

The watchword here was terror. Unable to rule by consent and close control, the early-modern state sought to rule by fear. Death, the greatest terror, became a technique of rule, and early-modern states were endlessly inventive in their elaboration of scaffold torments.

The chief targets of this ferocity were enemies of the state and those who threatened public order: above all offenders convicted of *lèse-majesté*, treason, riot, or sedition. The most horrendous executions were reserved not for murderers or common criminals but for political offenders. Traitors were hung, drawn and quartered, their heads placed on spikes, their body parts displayed around the kingdom. Treasonable offenses of a lesser kind—"petit treason" against masters or husbands—also drew unusually severe punishments such as burning at the stake.[23]

Political purposes continued to define the death penalty well into the eighteenth century, even in nonabsolutist states such as England. Speaking of seventeenth- and eighteenth-century English executions, V. A. C. Gatrell notes, "The order of the world depended on these slaughters," and "the sanction of the gallows and the rhetoric of the death sentence were central to all relations of authority in Georgian England." Douglas Hay makes the same point when he writes that "rulers of eighteenth-century England cherished the death penalty" and argues that "the criminal law, more than any other social institution, made it possible to govern eighteenth century England without a police force and without a large army."[24]

Throughout this period, the use of the death penalty was adjusted to sustain unstable regimes in the face of insurrection. Political crises, threats to the state, acts of insubordination—all were occasions for the harsh deployment of scaffold punishments and the setting of ruthless examples. In sixteenth-century England under the Tudors, execution ceremonies became more elaborate and traitors were singled out for especially horrific treatment. But later, when the state's power was better established and its authority grounded in consent as well as coercion, the gallows became a less prominent instrument of rule. Thus in England by the late eighteenth century, the guiding principle of state killing was more restrained: "public policy demanded examples, not a charnel house."[25] Governing authority in these more settled times was displayed by merciful pardons as well as by spectacular deaths.

The predominant model of rule on the European continent in the early-modern period was that of the absolute monarch. This absolutist conception of power colored the process of law, leading to secret charges, state-directed prosecutions, torture, *lettres de cachet,* and an absence of procedural protections for the individual accused. Investigative torture took place in secret, and the processes of trial and conviction were shrouded in darkness: not until the execution was the outcome brought into broad daylight. Even in nonabsolutist England, with its parliamentary monarchy and its tradition of the rights of freeborn individuals, it was not until the Treason Act of 1694 that any suspect was granted the right to counsel or the right to hear the charges ranged against him.[26]

In that age of faith, secular and religious forms of authority were closely integrated and state officials leaned on the church to augment their power. Like all state ceremonies of this period, the execution was also a religious event, framed in a discourse of eternal verities as well as of worldly power, presided over by clerics as well as by state officials. Writing of English executions, McGowan notes that "theology structure[d] and infused the gallows."[27] Discussing the German experience, Evans says, "The language by which condemned people were described emphasized above all the moral and religious aspects of their status. They were known as 'poor sinners.'" The condemned were allowed priests or pastors, encouraged to repent, and urged to take communion.[28]

Early-modern execution ceremonies focused on the state of the condemned's soul: his every word and gesture was scrutinized by the crowd for signs of atonement and the prospect of redemption. In the ritual of execution, larger questions of eternal judgment were also at stake. The condemned was going to die and meet his maker—a fate that every onlooker feared and that each would one day experience—and he was groomed and prepared accordingly. His last meal recalled the Last Supper. His procession to the scaffold recalled the procession to Calvary. His last words—prepared with the help of a cleric—were usually those of a remorseful penitent offering himself up to God's mercy. His torment on the scaffold symbolically repeated that of Christ on the Cross and suggested the fate of all believers at life's end. In addressing the themes of crime and the relation of subject to sovereign, the scaffold drama also raised the question of death and man's relation to God. The authority of one great power flowed into that of the other.[29]

As well as being an age of faith, the early-modern period was also an age of folk superstition and magical belief. As with funerals and other death rites, myths and magical practices surrounded the scaffold; these included the drinking of the corpse's blood and the taking of relics (pieces of the rope, amputated fingers, and so on) as magical cures. The execution sometimes took on the status of a totem, and practices of avoidance and respect (touching the apparatus, staying away from the site afterward, and so on) are reported from France, Germany, England, and early America.[30]

Despite their importance, making and maintaining state power were not the only purposes of capital punishment in the early-modern state. Common criminals were also put to death for a great variety of offenses, though these "enemies of the people" were executed without the ceremony and intensity reserved for enemies of the state.[31]

In his discussion of eighteenth-century English judges, Hay describes their dual role, sometimes meting out "ordinary criminal punishment," sometimes serving a more political function in the maintenance of state security: "The fine-tuning of ordinary criminal punishment was part of their semi-annual role in the assize courts, and eight times a year in the Old Bailey." There they "adjusted the weight of the law accordingly, usually pardoning sheep and cattle thieves, always extending mercy to pickpockets, hanging coiners and deferring to the Bank's determination to hang forgers, and increasing the overall number of executions when high crime rates seemed to require more examples at the gallows." But in times of danger, when faced with treason, insurrection, or dissent, these same judges functioned "in their role as rulers." They believed that in times of popular insurrection capital punishment "was the ultimate guarantee of the survival of the oligarchic, monarchical, aristocratic, and profoundly undemocratic state they served."[32]

Over the course of time, as state rule became more legitimate, state officials represented executions as the enforcement of law rather than the display of power. Authorities increasingly represented themselves as serving the broader ends of crime control, criminal justice, and public safety. Indeed, as Esther Cohen notes, "In many European languages, the term for executions was derived from the word for justice: 'faire justice' in French, 'giustiziare' in Italian, 'Hinrichtung' in German." Cohen further observes that "although the King's justice and the people's interests were by no means identical, the association between the two was constantly asserted."[33]

The early-modern state's death penalty also had a penal function: the scaffold was used to dispatch criminal wrongdoers as well as political offenders. Terror served a deterrent purpose, aided by the speed with which executions followed convictions. (English statutes specified that executions take place on the next day but one following the imposition of the sentence.[34]) Early-modern governments lacked much of the institutional infrastructure needed for the generalized use of penalties such as imprisonment, transportation, or public works (though all of these sanctions were beginning to be used in this period), so the death penalty, supplemented by corporal and shaming punishments, formed a mainstay of the criminal justice they meted out.

The early-modern death penalty sometimes had a further use besides shoring up state power and controlling crime—one that reached beyond the emerging public sphere into the world of private interests and market relations. Early-modern states were always amalgams of public and private interests, and sections of the ruling class were able to appropriate the death penalty to their own use. Economic stability was also a state interest, and offenses such as forgery and smuggling that directly threatened the exchequer were ruthlessly suppressed.[35] The pattern of criminal law-making in that era suggests that death was often doled out to protect the commercial interests of particular groups rather than those of the general public.

Take, for example, the expansion of England's capital laws between 1688 and 1820, when the capital code grew from about 50 to more than 200 offenses, almost all of them against property, creating a "Bloody Code" that shored up private interests using the state's power to kill. As Hay puts it, "the death penalty was routinely added to protect . . . investments." Perhaps the most striking evidence of this can be found in instances where the intended deterrent backfired, prompting appeals from the property owners to *lessen* the severity of the law. When juries began to nullify crimes in capital cases involving theft from bleaching grounds—the plots of land where fabric was bleached in the open air—because they regarded the mandatory death sentence as too severe, the bleaching merchants demanded that the penalty be downgraded so that juries might convict and their property be protected.[36]

The pardon system was another mechanism that facilitated the private uses of capital punishment. The pardon process helped generate an informal system of gift-giving and return benefits that amounted to a usable system of social control operating in the shadow of the scaffold. The power to intercede on behalf of a servant, employee, or tenant—a power that might result in grants of mercy by the Crown—gave landowners and the propertied classes an additional claim to personal authority. "The pardon [was] important," Hay notes, "because it often put the principal instrument of legal terror—the gallows—directly in the hands of those who held power." These acts of mercy, which over time occurred with some frequency, helped create "the mental structures of paternalism."[37] The ability to act on behalf of "their people" in matters of life and death was of great importance to the eighteenth-century English gentry. It enabled them to give highly valued gifts to their subordinates and provide favors that would not easily be forgotten. The death penalty thereby provided already powerful individuals with an additional source of authority and prestige.

To this day, the forms in which the death penalty is enacted are, to a considerable degree, dictated by the institution's purposes. To deter potential enemies, the state must threaten certain death and mount a terrifying spectacle. To project state power, it needs majestic display and the trappings of authority. To communicate abstract principles ("justice," "sovereignty," "divine retribution") requires performative rituals that give flesh to abstractions and concrete embodiment to inchoate ideas.[38] An examination of the forms in which early-modern capital punishment was enacted can help identify what the institution was intended to do as well as how it appeared.

There were many ways to die on the early-modern scaffold. Judicial killings were carefully calibrated events, and the form of death was modulated, depending on the condemned person's rank, status, sex, and offense. Instead of a single death for all, there were lesser deaths and greater deaths, aggravated deaths and mitigated ones. For the most serious offenders, the punishment continued beyond death, in the form of postmortem desecrations and the display of body parts. The English practice of gibbeting, for example, proceeded thus: "However killed, the corpse was treated by boiling or tarring and hung up in a chain or wicker suit at the scene of the crime, along heavily traveled roads and rivers, or at a special gibbet place. The preservative retarded decay and the chain or wicker suit prevented large parts of the corpse from detaching. By such means the corpse's public display was prolonged until carrion birds eventually picked the bones clean."[39] For less serious offenders, the execution might be enacted in a symbolic form that stopped short of death; for example, standing criminals on a scaffold for a period of time with a noose around their neck, without proceeding to hang them.

For those put to death, different methods were reserved for different classes. As a French legal saying put it, "The axe for the noble, the rope for the villain"—a status-based distinction grounded in an old tradition that viewed hanging as "the most shameful death" and beheading the "most honorable and mildest."[40] Such distinctions were characteristic of this period, though the symbolic connotations of each method varied from place to place. In France, there were five ways to be put to death: "decapitation for nobles; hanging for common criminals; drawing and quartering for offences against the sovereign known as *lèse majesté*; burning at the stake for heresy, magic, arson, poisoning, bestiality, and sodomy; and breaking on the wheel for murder or highway robbery."[41] In the Netherlands, there were three: "the gallows, the wheel, and fire." Blok tells us that "[o]rdinary thieves were hanged; murderers and bandit leaders were broken on the wheel; and arson and sacrilege (e.g. church robberies) were punished by various forms of burning." In Italy, according to Merback, "penalties perceived by both elites and popular culture as disgraceful included hanging, breaking with the wheel, burning and every variety of dismemberment. In contrast, decapitation by sword epitomized the honorable death; unlike its opposites, it brought no stain of infamy on either the condemned or, just as important, his or her family."[42] Death by sword—an echo of death on the battlefield—was everywhere the entitlement of noblemen and high-ranking patricians.[43]

The many forms of the institution expressed the stratified nature of early-modern society. Even when being punished for criminal wrongdoing, the rank of a nobleman entitled him to greater respect than a commoner, just as a clergyman could expect to be treated differently from a layman, and a man from a woman. But the differentiated death penalty was more than an expression of social hierarchy. The variety of its forms—aggravated and mitigated, with and without torture, with and without degradation, going beyond death or stopping short of death—also points to its multiple uses and the wide range of offenses for which it was prescribed. In a political context in which it was viewed as essential and a penal context with few alternatives, the death penalty became varied and versatile.

Early-modern executions were meant to be seen. They took place on elevated platforms in town centers, were preceded by lengthy processions, and were performed with great ceremony. Executions in Paris occurred in the Place de Greve, the same public square where fireworks displays were staged to celebrate births and deaths in the royal family.[44] The stress was on making examples, on demonstrating a claim, on communicating with the watching crowd. And that communication was achieved by dramatic theater and symbolic gesture encoding cultural understandings of power and authority. Executions, in short, were rituals of power, and their form was designed accordingly. David Cooper's description of an eighteenth-century London execution gives a sense of this dramatic rite:

> Capital convicts of the City of London and the County of Middlesex were drawn in open carts, pinioned ropes dangling necklace-like from their necks, a distance of two miles from Newgate Gaol to Tyburn. A procession led by the City marshals on horseback, the under-sheriff, a group of peace officers and a body of constables with staves accompanied the convict and his executioner who rode in the open cart. A number of javelin-men brought up the rear. If the criminal was well known, the entourage had two sheriffs in their coaches, each holding his sceptre of office.[45]

Capital punishment and executions varied from place to place (more secular here, more religious there) and from time to time (more unruly on this occasion, more solemn another time). Scaffold speeches by the condemned were standard in England, Germany, and France but not in the Netherlands, where the condemned was allowed to pray or sing a psalm but not to make a speech.[46] Sharpe tells us that in England, executions after 1700 became less religious and more secular, though the evidence for this is contested.[47] Eighteenth-century English executions also became more likely to attract unruly and resistant crowds—or so the authorities complained—until in 1783 the execution venue was moved from Tyburn Field to Newgate Prison, a move that permitted the authorities to impose tighter control over the event.[48]

The historical evidence from Western Europe and colonial America leaves some doubt as to the nature of the interaction that occurred around the gallows. Historians debate how these executions were experienced by onlookers and the extent to which authorities succeeded in controlling the events and their meaning. Depending on which interpretation one prefers, the execution was a solemn state theater, a pious religious ritual, or an unruly popular carnival—and any specific execution probably displayed traces of each.[49] What is not in doubt, however, is that the early-modern execution was enacted as a public spectacle in full view of the assembled populace.

Rituals deal in symbolic meaning. Their staging, scripts, and performances are designed to embody ideas and to communicate with audiences. Symbols—whether in the form of words, dress, gestures, or choreographed conduct—were the medium through which these communications operated, and executions were always scenes of symbolic action and meaningful gesture. Some of the most common had a standard meaning that was widely understood by people everywhere: the signs of military and religious power, for example, or the brutal significance of physical degradations and dismemberments. People understood that execution by the sword echoed death on the battlefield and was nobler than hanging or burning at the stake. And they understood the religious parallels between the sinner's execution and Christ on the Cross. The early-modern execution utilized a stock set of ritual gestures and symbols that endured over long periods because popular culture ensured their intelligibility.[50]

The execution's symbols had to be understood, but this did not mean they had to be simple. Here is Chief Justice Coke's exegesis of the capital sentence he imposed on the defendants in the English Gunpowder Plot case of 1606:

> At first, the traitor shall be drawn to the place of execution, as not being worthy any more to tread upon the face of the earth, whereof he was made; and with his head declining downwards, and as near the ground as may be thought unfit to take the benefit of the common air. He shall next be hanged up by the neck between heaven and earth, as deemed unworthy of both or either, as likewise that the eyes of men may behold and their hearts condemn him. Then is he to be cut down alive, and to have his parts of generation cut off, and burnt before his face, as being unworthily begotten, and unfit to leave

any race after him. His inlayed parts shall be also taken out, and burnt, for it was his heart, which harbored such horrible treason. His head shall be cut off, which imagined the mischief; and lastly, his body shall be quartered, and the quarters set up in some high and eminent place, to the view and detestation of men, and to become prey for the fowls of the air. And this is the regard due to traitors, for it is the physic of government, to let out corrupt blood.[51]

The torments imposed on the condemned were more than just greater or lesser degrees of pain. Each specific action was instead designed to signify, to convey a message, to embody a statement. As Merback puts it, "the signs of the body in pain were not . . . simply a 'shameful side effect' to be tolerated for the sake of justice; they were instead the focal point of comprehension which gave the spectacle its religious meaning." Randall McGowen makes the same point when he says, "The violence of punishment was a language employed by authority to write the message of justice."[52]

If these public rituals depended for their effectiveness on the existence of commonly understood symbols, they also depended on the existence of a community for whom these symbols were meaningful. Such communities existed in early-modern towns and cities, and in the wider community of Christian believers, which is why rituals and symbols could be such an important aspect of secular and spiritual authority. Ritualized processions, scaffold ceremonies, choreographed performances, gallows literature, broadsheets, woodcuts, and final speeches were among the many means of communicating to a populace primed and ready to engage with the event and reflect on its meaning.[53]

Early-modern authorities gave few signs that they felt compassion toward the individuals they sentenced to die. Gatrell tells us that Edward Coke and his contemporaries cared little about the condemned man's fate and "would neither have contemplated the biographies of the humblest who hanged nor thought the worse of the law for their hanging."[54] But though there is scant evidence of sympathetic identification, the condemned man was not represented as alien or "other" in the way he sometimes is today. Criminals were regarded as sinners, as law-breakers, as individuals who had forfeited their right to live, but they were not characterized as inhuman. To members of the political elite, a lower-class criminal may have been beneath notice, but he was not demonized. That came later, when a widespread commitment to the "sanctity of the individual" and the "dignity of man" rendered it more problematic to put human beings to death.

Executions were rituals not only of punishment but also of death. As Evans says of the early-modern German institution, "The ceremony of execution would have been popularly understood, among other things, as a variant of the normal ceremony of death and burial. Both were rites of passage from life to death." The killing of the offender proceeded against a background of belief that gave it a meaning rather different from that which prevails today.[55] The condemned man was not being launched into nothingness: he was going to God's judgment and perhaps to a life beyond. His death occurred within a system of belief that held out expectation of an afterlife, of heaven and of hell. That the condemned man died was less important to the watching crowd than the question of how he died. Did he confess his crimes? Did he plead for God's mercy? Did he express remorse and seek redemption? His suffering was less significant than the responses that his torments elicited and what they said about the state of his soul.[56]

In the early-modern period, the "sight of decaying human bodies was more commonplace. Everyone, including children, knew what they looked like; and because everyone knew, they could be spoken of more freely."[57] There was no attempt to disguise the dying that took place on the scaffold and little apparent embarrassment about the facts of pain and death it put on display. The death and its meaning were elaborated and amplified, vocalized by "death talk specialists" (the priests on the scaffold, the clerics who helped prepare the "last dying speech") and memorialized by broadsheets and gallows literature. This discourse seized on the death as a cautionary moral tale and an occasion for religious reflection, as well as an affirmation of the rulers' authority.[58]

Anyone who tested the authority of a great power in early-modern society could be made to pay with his life: the worth of a lowly individual was no match for an angered God or an injured sovereign.[59] No deep controversy surrounded the state's right to kill law-breakers. Writing of seventeenth-century England, Beattie notes, "There is little evidence of a serious disagreement in society about capital punishment itself. It was justified on grounds of both social utility and religious authority."[60] Radzinowicz suggests the same thing when he notes that virtually all capital offenses enacted by the British Parliament in the seventeenth and eighteenth centuries "were created more or less as a matter of course by a placid and uninterested Parliament. In nine cases out of ten there was no debate and no opposition." Moreover, according to Banner, no one seriously proposed that capital punishment be abolished in colonial America: "It fulfilled the moral expectations of most colonial Americans most of the time . . . Hardly anyone suggested that it be used more sparingly, much less that it be abandoned."[61]

Nor was capital punishment cause for anxiety or embarrassment on the part of the authorities. "The rulers of English society in the early modern period were . . . unembarrassed by the violence of their punishments,"

McGowen tells us. "Hanging, branding, flogging, the pillory, drawing and quartering, burning alive—all were accepted as legitimate forms." And Pieter Spierenburg describes the attitude of the Dutch authorities toward executions as "familiarity largely unhampered by feelings of repugnance."[62] In contrast to contemporary America, where death penalties are controversial and executions take place in semi-secret, laden with anxiety, in the early-modern West executions were highly integrated into the fabric of society.

Early-modern capital punishment had the character of a grand tragedy. Having been convicted of a capital offense, and in the absence of any merciful intercession, the rebellious law-breaker would inevitably be killed. His death on the scaffold was a tragic necessity, compelled by the scheme of things, ordained by the way the world was put together. "What is a public execution?" Jeremy Bentham asked at the end of the eighteenth century. "It is a solemn tragedy which the legislator presents to the assembled community; a tragedy made truly important, truly pathetic, by its sad reality and the grandeur of its object."[63] In an unstable political environment constantly on the edge of violence, with a barely elaborated criminal justice system offering few practical alternatives, the death penalty was, for rulers, a vital means to secure important political, religious, and penological ends. This dramatic social context and these functional purposes shaped the institution's forms, providing it with a richly symbolic set of rituals and representations, rendering it continuous with cultural assumptions and silencing all questions about its legitimacy.

This classical moment in death penalty history left a deep cultural legacy, a lasting mark in the collective memory. Divine Justice; Sovereign Power; Terror and Death; a sinner facing his fate; awesome engagements with higher powers staged before an enraptured crowd—these images have come down to us from the early-modern era, indelibly associated with the penalty of death. Subsequent modes of capital punishment are less explicit in their engagement with these larger issues, more focused on crime, criminal justice, and public protection, but the connotations remain there in the background. If terror, death, and God are nowadays the private nighttime fears of the condemned, in the early-modern period, they were exhibited in the bright light of day for all to see.

The Modern Mode

The old death penalty, early-modern style, had disappeared from most parts of Europe and America by the early nineteenth century. Several jurisdictions—Tuscany, Prussia, Austria, and Pennsylvania—had reformed

their capital codes in the last decades of the eighteenth century, either abolishing the penalty or else drastically limiting its use. Others made the shift
later: England's Bloody Code, for example, was not reformed until the
1830s. A spectacular reprise of the grand ritual occurred in Paris in 1757,
when the execution of Robert Damiens, the regicide, revived the fading genre for a memorable last performance.[64] (The sentence imposed on
Damiens copied, virtually to the letter, the sentence imposed on Francois
Ravaillac in 1610 for the assassination of Henry IV, including the elaborate scaffold tortures that had been designed to force Ravaillac to name his
co-conspirators.) But by 1800 the shift was already well under way, and by
1900 it was virtually complete.

The transition from one mode of capital punishment to another occurred within a larger arc of development: the transformation of the European state system. The newly stabilized states of the late seventeenth century gave way to the enlightened monarchies of the eighteenth century and
eventually to the unified and bureaucratized nation states of nineteenth-
century Europe. But the reform of capital punishment was also reinforced
by developments internal to criminal justice, notably, the development of
alternative punishments such as transportation and imprisonment, and
later the rise of a progressive penology.

During the last part of the eighteenth century, rulers regularly commuted death sentences, substituting transportation to the colonies, forced
service on public works, or even long-term confinement in the new penitentiaries that were beginning to appear. Within a few decades, all across
the West the new disciplinary prison became the punishment of choice for
all kinds of offenses, from the most trivial to the most serious. The nineteenth century would become the age of the penitentiary, and, with the decline of transportation and public works, long-term imprisonment eventually replaced death on the scaffold as the punishment for all but the most
serious criminals. As national prison systems developed, becoming more
secure, more disciplinary, and more austere, penal reformers pressed the
idea of imprisonment as punishment for serious crime. Out of the penitentiary experience grew a new penology that rejected retribution, embraced
reform, and stressed the positive, utilitarian character of penal sanctions.
These ideas—which quickly spread across Europe and America—reinforced the shift away from the old death penalty and raised questions
about the value of capital punishment in a reformed criminal justice system. During the course of the nineteenth century, the number of executions
in many Western nations declined—at first because of *ad hoc* commutations and later because sentences of death were replaced by "life" sentences of imprisonment. By the 1890s, Western nations had begun to establish criminal justice institutions (probation, reformatory prisons, parole,

indeterminate sentencing) that stressed reformatory and even welfarist goals—a development that placed new ideological pressure on an already embattled institution of capital punishment.[65]

By the start of the twentieth century, capital punishment in the West was operating in a transformed political and penological context. Changes in the structures of state power and penal control had rendered death sentences less necessary, while changes in the dominant culture rendered them less legitimate. During the course of the nineteenth century, most Western states consolidated their monopolies of violence, disarmed and pacified the population, and created standing armies and extensive police forces. The new nation states institutionalized their social-control capacities—through taxation, government bureaucracies, and legal regulation—and fostered new sources of popular consent such as nationalism, limited democracy, and citizenship. By the 1890s, Germany and Britain were providing rudimentary social insurance and welfare benefits.

The result was that terroristic displays of state violence ceased to be regarded as a vital tool in the armory of Western nations. As Lamartine had declared to the French Chamber of Deputies in 1837, "Today society is armed with powers of repression and punishment that do not require the shedding of blood."[66] Being less vital, such displays came to seem less legitimate as well. They clashed with the new liberal-democratic politics that defined the state's relationship to citizens and with the civilized, humanitarian sentiments that increasingly shaped the self-image of the ruling elites. As states became more secure, political restraints on violence more robust, and individual lives more valuable, the institution of state killing began to lose its moorings.

The rise of the rational-bureaucratic state brought with it a more developed criminal justice apparatus of professional police and prosecutors, adult and juvenile courts, and a penal system of prisons, reformatories, probation, and parole. This, in turn, moved decision-making about punishment away from political actors and placed it increasingly in the hands of criminal justice professionals. Over time, capital punishment was transformed from a state-controlled political institution geared to state maintenance to a legally controlled criminal justice institution geared to crime control and penal justice. With this institutional reorientation came new rationales and representations. "Justice" continued as a central purpose, but that value came increasingly to be phrased in terms of the protection of individual life and public security rather than the king's justice or the maintenance of state rule. What had once been an explicitly political exercise of state power came to represent itself as a form of apolitical penal practice.

By the end of the nineteenth century, the ancient rites of state killing had largely disappeared and been replaced by an "enlightened" death penalty, a criminal punishment forming one penal sanction among others in an increasingly professionalized criminal justice system. This new death penalty was less a ceremonial of power and a technique of rule than a policy instrument, rationally adapted to the ends of criminal justice and crime control. Having lost its grounding in absolutist *raison d'état* and the imperatives of divine justice, the death penalty's rationale now became more subject to moral debate and utilitarian dispute. The modern death penalty was no longer an unquestionable expression of sovereign power but a policy tool like any other. If it was deployed, in the face of ideological doubts, it was because it was seen to serve human purposes: to deter crime, to save innocent lives, to inflict pain with a view to creating benefits. What had once been a tragic necessity now became a contingent and conditional choice.

The modern death penalty functioned primarily as an instrument of criminal justice, an "ultimate" penalty reserved for the most serious criminal offenses. Its purposes were represented in penological rather than political terms—as a matter of justice and crime control rather than as an exercise of state power. Executions took place in a penal space, inside the prison, rather than in the political space of the public square. Their chief targets were criminal wrongdoers rather than political enemies. During this period the institution came to be seen as less essential and more controversial. This led to a greater concern with questions of justification, and these legitimacy debates were framed by questions of social welfare and criminal justice. Putting offenders to death was no longer discussed as an essential support for secular or religious power but instead as one means among others of doing justice and reducing crime.

The fact that modern capital punishment was located within what one might call "ordinary" penal policy and, for the most part, administered accordingly did not mean that it lost its connection to the political process. In contrast to other criminal sanctions, which were routinely imposed without any direct involvement on the part of government ministers, the execution of death sentences typically required the approval of some high-ranking government official—the home secretary, the minister of justice, the state governor, and so on. As a result, political considerations always played a role in decisions about executions and pardons. But the political character of these questions had changed. The considerations involved were now matters of party advantage rather than anxieties about the preservation of state power. "If a government wished to signal its determination to crack down on crime and disorder and to brook no opposition to its policies, what better way of doing so than to consign the majority of capital offenders to the block?" Richard Evans writes, discussing the German institution in the nineteenth century. "On the other hand if, perhaps, under liberal pressure, a government wished to signal its humane and benevolent intent, an increase in the number of capital offenders granted the royal clemency was a simple and striking way of doing so."[67]

"Political uses" are to be distinguished here from "state functions." The modern death penalty might be manipulated for partisan political purposes—and might sometimes be used against traitors and enemies of the state—but in stable Western nations it was no longer an important tool of state maintenance. These political party uses should also be distinguished from the private uses common in the early-modern institution. In the modern mode, pardons and commutations were no longer triggered by private interventions, nor were they used as forms of giving and getting linked directly into private hierarchies of status and deference.

The modern death penalty was used for a narrower range of offenses than hitherto. Property crime, moral offenses, and crimes against religion were no longer punishable by death, which was now reserved for the most serious crimes against the person—above all for murder. Its chief targets were individuals who harmed others or threatened public safety, not individuals who threatened the state.[68] Treason remained a capital offense, as did other crimes against the state, but these were rarely prosecuted outside of wartime. Capital punishment was now deployed in the name of the public, not as an expression of a ruler's power. It became an "ultimate" penalty, an exceptional measure of last resort, not a multipurpose sanction to be routinely deployed across a range of offenses. Justified only at the extremes of criminal wickedness, incorrigibility, and danger, it was now regarded as too severe for the property offenders and public-order violators who had previously mounted the gallows.

By the modern era, executions had come to be administered in a single format, with the same uniform death for everyone. This change resulted not just from the leveling of status distinctions in nineteenth- and twentieth-century Western society but also because a variety of other sanctions were now available to deal with the range of offenses. And of course modern sensibilities acted as a barrier to the use of torture, postmortem torments, and other forms of aggravated death sentences.

Over the course of the nineteenth century the Western death penalty also lost much of its religious character and became predominantly secular in orientation and organization. "Penal policy was rationalized," writes Richard Evans of the German institution. "Enlightenment monarchs and bureaucrats . . . rejected the divine aspect of punishment as irrelevant, even counter-productive. Punishment was to be based on a rational degree of pain, a calculus of terror, a system of punishment graded according to the degree of deterrence required."[69]

Clerics remained at the scene of modern executions, and the traditional rites of the "last meal" and the "last words" continued to be administered. But these were less a mark of presiding religious authority than a private consolation to the condemned and a means of smoothing the execution process. Wherever religious traditions clashed with the more secular objectives of the modernized institution, the former tended to give way.[70] Arrangements once regarded as politically and culturally essential came to seem counterproductive as the institution adapted to its new context and purposes.

Secularization deprived the event of many of its larger meanings. It reduced the execution to a state killing, pursuant to a contingent decision by fallible social actors, rather than an instantiation of God's justice. At the same time, the fate of the offender came to seem more grimly horrifying, since he was now being condemned to nothingness rather than commended to God's mercy: "Gone . . . is the construction of the hanging as a drama of salvation."[71] In its place was a bureaucratic procedure that offered little solace or hope of redemption.

In a discussion of two New York execution reports, one in 1825 and the other in 1892, Michael Madow captures something of this shift. The earlier report depicted the execution as a drama of sin and atonement in which the offender's spiritual fate was in the balance: "It was Reynold's soul, not his body that claimed the narrative's center." In contrast, the 1892 report focused on the physical aspects of the event: "when Charles McElvaine was privately executed at Sing Sing some sixty-six years later, physicians, not clergy, dominated the scene, and the question posed by journalists assembled outside the penitentiary all presumed this event's medicalized construction: 'Exactly when did McElvaine die? When did he lose consciousness? Did he feel any pain? Was there any burning of the flesh?'"[72]

The modern execution aimed not to terrorize onlookers with a spectacle of suffering but to carry out the court's death sentence in an efficient, humane manner. The sights, sounds, and smells of the body in pain ceased to be an essential part of the institution and became a problem to be minimized out of concern for the offender and for witnesses. Death, and death alone, became the punishment. The offender's life was to be terminated, but beyond that, no supplementary suffering was to be imposed. All additional torments, degradations, and postmortem aggravations were avoided. In a secular world, the finality of death meant that additional, postmortem punishments were harmful superstitions. As a German appeal court put it in 1853, "Death expiates all guilt here on earth; the human judge's hand should not stretch out beyond it."[73]

The shift from an extended ritual of death to a curt termination of life meant that the modern execution would become increasingly oriented toward speed and efficiency. Evans observes in his study of nineteenth-century German executions that "the emphasis was above all on speed." Modern executions were "simple straightforward affairs, with a minimum of speechifying," their "formulaic brevity" standing in stark contrast to the "spectacular, semi-sacral procedures of an earlier day." As Simon Schama writes, the introduction of the guillotine in France was a disappointment for the execution day crowds, for whom the event was now too expeditious to be satisfying: "A swish, a thud; sometimes not even a display of the head; the executioner reduced to a low-grade mechanic like some flunkey pulling a bell rope."[74]

As early as the late seventeenth century, permanent stone scaffolds were replaced with temporary structures that were removed from sight when not in use. The procession to the gallows was first shortened, then abolished altogether. The scaffold was partly covered so that the dangling corpse would not be visible. Later the scaffold was moved from the public square to the closed jail yard. The large hanging-day crowd disappeared, replaced at first by an invited audience given access to the jail yard, eventually by a smaller number of "witnesses" whose access was closely controlled. By moving the event from the public square to the interior of a state prison the authorities were, as Elias would phrase it, putting the execution "behind the scenes of social life," rendering it distinct from the everyday life with which it had previously been integrated. The execution ritual became "defensive not demonstrative," its visibility and audibility greatly diminished, its performative character changed from noisy public event to silent, backstage procedure.[75]

As Michael Madow sums up the transformation, the modern execution was thrice removed from the life of the community: *spatially*—from an outdoor open space to the interior of a high-walled prison; *geographically*—from the local county where the murder occurred to a state prison that might be many miles away; and *epistemologically*—from "the domain of first-hand, everyday experience," where people apprehended capital punishment with their own eyes and ears, to the sphere of "abstract consciousness," where people learned of the event through newspaper accounts, literature, and other second-hand cultural representations.[76]

As the early-modern death penalty developed into the modern death penalty, its symbolic communications changed. The offender's death and the staging and discourse surrounding it were no longer designed to evoke images of a soul in torment or metaphors of the body social. By the early nineteenth century, the institution had become disenchanted, stripped of its religious character and its status as communal ritual. Allusive, metaphoric communication was increasingly shut down. The execution came to be merely about itself, a matter of imposing death without further ado.[77]

Some traces of the old religious practices survived, of course—the "last meal" and "last words" continue right up to the present—but without much collective meaning other than a bland sense of "tradition." And whereas the early-modern execution had been an occasion for extensive and elaborate discourse, the modern execution generated few official statements and permitted little in the way of speech-making or narrative performances. To some extent, the press took up the slack, providing a steady stream of sensationalist reports and formulaic narratives. Journalists represented the execution as a horror, a terror, a fate to be avoided, but no longer as a symbolic communication about man, the state, and the cosmos. Stories about modern executions concerned themselves with the physical details of the procedure and the legal process that led up to it. Little space was given to larger political or religious lessons that might be drawn from the event.[78]

If the early-modern institution was legitimate, confident, and taken for granted, modern capital punishment operated in a more troubled environment. In the modern era, capital punishment came to be regarded as inherently problematic, the more so as nations moved toward liberal democracy and later toward welfarism. From the Enlightenment onward, the death penalty had been challenged by the liberal ideas and humanitarian sentiments of the professional and middle classes and their religious and political leaders. Whereas the early-modern institution had been continuous with the background assumptions of political and cultural life, the modern institution came to seem increasingly incongruous, caught in a contradiction between traditional conceptions of absolutist justice and a newer insistence that state violence should be strictly limited and human life preserved.

Throughout the modern period, this contradiction between absolutist tradition and liberal modernity exerted a steady pressure for reform. But its most immediate effect was to give rise to criticism challenging the institution, which, in turn, prompted new and more elaborate efforts to justify it. The late eighteenth and early nineteenth centuries became a period of forceful critique and debate. In 1764, Cesare Beccaria published his treatise *Dei delitti e delle pene* [Of crimes and punishments], an Enlightenment critique of the death penalty and absolutist criminal justice that resounded across Europe and America and became a standard reference for reformers everywhere. This critical challenge energized a conservative reaction, moving death penalty supporters to an intensified concern with justification. In England, for example, William Paley mounted a powerful defense of the institution that took nothing for granted. Leaving behind the "uncomplicated vindictiveness" of earlier writings such as the early eighteenth-century pamphlet *Hanging Not Punishment Enough,* "Paley advanced the political and moral justifications for capital punishment with unprecedented ambition." As Gatrell comments, Paley's "elaborate pleading" was necessary "because older certainties had become uneasy."[79]

Rationales that had previously gone unstated were now made explicit, and new justifications were developed in response to the Enlightenment critics. The modern philosophy of punishment mostly dates from this time, with the writings of Kant, Hegel, Bentham, and Mill serving as its foundations. Among the institution's supporters, the death penalty was no longer discussed as an unquestioned necessity. Henceforth, its use would be framed as a moral duty that accorded individual moral agents their just retribution, or a deterrent that saved human lives—each account striving to represent state killing as somehow aligned with the cause of humanity. For the first time, the death penalty came to be represented as a humanitarian institution. To condemn killers to death was, so its supporters said, a way of expressing respect for human life. The executioner took lives in order to save lives. The savage will of the sovereign had become a means of social welfare.

At the same time and for the same reasons, the institution came increasingly to be surrounded by anxiety and embarrassment. By the 1960s, and the beginning of what I will term the "late-modern" contemporary era, this ambivalence had become quite pronounced. "No one dares speak directly of the ceremony," Albert Camus observed in 1961. "[W]e read at breakfast time in a corner of the newspaper that the condemned has 'paid his debt to society' or that he has 'atoned' or that 'at five A.M. justice was done.' The officials call the condemned 'the interested party' or 'the patient' or refer to him by a number." What had once been a demonstrative public ritual had become a topic for reticence and euphemism: "People write of capital punishment as if they were whispering."[80]

The waning of religious understandings, together with renewed efforts to justify the institution, prompted new representations of the condemned. In his discussion of nineteenth-century Germany, Richard Evans notes the emergence of a new language of justification centered on the dangerousness, bestiality, and inhumanity of the murderer. Foucault reports similar developments in nineteenth-century France, noting that the "monstrosity" of the offender now became a key justification for a sentence of death. In order to kill the condemned person, it had become necessary to distance him from the human race.[81] Karen Haltunnen observes the same thing even earlier in the United States: "By the end of the [eighteenth] century, the cult of horror was replacing an earlier, sympathetic view of the condemned criminal as moral exemplum with a view of the murderer as moral alien." And in nineteenth-century England, according to Gatrell, "[i]t seems also to have been necessary to insist on the 'otherness' of the hanged man or woman. . . . [Henceforth] the condemned were to be defined with increasing explicitness as social others (poor people and thieves) or political others (subversives or traitors) or psychological others (monsters, murderers)."[82] To see hanged men or women as human was to create a friction between capital punishment and modern liberal culture. Rendering them monstrous served to reduce dissonance and lubricate the machinery of death. Medicine, psychiatry, abnormal psychology, and positive criminology—the new human sciences that emerged in this period—helpfully supplied a new language of monstrosity, each of them providing a positive source of scientific legitimacy for the institution, much as they do in the sentencing phase of American capital trials today.

The Late-Modern Mode

By the 1960s, the political contradictions that had long affected capital punishment in its modern mode had grown more intense, the cultural environment in which it operated, less hospitable. By that time, the politics of liberalism, democracy, and welfarism had become dominant across most of the Western nations, and these governmental rationalities rendered the death penalty increasingly outmoded and illegitimate. Of course these developments unfolded unevenly, their timing and extent determined by the balance of political forces in the different nations and by the contingency of events. While most of Europe moved toward social democracy in the postwar decades, Spain, Portugal, and Greece were under military rule until the 1970s, during which time they retained capital punishment. And though America added to its New Deal welfare state with President Johnson's Great Society programs of the 1960s, the nation remained decidedly less welfarist and social democratic than its European equivalents. Instead of European-style social democracy, with citizenship, solidarity, and redistribution organized through a powerful state apparatus, the United States sustained its long-standing commitment to radical local democracy, devolving most social and penal policy decisions to local political actors—an arrangement that fostered local variation and populist politics rather than uniform national governance by professional elites. But in general, compared with the modern period, and across the whole of the West, this era saw the enhancement of liberal democracy, the growth of welfare states, and the further decline of capital punishment.

In the wake of two world wars, the experience of fascism, and the searing horror of the Holocaust, Western societies set themselves on a path toward a new form of social organization. All across the West there emerged liberal-democratic institutions, welfare states, anti-authoritarian cultures, and international institutions dedicated to the cause of human rights. In this context the death penalty grew increasingly problematic, increasingly at odds with the "politics of life" and the humanistic culture that were defining features of welfare societies.[83] At the same time, the professionalization of police and criminal justice, and the rise to dominance of a more reformative style of penal policy, exerted new pressure on capital punishment as an institution. If the proper purpose of penal sanctions was not retribution but reform, as most penal experts now insisted, then the death penalty was an outmoded anomaly. In this developing context, the death penalty grew increasingly marginal. By the 1960s, many nations—America, France, and Britain among them—reported declines in their annual execution tolls.[84]

An institution that had been contested ever since the Enlightenment now became more controversial than ever. Schoolchildren everywhere debated the subject, and every adult citizen came to have an opinion on the matter.[85] Governments in every Western nation were pressed to end the institution once and for all. Being in favor of capital punishment was increasingly regarded as a sign not of common sense or moral rectitude but of social and political conservatism.

By 1965, the death penalty had been completely abolished in only a handful of nations, but its use had declined everywhere and none of the Western nations any longer relied on it as a normal penal sanction. Those nations that continued to impose and execute death sentences did so rarely and somewhat reluctantly, and only for the worst crimes of violence, usually heinous intentional murder. And when executions did take place— which happened more and more rarely—they were surrounded not just by solemnity, as before, but by intense controversy and palpable discomfort.[86]

One by one, the Western nations resolved these contradictions by means of national legislation that abolished the institution. As the postwar wave of abolitions took hold, it changed the context in which the death penalty existed elsewhere. Each new act of abolition made each subsequent one easier to accomplish, and each refusal to abolish more difficult to justify. In nations where the death penalty survived into the 1960s and 1970s, its use became ever more controversial and problem-laden.

The death penalty systems that operated during this late-modern period —in Britain until 1965, Spain until 1975, France until 1981, the United States still today—were structured in much the same way as before. The discussions surrounding them, with their formulaic arguments and textbook debates, were the same as those that had emerged in the eighteenth century, though by the 1960s the American debates had begun to focus on questions of constitutional law. The cultural and political contradictions that challenged the legitimacy of the death penalty continued to operate, rendering its use ever more narrow, restrained, and refined. In short, these death penalties were still recognizably modern.

But all the earlier contradictions continued and grew more intense. The institution became increasingly at odds with the political and cultural institutions that surrounded it. Alternatives—especially life imprisonment and, later, life imprisonment without parole—became more routinely available, making it possible to impose harsh retributive punishment and incapacitate dangerous individuals in ways that stopped short of death. Legal reforms narrowed capital codes still further, until only aggravated murders warranted a death sentence. Mandatory capital punishment disappeared. Homicide was reclassified into capital and noncapital offenses. Capital cases attracted more legal process, more appeals, and consequently generated greater delays. Death sentences were commuted or overturned more often than before, so that executions became rarer still.

The growing rarefaction of death sentences and executions increased the institution's marginality and further diminished its effectiveness as a means of crime control or retributive justice, thus providing more fuel for the critics. When executions did occur, they attracted a great deal of negative publicity and criticism, sometimes from foreign audiences and international authorities as well as from domestic critics. Each event was carefully scrutinized by opponents for the least sign of inhumanity, watched anxiously by ambivalent authorities for fear of mishap or a botched procedure. Increasingly the death penalty became a divisive issue rather a functioning institution.[87]

In nations such as France and the United Kingdom that retained their old execution methods—the noose and the guillotine—capital punishment came to seem especially archaic and outmoded.[88] In the United States, where most states had already updated their execution technologies in the course of the twentieth century, setting aside the noose in favor of the electric chair or the gas chamber, most of them did so again after the 1980s, when lethal injection provided a way of making the death penalty seem less objectionable. But even the reformed institution—used sparingly, for the most unpopular murderers, after an elaborate show of due process and administrative review—could not avoid appearing problematic in the context of late modernity. The continued practice of capital punishment placed officials and their supporters in a cultural contradiction, obliging them to behave in ways that were at once lawful and transgressive. It trapped them in the uncomfortable space between the cultural norms of liberal humanism and the legal practice of execution. This difficult status marked death off as "different." Other criminal penalties might sometimes become a subject of dispute, but by the end of the twentieth century, the death penalty was always and everywhere controversial. Whenever and wherever a death sentence was imposed, the legitimacy of the institution was liable to be called into question.

Eventually, all the major European nations became abolitionist, with Britain making a provisional abolition permanent in 1969, Spain repealing its capital laws in 1975, Portugal in 1976, and France in 1981.[89] Each of these national abolitions was brought about by reform forces internal to the society in question, with only occasional reference to the experience or preferences of other nations. But once all the major European nations had come into line, they proceeded to regard the new abolitionist consensus as a transnational norm, a human rights principle that ought to be observed by all nations everywhere. Countries that were once retentionist holdouts now became abolitionist proselytizers, thereby increasing the pressure on nations that had not yet abolished. By the 1980s, the United States—or rather a majority of American states plus the U.S. government—was left as the only remaining retentionist nation in the West. When the International Criminal Court was established in 1998, the death penalty was excluded from the punishments it was authorized to impose, even for offenders convicted of genocide or crimes against humanity.

Western capital punishment in the late-modern era no longer performs the functions associated with the institution in its modernist phase, or at least not with the same degree of effectiveness. Too rare and uncertain to deter and too averse to bodily violence to deliver harsh retribution, it has lost much of its modern *raison d'être*. Where it still exists as a legal sanction—which is by now only in the United States, though European laggards such as France, Spain, and Britain displayed similar patterns in the 1960s and 1970s, as do non-Western retentionist democracies such as Japan and India today—we see institutional ambivalence surrounding its use. The visible signs of this ambivalence are laws that go unenforced, sentences that go unexecuted, legal proceedings that create endless delays, and a great deal of discomfort on the part of the judges, government ministers, and penal officials charged with administering the punishment. The death penalty that exists in the public imagination and in justificatory argument grows ever more distant from the death penalty as it is actually administered. What was once a practical instrument of penal policy has become something quite different.

FOUR

The Death Penalty's Decline

State-sanctioned killing . . . is becoming more and more anachronistic.

JUSTICE JOHN PAUL STEVENS, *BAZE V REES*, 2008

The decline of capital punishment in the West involved a sequence of developments that began slowly in the years after 1700 and gradually accelerated during the nineteenth and twentieth centuries. These developments threw into reverse the expansion and intensification that had characterized the institution in previous centuries. The late-medieval and early-modern periods had seen a marked increase in lethal punishments all across Europe as emerging nation states struggled to defeat their enemies, pacify their populations, and monopolize legitimate violence. But over time the death penalty became less essential in routine governance, and its use came to be dictated by the varying political fortunes of ruling groups and their governmental regimes. Upswings in the frequency and intensity of capital punishment were features of unstable phases of state formation; downturns tended to occur during more stable periods. Restraint, refinement, and reduction became the norm in the early eighteenth century, and the trend has continued ever since, all across the West, albeit with many reversals and much unevenness.

Decline in Europe

From the seventeenth century onward, punishments such as breaking on the wheel, burning at the stake, hanging, drawing and quartering, and gibbeting began to fall into disuse. By the mid-nineteenth century, postmortem torments had mostly ceased, as had the practice of exposing corpses or subjecting them to medical dissection. By the mid-twentieth century, even the ancient ignominy of burial in an unmarked grave was gone. There had been, to use Jeremy Bentham's apt terminology, a movement from "afflictive" to "simple" capital punishment.

We can trace this process through time, as first judicial torture, then aggravated methods of execution, then postmortem afflictions were abandoned in one country after another.[1] The abolition of judicial torture began when Voltaire's patron Frederick the Great abolished it in Prussia in 1754. Other rulers soon followed, and the practice was abandoned in Saxony in 1770; Sweden in 1772; Austria and Bohemia in 1776; France between 1780 and 1778; the Southern Netherlands in 1787–1794; and the Dutch Republic in 1795–1798. By 1820, all of the German states had abolished it.[2]

The decline of aggravated execution methods got under way even earlier, beginning in the early seventeenth century, though it was concentrated mostly at the end of the eighteenth and the start of the nineteenth centuries. In the Dutch Republic, the use of scaffold torture became less common after 1750, with a sharp decline in the use of burning at the stake and a turn to simple hanging.[3] In England, pressing to death— *peine forte et dure*—was abolished in 1772, and the burning of women at the stake was abolished in 1790, the last such execution having taken place the year before.[4]

England ended its use of aggravated executions in the early decades of the nineteenth century, though historians disagree about the date of the last "absolutist-style" execution. Radzinowicz tells us that it was 1817 when Jeremiah Brandeth and two others were hung and then beheaded for the crime of high treason. Gatrell places the event three years later: "1820 saw the last executions for high treason in the old fashioned way. In that year eight men were publicly hanged and decapitated . . . each head was held up to the spectators, the executioner crying out his name."[5]

The French Assembly abolished all aggravated death penalties in 1791, when it made death by guillotine the sole method of capital punishment. As early as 1750 the French *parlements* had begun to impose the death penalty less frequently and increasingly ordered that the condemned "be strangled before being burnt at the stake or placed on the wheel."[6] In Portugal torture and cruel executions were forbidden by law in 1802.[7] The Spanish Penal Code of 1822 specified that execution would henceforth be solely by garrote, without additional torture or aggravation. Germany persisted longest with afflictive executions, retaining breaking on the wheel until about 1850.[8]

This movement away from bodily torments, mutilation, and dismemberment was a more general one, not confined to capital punishment. The corporal punishments of cutting off of ears and hands began to decline in the seventeenth century. Branding—a means of identification as well as an afflictive punishment—was abolished in England in 1779, in France by 1832, and in the Netherlands in 1854.[9]

Postmortem punishments disappeared as part of the same process. According to Spierenburg, "The display of the dead bodies of capitally punished delinquents was discontinued in Western Europe around 1800." In England, the practice of gibbeting was ended in 1834, its last use being in 1832, when the bodies of two executed criminals were hung in chains.[10] The practice of "anatomizing" or dissecting murderers—a mark of infamy for the condemned and a convenient source of cadavers for medical students—ended around the same time with the Anatomy Act of 1832.[11] The exposure of corpses was ended in Germany in the early nineteenth century.[12]

As capital punishments grew less cruel, they also grew less diverse. The variegated death penalties of the early-modern period gradually disappeared in the seventeenth century, giving way to a single, standard death that was the same for all. In France, the Revolutionary Assembly introduced this reform, insisting on "the simple privation of life, without torture, for all kinds of murder" and representing it as a reform that was at once enlightened, egalitarian, and democratic. Spanish liberals enacted a similar reform in 1822, only to have it reversed six years later when Ferdinand VII reestablished an absolutist monarchy. Standardization had begun earlier in Germany, where reforms began in the late seventeenth century. In place of hanging, breaking on the wheel, burial alive, burning at the stake, and drowning, the German states increasingly turned to a single method—decapitation by the sword: "Once the traditional privilege of the nobility, [decapitation] was used by the later seventeenth century for all classes of offender."[13] What in the early-modern era had been a complex repertoire of differentiated executions became, by the nineteenth century, a single method, uniformly applied.

A key development enabling modernizing states to reduce their reliance on the death penalty was the emergence of alternative or "secondary" penalties that could serve as effective substitutes in the punishment of serious offenders. In the seventeenth and eighteenth centuries, banishment, transportation to the colonies, and forced labor on public works projects emerged as alternative sentences having first been used as substitutes when the offender's capital sentence was commuted. In the nineteenth century, lengthy sentences of imprisonment, sometimes for life, became the standard alternative as states gradually built an infrastructure of secure disciplinary prisons.[14] The same process of substitution is still at work today, as one American state after another enacts laws that permit sentences of life imprisonment without parole. As usual, the emergence of this alternative has led to a decrease in the number of death sentences imposed.[15]

From the mid-sixteenth century onward, European states developed punishments that would later substitute for capital punishment: galley slavery in the Mediterranean states; houses of correction in Germany, Austria, and the Netherlands; and transportation abroad in states such as Britain, France, and Spain that possessed foreign colonies. The houses of correction later evolved into modern prisons. These were used at first for petty offenders, then—combined with transportation—as a means of commuting capital sentences, and finally as the standard punishment for even the most serious offenders. Each of these new punishments required a certain level of state capacity and resources—convicts had to be selected, assembled, provisioned, chained, and marched to the ports; carceral institutions had to be built, staffed, and maintained. The decline of capital punishment was facilitated by the states' growing infrastructural power.[16]

The first substitution—replacing death with transportation to the colonies—took place in most European nations in the eighteenth century. John Langbein tells us that, on the Continent, "[t]ransportation of felons began as a trickle in the years 1615–1660, became substantial in the period 1660–1700, and expanded greatly after 1717." John Beattie shows that although the English authorities were sending felons to the colonies as early as 1600, transportation became a regular sentence of the courts only after the Transportation Act of 1718—a development that brought a marked reduction in the frequency of executions. The interruption of transportation by the American Revolution accelerated the development of England's use of imprisonment. And although the transportation of convicts later resumed, this time to Australia, sentences of imprisonment with hard labor soon became the standard secondary punishment. A similar pattern was evident in eighteenth-century Germany, where the construction of penitentiaries led to a decreased use of corporal and capital penalties.[17]

The range of offenses to which the death penalty might be applied was narrowed over time, as was the range of eligible offenders. In the early-modern Netherlands, it was common for burglars and robbers to be executed, especially if they were recidivists. After 1750 that practice declined and capital punishment "was increasingly reserved for manslaughter and murder." In Spain, the penal code of 1848 limited the variety of crimes considered capital offenses.[18] In England, "capital punishment was abolished for cattle, horse and sheep stealing in 1832, for housebreaking in 1833; for sacrilege and stealing letters by Post Office employees in 1835; for coinage and forgery in 1836; and for burglary and stealing in dwelling houses in 1837." By the time of Queen Victoria's coronation in 1838, the number of capital offenses had been reduced from more than two hundred to fifteen. By 1860, this number had been further reduced, making murder the only common crime for which the death penalty was available—although the political offenses of treason, piracy with violence, and arson in government dockyards and arsenals also remained capital.[19]

North of the border in Scotland, an act of 1887 removed robbery, rape, incest, arson, piracy with violence, and destruction of shipyards from the capital class, though most of these had been in desuetude for some time before. The number of executions declined as these changes took effect. In Middlesex and London, executions averaged 140 per year between 1607 and 1616; 90 per year during the reign of Charles I; 85 per year during the Commonwealth; 36 per year between 1749 and 1758; 22 per year between 1790 and 1799; and 12 per year between 1800 and 1810.[20]

In France, Napoleon's Penal Code of 1810 made 36 crimes punishable by death. That code was revised in 1832, reducing the number of capital crimes to 22 and permitting the courts to consider extenuating circumstances. The result was a decline in the number of death sentences and executions: from an annual average of 264 executions during the later years of the empire (1804–1815); to an annual number of 111 death sentences and 72 executions between 1826 and 1830; and, in the period following the reforms of 1832, an average of 51 death sentences and 32 executions.[21] A similar narrowing occurred in Germany over the same period. The new criminal codes of Prussia and the other large German states had, by 1851, "drastically restricted the number and range of capital offences, such that murder and treason were the only grounds for a death sentence in most parts of Germany." The liberal codes enacted in the aftermath of 1848 also introduced a higher minimum age at which the offender could be executed, effectively abolishing the death penalty for offenders younger than eighteen.[22]

Moral and religious offenses were rarely capital in Europe after the eighteenth century, and property crimes were largely excluded during the nineteenth century. By the twentieth century, only the most serious offenses against the person—rape, robbery, arson, and homicide—were capital.[23]

By the second half of that century, this list was narrowed further until the death penalty was reserved exclusively for murder, or for the still narrower categories of "first-degree" or "aggravated" murder.

Over time, the range of eligible offender types was also narrowed, either *de facto* or *de jure*. In the seventeenth and eighteenth centuries, the courts used legal fictions such as "benefit of clergy" or "benefit of belly" to spare the lives of first offenders and women.[24] Later, statutes were passed excluding children and young people, and courts developed doctrinal arguments that deemed the mentally ill to have "diminished responsibility," thus allowing them to escape capital punishment. In England, the Children's Acts of 1908 and 1933 prohibited capital punishment for young persons, first drawing the line at sixteen years, and then eighteen. The Infanticide Act of 1922 effectively abolished capital punishment for mothers who killed their newborn infants, removing yet another category from the list of offenders who might mount the gallows.[25]

This process of narrowing and reduction continues in the United States today, where state legislators and the Supreme Court have recently removed minors, the mentally deficient, and child rapists who did not kill their victims from the ranks of those who may be eligible for the death penalty. Again, the practical effect is to further reduce the frequency of death sentences and executions.

Whereas the early-modern period saw the emergence of the execution as a ritualized spectacle of state power, the period from 1700 to the present saw that process reversed. The diminution of the institution's more visible, dramatic aspects begins with the dismantling of the permanent gallows and ravenstones that stood in the entrance gates and public squares of early-modern towns. As early as 1600, Henry IV of France had the stone gibbet in the Place de Greve replaced by a fountain. The forbidding stone structures had all but disappeared in the Netherlands, too, by the end of the seventeenth century. Elsewhere, the process began later. The permanent gallows structure at Tyburn outside London was replaced by a mobile structure in 1759. Later, when the execution site was moved to Newgate Prison, the gallows were kept in a shed in the prison, to be dragged into the street by horses on the day of the execution and hidden away again thereafter.[26]

Next came the shortening of the procession to the gallows and the public rituals associated with it. The traditional procession to Tyburn Field on the outskirts of London was ended in 1783. What had been an hours-long public event with the condemned being paraded through the city streets for all to see now became a short, unceremonial walk from the Newgate death cell to the street outside.[27] The introduction of the trap-door hanging—first used in 1760 for the execution of Lord Ferrers—reduced the event's visibility still further by hiding the dying body from view. This development was consolidated in the 1860s, when the authorities draped a black cloth around the Newgate scaffold, hiding all but the heads of the condemned after their drop.[28]

Given that it retained public executions until 1939, France must be considered an outlier in this general pattern. But in France, too, the authorities took steps to reduce the event's visibility. In 1832, officials in Paris moved the public execution to a less visible location, shortened the procession, scheduled it for a less accessible time, and closed off streets to restrict the size of the viewing crowd. In 1851, they abandoned the raised scaffold and placed the guillotine on the ground, thus restricting the crowd's view of the decapitation process. After the beheading of the mass murderer Eugen Weidmann in 1939, the guillotine was hidden behind prison walls, and it became an offense for witnesses to report what they had seen. France was a laggard participant in the general process rather than an exception to it.[29]

As executions retreated from the public stage to a more private setting, public gestures and pronouncements were simultaneously silenced. In England, a series of administrative reforms ended the sights and sounds that had once proclaimed an execution in progress. In 1901, the practice of tolling the prison bell prior to an execution was discontinued. In 1902, the law requiring a black flag to be hoisted was revoked. In 1925 the press was excluded and a simple death notice posted on the prison gate.[30] Over time, even the death sentence pronounced by English judges was changed to make its phrasing less dramatic. The customary language had been direct and graphic: "The sentence of the Court upon you is, that you be taken from this place to a lawful prison and thence to a place of execution and that you be hanged by the neck until you be dead; and that your body be afterward buried within the precincts of the prison in which you shall have been confined before your execution. And may the Lord have mercy on your soul." After 1945, the sentence became simply, "You shall suffer death by hanging." Even that phrasing still seemed too "grim" for the Royal Commission of 1953, which recommended that the formula be "as brief, simple and colorless as is consistent with the solemnity of the occasion."[31] Right up to the end of British hanging in the 1960s, the ritualistic aspects of sentencing and execution continued to be curtailed, with the traditions of the judge's black cap and the unmarked prison grave also eventually abandoned.

A similar process occurred in Germany. In 1863, authorities introduced an execution bell to ensure that the new jail-yard executions would not be perceived as secret procedures. By 1915 officials had come to regard the tolling bell as embarrassing and overly theatrical, and recommended its abolition. In the event, the bell was retained, but only because the authorities were persuaded that its tolling covered up another, more embarrassing sound—the thud of the guillotine's blade as it crashed down on the condemned man's neck.[32]

The long-term restriction of spectacle and ritual also reduced the official discourse generated around the scaffold. Between the nineteenth and the twentieth centuries, the publication of execution broadsheets, last dying speeches, and scaffold sermons became a thing of the past. The execution became less public over time, but it also became less voluble, less demonstrative, and less eager to communicate. Between about 1830 and 1870 most Western nations ceased executing offenders in public, though Spain continued the practice until 1894 and France until 1939. One by one— usually after extensive debate and in the face of public protest—Western authorities moved the event behind the scenes of social life and reduced the number of people allowed to witness it. In Germany, abolition of the public execution occurred in one state after another during the 1850s and the early 1860s. In the Netherlands, the last one took place in 1860. Both Austria and England abolished the practice in 1868. According to Spierenburg, all the Western countries witnessed much the same pattern.[33] Britain's overseas colonies were affected, too, with South Australia, New South Wales, Tasmania, and Queensland abolishing public executions from 1858 onward and Canada ending the practice in 1869.[34]

Over time, executions went from being a community ritual, controlled by local officials close to the scene of the crime, to being a state event controlled by national or state authorities and enacted at a location some distance from the affected community. In most Western nations this process of "delocalization" started in the seventeenth century and continued into the twentieth, proceeding alongside broader processes of administrative centralization.[35] By the start of the twentieth century, executions in most countries took place in a few central locations under the supervision of national authorities. Local officials had lost control of the execution, which was now administered at a central site by their superiors in central government.

Spierenburg notes that the shift from local to more centralized executions began with the emergence of large European cities: "During the last phase of pre-industrial society in Europe a regular location prevailed. Notably this is true for its three biggest cities. In London executions came to be performed at Tyburn, in Paris at the Place de Greve, in Amsterdam at Dam Square." He links these developments to the growing rationalization of criminal justice: "The step towards unilocality marks the routinizing of public punishment."[36]

Delocalization affected the whole capital process, not just the staging of executions. It gave rise to centralized review of capital sentences by national officials—the home secretary, the kaiser, the president, a panel of the nation's high court—who might choose to grant pardon or mitigate the sentence. Though national politics could shape capital decisions and may sometimes have increased the likelihood of an execution, the usual effect of delocalization was to rationalize the process, reducing disparities between regions, interposing dispassionate middlemen between the crime and the punishment, and reducing the frequency with which death sentences were actually carried out.[37]

For much of human history, the creative energy expended on execution methods was directed toward ever-more fearsome and spectacular deaths. But after the eighteenth century, human inventiveness was mostly applied to the opposite purpose, as criminal justice authorities sought to make executions more rapid and reliable. Over the last two hundred years, there has been a sustained shift away from direct hands-on methods whereby an executioner—often a butcher or a skinner by trade—set upon the condemned man's body with a crude weapon such as a rope, an axe, a club, or a wooden wheel. In their place we see the emergence of more mechanized methods intended to make the process more expeditious, less painful and less messy, with minimal direct contact between executioner and executed.

The refinement of decapitation technology exemplifies this process—with first the sword being replaced by an axe, then a mechanized axe (the guillotine) replacing the hand-held version. When the French Constituent Assembly decreed in June 1791 that death by guillotine would henceforth be the sole mode of execution—a death without torture, the same death for each—it declared: "The punishment of death shall consist in the mere privation of life." The instrument's promoter, Dr. Joseph Ignace Guillotin, put it more graphically: "The blade hisses, the head falls, blood spurts, the man exists no more. With my machine I'll cut off your head in the blink of an eye and you will feel nothing but a slight coolness on the back of your neck."[38] The guillotine's sharp steel and greased pulleys were to execute death sentences with "zero-degree torture."[39]

Elsewhere, the reworking of traditional methods in pursuit of rapid, silent deaths produced other innovations. In the nations that relied on the rope, the gallows were redesigned, hanging techniques refined, and the hangman's know-how improved. By the end of the eighteenth century, the ancient hanging tree (from which a noose was suspended with a cart or ladder below for the condemned man to stand on prior to being launched into eternity) was being replaced by the more reliable trap-door gallows. In this new contraption, the condemned was positioned on a trapdoor built into a raised scaffold platform. Once the noose was in place, the executioner pulled a bolt to release the trapdoor and cause the sudden drop of the condemned into the space below. In England in 1876 this arrangement was further refined by the introduction of a scaffold-top lever for releasing the drop.[40]

In 1886, a British government committee appointed to report on the best way to carry out executions "in a becoming manner without risk of failure or miscarriage in any respect" made recommendations about the length of drop, improvements in the apparatus, and the adoption of preliminary tests and precautions. Following the committee's report, the British government reformed its techniques, producing tables of "calculated drops and standardized ropes and scaffold structures" and introducing the "long drop" as a means to "dislocate the cervical vertebrae and rupture the spinal cord." Professional hangmen like Albert Pierrepoint further improved hanging techniques, using height and weight charts to increase the likelihood that death would be caused by severing the spinal cord rather than by strangulation or decapitation, and organizing the execution process for maximum speed and minimum disruption.[41] In his testimony to the Royal Commission, Pierrepoint claimed that it took between nine and twelve seconds to get the condemned man from his cell into the execution chamber, apply the noose, and pull the lever.[42]

In its 1953 report, the British Royal Commission on Capital Punishment noted that these improvements contributed to a change in the meaning of hanging. An execution method "whose special merit was formerly thought to be that it was peculiarly degrading is now defended on the ground that it is uniquely humane." In a series of remarks that neatly captures the key elements of this transformation, the commission insisted that the requisites of a modern British execution were "*humanity, certainty* and *decency* and those alone":

> *Humanity* . . . The requirements of humanity are essentially two. One is that the preliminaries to the act of execution should be as quick and as simple as possible, and free from anything that unnecessarily sharpens the poignancy of the prisoner's apprehension. The other is that the act of execution should produce immediate unconsciousness passing quickly into death . . . *Certainty* . . . which method is most likely to avoid mishaps? . . . *Decency* . . . In using this term, we have two things in mind. One is the obligation that obviously rests on every civilised state to conduct its judicial executions with decorum. The other is the regard that should be paid to the feeling, which we believe to be

generally prevalent, and which we share, that as far as possible, judicial execution should be performed without brutality, that it should avoid gross physical violence and should not mutilate or distort the body.[43]

"The history of executions," declared a United Nations report just a decade later, "is one of gradual diminution of the infliction of pain and degradation and of increasing insistence upon speedier and more painless methods."[44] This process is not yet at an end, at least where Western executions still occur. The medicalization and bureaucratization of today's American executions are clearly oriented to the same ends, and lethal injection represents the high point, thus far, of that development.

The movement of Western states toward the complete abolition of capital punishment began, haltingly, in a few small jurisdictions in the late eighteenth century. It spread to a handful of larger nation states in the course of the nineteenth and early twentieth centuries, often producing complete abolition only for "ordinary" crimes (as opposed to "extraordinary" or political offenses) with many of these abolitionist developments subsequently being reversed. Then, in the last third of the twentieth century, the movement greatly expanded until it encompassed all the Western nations with the exception of the United States, each of which had abolished the death penalty entirely by the end of the century.

Like the other transformations, abolition was a process that unfolded over an entire region and over a long period of time. In the great majority of cases where sustained and comprehensive abolition occurred, it emerged as the final phase in a reform process that had already restricted, restrained, and refined the practice and greatly reduced its frequency. Except in a very few instances, complete and sustained abolition has been a late twentieth-century development that capped a much longer process of transformation.

The Grand Duchy of Tuscany—a Hapsburg possession, ruled by Leopold II, the future emperor of Austria—was the first Western jurisdiction to declare the abolition of the death penalty, doing so in its reformed criminal code of 1786.[45] A few years later, the penalty was also abolished in Russia, at the behest of the Empresses Elizabeth and Catherine II. In each case, the punishment was held in abeyance for several years before being reintroduced.

In the nineteenth century, more abolitions occurred, most of them later reversed but a few lasting until the present. In 1849, a law abolishing capital punishment was adopted by several German states as part of the nation's "liberal revolution," though the law was repealed soon thereafter. Temporary abolitions also occurred in Greece in 1863 and Romania in

1864. In 1866, the death penalty was deleted from the Belgian Law Code after a decade during which the king had commuted all capital sentences. A similar pattern occurred in the Netherlands, which legally abolished capital punishment in 1870, fifteen years after King Willem III began his practice of refusing to sign death warrants. In 1872, this process was repeated in Norway and Sweden, when the king declared himself opposed to the death penalty and unwilling to impose it. Italy's liberal monarch adopted the same position in 1863, leading to twenty-five years without executions. That country's *de facto* abolition process was rendered *de jure* in the Criminal Code of 1888, though it was later reversed during Mussolini's fascist administration.[46] Portugal abolished capital punishment for ordinary crime in 1867, having carried out no executions after 1846.[47] Switzerland's Federal Council abolished the death penalty in 1874, and though two cantons reinstated the punishment five years later, neither subsequently executed anyone.[48]

Abolition was pursued elsewhere with less success. The British House of Commons put abolition bills to a vote on at least eight occasions between 1840 and 1869—the most lasting result being the ending of public executions in 1868.[49] Members of the French Chamber of Deputies, for their part, pursued an abolitionist parliamentary campaign, defeating reform attempts that fell short of total abolition—with the result that France retained public execution longer than any other Western nation.

The majority of Western European abolitions occurred in the second half of the twentieth century, either in the years immediately after the Second World War or in the 1960s and 1970s. Italy, Germany, and Austria included abolitionist provisions in the new liberal constitutions they enacted following the collapse of fascism. After the war, nations such as Britain, Spain, France, Ireland, Australia, New Zealand, and Canada experienced a decline in the frequency of executions, though legislative attempts failed to bring about complete abolition for decades thereafter.[50]

In several nations where capital punishment had long been abolished for "ordinary" crimes, the death penalty remained on the books for political offenses against the state—a reminder of capital punishment's historic role in the maintenance of state power. In the relative stability of Western Europe in the postwar years, these "extraordinary" penalties were never invoked, and they, too, were eventually abolished: by Portugal in 1976, Denmark in 1978, Luxemburg and Norway in 1979, the Netherlands in 1982, Ireland in 1990, Italy in 1994, Spain in 1995, Belgium in 1996, and the United Kingdom in 1998.

Since the 1980s, anti–death penalty provisions have increasingly been embodied in human rights conventions, transnational treaties, and inter-

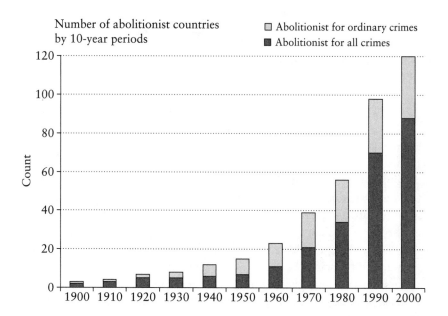

Number of abolitionist countries by 10-year periods

□ Abolitionist for ordinary crimes
■ Abolitionist for all crimes

national law. Protocols 6 and 13 of the European Convention on Human Rights (1983 and 2002) prohibit the death penalty, as do the United Nations' 2nd Optional Protocol to the International Covenant on Civil and Political Rights (ICCPR), which was passed in 1989, and the American Convention on Human Rights Protocol to Abolish the Death Penalty, adopted in 1990 by the General Assembly of the Organization of American States.[51]

The emergence of these international legal norms has changed the nature of the death penalty as a political issue. Their existence exerts abolitionist pressure on other nations, and in some cases provides them with political and economic incentives to abandon the death penalty. They have internationalized death penalty politics, transforming a domestic matter into an issue that has a bearing on international relations. They "lock in" death penalty abolition in those nations that are signatories to the ICCPR, or members of the European Union and the Council of Europe, making continued abolition an international obligation rather than merely a domestic policy choice. As a result, capital punishment has tended to fade from national political debate in these nations, and popular opinion in some countries has begun to shift away from the death penalty.[52] The new reform movement has succeeded in elevating death penalty abolition to the status of an international human rights principle.

The long-term history of the death penalty in the West thus approaches its absolute antithesis: what was once an unproblematic institution, universally embraced, is fast becoming a violation of human rights, universally prohibited. Except, of course, in the United States, where capital punishment remains constitutionally permissible and executions continue to be carried out.

Decline in America

The history of capital punishment in America is, in its overall pattern and direction, largely the same as that of other Western nations. Contemporary conversations about American Exceptionalism and America's cultural commitment to capital punishment convey a rather different impression, but the truth is that for much of the last 200 years, America and the other Western nations have marched in lockstep, continually restraining, refining, and reducing the use of the death penalty.

Like their counterparts in Europe, the American states abandoned the use of aggravated execution methods toward the end of the eighteenth century. As Stuart Banner tells us, "Burning, gibbeting, and dismemberment all dwindled away," and though the dissection of the condemned person's corpse continued longer than these other practices, this postmortem affliction was not for public viewing. Dissection, too, would eventually disappear during the course of the nineteenth century.[53]

The diversion of serious felons from the scaffold to secondary punishments also occurred in the United States in much the same way and at much the same time that it occurred elsewhere. Neither the American colonies nor the states that they became ever utilized transportation as a substitute for capital punishment, though the colonies had received transported convicts from Britain before the War of Independence. But America's Northern states were in the forefront of the penitentiary movement, and from the 1790s onward, sentences of imprisonment were used to deal with offenders who would previously have been sentenced to death. Banner reports that "Massachusetts, New York, and Pennsylvania . . . established their first prisons in the 1780s," and that when New Jersey, Virginia, and Kentucky narrowed their capital codes in the 1790s, "each state simultaneously appropriated funds for its first prison."[54]

As for restricting the offenses to which capital punishment might be applied, it was widely acknowledged in the early nineteenth century that American states were in the vanguard of this movement. European visitors to the United States expressed surprise at the mildness of the new nation's punishments. Alexis de Tocqueville was particularly impressed that "the Americans have almost expunged capital punishment from their codes."[55]

That a young nation could exhibit such civilized laws became a matter of pride for Americans like James Dana of Connecticut, who remarked, "It doth honor to the wisdom as well as the lenity of our legislators that not more than six crimes are capital by our law."[56] And of course the contrast with England—where the Bloody Code still survived—gave great satisfaction to the former colonists. One of the first justices on the new United States Supreme Court declared: "How few are the capital crimes, known to the laws of the United States compared with those known to the laws of England."[57] Nor was this an idle boast. As David Brion Davis later noted, several American states had abolished capital punishment for every crime except murder "at a time when Sir Samuel Romilly was desperately trying to persuade Lord Ellenborough that the British character would not be hopelessly corrupted if Parliament repealed the death penalty for thefts from bleaching grounds or for stealing five shillings from a shop."[58]

America's curtailment of the capital code began early. In 1682, William Penn's Great Act limited the application of the Pennsylvanian death penalty to premeditated murder only—a reform that lasted until 1718, when a new penal code expanded the gallows' reach to a further twelve offenses. Toward the end of the eighteenth century, Pennsylvania once again introduced a series of narrowing reforms. In 1786 the state eliminated capital punishment for robbery, burglary, and sodomy, and by 1794 the death penalty was permitted only for those convicted of first-degree murder. Other states followed Pennsylvania's lead. In 1796, legislators in New York, New Jersey, and Virginia voted to reduce the number of capital crimes. In 1815, Ohio joined these states in restricting capital punishment to "first-degree" murder, and within twenty years most of the other states had followed suit.[59] "By 1860 no Northern state punished with death any offense other than murder and treason.[60] Southern states also narrowed their capital codes, but only as they applied to whites.[61]

In this narrowing process, the introduction of legal distinctions between degrees of homicide was especially important because it permitted juries to convict capital defendants of a lesser offense, thus giving juries discretionary control in the matter of death sentencing. Davis makes this point when he notes that Pennsylvania's division of murder into two degrees was followed by a broader American trend toward leniency for lesser murders: "When states went still further and defined four degrees of manslaughter, which along with excusable and justifiable homicide, allowed eight different interpretations of killing, juries were, in effect, given the power to commute the penalty for almost any specific act of homicide." This *de facto* shift of capital sentencing power from judge to jury was consolidated when states enacted laws repealing mandatory death penalties in favor of discretionary penalties. This reform began in the mid-nineteenth century—prompted by Southern legislators aiming to give white juries power to discriminate against blacks—and quickly spread across the whole country until by the 1920s most of the states had adopted it.[62]

The movement to restrict death-eligible offenses developed faster in some regions than in others. As late as the 1960s, many Southern states retained capital penalties for rape and robbery (reserving these, in practice, for black defendants), whereas states in the rest of the country had long before limited capital punishment to first-degree murder. By the late 1970s, following a series of Supreme Court decisions, the American death penalty was effectively available only for aggravated murder.

The process of privatizing the execution—rendering it less visible, less ritualized, and less accessible to the public—also occurred in the United States, sometimes in advance of developments in Europe. In 1787 Benjamin Rush lectured on the counterproductive effects of public executions, and in 1830 Connecticut abolished the practice—several decades before England, Austria, Germany, and the Netherlands followed suit.[63]

Again there was considerable variation across American regions, with some Southern states continuing to stage public executions more than one hundred years after they had been abandoned in the North. But then developments were uneven in Europe as well: the last public execution in America occurred in Missouri in 1937; the last European execution was in France two years later. Between 1830 and 1860, all the Northern states—and some Southern ones such as Mississippi and Alabama—had moved hangings into the jail yard or, like Iowa in 1838, given their courts discretion to order hangings in public if they saw fit.[64]

Some state authorities—New York in 1888, followed by Colorado, Minnesota, Virginia, Washington, and Arkansas—went so far as to refuse press access to executions and prohibit the circulation of execution reports. These laws were widely flouted, however, and litigation eventually rendered them void. Elsewhere, officials were less restrictive, sometimes issuing "invitations" to large numbers of citizens to attend jail yard executions. American states today typically permit a small number of selected individuals to witness executions but bar them from photographing or recording the event.[65]

The process of delocalization, whereby the control and location of executions shifted from local to central authorities, occurred in the United States as it did in other Western nations, though again, with a great deal of regional variation and significant time lags between first and last. But American delocalization was, in important respects, only ever partial, shifting the location and control of executions but leaving prosecution and sentencing decisions under local control. Even today, the most important decisions about capital charging and sentencing remain matters for county-level decision-makers.

Prompted by the growth of state prisons and by the administrative centralization that occurred after the Civil War—and later by the advent of electric chairs and gas chambers—states increasingly insisted that all executions within their boundaries "be performed under state authority at a single state facility." Again, as with privatization, the delocalization process took hold earliest in the American Northeast and latest in the South.[66] "This movement began," Bowers tells us, "in 1864 when Vermont and Maine imposed the first executions under state authority; it was still in progress in 1955 and 1957 when Mississippi and Louisiana brought their executions under state authority; and it was never fully completed, with Delaware and Montana continuing to execute under local authority until the *de facto* cessation of executions in these states."[67] The designation of a specific facility as the place where all death sentences in the state would be carried out—together with the practice of conveying condemned offenders there, immediately after sentencing, to await execution—led to the creation of the modern "death row."

The reform of execution technologies to hasten death, avoid mishaps, and minimize the appearance of suffering was also a prominent aspect of American history. Indeed, the search for the painless, problem-free execution was more marked in the United States than elsewhere, and produced a series of innovations that were distinctively American. Most of these methods emerged in the last 120 years—the electric chair (first used in 1890), the gas chamber (1924), and the lethal injection (1982)—but the process began earlier with efforts to improve hanging techniques.[68]

The trap-door hanging was used in America beginning in 1822, and in the years after 1831, a contraption known as the "upright jerker" (which used pulleys and weights to effect a sudden upward pull on the noose) was employed in several states, including New York, New Jersey, Pennsylvania, Illinois, South Carolina, and Massachusetts. Before the invention of the electric chair, there were various proposals to ease the suffering of a condemned man, for example, by administering chloroform prior to execution, or by replacing the noose with a guillotine.[69]

The movement to abandon hanging and adopt a new execution method spread rapidly across the states from 1890 onward. Within twenty-five years, fourteen states had followed New York in adopting electrocution as their execution method. A further eleven plus the District of Columbia had done so by 1950. Nevada's introduction of the gas chamber in 1921 led to that new method being adopted in a further ten states by 1955. As Banner remarks, "Hanging had been the universal American method of execution in the late nineteenth century, but by the middle of the twentieth only a handful of states retained the gallows."[70]

Hanging continued in a few states, including New Hampshire and Washington—the last hanging being carried out in Delaware in 1996—and two states, Nevada and Utah, permitted execution by shooting.[71] But from the 1980s, the noose, the electric chair, and the gas chamber were increasingly replaced by the latest in supposedly pain-free execution, the lethal injection. This method was first developed and authorized by Oklahoma in 1977 and first used by Texas in 1982. By the beginning of the twenty-first century lethal injection was standard in every death penalty state.

America's turn to new technologies can mostly be understood as an attempt to reduce the pain and suffering of executions. But the decision to abandon the age-old method of hanging raises a question: why did the American states choose to *abandon* the traditional method rather do what other hanging nations did and try to *improve* it? Why did they suddenly find the noose to be intolerable, rather than follow other nations in seeking to improve the skills of the hangman or devise guidelines to regulate the procedure? And why did this shift occur where and when it did—in the Northeastern states in the late 1880s? The answer may have to do with Southern lynchings and the taint that lynch mobs left on an execution method previously favored by American state officials.

In his 1885 address to the New York legislature, Governor David B. Hill announced his intention to review execution methods to see if a technique "less barbarous" than hanging could be developed.[72] The next year he appointed a state commission charged with finding a suitable alternative. What is not made explicit, either in the governor's address or in the commission's report, is precisely why the centuries-old method of hanging had suddenly become unacceptable and beyond repair. Certainly, the report sets out a list of objections to hanging—it can be "degrading and revolting" to watch; it can fail, allowing the condemned to be resuscitated; it can decapitate; it seems inappropriate for women; and so on—citing anecdotes to illustrate these concerns. But these problems were long-standing ones, as attested by the fact that the anecdotes are taken from England as well as from America, and often date from decades or even centuries before. Moreover, there is no disclosure of any immediate reason for the turn against hanging.[73]

Circumstantial evidence suggests that the Northern officials felt the need to distance lawful state executions from lynch-mob killings—and the disavowal of the noose was a means of drawing that distinction. In the decades after the collapse of Reconstruction, Southern lynch mobs killed with more frequency and ferocity than ever before.[74] During the postbellum period the *New York Times* carried more than 1,000 reports of lynchings, and the 1880s saw a sharp increase in the number of spectacular events that caught national attention. In an editorial of December 17, 1887, anticipating the findings of the state commission, the *New York Times* referred to the gallows as a method best suited to lynch mobs and pressed the state to adopt "the electric bolt" as a more solemn and impressive method: "An execution by lynch law is itself an act of passion and revenge rather than of deliberate justice, and the gallows is its appropriate instrument. An execution under the law ought to be the more terrible for the solemnity and impressiveness with which it is performed." As far as the *Times* was concerned, the nation's traditional method had been appropriated by lawless mobs, and the state ought to find an alternative.

The commission's report alludes to the same problem when it states, "The strong and general prejudice among cultured or high-minded persons against executions by hanging has undoubtedly been fostered by the multitude of accounts which have been published of such scenes which have occurred, not necessarily connected with the death penalty."[75] This reference to a "multitude" of reported hanging scenes "not necessarily connected with the death penalty" is likely a reference to lynchings. The spate of Southern lynchings had changed the social meaning of the noose, generating a "strong and general prejudice" against execution by hanging. A century later, American legal officials were still conscious of this association. As Judge Reinhardt wrote in 1994, "Hanging is associated with lynching, with frontier justice, and with our ugly, nasty, and best-forgotten history of bodies swinging from the trees or exhibited in public places. To many Americans, judicial hangings call forth the brutal images of Southern justice."[76] It was not that hanging techniques were beyond improvement—as demonstrated in other nations where hanging was reformed and retained. It was that in parts of America the social meaning of the noose had been spoiled.

With respect to total abolition—the final stage of Western development—the various American states stand in very different relationships to the general historical pattern. Several states, most notably Michigan, Rhode Island, and Wisconsin, were in the vanguard of the abolitionist movement, repealing their capital statutes in the middle of the nineteenth century. Others retain and use the death penalty today, thirty years after the practice was abolished throughout the Western world.

The vanguard abolitions of Michigan, Rhode Island, and Wisconsin were not the first American moves toward total repeal. In 1821, Edward Livingston submitted a revised criminal code to the Louisiana state legislature that included a provision that eliminated the death penalty. In the event, this provision was rejected by the state, but the Livingston report became a model for death penalty reform that was cited time and again during the nineteenth century. It influenced the New York state legislature, for example, which set up a committee in 1832 to consider the expediency of abolition, leading to abolitionist bills in 1832 and 1834. In 1837, the state of Maine moved close to abolition when its legislature passed a law requiring that death-sentenced criminals not be executed until a full year had elapsed following sentencing and a written warrant had been issued at the discretion of the state governor. The result of the Maine Law, later adopted in several other states, too, was that few executions were carried out.[77]

Following the lead of Michigan, Rhode Island, and Wisconsin in the 1840s and 1850s, other states moved to total or near-total abolition. Maine became totally abolitionist in 1887, Minnesota in 1911, Alaska and Hawaii in 1957, Iowa and West Virginia in 1965, New Mexico in 1969, and California—as a result of a state court ruling—in 1972. Several others—North Dakota (1915), Vermont and New York (1965), and New Jersey (1972)—introduced laws abolishing the death penalty for all murders except those of on-duty police and prison officers and those committed by individuals under sentence of life imprisonment. Others still abolished capital punishment only to reintroduce it later: Colorado was abolitionist from 1897 to 1901; Kansas, 1907–1935; Washington, 1913–1919; South Dakota, 1915–1939; Tennessee, 1915–1916; Arizona, 1916–1918; Missouri, 1917–1919; and Delaware, 1958–1961.[78]

The movement of states toward total abolition was staggered, with successive waves of abolitionist reform in the mid-nineteenth century, the Progressive period, and the mid-twentieth century. Abolition was sometimes followed by the reintroduction of death penalties shortly thereafter. But the 1930s onward saw a sustained thirty-year decline in executions. The peak year for executions in the twentieth century was 1935, when there were 199 nationwide. Thereafter, the annual numbers begin to drop, going below 150 in 1948, below 100 in 1952, below 50 in 1961, and down to zero in 1968.[79] By the late 1960s—against a backdrop of decreasing executions, a *de facto* moratorium across the whole country, litigation challenging the death penalty's legality, and public and political opinion turning against capital punishment—America seemed on the verge of nationwide abolition. At that moment, like so many over the last 200 years, no one would have viewed the United States as an exception to the general pattern of Western development.

Convergence and Divergence

These convergent developments and common chronologies show that America participated in the broad Western historical transformation of the death penalty. They also suggest, following the principle of "same effects, same causes," that the underlying causes that brought about death penalty reform and abolition in Europe were probably operative in the United States as well.

That America's participation in the Western process of death penalty reform has been deep and enduring has implications for the contemporary institution. Not the least of these is that today American capital punishment operates in an environment that is, in important respects, hostile to its existence. It exists in a political and cultural context that has produced abolition elsewhere, has drastically curtailed the practice in the United States, and ensures that American capital punishment is inherently controversial. Capital statutes, capital indictments, death sentences, and executions occur in contemporary America and command popular and political support. But they take place in a social context shaped by historical processes that produced abolition throughout the Western world and in many parts of the United States.

If there is a common history that places America in the mainstream of Western reform, there are also definite divergences that mark America as an outlier in certain respects. The most important of these—the nation's continuing use of capital punishment thirty years after the rest of the West abolished it—has already been identified. But there are three other significant differences that must figure in any comparative account of the American present, each of them inter-related in certain respects. First, in matters of criminal justice, is the general and long-standing predominance of local community control relative to central state and federal control. This is a distinctively American power balance that limited the extent of delocalization and allowed the continuation of state- and county-level control of capital law and sentencing. Second is the importance of regional differences in death penalty development: the three most notable examples being the late persistence in the South of public executions; the late persistence in the South of racial distinctions that determined whether an offender was eligible for the death penalty and how he would be executed; and the concentration of executions in the South in the period since 1976.

Third is the phenomenon of extra-legal executions, most notably public torture lynchings, which continued into the twentieth century, were concentrated in the South, and were organized around racial divisions. Each of these distinctive characteristics marks America's divergence from the mainstream of Western reform. And each one provides us with clues about the institutional structures and social divisions that have shaped America's capital punishment complex in the past as well as the present.

From colonial times onward, the American death penalty (and crime policy more generally) was controlled by local rather than central authorities and presided over chiefly by religious rather than secular officials—in contrast to most European nations, where the balance was the opposite. In colonial New England, for example, "the power of the state was clearly at work in the system of justice that convicted a felon and put him to death." But, as Karen Haltunnen points out, "the explicit purpose of the spectacle, as expressed in the execution sermons, was the moral and religious edification of the community, not the display of political power." Haltunnen goes on to show that "[i]nstead of reflecting a distant state and an isolated victim in a drama of monarchical authority before terrified witnesses, the New England execution sermon shaped a more intimate drama of an exemplary sinner standing before compassionate spectators who joined with him in a collective struggle against sin."[80]

Religious officials, speeches, and symbols stood at the center of the American scaffold, giving its rituals a different shape from those of early-modern Europe: "The transcendent drama of collective sin and redemption took clear precedent over the worldly performance of the power of the state." Before the delocalization of executions in the late nineteenth and twentieth century, the American people, not the state, were the punishing authority. The contrast here is with European nations such as England, France, and Germany, where the presence and control of the early-modern state were much more marked than in the United States.[81]

A key variable shaping American executions was the fact of local, community control rather than state control. What distinguished the American execution was not so much its "religiosity" (which, in European settings, was closely aligned with state power) so much as local, personalistic, power, expressed then, as now, in the language of faith and sectarian belonging. In this respect, the colonial character of early-modern America and the great distance that separated the American periphery from the British state across the Atlantic explain the devolved power that American county officials enjoyed. On the American scaffold, the state was less prominent and the death penalty less directly linked to state purposes than was the case in European nation states. Early American executions were community events, and local religious and political leaders shaped their form and their projected meaning.

The powers enjoyed by colonial Americans were not willingly given up. Local autonomy was a key consideration in the framing of the federal Constitution, which took pains to preserve it, and in the radical brand of localism that came to define the American polity. As a consequence, capital (and noncapital) prosecutions continued to be controlled by elected county officials, capital cases continued to be decided by county-level decision-makers (elected trial judges, local jurors), and, as late as the 1930s in some jurisdictions, the staging and control of executions continued to be a matter for the local sheriff and his deputies. (The private police powers of slave masters gave added force to this localist tradition in the Southern states.) Processes of rationalization, centralization, and professionalization occurred in America as elsewhere, imposing the power of the state and curtailing the power of local mobs. But they always encountered greater and more effective resistance in the United States than in other Western nations.

Between about 1890 and 1930 most American states sought to bring executions under more centralized authority, shifting administrative control from the county to the state level. In this they were largely successful—though control of prosecution, trial, and sentencing remained in local hands—in part because new execution technologies required greater levels of funding and expertise. But the will to retain local control was powerful, and local authorities sometimes succeeded in resisting this process. In Mississippi and Louisiana the state authorities were persuaded to introduce portable electric chairs that were taken (on a truck, together with a mobile generator) from the state penitentiary to the various county jails as the need arose.[82] And in Kentucky, which had previously moved to state-administered electrocutions, the legislature passed a law that reintroduced local hanging for capital rapists—a measure that returned executions to the county crowd for precisely those cases that aroused the most local passion: those involving black men convicted of sexual offenses against white women.[83]

It is not uncommon for federated nations to exhibit internal variation in the development of death penalty policy: the history of Germany, Switzerland, and Australia all manifest subnational variation of this kind. But the divergent trajectories of the American regions are more marked than usual, exhibiting movement in opposite directions as well as an uneven pace of reform.

Thus while Northern American states were in the vanguard of abolition 160 years ago, Southern states still execute offenders today. Similarly, while Northern states led the world in the privatization of executions, with states such as Connecticut and New York abolishing public executions in the 1830s, Southern and border states such as Kentucky and Missouri continued to stage public hangings as late as 1936 and 1937, long after most Western nations had abandoned the practice.[84] And Southern states continued to put offenders to death for crimes such as rape, robbery, burglary, and arson up until the 1960s, while the rest of the country (and most Western nations) had long before restricted the death penalty to first-degree murder.[85]

The use of racial characteristics to determine death penalty eligibility and mode of execution—continuing long after it had disappeared elsewhere—was another practice that distinguished the South from the rest of the country. The origins of this practice lay in slavery, when every Southern state specified a substantial number of felonies that carried the death penalty if committed by a slave and a lesser punishment if perpetrated by a white. But *de facto* race discrimination in capital proceedings continued long after the Civil War and despite the Reconstruction Amendments that rendered it illegal.[86]

This discrimination was evident in 1901, when "Arkansas abolished public hangings except for rape, a crime for which capital punishment was in practice largely limited to blacks," and in 1920 in Kentucky, when, as noted above, public hanging was reintroduced for rape and attempted rape.[87] It was also apparent in the middle of the nineteenth century, when Southern states were the first—beginning with Tennessee and Alabama in 1841—to give juries discretion in bringing in capital verdicts, thus enabling them to mete out different punishments for black and white defendants.[88] In American criminal justice, discretionary sentencing decisions nearly always produce racial discrimination in punishment, and this was a major consideration in the 1970s and 1980s, when reformers sought to reduce discretion and establish stricter legal guidelines in all areas of criminal sentencing.[89]

In the Southern states of the United States, the lynching of blacks was tolerated well into the twentieth century, with more than 3,000 such events being recorded between 1880 and 1930.[90] Many of these lynchings were little more than murders tolerated by Southern communities because the murderers were white and their victims black. But others—like the spectacle lynching of Henry Smith—were much more public in character and occurred in response to allegations of heinous crimes supposedly committed by black perpetrators against white victims. When these black suspects were lynched, often in front of large crowds following a brutal summary process aimed at extorting a "confession," the events were, in effect, quasi-legal executions—instances of "popular justice" undertaken in the name of the local community and openly tolerated by local officials.[91]

The widespread occurrence of these collective killings and the singular failure of the state or federal authorities to prevent them spoke to the limits of governmental power in the Southern states—still severely dislocated by the Civil War and Reconstruction—and to white dissatisfaction with how the state's criminal justice institutions dealt with black offenders. But even when blacks were spared lynching and given an official trial, the difference was not always great. "The line between a lynching and an official execution could be thin," Stuart Banner writes. "The participants in lynchings often included the very same people who, in their official capacities, administered the criminal justice system." Official trials and executions in the South "could take place astonishingly fast, so fast as to closely resemble lynchings, when a case carried racial implications. In Kentucky in 1906 a black man convicted of raping a white woman was hanged only fifty minutes from the time the jury was sworn. In Galveston, Texas, a black defendant was indicted, tried, and hanged in less than four hours."[92] From the 1890s onward, Southern state legislatures and the U.S. Congress endeavored to end this scandal, the former passing antilynching statutes, the latter failing to do so because congressional Southern Democrats opposed them. But little real progress was made until the 1940s, by which time Jim Crow social controls were well established and white supremacy had less need of brutal violence.

The United States was not unique in experiencing lynching and collective vengeance, even in the twentieth century. Hundreds and perhaps thousands of collaborators and others were killed by mobs at the end of the Second World War in nations such as France, Belgium, Italy, and the Netherlands.[93] But these European instances of "popular justice" occurred during the upheaval of war and its aftermath. None of these nations experienced a widespread and decades-long practice of extra-legal executions during peacetime. In this respect, too, the United States was an outlier.

America's relation to the general process of Western change is, like that of other nations, both convergent and divergent. The United States partakes in a common Western history but also exhibits unique characteristics. It is caught up in the same broad processes, exhibiting the same direction of change, the same developmental sequences, and the same patterns of reform as the other Western nations. But it also exhibits important differences. These international differences, which distinguish America from other Western nations, are linked to internal subnational differences, distinguishing some American states from others—hence the fact that some American states have been in the vanguard of Western reform, while others lag far behind.

FIVE

Processes of
Transformation

We may further observe, that sanguinary laws are a bad symptom
of the distemper of any state, or at least of its weak constitution.

<small>SIR WILLIAM BLACKSTONE, *COMMENTARIES ON THE LAWS OF ENGLAND*, 1853</small>

The decline of the death penalty is often attributed to the coming of
modernity. This is not altogether wrong: abolition is a phenomenon of
the modern period, and today's less developed nations are much more
likely to retain capital punishment than are modern, developed countries.[1]
But a simple modernity thesis does not stand up to inspection. The Soviet
Union was a modernized society, as were the totalitarian regimes of Nazi
Germany, fascist Spain, and fascist Italy, but all of them embraced the
death penalty and used it with great frequency. Contemporary nations that
are thoroughly modernized, such as the United States, Japan, and Singapore, continue to execute offenders. And nations that revert to capital
punishment after a period of abolition—as both Japan and the United
States have done—do not do so because they have become less modern.

A more powerful explanation for the death penalty's decline can be
found in a series of social transformations that altered the character of the
state in Western society, its strategic interests, and the social fields in which
it operated. This theory focuses on state institutions and the political and
cultural processes that bear on state action. The death penalty is always
and everywhere an exercise of state power. Officials may represent the
death penalty as a community response to crime, the application of a legal rule, or the expression of a moral imperative—and it may have all
these characteristics. But the defining feature of capital punishment is that

state officials put individuals to death while exercising the state's power to punish.

The use and character of capital punishment are—and have always been—shaped by the structure of state institutions and the decisions of state officials acting in accordance with their perception of strategic governmental interests. State actors strive to maintain control and deploy power in the interests of their institutions, their allies, and their constituents. The death penalty is one more tool to be deployed—or not—in the furtherance of these ends. As the nature of the state and its context of action have changed over time, so too has capital punishment.

Over the course of the last 300 years, a series of political and cultural forces has altered the state in Western societies in ways that have had major consequences for capital punishment. State formation and state building have expanded the institutional capacities of government and the ability of state actors to exert social and penal control. The struggles of liberal and democratic forces have transformed political institutions, forged new power balances, and exerted pressure on state policy. The emergence of cultural practices embodying civilized and humanitarian sensibilities have softened state power, establishing new criteria of legitimacy and imposing new limits on the use of violence.

Over the same period, the social environment in which the state deploys its powers has been continuously transformed. Throughout the West, societies have tended to become more pacified, more orderly, more market-dominated, and more individuated, though these developments have frequently been accompanied by violent upheavals, challenges to state authority, group hostilities, and disruptions of social order. All these processes have been consequential for the shape and deployment of capital punishment. International relations have also impacted death penalty practice, especially in the context of war, imperial conquest, and decolonization. Since the last decades of the twentieth century, transnational pressures for abolition have been exerted by organizations such as the Council of Europe, the European Union, and the United Nations.

State Formation and the Death Penalty

State formation played the leading role in shaping the pragmatics of death penalty deployment. Early-modern processes of state-making—involving brutal struggles to defeat political rivals, pacify populations, and establish sovereign monopolies of violence—led to a widespread intensification of capital punishment. Once state authority was secured and social order established, changes in capital punishment were instituted by state actors eager to increase their control over events, minimize disruption, and enhance their legitimacy. As Anton Blok observes, "with the political integration of various territories and the formation of modern bureaucratic states, central control over larger populations became more stable and effective . . . it was precisely in such states as Prussia and Austria . . . that death sentences were often substituted by extraordinary punishments involving various forms of confinement."[2] Death penalty reforms were sometimes undertaken in the wake of disruptive events—unruly crowds, botched executions, and spoiled rituals. But the causes that pushed for change were mostly liberal forces demanding limits on state power, democrats demanding equal treatment, cultural elites demanding more civilized or humane procedures, or lawyers pushing for due process of law.

The state's control imperatives have shaped the death penalty at every turn. But the nature of these imperatives has changed over time, from the brutal assertion of violent power in the formative phase; to a more restrained use once state power was well established; to an attenuated, ambivalent deployment when the death penalty became embroiled in problems of legitimacy and efficacy.

Shifts in political relations and cultural sensibilities shaped the changing character of the state and its strategic interests. In particular, liberalism (with its commitment to the freedom of the individual and the restriction of state power) and humanitarianism (with its concern for the sanctity of human life and the minimization of human suffering) have operated as powerful forces of reform, pressing for the restriction of capital punishment and ultimately for its abolition. Democratization (the process of extending the franchise and establishing elections, majority rule, and egalitarian values) and "civilization" (the cultivation of refined sensibilities, together with a characteristic squeamishness and an embarrassed avoidance of brutish sights, sounds, and smells) have also been historically influential, but their impact on the death penalty has been more ambiguous.

Democratic leaders often demanded that liberal protections be extended to all citizens. They spoke out against "monarchic" punishments, exerting downward pressure on the use of capital punishment. But in some settings the effect of democracy has been to valorize populist sentiment and to authorize the death penalty because it is supported by a majority of "the people." Similarly, the civilized sensibilities of cultural elites caused state officials to refine death penalty methods and reduce the institution's more visible, violent practices—sometimes resulting in the reduced use of capital punishment. But civilizing reforms are often more intent on concealing distressing events than on abolishing them, and their effect has sometimes been to sustain capital punishment by making it less visible and therefore more tolerable.

The death penalty is inscribed in the politics of state violence and violence control—and is deployed and developed accordingly. In Western societies, improvements in violence control, together with cultural prohibitions on the use of violence, had, by the end of the twentieth century, rendered capital punishment practically inessential and politically problematic. The penalty of death was made inessential by the formation of a stable bureaucratic state, secure in its monopoly of violence, supported by a criminal justice apparatus of police and prisons, and relatively effective in its control of interpersonal violence. It was made problematic by the development of liberal-democratic and welfare state institutions, and by an associated culture of civilized refinement and humanism, all of which worked to limit state violence and surround it with prohibitions and taboos. These institutional and cultural conditions set the scene for the eventual abolition of the institution, a step that all but one of the Western nations had taken by the last decades of the twentieth century.

Because modern capital punishment is a state sanction, the decisions that shape its use are made by state actors—by governors, government ministers, legislators, prosecutors, judges, jurors, and prison officials—acting within the context of state institutions. Every execution, every grant of mercy, every reform or adjustment to procedure is carried through by individuals acting in the name of the state. Other social forces influence state action, of course, the more so as society becomes more democratic and power is more extensively shared. But social forces affect death penalty outcomes only to the extent that they act on and through state officials and their legal and administrative procedures. Historians debate the causes of death penalty reform, counterposing cultural explanations to explanations that stress the control interests of state actors. But these interpretations ought not to be seen as mutually exclusive. State actors respond to cultural and political reform pressures, but they do so at specific times and in specific ways in order to further state interests.

When the death penalty was first repealed in eighteenth-century Europe, the abolitions were *ex cathedra* decrees of "enlightened" monarchs. In subsequent centuries, abolition was typically enacted by majority vote in a national parliament or legislative assembly. More recently, the decision has sometimes been made by national constitutional courts. In each case, abolition has been a top-down, countermajoritarian reform, imposed with limited popular support and usually in direct contravention of majority public opinion. State officials, political leaders, and high court judges who were previously responsible for using capital punishment subsequently became responsible for ending it.

Different kinds of states, and states at different stages of development, deploy different kinds of punishment. The personalistic regimes of dynastic, patrician, and monarchical states made heavy use of corporal and capital punishments—in part because they had few alternatives but also because rulers regarded disobedience as an insult to their personal authority.[3] Reliance on imprisonment, fines, and penal supervision, with little or no use of capital punishment, is more typical of bureaucratized liberal-democratic states, where the welfare of citizens is a primary governmental concern.

Processes of state formation are fundamental to understanding the development of capital punishment. But state formation is intertwined with other social developments, such as the expansion of the division of labor, the growth of towns and trade, and increases in the population. Indeed, "Internal pacification of territory facilitates trade, which facilitates the growth of towns and division of labor and generates taxes which support larger administrative and military organization, which in turn facilitate the internal pacification of larger territories and so on." In this cumulative economic and political process, denser webs of interaction tend to produce tighter social controls, alter power balances between groups, and exert pressure on individuals to maintain higher standards of self-restraint. These new controls, in turn, make possible "more effective and calculable administration" and the further rationalization of state and society.[4]

Histories of state formation are also histories of shifting power balances and of social relations between groups and individuals. State formation begins when a political elite becomes the dominant force within a territory and proceeds to institutionalize that dominance.[5] "Liberalization" describes the institutionalization of restraints on state power and the protection of individual freedom through the rule of law. "Democratization" is the struggle of successive social groups to share in the control of government and establish political institutions (such as elections, political parties, a widening franchise, and so on) that facilitate this development. The "civilization" of the state occurs when bourgeois cultural elites succeed in imprinting their sensibilities on state policy and social conduct. And "humanitarian" reform aims to prohibit unnecessary cruelty and suffering and establish practices oriented to the welfare and flourishing of persons—most recently in the form of human rights. Each of these processes has consequences for the relative position, power, and life chances of groups and individuals. And each of them is, in turn, conditioned by economic developments—especially changes in productive relations, the division of labor, and the structure of markets—which play a central role in shaping group relations.

If the fundamental dynamics of group relations—balances of power, interaction and interdependencies, solidarities and schisms, hatreds and fellow feeling—are crucial in shaping the state, they also play a major role in shaping its use of the power to punish.[6] Group belonging and group hostilities—especially racial identities and racial divisions, but class relations, too—are powerful social forces that shape who may be punished and to what extent. Love and loyalty, hatred and fear, fellow feeling and ethnic enmity are visceral emotions that find expression in the ways that members of one group condemn and punish members of another. Whenever state policy has been responsive to public opinion, the character of group relations and the intensity of communal fears and hostilities have determined the severity of punishments and the direction of their use. Social distance, status hierarchy, cultural difference, and racial division tend to prompt more intense punishment—such as the death penalty—while interdependence, equality, shared values, and group identity tend to inhibit it.[7]

Long-term processes of state formation are the fundamental context within which we can understand the rise and fall of capital punishment in the modern West. The early phases of state formation—when ruling groups struggled to achieve and consolidate sovereign power—saw the increased use and intensification of capital punishment.[8] The state execution, with its elaborate cruelties and ceremonials, was designed to teach political lessons to enemies and to impress the state's power on the population. Given that purpose, we can appreciate why the most horrifying torments were reserved for those convicted of treason and *lèse-majesté*.[9] We can also see why the death penalty came to be so closely linked with the question of sovereign state power.

Sovereign mastery required the subjugation of contending political forces, including powerful lords who claimed the right to raise private armies, keep armed retainers, feud, duel, exact revenge, and exercise "police powers" in their localities. Over time all these rights were rescinded. Resort to the king's courts replaced feud and revenge killing, while personal conflicts were gradually transformed into crimes to be prosecuted and punished by the state.[10] The displacement of private revenge by the king's justice was a long-term project of state officials, in which the ritual of execution formed an essential part.

A crucial building block of state power is the pacification of the territory over which that power extends. Effective pacification required not just superiority of arms but also the inculcation of habits of obedience and self-restraint, including acquiescence in the state's claim to control the power to punish. "Disarmament of the civilian population took place in many small steps," as Charles Tilly explains, including "general seizures of weapons at the ends of rebellions, prohibition of duels, controls over the production of weapons, introduction of licensing for private arms, restrictions on public displays of armed force . . . At the same time, the state's expansion of its own armed force began to overshadow the weaponry available to any of its domestic rivals."[11]

Over time, with the seventeenth century as a "decisive turning point" and with Northwestern Europe leading the way, these efforts succeeded in driving down levels of interpersonal violence. The reduction occurred first among elites and later in the population as a whole. According to the leading authority, homicide rates declined substantially from the late middle ages to the middle of the twentieth century.[12] The timing of these developments helps identify their causes: as Manuel Eisner puts it, "phases of accelerated decline in homicide rates often seem to coincide with periods of rapid expansion and stabilization of state structures," particularly the creation of professional armies and eventually civilian police forces.[13]

This was a massive social change. Our best estimates suggest that, between the fifteenth and the twentieth centuries, homicide rates declined by a factor of between ten and fifty. Capital punishment was deeply implicated in this social change, at first as cause (when frequent executions helped establish the state's monopoly of violence) and later as effect (when a peaceable civil society made executions appear brutal and unnecessary). The first signs of capital punishment's shifting status—from being an essential tool of state power to being neither "just or useful in a well-governed state"—emerged toward the end of the eighteenth century in stable states with relatively peaceful populations.[14]

That capital punishment was long considered an indispensable tool of statecraft meant that it was spared critical attacks: an essential practice could hardly be abolished. But once capital punishment became inessential to state maintenance, or at least was perceived as inessential, the politics of the death penalty were fundamentally transformed.[15] We can date from that moment—sometime in the eighteenth century—the emergence of a powerful antigallows critique.

The new institutions of criminal justice that became established in most Western nations during the nineteenth century had important consequences for capital punishment. Professional police forces, public prosecutors, and reformed prisons brought crime and violence under greater control, increased the likelihood of punishment, and so lessened the need for severity.[16] Sentences of transportation to the colonies and disciplinary imprisonment functioned as effective alternatives for punishing routine crime, allowing the death penalty to be reserved for the most serious offenses.[17]

The emergence of a criminal justice bureaucracy changed the character of state punishment, reducing its personalistic elements and allowing a more rational, utilitarian approach to develop. From the late nineteenth century, bureaucratic sensibilities and criminological expertise altered the nature and direction of criminal justice, moving it from a local, personalistic process to a more formal, rational one. Increasingly, "indifferent middlemen" administered the business of punishment, thus reducing its emotive, reactive character and introducing new levels of impartiality, self-control, and rationality.[18] By the mid-twentieth century, these professionals were espousing penal-welfare ideologies with a stress on reformation and correction that posed new challenges for capital punishment.[19] The build-up of the state's control capacity thus reduced the necessity of capital punishment and introduced new norms of penological reform and bureaucratic restraint.

Finally, the centralization that occurred in the nineteenth and twentieth centuries as national governments sought to divest local authorities of their powers and concentrate them in the center led to the "delocalization" of punishment and the creation of national prison administrations, national criminal codes, and uniform penal laws.[20] The death penalty was soon altered by these developments; it came to be administered by central government officials and was thus less affected by personal passions, local politics, and community prejudices.

Early-modern authorities used executions to project state power. But these events brought dangers for officials, since they put the state's power and authority on the line. The great ritual of state could be spoiled by an executioner's incompetence, a condemned man's recalcitrance, or a disruptive, unruly crowd. Instead of affirming state sovereignty, the execution could undermine it. An execution's meaning was inherently unstable, always vulnerable to resistance and reappropriation.[21]

State officials have always been motivated to increase their control over these difficult events—to minimize opportunities for disruption, to limit the impact of other actors, to develop protocols that can be carried through without fail. In fact, a large part of capital punishment history can be understood in these terms.[22] Consider, for example, the changing pattern of public access to executions. At a certain point in the nineteenth century, the benefits of public executions came to be outweighed by their attendant costs, and state authorities began to move scaffolds behind prison walls. But the process of "privatizing" the execution, of reducing its visibility and the extent of public involvement, began earlier and continued beyond this time. This process is best understood, not as a response to more refined sensibilities or a reaction to more unruly urban crowds, though these factors played a role. It is best viewed as the ongoing effort of government officials to exert ever-tighter control over a fraught undertaking and to manage the meanings that it put into circulation. Time after time in the nineteenth and twentieth centuries, officials moved to reduce the extent of the ritual, the size of its audience, the performative role of the condemned, the time taken for the offender to die, and the opportunities for viewing and communicating about what was seen. Official concern with avoiding spoiled public rituals eventually ended both ritual and publicity.

This same process continues today in places as far apart as Iran, where authorities recently declared an end to public executions, and the United States, where recent litigation challenging the lethal injection highlighted official concern over what execution witnesses are allowed to see.[23] Such reforms are often represented as the effect of a civilizing sensibility, but in addition to considerations of decency and propriety a more basic process is at work—that of a state modifying its procedures to better secure its authority and control.

State forms and state interests dictate the character and use of the death penalty. But state interests are shaped by political and cultural forces that influence state institutions and shape their operating environment. In the evolution of capital punishment, the most important such forces were liberalism, democracy, civilized manners, and humanitarian sentiments.

Political Processes of Reform

We easily conflate the terms "liberal" and "democratic." Most Western nations today are liberal democracies of one kind or another, and modern liberal thought has become infused with democratic ideals. But liberalism and democracy, for all their modern overlap, are distinct political traditions with different histories, values, and priorities. Paul Starr reminds us that, "by and large, the classical liberals were not democrats," or at least not democrats in the full modern sense of the term: "Classical liberalism sanctioned the denial of rights to women, men without property, and people of color."[24] Eric Neumayer makes a similar point when he observes that "not all democracies are necessarily respectful of human rights. The simple fact of electoral competition and democratic participation need not coincide with human rights protection."[25] When it comes to the death penalty, liberalism and democracy have sometimes pressed in different directions.

As a political tradition, liberalism has many strands, including religious tolerance, abhorrence of cruelty, opposition to fixed hierarchies, support for market freedoms, and an intellectual attitude that values doubt, open-mindedness, and intellectual exchange.[26] It has evolved over time, coming eventually to embrace democratic ideals and to reconstitute itself as modern democratic liberalism.[27] But at the core of classical liberalism are two essential commitments: a conception of social order that values individual freedom and autonomy; and a commitment to limiting governmental power by means of the rule of law and the separation of powers. Liberal institutions aim to restrain the coercive power of the state and to uphold the rights and freedoms of individuals. Little wonder, then, that liberals have always been among the death penalty's chief critics.

Liberalism is opposed to capital punishment in a number of respects. For Enlightenment liberals, the cruelty of judicial torture and execution made them favorite targets of criticism. For thinkers such as Montesquieu, Voltaire, and Beccaria, the death penalty was emblematic of the absolutist *ancien regime* with its arbitrary use of power and crushing disregard for individual life and liberty. "The severity of punishment is fitter for despotic governments whose principle is terror than for a monarchy, or a republic, whose spring is honor and virtue," Montesquieu famously wrote, and liberals as diverse as Hume, Franklin, Paine, Rush, and Bentham evinced the same sentiment.[28] This liberal aversion to cruel or unusual punishment also finds expression in the Eighth Amendment to the U.S. Constitution and formed the basis for contemporary challenges to America's death penalty.

The growing power of liberal ideas and social forces impacted the death penalty from the eighteenth century onward. In early-modern Europe, punishments would sometimes be collective, as when in 1757 the relatives of the regicide Robert Damiens were deprived of their family name and banished from France.[29] Against this, liberals insisted that crimes were an individual responsibility and that only the offender ought to be subject to official punishment. Liberals reformed the procedures whereby capital punishment could be imposed. Reacting against the arbitrariness of personalistic rule, the political opponents of absolutism demanded procedural protections for those accused of crimes and the establishment of legal rules and principles of fairness that would limit the reach of state power. As early as the thirteenth century, English nobles pressed for *habeas corpus* and trial by jury, and by the seventeenth century these "rule of law" principles—together with rights to counsel and to public indictment—had become central to liberalism's agenda.[30] Liberal demands for procedural propriety and due process remain a mainstay of death penalty reform in America today.

In addition to generating new criticisms of capital punishment, the rise of liberalism also changed how the institution was justified. The early-modern death penalty had been phrased in the language of tradition, of religion, and of the divine right of kings, none of which invited criticism or argument. From the eighteenth century, liberals applied tests of utility and reason to the ancient institution and argued that if it could not be justified in these terms it ought not to exist at all. The justification of capital punishment came to be framed in the language of liberal moral discourse, above all, that of utilitarianism. From the nineteenth century onward, authorities justified the death penalty by pointing to its capacity to deter criminals and control crime, thereby enhancing the general welfare. This way of thinking prompted empirical inquiries and the accumulation of scientific evidence—about its deterrent effects and also its discriminatory nature and financial costs. Such evidence eventually became an important basis for further challenges to the institution.[31]

The individualism at the heart of liberalism has deep roots in Western history, stretching back to Greek conceptions of the person, Roman legal categories, and Christian doctrines of the soul.[32] But political liberalism in its classic form emerged in the seventeenth and eighteenth centuries—the same period in which principled opposition to the death penalty first took shape. The emergence of liberalism is usually presented as the story of a rising bourgeoisie challenging the monopoly powers of autocratic states by demanding a political voice and the restraint of state violence. The historical process was actually more complex, with monarchs granting rights to bourgeois freemen in expanding cities in order to form alliances that would curtail the power of nobles and landlords. The process had an economic dimension, too, involving the rise of market trade and its individualizing effects. As commercial life became increasingly market-oriented and freed from guild monopolies and traditional restraints on trade, so did individualism become more powerfully rooted in social experience.

In the late eighteenth and nineteenth centuries, Western governments and legal systems underwent liberal reform, which placed the institution of capital punishment under increased pressure. The age of liberal revolutions (roughly from 1774 to 1848) coincided with laws abolishing capital punishment in small states and principalities such as Tuscany, San Marino, and Prussia. This earliest age of reform forged an association between liberal states and abolitionism that has persisted up to the present day.[33]

Antiliberalism forged the opposite association. Modern European history is deeply marked by periods in which political freedoms were rescinded by the rise of authoritarian governments, and the turn against liberalism usually entailed a return to capital punishment. As Evans says of Germany, "the rise and fall of the execution rate in nineteenth century Germany mirrored precisely the varying fortunes of liberalism and authoritarianism."[34] And the rise of fascism and Nazism in the twentieth century brought with it the vigorous deployment of death as an instrument of state policy.[35] But despite reversals, the predominant tendency of the modern West has been toward the institutionalization of liberal forms of law and government. As Durkheim remarked, in modern Western society liberalism is not a "drawing-room theory" or a "philosophical construct." It is a social fact that has "penetrated our institutions and our mores" and "blended with our whole life."[36] And as liberalism has been established, so has the death penalty been disestablished.

The rhetoric of death penalty reform has often been cast in the apolitical language of humanitarianism and civilization, the better to appeal to those who do not share a liberal viewpoint. But the earliest abolition documents made their liberal political credentials perfectly clear. In 1764 Beccaria declared that "the punishment of death is not authorized by any right," adding, "If it be objected that almost all nations in all ages have punished certain crimes with death I answer . . . [t]he history of mankind is an immense sea of errors."[37] When Michigan legislators came to draft the first American abolition some eighty years later, they, too, asserted that the state has no authority to impose capital punishment: "the law recognizes no right of taking away his own life as belonging to any man, and therefore no power to inflict death could be possibly surrendered by any man, nor delegated to any government."[38]

Thousands of miles away in Britain, France, and Germany, liberals were adopting the same stance, describing the death penalty as an affront to a free nation.[39] As the rule of law, procedural protections, and civil rights spread over the course of the nineteenth century, so, too, did death penalty reforms. The most committed reformers, in one country after another, were the lawyers, editors, writers, liberal clerics, evangelicals, and professionals who formed the mainstay of the liberal movement, just as the chief opponents were usually nobles, landowners, judges, and supporters of the old order.[40] By the late twentieth century, death penalty abolition had become a tenet of modern liberalism and a principle of the international movement for human rights.[41]

The values of democracy have become integral elements of modern liberal thought. When Supreme Court Justice Hugo Black observed that "the most fundamental individual liberty of our people" is "the right of each man to participate in the self-government of his society," he evoked a democratic principle—the importance of self-government—and rendered it as a liberal principle, the commitment to individual liberty.[42] This merging of democracy and liberalism is a comparatively late development: liberal rights and freedoms were originally claimed only for white male property owners. But by the end of the nineteenth century, the bourgeois fear of revolutionary mobs had subsided and liberals came to favor a universal franchise and political egalitarianism. Over the course of the twentieth century, constitutional liberalism evolved into democratic liberalism, and liberal democracy became the standard form of government in the West.

The central principle of democratic rule is well expressed in Lincoln's phrase "government of the people by the people for the people."[43] But its meaning has been understood in different ways and implemented through different arrangements, each of which produces different distributions of power and different effects.[44] Competitive popular elections and the citizen's right to vote are crucial features of any democratic system—augmented by supporting rights and conditions such as free speech, freedom of assembly, a free press, the right to organize opposition parties, the rule of law, and so on. We should think of "democracy" as a matter of degree—more or less, partial or full—and also as a question of kind: popular, direct, participatory, representative, parliamentary, presidential, and so on.

Democratization is a process of political change, usually carried forward by social movements (chartists, trade unionists, suffragettes, and civil rights activists, to name a few) struggling to secure political rights and the enhanced power that they bring. But it is also a broader story of social and economic change, since democratic advances are usually made possible by underlying changes in economic life or following mobilization for war—typically when rulers are forced to grant democratic concessions to groups of subjects in exchange for tax revenue, support in war, conscription, and the like.[45] In one nation after another, the franchise has been expanded to bring women, blacks, minorities, and poor people more fully into the national community. In the second half of the twentieth century, this more inclusive vision gave rise to welfare state institutions—a form of social organization and government that has influenced every Western democracy to some degree. In such a context, with its universal citizenship, solidaristic social organization, and welfare-oriented government, the death penalty has come to appear increasingly anomalous.

Democracy is above all a matter of power.[46] The expansion of the franchise generates equality by giving new groups (workers, women, blacks) a measure of political power that can be used to secure advances in the group's position. The capacity of newly enfranchised groups to bargain for economic gains explains the tendency of democratic governments to grant social and economic rights to all their citizens, gradually transforming liberal democracies into welfare states. Democratization processes such as the introduction of secret ballots, freedom of information laws, and primary elections shift the balance of power between the people and their representatives, rendering government more accountable and more subject to popular control.

For the most part, democratic writers and theorists of democracy have been unenthusiastic about capital punishment, often seeing it as a degrading practice emblematic of absolutist power and repressive rule. Like the lash, capital punishment suggests a kind of tyranny, an utter subordination of the punished by the punisher. As the American Benjamin Rush argued a year after the guillotine was installed in the Place de la Revolution in Paris: "capital punishments are the natural offspring of monarchical governments . . . the principles of republican government speak a very different language."[47] One hundred and fifty years later, European democrats were making much the same argument. As Reginald Paget MP told the British House of Commons in 1947, "Let the dictators have their gallows and their axes, their firing squads and their lethal chambers. The citizens of a free democracy did not have to shelter under the shadow of the gallows tree."[48] In 1948 a fellow Labour MP made the same declaration: "[the gallows] have no proper place in the institutions of a free democracy. By their very nature, by their inherent quality, repressive punishments belong to the systems of totalitarian states and not democracies."[49] And when in 1981 the French state finally abolished the guillotine, the Socialist minister of justice, Robert Badinter, declared that his government abolished capital punishment because it "expresses a totalitarian relationship between the citizen and the state."[50] It is notable, however, that the view of the relationship between the death penalty and democracy expressed by these leaders is at odds with the fact that a majority of citizens supported capital punishment. Though they couched their critique in the language of democracy, the central objection being expressed is not that the death penalty lacks popular support but that it has been used by authoritarian governments to suppress liberty and dissent—a historical fact that European writers had good cause to remember in a century that witnessed state killing on an unprecedented level.

Democracy, too, has a long lineage. Democratic values and practices were characteristics of classical Athens, the Protestant sects of the seven-

teenth century, and the American and French revolutions of the late eighteenth century. But it was not until the nineteenth century that societies began to expand their franchise and not until well into the twentieth century
that universal suffrage became an established feature of all Western nations. The development of modern democracy closely parallels that of
death penalty abolition, with the nations of Northern Europe and Scandi-
navia taking the lead in both respects.[51] In many ways, democracy did not
fully come of age until the late twentieth century, the period in which abolition became the norm across the Western nations.[52]

But death penalty abolition did not occur because the newly enfranchised masses demanded it. Rather, their parliamentary representatives—
whose background, education, and culture were generally more elite than
those of their constituents—felt an elective affinity between democracy
and death penalty reform and were able to act on it, with or without popular support. Although a few abolitions occurred during the nineteenth and
early twentieth centuries, the majority took place in the decades after
World War II, with the abolitionist trend accelerating in the 1990s.[53] The
temporal pattern of death penalty reform matches the temporal pattern of
democratization. The end of fascism in the 1940s prompted constitutional
abolition in Italy, Germany, and Austria. The Iberian transition from authoritarian corporatism to democracy in the 1970s led to abolition in
Spain and prompted Portugal to repeal all its residual capital offenses. The
Soviet Union's collapse in the late 1980s led to abolition in East Germany
(GDR), Romania, Hungary, and the Czech and Slovak republics, and later
in countries such as Poland, Serbia, Croatia, Macedonia, and Slovenia
(though this last group was also motivated by a desire for European Union
membership). The same pattern is visible outside Europe: South Africa and
the Philippines both marked the commencement of democracy by ending
capital punishment.[54]

At the level of values and ideals, there is something of a tension between
democracy and the death penalty. Wherever democratic institutions have
merged with liberal ones, this tension has been heightened, usually resulting in a total rejection of capital punishment. (This affinity between liberal democracy and death penalty abolition is negatively confirmed by the
fact that the communist nations—neither liberal nor democratic—each retained capital punishment and used it extensively.[55]) But between democracy and death penalty abolition there is no straightforward link. A nation
such as France, which led the European continent in its march toward democracy, was the last European nation to give up its death penalty.[56] And
no one denies that the United States is a democratic nation—and *fully*

democratic since the 1960s and the end of Jim Crow—but its commitment to capital punishment continues. Indeed, that commitment is nowadays justified in the name of democracy and the "will of the people."

Recall that liberalism and democracy, though today usually conjoined, are not quite the same thing. Democracy's central commitment is not to equality, nor to civil liberties, nor even to limited government, but to a form of rule in which "the people" govern themselves. This commitment has given rise to many different kinds of democratic government—direct, participatory, representative, parliamentary, local, plebiscitary, and so on. Each of these forms sets up a different balance between popular will—as expressed by a majority of voters—and other political values, such as equality, or minority protections, or individual freedoms, or human rights. Wherever popular will is relatively unconstrained by such considerations, democracy may press in favor of capital punishment rather than against it, since majorities often favor capital punishment. Wherever popular majorities rather than liberal elites control law and policy, the death penalty is more likely to persist.

Cultural Processes of Reform

The decline of capital punishment is commonly viewed as an effect of cultural change. If we no longer hang, draw, and quarter offenders in the public square, it is because—on this conventional view—our society has become more civilized and our sensibilities more refined. Nor is this understanding a recent one. For more than two centuries now the standard reform narrative has been a story of how cultural change—more refined manners, less tolerance for violence, more sensitivity to the pain of others—has led to changes in capital punishment.

From Beccaria onward, critics of capital punishment have viewed themselves as aligned with "the cause of humanity"—expressed in both religious and secular terms—and seen each reform as a progressive step in the advance of civilization.[57] From the Enlightenment to the present, moreover, the language of civilization and humanitarianism has framed the reform effort, with each step toward abolition being understood as the result of our "evolving standards of decency."[58]

Historians agree about the civilization idiom and humanistic understandings in which death penalty reform has been articulated, but they lack consensus about the causal weight to be given to this language and the cultural currents to which it refers. When we turn from describing normative debates to developing historical explanations, the status of "culture" becomes more problematic. The question becomes how to assess the causal role of cultural currents such as humanism and the refinement of sensibility. Should we regard culture as a real cause of action or merely as a glossy surface that overlays more basic causal processes? Are civilizing and humanizing sentiments distinctive engines of historical change or merely the incidental music that accompanies the real action?[59]

Recall that the death penalty is a state practice and is altered only when state officials adjust their laws or procedures. Cultural currents and group sensibilities became effective in reforming capital punishment only when they had an impact on the strategic orientation and control imperatives of state officials. Whether by political pressure (when protest and criticism altered the state's operating environment) or by persuasion (when the beliefs and sensibilities of officials were altered) or by strategic alignment (when criticisms provided opportunities for officials to make changes that worked to their benefit), cultural processes had first to be translated into political forces before they could bring about death penalty change. Civilizing and humanizing pressures were most effective when they promised to help officials improve their control. The power of refinement was greatest when it led to the refinement of power.

The changes in norms, habits, and dispositions brought about by the emerging cultures of civilization and humanitarianism were real enough and affected upper-class elites across much of Europe and America beginning in the eighteenth century.[60] Grounded in the new ways of life of increasingly commercial societies, these norms motivated reform campaigns, put pressure on state officials, and changed the way that social elites experienced the execution of offenders. To that extent, the conventional wisdom is correct: cultural change did indeed prompt death penalty reform. But a closer look adds nuance to this general view: the cultural shifts that mattered affected social elites and not the mass of the people; processes of reform operated on and through state actors, so cultural preferences had to be aligned with political realities; and different strands of enlightened culture had quite different implications for capital punishment reform.

We can trace the decline of the absolutist death penalty from the late seventeenth century, when European elites began to turn away from the traditional sights and sounds of the gallows, expressing a new revulsion and embarrassment. Spierenburg reports the complaints of the poet Constantin Huygens, who wrote to William III in 1674 to protest that an area of The Hague was "a too noble and glorious place to be perpetually embarrassed by the sight of wheels and gibbets, to the great chagrin of many residents of quality."[61] But the movement against the death penalty really took off a century later, when Beccaria articulated these growing misgivings in the form of an Enlightenment critique that aligned "the cause of humanity" with the benefits of a more utilitarian scheme of punishment—at which point an antigallows movement began to take shape all across Europe and North America.

The reform movement drew support from a relatively narrow social group—above all from upper–middle-class professionals such as lawyers, newspaper editors, writers, liberal politicians, liberal Protestant ministers, and evangelical clerics. And though its campaigning literature often invoked liberalism and democratic republicanism, its abolitionist arguments were mostly phrased in the cultural idiom associated with the educated bourgeoisie—which is to say, the languages of civilized refinement and humanitarian sensibility.

More refined sensibilities were the cultural corollaries of new forms of social organization that flourished in eighteenth-century Europe and America. With the decline of chronic warfare and the rise of commercial society came shifts in class relations—above all the rise of an urban bourgeoisie and a decline in the power of landed aristocracy—and correlative changes in the forms of life around which elite culture was organized. Increases in trade and communication, the growth of cities, and a vastly extended division of labor brought more interdependence between groups and individuals and shifted the balance of power between them. Over time, these dynamic economic forces shook up the fixed ranks and status differentials of traditional society and made possible more direct and egalitarian relations between social groups, as well as more individualistic forms of enterprise and culture. These cultural changes included new class distinctions marked less by honor and military prowess than by civilized manners and dignified comportment, as well as a new morality centered on the sacredness of human life and the worth of each individual. The remarkable wave of humanitarian reform that emerged in the nineteenth century—challenging the slave trade and slavery, child labor, cruelty to animals, corporal punishment, and much else—originated in these social changes and the sensibilities they made possible.[62]

The refined manners and civilized sensibilities cultivated by Western bourgeois elites were shaped by the demands of commercial society, but they were also a reaction against the military mentality and honor culture of the old ruling class. Whereas warrior elites had cultivated an ethos of bodily strength and physical courage, reveling in the thrill of battle, openly enjoying the primitive pleasures of sex and food, regarding death as an event to be publicly ritualized and witnessed, the new commercial upper classes developed a very different sensibility. Bourgeois elites cultivated a horror of violence and revulsion at the sight of pain and suffering. They treated the bodily aspects of the human condition as sources of anxiety and embarrassment, surrounding them with strict behavioral codes and taking elaborate steps to reduce their visibility. The facts of death and violence went from being the visible center of a warrior culture to the unspeakable secrets of bourgeois society, surrounded by anxiety and taboo, taken care of by specialists and hidden, well away from public view.[63]

To be a "civilized" person in eighteenth-century Europe and America was to disavow the crude, "barbaric" habits of traditional agrarian society with its ethos of manly honor and violence and instead cultivate refined manners, urbanity, and habits of decorum and self-restraint. It was to develop good taste and proper etiquette and comport oneself in a manner that avoided embarrassing or offending others, particularly other people of refinement. Civilized ladies and gentlemen would draw back in disgust at the sight of vulgarity or unpleasantness, above all from scenes of violence or brutality. They recoiled with horror or embarrassment when confronted by bodies and bodily functions, death and decay, physical violence and suffering flesh. When faced with these disturbing facts of life, the impulse of civilized people was to cover them with shame and embarrassment, or else usher them "behind the scenes" of social life.[64] Hence the elaborate, anxiety-laden formality of bourgeois social etiquette, the prudishness of Victorian dress codes and sexual conduct, and the emergence of institutions—the privy, the marital bedroom, the asylum, the hospital ward, the hospice, the prison—designed to "privatize" such behavior and remove it from public view. "One of the effects of civilization (not to say one of the ingredients in it)," John Stuart Mill remarked in 1836, "is that the spectacle, and even the very idea of pain, is kept more and more out of the sight of those classes who enjoy in their fullness the benefits of civilization." As Mill explained, "it is in avoiding the presence not only of actual pain, but of whatever suggests offensive or disagreeable ideas, that a great part of refinement consists."[65]

This Western bourgeois culture, which became increasingly widespread during the nineteenth century in both secular and religious forms, had important consequences for the place of physical violence in social life—consequences made all the more powerful because they reinforced the state's efforts to subdue the old warrior classes and their aristocratic culture. Private feuding and dueling declined, as did the routine use of violence to chastise wives, children, and servants.[66] Torture was prohibited. Corporal punishments such as maiming, branding, flogging, and whipping were used less widely. Punishments involving bodily exposure or suffering—the stocks, the pillory, flogging, birching, and branding—were mostly abandoned.[67] The death penalty grew less frequent and less violent, so that from the eighteenth century onward, execution practices that disfigured, dismembered, or displayed the condemned's body became much less common and the suffering of the condemned on the scaffold was greatly reduced. By the middle of the nineteenth century, long after scaffold tortures had been abolished, middle-class commentators complained that the sight of a person being put to death was too disturbing to watch and criticized the callous vulgarity of those who continued to attend public hangings.[68]

Beginning in the late eighteenth century, Western elites denounced public executions in the name of civilization, criticizing state officials for staging such "barbaric" displays and providing occasions for "vulgar," despicable conduct.[69] By the mid-nineteenth century, a practice once supported by ruling groups everywhere was now being criticized by them.[70]

These new sentiments troubled the conscience of state officials. Lawmakers and high-ranking government ministers, raised in the same bourgeois culture and socialized into the same sensibilities as the antigallows elite, began to deploy the death penalty with more reticence and to distance themselves from the unpleasant business of killing. Banner gives striking evidence of this new reluctance when he describes a number of contraptions invented in nineteenth-century America to enable the condemned person to trigger his or her own execution. As he observes, these auto-execution technologies (which were used on at least one occasion) suggest that "the government employees who carried out hangings, like the spectators, were becoming more and more uneasy about the prospect of inflicting pain."[71]

This culture of refinement, with its fastidiousness about the body, its squeamishness about physical violence and suffering, and its urge to hide disturbing events from public view, brought powerful pressures to bear on the death penalty, subjecting it to new critiques and demands for reform. That these cultural demands often meshed with the interests of state actors, allowing officials to extend control over executions and minimize their disruptive possibilities, only added to their influence. The result was a major transformation in the dramaturgy of the execution, changing it from an open, violent death ritual into a covert procedure designed to disguise the fact of death and suppress all signs of violence.

We could certainly explain this transformation as an effect of civilization and the softening of manners, which is how the reformers themselves understood it. But we could equally regard it as a strategic shift in the exercise of state power—an arrangement that gains more by concealing death and violence than by showing them. The sociologist John Lofland describes the strategy of concealment as it applies to state executions:

The perfectly concealed technique of death is one in which the condemned's body instantly disappears, never again to be seen. Short of this, the act of dying can be diminished in several ways. First, the technique of death should be speedy. The quicker it is over, the less there is to see, and the less death need be thought about. Second, a death in which the condemned dies immediately and therefore without pain is somehow less openly a "death" than one in which the condemned dies slowly and painfully, with attendant struggles, facial contortions, and screams. Third, a death without mutilation of the body appears to be less a death than one which does involve clear mutilation. Fourth, to conceal lingering, painful and mutilating deaths which might occur despite all precautions, the body can be shielded from view during dying. Fifth, the machinery of death had best not only work with unfailing effectiveness and swiftness, but also quietly. Banging gallows trapdoors, thuds of dropped bodies, sizzling flesh, and the like, all communicate too clearly the presence of death.[72]

The lethal injection protocol used in America today is certainly the most "civilized" execution yet invented, and cultural refinement has surely helped bring it about. But it is also the most effectively concealed and managed, and to understand this dimension we need to think in terms of power and control as well as culture and sensibility.

The grip of bourgeois culture became increasingly relaxed during the twentieth century as societies became more democratic and public culture less dominated by elites. The norms of contemporary culture now push in the opposite direction, urging us toward exposure, revelation, and display, especially where sex and the body are concerned. This countercurrent of revelation and exposure has occasionally impinged upon the death penalty, demanding to see behind the scenes, litigating to allow executions to be televised, pressing to permit the public to view the fatal moment. But as yet to no avail.[73]

Refinement was not the only cultural foundation of the antigallows movement. An equally important strand in the movement's make-up has always been humanitarianism: a moral—and often religious—sensibility that regards human life as sacred, presses for an end to cruelty, and aims to extend compassion to all fellow creatures.[74] This sensibility has been a constant theme of penal reformers: from Beccaria and his "cause of humanity" in the eighteenth century to Norval Morris and his "decency, empathy," and concern for "human suffering" in the twentieth.[75]

Humanitarianism has many sources—the Enlightenment writings of Montesquieu and Voltaire; the moral individualism of liberalism; the credos of eighteenth-century Quakers and nineteenth-century evangelicals; the Romantic movement in fiction and poetry.[76] Its characteristic sentiments of empathy and identification with others were acquired and transmitted through cultural practices such as reading novels, keeping diaries, and putting oneself in the position of others. But its central principle is the simple moral imperative that human life is sacred and ought not to be violated—and this imperative has emerged most fully as an organizing principle of governance and social life in modern liberal democracies.[77]

Humanitarianism has at its core a fundamental respect for individuals and for personhood. Such values may seem obvious and unavoidable today, but their emergence marked a new phase in Western history: an epochal revaluation of morals in which the claims of kin, tribe, sect, and state were downgraded and those of autonomous individual persons made paramount.[78] In its implacable opposition to killing and violence, humanitarianism is a decidedly antimilitary sensibility, grounded in peaceable forms of life and commercial social relations. In contrast to the warrior ethos of the preceding era—with its history of blood and cruelty, its idea of honorable violence, and its enjoyment of killing and blood sports—humanitarianism regards human suffering as unconscionable and utterly deplores violence. Its horror of cruelties even extends to those perpetrated by God: it is the New Testament doctrine of compassionate forgiveness that appeals to the humanitarian, not the fire-and-brimstone vengeance of the Old.

In the cultural scheme of the early-modern period, values such as sovereign power, religious faith, and social order counted for more than any ordinary individual, especially a lower-class criminal. Offering up a condemned man's life to avenge an injured sovereign or appease an offended God was a sacrifice that could be regarded as just and necessary. The spread of humanitarianism made such practices more difficult to justify and raised questions about any authority that failed to respect the sanctity of human life.[79]

With the decline of traditional honor codes and the spread of humanitarian ideals, physical violence became the new taboo of liberal-democratic societies—the more peaceful and stable the society, the more problematic the violence.[80] As Haltunnen writes, the culture of refinement "steadily broadened the arena within which humanitarian feeling was encouraged to operate, extending compassion to animals and to previously despised types of persons including slaves, criminals, and the insane." The result was that "forms of cruelty that had once gone unquestioned" were now brought into the open and subjected to criticism.[81] Over time, humanitarian sensibilities reshaped criminal codes, placing the heaviest prohibitions on physical violence, and above all on murder, the "ultimate" offense against life itself.

The moral horizons of humanitarianism stretch, in principle, to all human beings. But in practice, its sentiments run up against socially determined limits and failures of moral imagination. People tend to regard others who strike them as ugly, dangerous, or alien as less than fully human. The same perception is applied to members of poor or disreputable social groups, especially those of other races or ethnicities who are associated—either in fact or in folklore—with crime, disease, or danger. These "others" are often dehumanized, banished from the community of fellow creatures. The setting of horizons and boundaries, the delineation of inclusion and exclusion, is an ongoing moral task, but in practice, the answer to the question, "Who is entitled to humane treatment?" has been determined in the context of group relations and the solidarities or social divisions that characterize them. The widening of solidarities extends identification and institutionalizes it, first as moral rules of compassionate regard and later as legal entitlements to citizenship and state welfare. Shifts in sensibilities develop along with shifts in solidarities. The extension of humanitarian treatment flows along lines of solidarity, which is why humanitarianism is so closely tied to the politics of liberal democracy and welfarism.[82]

The capacity to see the defendant as a sentient, suffering human being, and not just as an evil, dangerous enemy, is an important precondition for restricting the death penalty's application. Wherever relations of solidarity exist, pain takes on a kind of conductivity: the pain of another is directly transmitted to us. We feel what he feels.[83] In a culture committed to humanitarian norms that cherish human life, the execution of human beings depends on their being thought of as somehow outside the human community or less than human. The use of the death penalty in such situations is typically accompanied by dehumanization and demonization.

The rise of humanitarian sensibilities had clear and direct consequences for capital punishment. Humanitarianism generated a new sympathy for the scaffold's victims and their suffering. Members of the governing classes who once regarded the sacrifice of felons as a necessary tonic for social order began to consider the suffering of the man facing death. Their moral horizons were extended, and with them, their moral imagination and ability to empathize.[84] Humanitarian concerns helped to put an end to torture and afflictive executions and prompted the search for a painless execution technique. Humanitarian sentiments changed the attitudes of legislators, judges, and juries, encouraging them to see a fellow human being where they had once seen only a lower-class felon.[85] This recognition was eloquently expressed by Benjamin Rush, when he insisted that criminals are "bone of our bone," possessing "souls and bodies composed of the same materials as those of our friends and relations."[86]

By the second half of the nineteenth century, the humanitarian sensibility was so widespread that even supporters of capital punishment were phrasing their arguments in these terms.[87] Thus Spencer Walpole, the home secretary in the British Conservative government, announced in 1866 that "human life ought to be regarded as so sacred a thing that anybody who attempts to take it away from another ought to feel that he does so at the risk of losing his own."[88] But if "sanctity of life" arguments could be made for *and* against the death penalty for murderers, the sacred place now accorded to human life discredited the use of capital punishment for lesser offenses. Capital codes narrowed accordingly. By the twentieth century, the opposition between humanitarian sentiment and capital punishment was being expressed in a new and more powerful form by a human rights movement that viewed the death penalty as a violation of the most fundamental right of man.

From the eighteenth century to the present, death penalty debates have been framed in the language of civilization and humanity. Civilized sensibilities might best be understood as an aesthetic of refinement, delicacy, and self-restraint, combined with social norms designed to minimize unpleasant encounters with vulgar and disturbing behavior. Humanitarian sensibilities, in contrast, are feelings of human sympathy and compassionate identification with others, and the moral imperatives that flow from such identification. These two sensibilities may run alongside each other and draw on the same language of refined feeling, but at a certain point their effects diverge. One is concerned with reducing the aesthetic affront involved in putting a person to death while the other fundamentally objects to human suffering. One aims to reduce the sight of pain, the other aims to reduce its infliction. One is primarily about manners and appearances, the other about underlying moral substance.[89] In terms of the death penalty, both push in the direction of reform, restraint, and refinement, but humanitarianism is more clearly abolitionist. Civilized objections to the sight of suffering can be accommodated by hiding the suffering away, rendering it less visible or less gross in appearance. Humanitarian objections, by contrast, will not be satisfied by aesthetic reforms that hide suffering but do little to relieve it.

SIX

State and Society
in America

Some 300 million of our closest allies think capital punishment is
cruel and unusual.

FELIX G. ROHATYN, FORMER U.S. AMBASSADOR TO FRANCE, 2001

Contemporary America is a mature liberal democracy. It has a welfare
state of sorts and a government designed to secure the rights to "life,
liberty and the pursuit of happiness." Its culture values individual freedom
and well-being. Its use of the death penalty has become progressively more
restrained, reduced, and refined over the last two hundred years. In these
respects, America is in the mainstream of Western development. But while
every other Western nation had, by the 1980s, abolished capital punishment, the United States has not, and the death penalty remains a legal punishment in thirty-five states, in federal criminal law, and in the law of the
United States military. In this respect, America has come to stand outside
the Western mainstream and—insofar as death penalty politics now feature in international relations—in conflict with it.

One explanation for this situation points to an accidental concatena-
tion of events. On this account, nationwide abolition in the United States
has been temporarily delayed by contingent decisions, not permanently
blocked by deep, structural forces. The expected abolition may yet occur,
in which case the United States will appear to have been laggard rather
than exceptional, last in line but by no means out of line.[1] A contingency-
centered explanation of this kind is certainly plausible. In 1972, the Supreme Court in *Furman v Georgia* came close to declaring the death penalty unconstitutional, and we can imagine circumstances in which it could
have done so decisively, either in *Furman* itself or in subsequent cases such

as *Gregg v Georgia* in 1976 or *McCleskey v Kemp* in 1987. Consider what might have happened if the Court's composition had not been altered by Nixon appointees; if the homicide rate had not been increasing; if the Kennedy and King assassinations had not occurred; or if the American public had not, at that moment, become so unenamored of civil rights and so inflamed about "law and order."

Contingent events might provide an explanation for the fact of American retention in an age of abolition, but they can hardly explain its form, which has a definite pattern that is far from accidental. Happenstance and accidental events cannot plausibly account for the distinct geographical patterns exhibited by the death penalty's current use—such as the overwhelming concentration of executions in the South—nor can they explain the distinctive institutional and cultural forms that have developed around capital punishment in the period since *Furman*. Such phenomena demand a more positive and substantial explanation.

Capital punishment's contemporary patterns and forms are the outcome of definite struggles undertaken within the constraints and possibilities of a structured social field. Therefore, an analysis of this social field—the American social landscape with its distinctive state structures, legal institutions, group relations, and cultural commitments—must form the foundation for an explanation. To explain the contours of America's capital punishment complex, whether in the present or in the past, we must look to the unique structure of the American state and the political relations and cultural sensibilities that formed around it.

American State Formation

From its beginnings, America's state has been less centralized and more localized, less bureaucratized and more personalistic, and in important respects less powerful, at least internally, than the states of other Western nations.[2] As Seymour Lipset remarks "No other elected national government except the Swiss is as limited in its powers." John Sutton adds, "The United States has the most decentralized and fragmented polity, as well as the least bureaucratized central state administrative apparatus, of any modern democracy." The relative weakness of American government generally and of central government in particular is a product of the U.S. polity's original design, embodied in a written constitution, and reproduced over time (with periodic adjustments) by the balances of power, legal restraints, and political habits to which the initial settlement gave rise. So although a unified legal order was effectively maintained from the Union onward, and an American nation state "fought wars, expropriated Indians, secured new territories, carried on relations with other states, and aided economic development," the distinctive realm of the state, especially the central, national state, was never so developed nor so distinct in America as in other Western nations.[3] To a greater degree than elsewhere, governmental power in the United States remained local and personalistic, exercised by local political actors and dominant groups rather than by national bureaucracies and civil servants.

To describe the American state as lacking power invites a skeptical response. The United States is, after all, the world's dominant superpower and is capable of projecting massive military force and economic influence. But "state power" is always a differentiated and multidimensional phenomenon. Power directed externally must be distinguished from power exercised over domestic affairs. Military, economic, political, and social power are each somewhat distinct—as is penal power—and a state may have greater capacities in some areas than in others. As Theda Skocpol writes, any state is simultaneously "(i) an institutionalized set of powers and functions superior to other entities and capable of autonomous action; (ii) a unit in the field of international relations; (iii) a sector of society, employing officials, public servants, generating economic activity"; and "(iv) a socio-cultural phenomenon, an idea, a myth."[4] The American state is comparatively strong on some of these dimensions, notably in military power and in international relations, but relatively weak on others. In particular, the pluralist, federated, separation-of-powers structure of the American polity ensures that the central state's capacities for action are sharply limited when it comes to certain kinds of domestic policy, including its ability to control conduct and shape social outcomes.

We need to be careful not to overstate this claim and to acknowledge change and variation.[5] American government, at the federal, state, and local level, has changed over time and is now very much more powerful than previously. Indeed, in some respects, even in domestic policy, American state power is unmatched by other nations: the extent of its apparatus of prisons and punishments is a striking case in point. But over the long term, American government has been comparatively underdeveloped with respect to its capacity for economic and social action—and this historical fact has left important legacies. To this day, the exercise of U.S. governmental power encounters restrictions and restraints in certain spheres—health-care reform is a current example—that are more substantial and more limiting than those faced by comparable governments elsewhere.

The federated structure that the Framers created in the late eighteenth century was not designed to consolidate sovereign state rule on the European state model. It was designed instead to distribute power across a plurality of institutions, constituencies, and locales and to limit its exercise in all of them. The Constitution institutionalized the insistence of the revolutionaries that the highest political authority should be a limited authority, always offset by countervailing power. In place of the European conception of absolute sovereign power, the Americans instituted divided government, hence Justice James Wilson's dictum "To the Constitution of the United States, the term sovereign is totally unknown."[6] This federated structure counterposed a small national government with limited capacities to a large group of states and local authorities. Each of these states retained residual jurisdiction over matters not assigned to the central authorities; each of them was authorized to exercise "police powers" over the conduct of everyday life in their territories, and each of them could exert control over the central authority through their representatives in the federal legislature. As federal systems go, it was (and is) remarkable for the extent of local power it enshrines.

To that vertical division of authority was added a set of horizontal divisions. A separation of powers was established at every level of government to ensure that sharply differentiated legislative, executive, and judicial branches would keep one another in check. And to these structural constraints, the Bill of Rights added a series of explicit prohibitions on various kinds of governmental action, limiting federal power and later the power of the states, as it related to individual rights. Finally, institutions such as the United States Senate and the Electoral College were designed in ways that limited the capacity of larger, more populous states to dominate smaller ones.

This designedly limited form of government was a principled expression of the Founders' revolutionary republicanism and their libertarian reaction against an oppressive British state. But behind these republican ideals was also the hard realism of politicians seeking a formula of confederation that would be acceptable to the thirteen former colonies that had fought the War of Independence, each of them protective of their autonomy, each of them characterized by a different constellation of economic interests, political values, and religious beliefs. The Founders were obliged to find an arrangement that would command the assent of Southern landowners—whose wealth and power depended on slavery and free trade—and also prove acceptable to Northern manufacturers and commercial merchants, for whom free labor and trade regulation were economically essential. This need to bring conflicting interests together gave rise to a distinctive political structure, designed to check and balance power, multiply veto points, and thereby minimize the risk that one set of interests would always prevail over another. It also gave rise to arrangements that constantly empowered local decision-makers, a pattern of devolution that had its roots in the battle over slavery, which had taught the Framers that they "could most easily overcome political deadlock simply by delegating policy authority to the states."[7]

In forming the American central state, the Founders created a self-limiting machine that, if it did not generate compromise, was designed to generate nothing at all. In place of the concentrated sovereign power of monarchical rule and the parliamentary systems that succeeded it, the Founders built a federal system of checks and balances in which power would be shared and policy-making would be a process of bargaining, trade-off, and compromise.

The relative weakness of the American nation state was economic and logistical as well as political. State power always rests on a dual monopoly: over the power to use legitimate force and over the power to levy taxes. The American state's capacity to tax, like its capacity to use force, was limited from the start by the slave states and their resistance to federal government intrusion.[8] Any discussion of state apportionment (that is, tax based on the size of the state's population or on property holdings) immediately foundered on the question of slavery, discussion of which threatened to undo the Union. The importance of private police powers to the institution of slavery similarly limited the extent to which these powers would be given up in the interests of a state monopoly of legitimate violence.

These original characteristics have had long-term consequences, preventing American central government from building the kind of institutional infrastructure that characterized nation states elsewhere, and limiting the extent of its role in the nation's economic development.[9] Compared with other Western nations, the United States government has been, until recently, a less prominent economic and criminal justice actor, leaving a much greater role to the market and to local regulation.

Much earlier than elsewhere, the power of voters was another important constraint on government in America. When Vermont entered the Union in 1791, any adult male who took the "Freeman's Oath" could vote. Pennsylvania's state constitution gave the vote to all tax-paying freemen, and since the state imposed a poll tax, this effectively enfranchised the great majority of adult white males. By the mid-nineteenth century, following the democratization of the Jacksonian era, universal white male suffrage was standard across the whole country. This early democratization also set American state formation on a path that was quite different from that characteristic elsewhere.[10]

America's franchise was initially confined to adult men, as it was in every Western nation.[11] American women won the vote in the early twentieth century, around the same time that female suffrage was achieved in most of Europe. Much more distinctive was America's overwhelming exclusion of blacks. At the time of the nation's founding, only a few states formally excluded free African Americans from the franchise, but between 1790 and 1850 more and more states disenfranchised them. By 1855, "only five states (Massachusetts, Vermont, New Hampshire, Maine and Rhode Island) did not discriminate against African Americans and these states contained only 4% of the nation's free blacks."[12] Even after the Fifteenth Amendment was ratified in 1870, prohibiting exclusion from the franchise "on account of race, color, or previous condition of servitude," practical barriers and intimidation prevented many blacks from voting right up to the 1960s.

This exclusion of African Americans was so distinctive and so enduring in the United States because white-black relations were grounded in racialized slavery and in the continuing legacy of that "peculiar institution." As a result, race relations involving blacks have been less about ethnic or cultural differences than about degradation, subordination, and segregation—and correlatively, about white fears of losing privilege or attracting violent reprisals.

The enslaved status of most black Americans meant that they were effectively excluded from the franchise at the time of the original constitutional settlement in 1787. This denial of citizenship was undone by the Civil War and the Reconstruction amendments only to be reimposed soon after by the Jim Crow laws of the Southern states—a *de facto* exclusion that continued up until the Voting Rights Acts of 1965. Black disfranchisement and segregation were justified by reference to "states rights" and by the majority preferences of local electorates in the South. They were shielded from federal intervention by a phalanx of Southern Democrats in the Senate who used their committee positions and voting bloc power to veto the passage of civil rights and antilynching laws. These Southern congressmen defended social segregation and political disfranchisement "as a constitutionally protected exercise of state 'police powers,'" and they objected to federal legislation as "a usurpation of state sovereignty."[13]

In most European nations, the sequence of events was first, the formation, extension, and consolidation of state power; second, the emergence of bureaucratic rationalization; and third, the growth of popular participation. Because democratic politics emerged only after a powerful bureaucracy was already in place, state bureaucrats were able to establish nonpartisan rules and practices that preserved their power and provided a degree of insulation from the political process. In the United States, the sequence was the opposite, which meant that the growth of state institutions was always limited and shaped by the prior claims of democratic controls and elected officials, resulting in a highly politicized state sector and a relative absence of nonpartisan institutions.[14] Moreover, American state formation occurred in relative isolation, with no strong nations competing in the region and no constant threat of border war. One of the key dynamics of European state building—preparation for war—was largely absent in America until the First World War, though the Indian wars on the Western frontier gradually built the U.S. Army over the course of the nineteenth century.

From the beginning, and to a degree not experienced elsewhere, electoral competition and democratic controls restricted the capacity of America's national government to raise revenue, impose regulations, or exert control over everyday life. And at several historical moments—most notably the Progressive period in the late nineteenth century and the years immediately following the Watergate scandal in the 1970s—many states passed laws establishing referenda, voter ballot initiatives, term limits, and open primaries in order to strengthen the power of the popular vote and to further limit the power of government incumbents. This distinctive path of political development continues to have significant consequences. As Robert Kagan observes, the national government in the United States "shares more power with states and municipalities" than most economically advanced nations, "and at every level of government chief executives share more power with legislatures, legislative party leaders with the subcommittee chairs and back-benchers, administrative agencies with judges, and judges with lawyers and juries."[15]

Compared with the parliamentary systems of most Western nations, where a solid majority in the national legislature allows the dominant party to enact laws and impose policies with little need of cooperation from other political actors, America's national government lacks a capacity for swift, decisive action with respect to domestic policy.[16] Multiple veto points impede the passage of national legislation, making social and economic reform difficult to achieve. (Executive power relating to war and foreign relations is a different matter, as are laws designed to increase the punishment for crime where there is often no organized opposition.) Even when one party controls the presidency, the Senate, and the House of Representatives, its capacity to enact reform legislation will be limited by procedural rules designed to prevent nonconsensual law-making—such as the allocation of committee chairs by seniority, or today's sixty-vote rule in the Senate—and by the relative weakness of party discipline, which enables representatives to vote for their state's specific interests (or those of their financial backers) rather than obey party leaders. The log-rolling and deal-making that this situation promotes, together with the gridlock that occurs whenever compromise fails, add to the low esteem in which many Americans hold their political representatives and reinforce the ideology of anti-government libertarianism.

The relative weakness of the American state has been reproduced over time despite significant changes in the nature and reach of government. To be sure, America's pluralist state has greatly expanded its functions and institutional infrastructure, as have the states of all Western nations. From the late eighteenth century onward, local authorities in towns and cities regulated local trade, commerce, building, and safety in the name of "the people's welfare." During the Civil War, the federated governments of both the North and the South arrogated extensive powers to direct economic and social affairs in the service of the military effort. Likewise, the coming of industrialism and urbanism in the late nineteenth century, the turn-of-the-century Progressive movement, the New Deal of the 1930s, two world wars, and the Great Society policies of the 1960s all expanded the reach of state and national government. In these respects, the American state joined the governments of other developed nations in acquiring extended means to govern the economy, regulate the social realm, and secure the population's welfare through compulsory social insurance and welfare transfers.[17]

The American state grew at every level—from county, city, and state up to the national government in Washington, DC—and by the early twentieth century, its vast military capacity and economic production placed the nation in the first rank of world powers. But with respect to domestic policy, and compared with the centralized states of continental Europe, the United States government has remained relatively small and sharply limited, with powers that are layered, fragmented, and contested rather than fused into an effective capacity for sovereign action.[18] Whereas policy directives in modern France, Britain, and Germany often descend from a central administrative state to be uniformly implemented across the nation by government officials, in America the details of social policy provision are more often forged at the local level, or in the courts, and tend to vary greatly from region to region.

Localism

A distinctive feature of the American polity is what Thomas Sugrue calls "the persistence of localism." Even during the New Deal and the Great Society, when Congress established nationwide welfare programs such as Social Security, Aid to Dependent Children, Medicare, and Medicaid, the implementation and delivery of these policies depended on local institutions. "States and localities," as a result, "became battle-grounds over the meaning and implementation of federal policies," as did the Supreme Court, which frequently adjudicates on the proper balance of power between central and local actors in different areas of government. Instead of a uniform, nationwide program, American government benefits have been channeled through local power hierarchies, leading to marked racial and class disparities in their allocation. "Federal assistance and federal social programs did not flow smoothly to localities," Thomas Sugrue argues, "instead local jurisdictional boundaries directed the stream of governmental assistance, channeling it to some places and away from others."[19]

The persistence of local autonomy—which has been especially marked in regard to race, education, social welfare, and criminal justice—provides opportunities for progressives and conservatives alike to diverge from national policy preferences. Progressives who pass state legislation permitting same-sex marriage and medical marihuana use are the beneficiaries of this local power as much as are conservatives who press for school prayer or the teaching of creationism in local public high schools. Local autonomy also allows for variation and difference within the same state, since local county and city authorities possess powers of their own. (There is, for example, a substantial county-to-county variation in the rate at which local prosecutors seek the death penalty.[20]) As a speaker of the U.S. House of Representatives once declared, in America, "all politics is local."

Given these central-local relations, it is hardly surprising that the power and prestige of national government—of what Europeans call "the state"—are less exalted in America than elsewhere. At the same time, the countervailing force of local powers ensures that local authorities and the political processes that control them are more important in the United States and present more of an obstacle to effective national government. Within this country, the commitment to state's rights, local autonomy, and antigovernmental ideology is especially strong in the Western frontier states and in the former Confederacy states of the South. For many Southern states, antipathy to "external" government interference is a powerful legacy of long-term sectional conflicts, though the original rationale for these habits—a desire to preserve slavery and the plantation economy—has given way today to a desire to preserve the "Southern way of life" with its racial hierarchies, religious beliefs, and traditionalist attitudes.

The stamp of localism is nowhere more apparent than in criminal justice administration. The Constitution allocates "police powers" to the states, together with responsibility for the enactment and enforcement of criminal law—a structure that has produced a radical devolution of the power to punish and a remarkable fragmentation of law enforcement. As Tim Newburn observes, "there are something in the region of 21,000 police agencies in the United States, of which 49 are state agencies, nearly 15,000 are local, over 3,000 are Sheriff-headed, and a further 3,000 are special agencies." More than 85 percent of police department employees work in state or local settings, and more than 95 percent of prisoners are housed in state prisons and local jails.[21]

To understand the peculiarities of American punishment we need to appreciate the radical character of local control in the American polity and its consequences for policy-making. In Europe, we look in vain for traces of such arrangements. If we find them at all, it is not in actual constitutional arrangements but in documents such as Karl Marx's commentary on the Paris Commune, where Marx makes the radical proposal that the police, judiciary, and other officials ought to be "elective, responsible and revocable."[22] In the United States, Marx's ultrademocratic reforms have been realized.

America's federated system has produced a great deal of state-by-state variation in the development of governmental institutions. States in the Northeast, the Midwest, and on the West Coast developed formally rational institutions and professionalized agencies earlier than did the poorer states of the South, where even today governmental institutions and criminal justice agencies (especially public defender's offices) remain comparatively underdeveloped. Part of the explanation for this regional pattern is economic, a consequence of the rural nature of the Southern economy and the relative poverty that characterized much of the region. But much of this differential is rooted in the legacy of slavery, segregation, and the disfranchisement of Southern blacks before the Voting Act of 1965—all of which retarded the growth of formally rational government. As Robin Eichorn observes, "From the beginning of the colonial era, American governments were more democratic, stronger and more competent where slavery was a marginal institution." Conversely, "American governments were more aristocratic, weaker, and less competent" wherever slavery played a major role in the economy and society.[23]

In much of the South, with its racialized franchise and its single-party government, local government was corrupt and inefficient for much of the twentieth century. Even today, when white supremacy and Dixie Democrats have long since given way to a more integrated New South, the region continues to be well below the national average in terms of taxation levels, provision of social programs, and levels of governmental resources —as it is in criminal justice spending on police and courts.[24]

State variation also extends to criminal law and punishment. A distinctive feature of the American Constitution's allocation of powers is that jurisdiction over police, criminal, and penal matters has, from the founding to the present day, been a matter for the state and local authorities rather than for the central government. This "penal law federalism," as Austin Sarat and Christian Boulanger call it, "is unparalleled in Europe."[25] America's states have exhibited considerable variation in their criminal codes, penalty structures, and enforcement policies, as well as great unevenness in the development of penal institutions and resources. So while Northeastern states established professional police forces, built reformative prisons, and developed professionalized correctional administrations in the nineteenth century, many Southern states did not do so until much later, relying instead on the private police powers of the slave master or the privately managed convict lease system. Similarly, in many Southern states, the administration of justice was, until recently, regarded as a position for political appointees and the party faithful rather than for trained professionals. As a result, Southern police departments have tended to be more politicized, less well resourced, and less fully professionalized, leading to comparatively high levels of corruption and brutality, and a style of enforcement heavily shaped by local politics.[26]

Legalism

The relative absence of state bureaucracies in the early years of the republic allowed courts to emerge as an important institution of American government, creating a tendency for political issues to become subject to litigation and court settlement rather than to top-down bureaucratic decision-making. As Alexis de Tocqueville observed, "Scarcely any political question arises in the United States that is not resolved, sooner or later, into a judicial question." If the model of government in most European states is a vertical hierarchy of bureaucratic authority, the American model is a more horizontal one in which courts and private actors play a much greater role. As John Kingdon puts it, the American way is not to deal with a task by creating a government program, but instead "to leave the activity to the private sector, but then to regulate it, either by government regulation or by private rights of action in court." A large part of the nation's notorious litigiousness is in fact social regulation by way of private actions in court. Using comparative case studies, Robert Kagan has traced the distinctive character of the American system of implementing policy and resolving disputes. Kagan concludes that, compared with other developed nations, the American system entails more complex legal rules, more adversarial dispute-settlement procedures, more costly legal conflicts, more punitive sanctions, more extensive judicial review, and more political conflict over legal rules and institutions.[27]

Compared with other developed countries, governmental power in America is less concentrated, less centralized, and less easily deployed uniformly across the nation. For better or worse, government in Europe is typically directed by national political elites who, backed by a parliamentary majority, are often capable of imposing their policy preferences on the nation as a whole despite public hostility to particular measures. In contrast, the American polity rarely permits top-down, countermajoritarian processes. Instead, it opens itself up to political conflicts that limit the impact of policy-making, devolve it to diverse local actors, or else find resolution through litigated settlements and court rulings. And once a policy issue becomes subject to litigation, the dynamic of adversarial legalism ensures that any rules and decisions that result will soon be challenged by further litigation.

A case in point is the recent litigation challenging the nationwide policy of using lethal injections as a method of execution. More than forty stays of execution were issued as this litigation wound its way through the state and federal court system, creating a *de facto* death penalty moratorium for much of 2007 and 2008. But instead of settling the issue—which concerned the constitutionality of Kentucky's lethal injection drug protocol—once and for all, the decision eventually issued by the Supreme Court in the case of *Baze v Rees* has left the question open for further litigation and debate.[28]

The Politics of Popular Democracy

If national and state government in America is often weak, the reach of politics and political patronage is comparatively extensive and powerful. Relative to European nations, political appointees play a larger role in government administration and occupy a larger segment of the administrative hierarchy. Whereas in Europe, government ministries are typically staffed by career civil servants up to the rank immediately below the government minister, in the United States, these positions are occupied by political appointees who owe their livelihood to political bosses and whose tenure in office stretches no further than the next election. As Edward Banfield and James Q. Wilson put it, "Our government is permeated with politics . . . there is virtually no sphere of 'administration' apart from politics."[29]

The politicization of administration is also reinforced by the fact that American political parties are relatively weak and do relatively little to finance individual politicians or to protect them from hostile public sentiment.[30] Since the advent of the primary process, party leaders no longer select election candidates—this power is now in the hands of small groups of primary voters.[31] To become a viable candidate, individuals must raise their own money, gain name recognition, and win over their constituencies. And since election cycles are short—two years in the House of Representatives—politicians are constantly in electioneering mode. Once elected, they owe little loyalty to their party and are not easily subjected to party discipline. Indeed, "In few other countries are elections and election campaigns as financially costly as they are in the United States. In none is the role of organized political parties so limited." As a consequence, America's elective politicians are placed in a highly vulnerable position: "Individually and collectively, they are more vulnerable, more of the time, to the vicissitudes of electoral politics than are the politicians of any other country." As Sven Steinmo observes, "In the absence of strong political parties, elected officials must cater to local or highly particularistic constituency interests to an extent that is truly unique in the democratic world."[32] Government by opinion poll, focus group, and special interest lobbying is the predictable result.

The weakness of parties, in turn, further limits the capacity of national elites to deliver national policies, even where the policy in question has widespread support. Wherever elected officials are dependent on their party, as they mostly are in European politics, they can usually be relied upon to vote in line with national party policy. But where the power base of elected officials is grounded in specific local interests or financial backers, as it is in the United States, it becomes exceptionally difficult for party leaders to assemble the votes needed to push new policies through Congress unless they command widespread popular support.

Most continental European nations emerged into the modern period bearing the legacy of their absolutist past in the form of strong bureaucracies, centralized governments, and powerful national elites—a legacy that would later be modified by liberalization and democratization. In contrast, liberalization and democratization were present at the start of the American state-building process and left their mark at the core of the nation's institutions. Liberal commitments—a limited state, local autonomy, the rule of law, guaranteed freedoms, individual liberties, private property—are at the heart of the United States Constitution and Bill of Rights. They are entrenched in the divided, pluralistic polity that the Constitution established. They are embodied in the market arrangements and expansive civil society that the Constitution protected. And they are expressed in the nation's legalistic mode of governing with its emphasis on procedural as opposed to substantive rights, the effect of which is to allow diverse interests to compete on a case-by-case basis. Democratic values also shaped the original design, and though conceptions of "democracy" have changed over time, expanding their reach and inclusiveness, America's democratic institutions have retained a distinctive coloring that stresses local decision-making, popular participation, and electoral accountability.[33]

These traits have became more important in the period since the 1960s, when political reforms "stripped away" the relatively thin insulation that had surrounded political institutions and processes, "leaving them more exposed to popular scrutiny and far more open to public participation."[34] Developments such as the recording of committee votes, open meetings, voter ballot initiatives and propositions, and the proliferation of opinion polls made representatives more accountable to electoral majorities and gave activists and ideological partisans—especially those with money—more power to influence outcomes.

In contrast to most European nations, where "intermediate institutions"—expert or advisory organizations located between the people and their government representatives—are regularly entrusted with authority and decision-making power, the United States lacks such arrangements.[35] American law gives regulatory agencies less discretionary power than is typical elsewhere, and permits more popular involvement in decision-making. This "hyperdemocracy" drastically limits the role of what the English call "the great and the good" and has tended to undermine institutions—such as the United States Senate—that were originally designed to function in this way.[36] Few issues are removed from partisan politics or the electoral process, and little trust is placed in bipartisan or apolitical decision-making bodies.[37]

These distinctively American arrangements, with their localized and racialized characteristics, were still operative during the most recent phase of state building: the growth of the American welfare state. Beginning with the Progressive reforms of the 1890s (veterans' pensions, widows' pensions, public schooling, and so on), expanding rapidly with the 1930s New Deal (social security, workers compensation, aid for families with dependent children), and again with the Great Society reforms of the 1960s (Medicaid and Medicare), these welfare-state processes culminated, most

recently, with the "welfare-reform" legislation of the 1990s and its wel-
fare-to-work legislation. All these programs—remarkably "statist" as they
were by American standards—were channeled along the established fault
lines of the American polity, varying in their implementation according to
state and region, often excluding blacks, relying on local channels of distribution, and offering less support to recipients than equivalent programs in
other nations.[38] Conversely, in the build-up of mass imprisonment that has
occurred over the last thirty years—itself an important form of state building driven by local dynamics, supported by broad popular majorities, and
unimpeded by organized opposition—young black males have formed a
disproportionately large segment of an incarcerated population that now
exceeds a daily average of 2.3 million people.

One consequence of this state structure is that electoral politics affect
criminal justice more directly and extensively in America than in any other
liberal democracy.[39] Rules and procedures vary from state to state, but in
most states—and in the great majority of death penalty states—the offices
of district attorney, state judge, county sheriff, and police chief are elective.
Candidates for these positions run for office. They raise campaign funds
from private donors and make electoral commitments to voters on issues
that would elsewhere be regarded as judicial matters or questions of impartial public administration. Because they are subject to election, legal officers seek to align themselves with majority sentiment and with popular
measures such as tough sentencing laws, harsh prison policies, and, of
course, capital punishment. In several states, penal policy has been enacted directly by popular referenda or voter ballot initiative, a process that
would be "unthinkable" in most of Europe.[40]

The criminal jury—selected from the local voting rolls—is a further
means whereby local majority sentiment finds expression in American
criminal justice. Whereas European nations have developed institutional
buffers that separate the administration of justice from electoral politics—
an apolitical judiciary, a professional civil service, nonpartisan selection
procedures for judicial appointments, and so on—most American states
have fewer barriers of this kind. Like much social policy in the United
States, justice is local and political and varies greatly from place to place.
Criminal justice processes are directed not by "impartial middle-men" but
by local political appointees.[41] Compared with most European nations, the
fate of an individual offender depends more on local community dynamics
and less on an apolitical rule of law.

The American predilection for local democratic processes and distrust
of "unelected experts" and "bureaucrats" also have important repercus-
sions for penal policy. As James Q. Whitman puts it, "Americans punish

more harshly because the management of the punishment system in the United States is more given over to democratic politics." Conversely, nations like France and Germany are generally less retributive because "European state apparatuses remain highly *autonomous*, largely steered by bureaucracies that are far more insulated from democratic pressures than are American bureaucracies." European states typically accord greater authority to criminological and correctional experts, an arrangement that tends to make criminal policy-making less populist and less directly expressive of community sentiment. As Whitman concludes, Europe's powerful bureaucracies work to "shield the state from the pressures of democratic politics and to manage prisons and other punishments in a sober and disciplined way." America, by contrast, experiences a "relatively easy translation of majority sentiment into policy"—there being little organized opposition to such policies—and officials rarely get ahead of public sentiment without being called to account.[42]

The death penalty is, first and last, an aspect of state power, shaped by state interests and by state officials. The distinctive development of the American state, its pluralism, its radical localism, and its popular democracy, are what have shaped the American death penalty. In the United States as elsewhere, any deployment of the death penalty is an exercise of state power. But in the United States this power is exercised at the local county level, by local political actors, and is co-possessed by the local electorate. Its exercise is determined by the interests and attitudes of local political actors and by the group relations and social situations in which they form their sense of justice and exercise their discretionary powers.

Anatomy of American Society

If the American state's distinctive character has had consequences for the shape and survival of capital punishment, so has the distinctive nature of the society and culture that have formed alongside it. America's characteristic form of social organization, its group and race relations, its high levels of interpersonal violence, and its cultural commitments have all played a role in shaping how the death penalty is deployed in the nation and its different regions. America's capitalist economy has changed over time, shifting from a predominantly agricultural economy, to a system premised on manufacturing, trade, and industry, to a late-modern economy dominated by its commerce, finance, and service sectors. Like other Western nations (though more reluctantly and less comprehensively) twentieth-century America established the economic and social controls of a welfare state, and like other nations (though here it led rather than followed) it subsequently pursued neoliberal policies of deregulation and marketization. Despite these commonalities, the United States displays some distinctive characteristics that have persisted over the long term and that distinguish the American economy from that of its Western neighbors.

The sectional divide that separated the cotton and tobacco slave-labor economy of the Old South from the manufacturing North and the corn-bowl Midwest had enduring consequences for the shape of America's political institutions and its economic and social policies. These sectional divisions persisted through a long and formative period of the nation's history and left their stamp on the nation's institutions. Southern senators used their power to sustain local control of policy administration and decision-making, and shaped legislation in ways that largely excluded blacks from political participation and social benefits. The result was that sectional divisions and race-based "color lines" long shaped economic and social policy and continue to do so in more muted ways today.[43]

American markets have been relatively lightly regulated in terms of trade and employment, a practice that has fostered intense competition and high levels of inequality. The fierce competition of American markets has not been balanced by powerful solidaristic institutions, such as social insurance or trade unions—neither of which are well established in the United States compared with Europe. The weakness of the American labor movement, together with the absence of a social democratic party, has tended to entrench free-market practices and limit the extent of welfare transfers and employment-based social benefits. Compared with other Western nations, poverty and social exclusion are more pronounced, and the population as a whole tolerates an economic inequality that sets the United States apart from most comparable nations.[44]

America's economic ethos is more individualistic and more entrepreneurial than is characteristic of other Western nations, and more likely to stress individual responsibility for economic outcomes. This ethos finds expression in the distinctive structure of the American welfare state—a structure that emphasizes the creation of generalized opportunity (through support for public schools and state colleges, for example) rather than income support for needy groups and individuals. The result is that, "compared to other countries, the American welfare system, at the federal, state, and local levels combined, remains less ambitious, provides fewer types of benefits, makes fewer people eligible for these benefits, and costs less *per capita* or as a proportion of gross domestic product."[45]

Whereas European welfare states have historically stressed solidarity, relative equality, and social inclusion, America's free-market economy and minimalist welfare state prioritize individual freedom and prosperity. The result is individual mobility and economic growth but also an enduring economic divide that marginalizes large sectors of the workforce, especially poorly educated black males. In periods and places where job opportunities are scarce, this division has hardened, creating an underclass of the "truly disadvantaged," many of whom end up in prison and jail or on probation and parole.[46]

Social solidarity—or its absence—shapes the use of capital punishment. Wherever legislators and juries identify with offenders, or with the groups to which they belong, the death penalty becomes less likely. Wherever punishers and punished are deeply divided by race or class, death sentences become easier to impose. The relations between social groups, and especially the balance of solidarity and compassion as opposed to hostility and indifference, are important determinants of death penalty politics.

It matters, therefore, that the United States has always been a diverse and divided nation. The thirteen colonies that created the new nation were divided by religious faith, ethnic background, and economic interest. The union they created established a shared national citizenship, but it also strove to preserve regional differences and ensure that no single interest would dominate others. For all the celebrated pluralism of the new federation, the union was, from the beginning, built around exclusion as well as inclusion.[47] A fateful dividing line was drawn when its founding document decreed that enslaved individuals—who were, of course, unenfranchised—would count as three-fifths of a person for the purposes of calculating a state's representation in the U.S. House of Representatives—thereby recognizing the institution of slavery. That original compromise held for seventy years, enabling the persistence of "the peculiar institution" and the large-scale (though never total) exclusion of blacks from citizenship.[48] Even after the Civil War and Emancipation, the relative autonomy of local decision-makers enabled Southern states to disenfranchise, segregate, and violate the constitutional rights of blacks with impunity. Concerned with preserving the regional, religious, and economic diversity of the original states, the Constitution effectively guaranteed the racial subordination of blacks, instituting a racial division that would endure for two centuries.

America's ethnic diversity was increased in the nineteenth and early twentieth centuries by great waves of foreign immigration and by the migration of blacks away from the South, a population movement that transformed once-homogeneous states such as Michigan and Ohio into racially mixed ones.[49] Many immigrant groups preserved their ethnic character and forged hybrid identities—Italian-American, Irish-American, Asian-American—using cultural practices designed to ensure group identity and mutual support. By and large, these groups successfully integrated into American society, though this process was easier for groups perceived as "white" than for people of color. The great exception to this integration process was African Americans, many of whom continued to experience the disadvantages and disrepute suffered by black slaves and their off-spring. Even when a successful black middle class emerged after the 1960s, it did little to alleviate the racial disadvantages endured by poor African Americans, who continue to experience the nation's highest rates of social and economic exclusion.[50]

Because it is market-oriented, regionalized, and pluralistic—and because it has no feudal legacy of fixed ranks, ascribed status, and aristocratic privilege—America has never given rise to the kind of cultural elites that dominate many European societies. America has no singular "establishment," no exclusive national elite to whom other classes look for leadership in matters of taste, honor, and distinction. Rather than a single elite, America has multiple elites. And since the waning of Southern white supremacy and the Northern WASP (White Anglo-Saxon Protestant) ascendancy, these have rarely coalesced into a cohesive bloc capable of stamping its mark on national politics and culture. Instead of being ruled by caste norms of elite taste and good breeding, America is ruled by money and markets. This makes for more fluid hierarchies and fiercer competition, but the absence of established status hierarchies also creates status competition and status anxiety.

Aspiration for upward movement and anxiety about falling back are inherent in a society that fosters ambition and mobility. Group differences and competition limit the reach of solidarity and foster suspicion and hostility. These divisions are sometimes articulated in economic terms (as when workers object to immigrants' competing for jobs or housing or schools), but more often they are given a moral phrasing, with the more established group regarding the outsiders as immoral, idle, dirty, or dangerous.[51] The Negrophobia and militant "white supremacy" of poor white Southerners in the 1890s, for example, were responses to the economic competition and status threat caused by the emancipation of Southern blacks.[52] And in the 1920s, rural white Protestants responded to the threat posed by Catholic urban immigrants by waging temperance campaigns that condemned the immigrant way of life and affirmed the superiority of the more established group. The late twentieth century's "culture wars"— in which the death penalty became embroiled—embodied the same kinds of status anxiety and group competition, this time expressed in the form of religious fundamentalism and the defense of "traditional ways of life."

America's radically localist federalism limits the social and economic power of national government. The same federalism limits the extent to which groups are prepared to enter into national bargains and devise broad-ranging social programs that utilize the national government as their means. Instead, American law provides the different stakeholders with multiple opportunities to contest the claims of others. Adversarial rather than mutual, procedural rather than substantive, legal rather than social, American institutions are geared to horse-trading or ongoing conflict. The issues most likely to command national consensus are not positive programs such as poverty relief, national healthcare, or public education but rather morally driven attacks on perceived wrongdoing or public threats such as crime, drugs, or terrorism. America's Prohibition laws of the early twentieth century are the classic example. A more recent case in point is the tough-on-crime sentencing laws of the 1980s and 1990s—passed in every state and by the U.S. Congress—that led to a build-up of mass imprisonment such as the world has never before seen.

Americans' distrust of the national state is also, at some level, a distrust of other groups who compose, or control, or benefit from it, especially other racial groups.[53] And the American reluctance to enter into a fully developed welfare state with generalized risk-pooling and far-reaching social transfers is partly a reluctance to recognize the worth and deservingness of other groups who would benefit from such arrangements. Rather than seek economic security by these means, the American electorate and its representatives have opted, time and again, for private and market-based arrangements. By contrast, when popular majorities seek security from the threat of crime, and regard that threat as emanating from lower-class minorities, they have little hesitation in demanding that the state take action. There is powerful evidence that racial attitudes are closely related to preferences relating to crime and welfare policy, with more negative attitudes toward African Americans being associated with support for harsher policies.[54]

Except in the face of enemy attack, American voters rarely view themselves as sharing risks or prospects with all of the nation's citizens and rarely seek comprehensive national mechanisms to address such problems. Solidarity-through-the-state (as distinct from local, family, religious, or ethnic solidarities) is consequently much more limited than its equivalent in Europe. While many European nations pursue solidarity through welfare institutions that are organized through the state, comprehensive, universalistic, and citizen-based, America's group solidarities tend to be more bounded and exclusive, restricted to insiders and hostile to outsiders. Rather than build universal, inclusive, nationwide programs, the Americans opt for localism, particularism, and ongoing group competition. State action is more readily invoked to deal with threatening enemies than with economic risks. The minimalism of America's welfare state is the best-known expression of this reality, but the harshness of its criminal punishment is equally telling.

The composition of American states varies greatly, with quite different levels of racial diversity, urbanization, and economic prosperity. Moreover, there is variation in each state's institutions, with some states (often, but not always, the smaller, more homogeneous ones) exhibiting developed welfare arrangements and solidaristic arrangements, and others (often, but not always, less affluent ones with white majorities and large black minorities) having few welfare transfers or social programs beyond those mandated by the federal government. Researchers have shown that states with generous welfare arrangements tend to rely less on the penal mechanisms of imprisonment and probation. Conversely, states that minimize welfare provision are more likely to impose harsh punishments.[55]

Violence in America

America's process of state formation—together with the group relations, power balances, and economic interests that infused it—has had continuing consequences for violence and violence control throughout the nation's history. The American state never fully succeeded in its efforts to monopolize legitimate violence, and its pacification of the population was more partial than was true in other Western nations. As Randolph Roth observes, "America became homicidal in the mid-nineteenth century because it was the only major Western country that failed at nation-building." This history has had continuing consequences, helping to produce America's high levels of interpersonal violence and distinctive patterns of violence control.[56]

The relative failure of the American state to control interpersonal violence had a number of causes. An armed population was a direct legacy of the Revolution and of the Framers' decision to preserve the right to bear arms.[57] For much of the nineteenth century, toleration of private violence and rough justice was a feature of frontier regions and of rural areas where effective government controls were lacking and where relations between settlers and Native Americans were often violent. In the South and the West, honor codes and a personalistic form of government encouraged the persistence of dueling, revenge killings, and lynchings, as well as casual fights that often became lethal because firearms were readily available. These violent traditions continued in the South and West long after they ended elsewhere, partly because local juries preferred to accept excuses of self-defense rather than convict white defendants of homicide.[58] They became less frequent during the twentieth century, only when they conflicted with the modernizing projects of Southern commercial elites, the emergence of more organized government, and the sensibilities of a more moderate urban middle class. A belated increase in federal law-enforcement efforts also contributed to their decline.[59]

For more than half the nineteenth century, long after such arrangements had disappeared elsewhere, American slave-owners reserved to themselves a private police power and a right to use violence to discipline their slaves. During the subsequent Jim Crow period, Southern whites claimed this private power as a means to maintain white supremacy: they exercised it in the form of casual violence against blacks, white race riots, and spectacular lynchings. Elsewhere, and well into the twentieth century, American employers used violence to deal with labor disputes, hiring private security forces to break strikes and disrupt unionization efforts. And in cities such as New York, Chicago, and Los Angeles, the Prohibition and Depression years of the 1920s and 1930s saw organized-crime gangs wield violence to enforce rackets and intimidate victims.[60]

Before 1945, the American government's armed forces were less developed than those of European states such as Britain, France, and Germany. Similarly, most American states were slow to establish full-time, professional police forces. Well into the twentieth century, violence and brutality were features of American police departments, many of which lacked professional training or effective oversight.[61] The very limited protection that these departments offered to poor African Americans meant that violence and insecurity were especially prominent features of black urban ghettos and rural communities.

The struggle to control crime and prevent violence is a serious challenge for every government, and no Western nation has entirely succeeded in this regard. But comparative evidence makes it plain that the American state has been less successful than others in violence control. Rates of homicide, violent crime (especially armed robbery), and collective violence in the United States have historically been higher than elsewhere, often four or five times as high as those of comparable Western nations.[62] The consensus among historians is that the United States has long been a comparatively violent nation. According to leading figures in the field, "the European/ American differences stretch back to the early modern or colonial era" with homicide rates that are "dramatically higher than in other industrialized countries."[63] And though long-term violence trends have moved in the same downward direction in the United States as in other Western nations, the actual rates of lethal violence have been consistently higher in America.[64]

This violence is a legacy of the American state-formation process and its incomplete pacification.[65] Pacification is more than temporary superiority of arms or military dominance over a territory. It means long-term success in inculcating habits of restraint and self-control in the mass of the population. Clearly, the American state has succeeded to some degree in this respect. And clearly, too, the demands of violence control have grown more effective and more wide-ranging over time. But sizeable sections of the American population have always escaped the reach of these disciplinary norms or been less effectively controlled by them, with the result that high levels of violence have long been part of the social environment.

This long-established characteristic has continued into the contemporary period. Over the course of the twentieth century, the average U.S. homicide rate of 7.6 per 100,000 was eight times that of England and Wales.[66] Even after the decline in violent crime rates that occurred during the 1990s, America's homicide rate was still four times as high as that of comparable nations. For the period 1997–1999, the U.S. homicide rate was 6.26 per 100,000, whereas the mean rate for seven comparable nations was 1.57. In 1999, 65 percent of U.S. homicides were firearm deaths, while the equivalent figure in England and Wales was 9 percent.[67] The widespread civilian possession of firearms in the United States sets the country apart from other Western nations and produces rates of gunshot death that are many times higher than its European counterparts. As Charles Tilly observed, "in the proliferation of private weaponry, the United States resembles Lebanon and Afghanistan more than Great Britain or the Netherlands."[68]

This elevated rate is a general feature of the American states, with only a few (New Hampshire, Iowa, and North Dakota) approximating European homicide levels or slightly above (Massachusetts, Minnesota, Idaho, and Delaware). High homicide rates are a national rather than a regional characteristic, though within these elevated levels, Southern states are consistently at the high end. According to Randolph Roth, a growing disparity emerged between the South and the rest of the nation in the late nineteenth century, when the collapse of Reconstruction gave rise to a political culture in which violence was endemic: "Conservative white-supremacist elites lost power briefly in a number of states, but they regained ascendency in the late 1890s and early 1900s and created a political regime that was more brutal, corrupt and nakedly anti-democratic than any the nation had seen since slave times. The consequence of political upheaval and the reaction that followed was . . . a rash of lynchings, vigilante killings, and everyday murders." Throughout the twentieth century, the South consistently exhibited higher homicide rates than the other regions, sometimes five times as high as the Northeast.[69]

America's extraordinary rates of lethal violence have institutional, cultural, and situational causes. They exist because of the historic limits of state power, the social norms shaping individual conduct, the availability of lethal weapons, and hostilities within social and racial groups. These causes are interactive and mutually reinforcing. In situations of underenforcement and insecurity, where disadvantaged groups cannot rely on government protection and criminally inclined individuals have little fear of state sanctions, habits of violence become endemic and create expectations to which everyone must adjust. Americans have made cultural adaptations in order to live with high levels of violence.[70] One adaptation is the swaggering "tough guy" or "gangster" persona that deploys violence to uphold honor, respond to offense, and pursue one's interests. Another is the custom of elaborate courtesy to strangers and the placatory attitude of "going along to get along." America's "take it easy" and "have a nice day" customs function, Cas Wouters argues, "not only to lubricate social intercourse but also to pacify it."[71] Chronic violence and its cultural adaptations are, of course, unevenly distributed, with the worst violence usually being located in neighborhoods that are economically marginal and racially segregated.

Cultural Scripts and Patterns of Action

To write in general terms about "American culture," "American character," or "the American creed" is necessarily to skim the surface of a domain that is complex, changing, and conflicted.[72] Such is the size and diversity of the nation that any claim about cultural patterns or attitudes can easily be confronted by evidence of its opposite. Like its poet, Walt Whitman, America is large, it contradicts itself, it contains multitudes.[73] The U.S. Constitution was designed to preserve regional differences and local mores—and in this it has certainly succeeded. But as a comparative matter, American culture, at least as expressed in the public sphere, contains certain distinctive dispositions that have emerged in interaction with the institutions just described. Institutional structures give rise to cultural scripts and patterns of action that are associated with and adapted to them. A brief description of these recurring patterns of choice and expression cannot begin to capture the richness and diversity of "American culture," but it can usefully point to some established habits of thought and evaluation that are prominent in the American public sphere and have a definite bearing on death penalty politics.

With these caveats, we can identify some cultural tropes and habits of thought that, while not peculiarly or exclusively American, tend to be more pronounced in the United States than they are elsewhere. These discourses and sensibilities have come to be crystallized in, and reproduced by, America's social structures. That Americans continue to think, talk, and act in accordance with these established scripts is, in large part, an adaptation to the institutional landscape within which they find themselves. And of course these cultural habits, like the history and institutional structures in which they are rooted, have important implications for penal policy and death penalty politics.

With these qualifications in mind, we can identify a set of recurring themes that feature prominently in the American public sphere: populism and anti-elitism; localism and community control; liberalism and anti-statism; individualism and responsibility; religiosity and moralism; and ruggedness and refinement. These are the paired values that routinely orient the standard preferences and habits of thought of middle America. And each of them has a bearing on the punishment of offenders and on death penalty politics.

There is, in American culture, a cult of the common man and an obligatory, abiding faith in "the people."[74] This is expressed in a strong commitment to institutions of popular democracy and an equally vehement anti-elitism. Communal belief, majority opinion, common sense, plain speaking—these carry a special weight in American political debate and cultural life, as Tocqueville long ago observed.[75]

This *vox populi, vox dei* attitude is closely aligned with a commitment to a form of democracy that is more direct, more participatory, and more populist than elsewhere. It also connects to the egalitarianism that forms part of the American creed—the self-evident truth that all men are created equal—and to a dislike of rank-and-status differentiations that hark back to European feudalism. As Crevecoeur wrote, the Americans' dictionary is "short in words of dignity, and names of honor."[76] There is a bitter irony here, of course. The most fundamental status division of all—that between freeman and slave—persisted longer in America than elsewhere, and marks of race continue even today to set off black from white in ways that belie this more general egalitarianism.

Populist attitudes are manifest in a lingering distrust of experts, of intellectuals, and of those who set themselves apart from the common people. In contrast to many European nations, America has no culture of deference toward elites or established groups. Americans pride themselves on their personal initiative and an ability to act without reference to higher authority. In American political life, attempts to exert authority by anyone other than elected officials are met with instinctive resistance. "Who are they to tell me what to do?" If the nation's hyperdemocratic culture were to have a motto, it would be, "Let the people decide!"[77]

One corollary is that the intellectualism, cultural refinement, and urbane sophistication that characterize the self-presentation of European governing elites are much less visible in American politics.[78] Political leaders, many of them from wealthy, privileged, and highly educated backgrounds, do their utmost to develop a "popular touch" and identify with the common people. In the American electoral arena, the merest hint of elitist taste or superior attitude can spell disaster. And while there are many *de facto* elites in America, occupying leadership positions in economic, political, and cultural life, these groups generally refrain from evincing elite manners and attitudes and usually lack the organized political influence that national elites exert elsewhere—a fact that has significant consequences for death penalty abolition.

The anti-elitism and anti-intellectualism of American culture are sustained and strong because the institutional structure of the polity allocates more power to local popular majorities than is the case in other nations. Elsewhere, power and decision-making normally drift upward to professional elites, bureaucrats, and experts who are acknowledged as "authorities." In the United States, more power is retained by local communities and voters, which in turn reproduces the populist rationale for these arrangements. Far from being free-floating "ideas" or abstract "values," these cultural traits, like others, are grounded in and reproduced by the solidity of power structures and institutions.

As we have seen, America devolves more power to local political actors than do other Western nations. This localistic structure is reinforced by a series of institutional arrangements organized on the same basis. Parties are organized locally. Taxes are raised locally. Services are delivered locally. Criminal justice is directed locally. This structure is also reinforced by public attitudes that value local autonomy, resist uniform nation-wide policies, and prefer local authorities to national ones. As Andrew Moravcsik writes, "Americans report suspicion about 'big government' in Washington and tend to trust state and local officials more." And Lipset observes that the American public "invariably indicate a preference for small governmental units to large ones."[79]

Insistence on states' rights, resistance to uniform national policies, respect for local folkways, and commitment to community control are habits rooted in the nation's diversity, in its pluralist ethos, and in local groups' preference for self-government. But these preferences are asserted selectively, depending on the locality and the issue in question. Every state and every locality has its particular interests, and claims of localism are most powerfully asserted when national policy puts them in jeopardy.[80] Historically, the most vigorous proponents of local autonomy have often been conservative white Southerners, for whom the principle of states' rights operated as a shield against federal incursions that threatened to undermine the region's slave economy—though localism has also provided opportunities for progressive reform at state and municipal levels, making it sometimes popular with liberals, too. Many Americans support states' rights not because they are principled localists but "because they favor a weakening of federal policies with regard to race, the death penalty, criminal rights, and welfare."[81] This persistence of localism is highly pertinent to death penalty politics, having shaped America's engagement with capital punishment from its abolition in nineteenth-century Michigan to its enthusiastic execution in twenty-first-century Texas. And since the 1970s, the right to retain capital punishment has come to symbolize for many the assertion of states' rights and local autonomy.

Louis Hartz famously described "all Americans" as "liberals of one sort or another." Discounting the hyperbole, it remains true that Americans are more prone than others to view government in a negative light and to express low levels of trust in government officials. American political discourse regularly equates government with corruption, inefficiency, bureaucracy, and oppression, viewing it as a "necessary evil" rather than as a positive social force. Minimizing government, cutting "tax-and-spend" programs, getting government "off people's backs"—these are the staple *desiderata* of the American electorate.[82] For this reason presidential candidates typically claim to be "outsiders," positioning themselves with the people and against "Washington," promising (however implausibly) to "clean up" politics and reduce big government.

For a majority of Americans, market mechanisms and private institutions are usually preferable to governmental ones. For all their flaws, markets are viewed as fairer, more trustworthy, and more efficient than the governments that seek to regulate or replace them. And if goods or services can be delivered by "the private sector" in a commercial, competitive manner, this is generally regarded as preferable to any public-sector alternative. Today all Western nations have mixed economies that combine state and market sectors, but the American mix is more heavily weighted toward the market, and this reflects the settled preferences of a majority of Americans.

Whereas many Europeans evince a suspicion of, and even a disdain for, the business ethos, in the United States, business and enterprise are embraced by both progressives and conservatives as core America values.

This current of antistatism raises an interesting puzzle about American capital punishment. We might have expected a society that is suspicious of state power to be unwilling to entrust government officials with the power to put citizens to death. But in American discussions—in contrast to European discourse—the death penalty is rarely framed as a question of state power, being viewed instead as an expression of local democratic process and popular will.[83]

The preference for market solutions is linked to the dominance of a certain kind of individualism in American political culture. The distinguishing feature here is not a belief in the sanctity and autonomy of the individual, which is common to all the Western nations. The distinctive element, rather, is a market-based understanding about how best to facilitate the flourishing of individual autonomy and welfare.[84] As James Bryce put it, "Individualism, the love of enterprise, and the pride in personal freedom have been deemed by Americans not only their choicest, but [their] peculiar and exclusive possession." The distinctively American mode of individualism is a market individualism, a vision of the individual as entrepreneur, as pioneering spirit, as restless soul, even, as one historian recently argued, as inveterate huckster.[85]

Americans have shown themselves to be less committed than the voters of other Western nations to collective transfer mechanisms and state-organized solidarity. They have a strong belief in the provision of opportunity for individual enterprise (public education, open markets, the absence of class restrictions) and a belief that individual talent and success ought to be rewarded. Once the basics have been provided, individuals are deemed to be in control of their own fates. Those who fare badly or are less successful have only themselves to blame; those who succeed deserve to reap the rewards, however large.[86] This habit of thought makes efforts to secure greater equality of outcome—progressive taxation, welfare transfers, income support, and affirmative action—seem misplaced, just as it makes individual deterrence and harsh retribution seem commonsensical, whether in welfare or in penal policy.

Whereas Europe became, in the twentieth century, increasingly secular and "dechristianized," the United States remains a religious nation, with a greater proportion of its population espousing religious beliefs than anywhere else in the West. As James Marone puts it, "Americans worship with a gusto unmatched in the western world." Belief in God is virtually universal, with 95 percent of Americans claiming to have faith, in contrast to

Britain, where the equivalent number is 76 percent, France (62 percent), or Sweden (52 percent). And according to survey research, 75 percent of Americans belong to a church, 40 percent attended services last week, and 10 percent claim to attend "several times a week." Crossnational opinion polls by Gallup and others suggest that "Americans are the most church-going in Protestantism and the most fundamentalist in Christendom."[87]

Unlike many Western nations that have moved from religious to secular, the United States has developed "from revival to revival." In the last third of the twentieth century, the nation went through just such a religious revival, with an increased number of the population describing themselves as "fundamentalist" or "evangelical." In recent years the religious enthusiasm of middle America has often been associated with a socially conservative politics, characterized by an enraged rejection of secular liberalism and an equally passionate defense of "family values" and traditional forms of life. Without an established church, and with a long tradition of religious dissent, America's religiosity is a source of group identity and division, with most believers being members of diverse sects rather than a single church.[88]

Nor does religion confine itself to the private realm.[89] Despite the constitutional separation of Church and State, religiosity infuses American political discourse, and religious groups are often mobilized around political issues—sometimes to the extent of deciding national elections. A vivid example is the way in which the fundamentalist "culture of life" has shaped political positions on abortion, stem cell research, and euthanasia, with important consequences for law and politics. The continuing support of the Christian conservatives and especially the Southern Baptist Convention for capital punishment is an important pillar of the institution, especially in Southern states where fundamentalism predominates.

Supreme Court Justice Antonin Scalia recently observed that American public life has "many visible reminders that . . . we are a religious people, whose institutions presuppose a Supreme Being":

> These reminders include: "In God we trust" on our coins, "one nation under God" in our Pledge of Allegiance, the opening of sessions of our legislatures with a prayer, the opening of sessions of my Court with "God save the United States and this Honorable Court," annual Thanksgiving proclamations issued by our President at the direction of Congress, and constant invocations of divine support in the speeches of our political leaders, which often conclude, "God bless America."[90]

Scalia went on to say that all of this is "most un-European" and that America's religiosity helps explain why the death penalty continues in this country. As he put it, "the more Christian a country is the *less* likely it is to regard the death penalty as immoral. Abolition has taken its firmest hold in post-Christian Europe, and has least support in the church-going United States."[91]

Particularly in Southern states, fundamentalist beliefs and religious language are prominent features of political discourse. Whenever a group's social position or way of life is perceived as being under threat, expressions of religious belief operate as metaphors for these cherished values and practices. As Gary Wills puts it, "It is fascinating to observe how effective religion can be as the medium in which all other forms of localism are fused, bathing them in an emotional glow of approval."[92]

A closely related feature of American public discourse is the tendency to transform political questions into moral issues, so that enemies are characterized as "evil," drugs are viewed as a "moral scourge," and outsider groups are deemed "immoral." Marone talks of "the roaring moral fervor at the soul of American politics" and argues that in "a nation made by immigrants, marked by social mobility, and home to a thousand religions, morality is dynamite. Visions of vice and virtue define the American community."[93] Lipset makes the same point when he suggests that this distinctive moralism is rooted in America's Protestant religious ethos with its assumption of perfectibility and intolerance of sin. The moral absolutism of much death penalty discourse illustrates the continuing power of this form of expression.

American culture is sometimes characterized by outsiders as rough, abrasive, and violent, as if the nineteenth-century frontier ethos still defined the habits and attitudes of daily life. In the face of that stereotype, we ought to recall that American people and institutions have sometimes taken a concern for civilized refinement and sensibility to lengths unknown elsewhere.[94] Think, for example, of the exquisite concern with hygiene (with bathing and showers and household cleanliness) that defined the American suburban household of the 1950s. Or look at the sanitized packaging of meats and poultry in American supermarkets and compare them with the blood-and-sawdust butcher shops still to be found in many small towns in France and Britain. Look at the speech codes enacted and enforced by American colleges and corporations, with their demanding norms of self-control and consideration of the sensitivities of others. And recall the euphemism and avoidance that surround death and sickness, as well as the reliance on specialists who remove such matters discreetly away from public view. In all these respects, American culture is thoroughly "civilized" in Norbert Elias's sense: exhibiting elaborate norms of self-control, delicacy, and mutual respect; avoiding indecency; and striving to put animalistic aspects of daily life "behind the scenes."

But another side of America regards such manners as effete and is more comfortable with the cruder, rawer aspects of the human condition. A sector of the America population still lives in rural farming communities and remains close to the blood-and-guts realities of traditional ways of life. Hunting is a major pastime of millions of Americans. Guns and firearms are widely distributed. And in the rural cultures of the South and West, as well as in the street culture of the big city ghettoes, there is a continuing glorification of masculinity, honor, and violence. That toughness, guns, and violence appall liberal elites elsewhere is, of course, part of their local appeal.

Urban and rural, white collar and blue collar, civilized and crude, refined cosmopolitan and red-neck good old boy—these are continuing antimonies in U.S. culture.[95] One of their expressions is the tension between the niceties of the rule of law and the visceral appeal of rough justice, a tension that finds repeated expression in American history, from the conflicts over lynching in the 1890s to the death penalty debates of the present day.[96]

None of these cultural scripts and patterned preferences, nor any combination of them, altogether shapes the beliefs or the day-to-day conduct of Americans. Each one is contested, each one coexists with its opposite, and each one is frequently violated by behavior that doesn't quite accord with the culture's espoused ideals. America's populist culture may promote suspicion of elites and experts, but millions of Americans worship sporting heroes or Hollywood celebrities, and millions more turn to experts and therapists for guidance about personal health and well-being. Older traditions of robust individualism and self-help bump up against the "therapeutic culture of vulnerable individualism."[97] The dominant American values may disparage state programs and prefer market distributions, but millions of Americans rely on the state to provide old-age insurance, mortgage support, and disaster relief, and many expect the federal government to bail out the victims of savings and loan scams, bank collapse, or foreclosure crises. In the same contradictory way, American juries are frequently persuaded by "abuse excuses" that absolve defendants of responsibility for their criminal acts; affirmative action programs continue to operate despite widespread criticism; the influence of religion on political life is periodically decried by secular critics; and moral turpitude is sometimes redefined as addiction or personality disorder and sometimes overlooked altogether.

And of course change occurs over time. The 1960s saw a shift to more secular, progressive, collectivist values—expressed in civil rights legislation, Great Society programs, the rise of moral relativism and situational ethics, a generation of young people critical of "corporate America," and the relaxation of sexual and social mores. The same decade saw a movement toward a less harsh, more reformative penal policy and a powerful challenge to the legitimacy of capital punishment that went all the way to the Supreme Court. In contrast, the period since then has seen the resurgence of religious fundamentalism and the declining power of the 1960s Social Gospel.[98] It has seen the political dominance of social conservatism and neoliberalism as well as a new form of racial segregation in the buildup of mass incarceration. Moreover, the period between the 1960s and the 1980s saw a steep increase in recorded rates of crime and violence and, not coincidentally, the emergence of harsh penal policies and a revival of capital punishment.

It is this complex social field—state institutions, group relations, culture, and history, operating as a changing, contradictory whole—rather than any single attitude or institution that has shaped the past and the present of American capital punishment.

SEVEN

Capital Punishment
in America

The United States stands alone on many issues. That does not
make us wrong.

DIANNE CLEMENTS, PRESIDENT OF JUSTICE FOR ALL, A PRO–DEATH
PENALTY VICTIMS' GROUP, 2000

The United States, which from the start has been a liberal, partially
democratic nation with a republican hostility to monarchical power, a
predominantly Christian culture, and a widespread cult of the individual,
did develop an abolitionist movement and *did* conform to the standard
Western pattern of increasing restraint, refinement, and reduction. Indeed,
it was frequently in the forefront of Western reform. The sanctity of the individual, an antipathy to sovereign power, the restraints of the rule of law,
a preference for a reformative penal system—these were liberal attitudes
that grew naturally in American soil nourished by the antigallows associations that formed in many parts of the nation.[1]

American liberal elites—lawyers, clerics, publishers, writers, progressives, and philanthropists—made significant contributions to the abolitionist cause, beginning with Benjamin Rush's reform proposals of the
1790s, continuing in the 1840s and 1850s with the vanguard abolitions in
Michigan, Wisconsin, and Rhode Island, and culminating in the constitutional litigation that led to the *Furman* decision in 1972. Each of the great
liberalizing moments of American history—the Founding, the Jacksonian
period, the Progressive era, the Civil Rights movement, the Great Society—brought advances in the cause of death penalty reform.[2] These same
social forces continue to press for abolition today through the work of
civil rights activists, progressive churches, human rights organizations, liberal Democrats, and *pro bono* defense lawyers.

But these antigallows sentiments have not resulted in national abolition nor even in extensive state-by-state abolition. Why did the processes
of transformation that fully abolished the death penalty throughout the
rest of the Western world not do so in America? And why did the reformative impulses of American liberalism fail to prevent public executions,
racialized capital codes, and public lynchings from continuing well into
the twentieth century?

American liberals were up against strong pro–death penalty forces.
Nourished by the anger that high homicide rates arouse, by racial hostilities that refuse sympathy to black defendants, and by righteous, moralizing dispositions that insist on harsh retribution, supporters of capital punishment not surprisingly remain dominant in many parts of the country.
But popular support for the death penalty is hardly peculiar to the United
States. Opinion polls indicate a majority in favor of capital punishment in
virtually every nation where the death penalty was abolished, both at the
moment of abolition and for long periods thereafter.[3] If popular support
for retention is more of a background constant than a determining variable, how do we explain the different outcomes? What allowed the political leaders of other Western nations to abolish capital punishment despite
popular support for retention? And why did the same process not occur in
the United States?

The explanation has to do with the distinctive structure of the American
state and the American polity. The U.S. Constitution allocates plenary penal powers to the individual states, thereby making European-style national abolition impossible. Moreover, the weak-party, populist nature
of American politics makes it politically difficult to enact European-style
countermajoritarian reform against the wishes of the American public.
The importance of these considerations becomes clear when we recall how
national abolition occurred elsewhere. In Germany, the 1949 Constitution
prohibited the death penalty despite the fact that two-thirds of the public
supported it. When President Mitterand's socialist government abolished
capital punishment in France in 1981, 73 percent of the French public supported its retention for "atrocious" crimes.[4] In 1995, thirty years after the
British Parliament abolished capital punishment for ordinary crime, opinion polls showed 76 percent support for its reintroduction. In the same
year, a poll in abolitionist Canada revealed that 65 percent of the public favored reintroduction of the death penalty.[5]

Politicians in these countries had the *political* capacity to carry through
this reform because the governing party could rely on broad support for its
other policies and need not face an election until several years later, or because bipartisan agreements, supported by effective party discipline, kept

the issue outside of electoral competition. They had the *legal* capacity to do so because the power to enact criminal penalties for the whole nation lay within the jurisdiction of the national parliament. Other than by a constitutional amendment—which requires a two-thirds majority in both congressional houses and the ratification of three-quarters of the states, and so cannot succeed without widespread support—America's national government lacks the legal authority to impose abolition on the country as a whole.[6] The constitutional mechanism that produced final-stage nationwide abolition in other Western nations is simply not available in the United States. Nor is it likely that a controlling majority in Congress would have the political capacity or inclination to undertake such a measure so long as a majority of state and local electorates objected to it. The political cover that European political parties provide to individual parliamentarians is not available in America. For an individual member of Congress to support an unpopular measure of this kind would be to invite defeat in the next party primary or general election. Where policy issues with high public salience are concerned, few American politicians are willing to move very far from the median voter preference in their districts. It is no surprise to discover, then, that most members of the U.S. Congress favor capital punishment and that Congress has enacted several federal death penalty statutes in the post-*Furman* period.[7]

Public opinion in most places tends to support the use of the death penalty for the most atrocious murders. The difference between other Western nations and the United States has less to do with popular ideas about punishment and more to do with the different political mechanisms that transmit—or do not transmit—majority opinion into public policy. It is not the distinctive views of the American public that are determinative here: it is the distinctive form of local democratic populism that shapes representative institutions and holds individual politicians directly accountable to organized majority sentiment.[8]

The United States does, of course, have an important mechanism for countermajoritarian law-making, namely, the U.S. Supreme Court: an unelected institution of government charged with upholding the federal Constitution and the individual rights it guarantees. This national institution became the focus of abolitionist efforts from the 1960s onward when political agitation in the state legislatures gave way to national litigation in the federal courts.

These litigation efforts could have succeeded, we might suppose, if the death penalty had been chiefly viewed as a penal measure, the instrumental utility of which was increasingly in doubt. But capital punishment soon became caught up in a series of political and cultural conflicts that altered its meaning. What had previously been a rarely used penal sanction dogged by moral controversy was rapidly transformed into a hot-button political issue with multiple meanings, all of them highly charged and deeply contested. The death penalty in 1970s America came to be seen as a litmus test in the politics of crime control, a powerful symbol of states' rights, and a prominent part of a conservative backlash against civil rights. Once this symbolic transformation occurred—and thirty-five states passed new death penalty laws—the probability of judicial abolition quickly receded. By 1976, the nation's abolitionist moment had passed and the social forces that sustained capital punishment asserted themselves anew.

The processes of transformation that shaped the history of capital punishment in the West shaped its American history, too. And the distinctive structure of American political institutions goes some way toward explaining America's partial divergence from the Western pattern. But our discussion of American society and culture points to other processes that have worked to conserve capital punishment even in an age of abolition.

Forces of Conservation

State-building and rationalization—together with the politics of liberalism and democracy and a civilizing and humanitarian culture—operated to corrode the death penalty in America just as they did elsewhere. These transformative processes generated reforms that reduced, restrained, and refined its use all across the United States and enabled full and sustained abolition in more than a dozen states. But capital punishment has shown, and continues to show, a remarkable resilience in the American context. The fundamentals of this resilience are rooted in America's distinctive political development and the social and institutional legacy it has produced. The causal mechanisms involved are, in effect, historical pathways that have allowed institutions, practices, and habits of thought established at earlier stages of development to continue into the present, influencing the contemporary structures that shape culture and guide action.

National, top-down, countermajoritarian reform imposed by governing elites is the basic mechanism through which national abolition has been achieved elsewhere in the Western world. But in the United States this mechanism is unavailable, with the result that American liberal elites have been unable to organize on a national level and enact nationwide reform. Even the Supreme Court is somewhat constrained in this respect, since the U.S. Constitution limits the circumstances under which capital punishment may be imposed but also limits the possibility of its being plausibly regarded as unconstitutional.

In the United States, the power to punish is controlled by local democratic processes. Local control can lead to abolition rather than to retention, as it did in more than a dozen states. But local democratic control, as exercised in the United States, has a tendency to produce more discriminatory enforcement than would typically be developed by the kind of national administration that governs criminal justice in most European nations. This is because local, politically accountable decision-makers are more likely to follow popular sentiment than are high-ranking bureaucrats who enjoy a degree of autonomy from the political process.[9] Locally administered justice (which operates close to the scene of the crime, to the aggrieved victims, and to the aroused and hostile community) is liable to be more personalistic, more political, more freighted with emotion, and more expressive than is justice determined by national, bureaucratized agencies that are less roiled by the emotional upheavals of the affected community.

America's commitment to localism has a further consequence of relevance here, namely, the relative strength of local communities *vis-à-vis* state power. This distinctive balance of power—a consequence of America's colonial past, its populist processes of representation, and the underdeveloped character of its state apparatus—has been of great significance in the history of American capital punishment. The American death penalty was always more local than state, more religious than military, more communal than official—all of which point to America's weak domestic state and correspondingly powerful civil society.[10]

The origins of this pattern lie in colonial times. American executions in the colonial period were not usually dominated by the imperial authorities.[11] It was not the king who presided over eighteenth-century executions: the local colonial communities and their religious leaders were the chief figures of authority. Thus there was more distance between American executions and the centers of sovereign state power than was typical of other nations. At an early stage in the country's development, capital punishment was less a ceremony of state power than a local, religiously inflected, community undertaking. These patterns were preserved after the Revolution and help explain why many Americans rarely associate capital punishment with overarching state power, viewing it as a community-based act of justice rather than as an act of state.[12] This long-standing contrast with Europe was reinforced by twentieth-century history. "Americans never lived through the Nazi era in the way that Europe did," as Hugu Bedau points out. As a consequence, they "never learned to see so clearly the abuses to which this punishment can be put. [They] have seen it only in the form of the normal instrument of criminal justice, rather than in the hands of obvious tyrants and murderers."[13]

The same pattern is evident in Southern lynchings, which were made possible by the limited power of state officials *vis-à-vis* local community actors. Wherever state apparatus was underdeveloped, local law enforcement was poorly trained and equipped, and local sheriffs owed their loyalties to county politicians rather than to state officials, communal mobs could often act with impunity.[14] The underdevelopment of state institutions and the relative powerlessness of state officials empowered community-level actors to disregard the rule of law and carry out summary killings in the name of "community justice." At the start of the twenty-first century, the relative empowerment of local communities continues to lend force and weight to popular demands for capital punishment.

Federalism, pluralism, localism, separated powers, devolved decision-making—all of these institutional structures express and embody a singular political fact about the United States, namely, the continued existence of fundamental disputes about the proper location of sovereign power. Sovereignty claims in the United States are more multiple, more contested, and more unstable than in other Western nations. The people's sovereignty is asserted over that of elected officials, county sovereignty over that of state authorities, state sovereignty over that of the federal authorities, and legislative sovereignty over the courts' powers of judicial review. Following the events of the 1970s and the involvement of the federal courts in regulating capital punishment, these conflicts are now sparked whenever the death penalty is debated. If the right to impose the death penalty is regarded as the stamp and signature of sovereign power—and it has long been so regarded, but never more so than in the wake of *Furman*—then each challenge to that right reaches beyond the immediate case to invoke a larger struggle.[15] For many local and state authorities across the United States, retaining the right to kill has become part of retaining their claim to sovereignty.

American political culture also plays a role in the retention of capital punishment. The relative weakness of national political parties, the existence of party primaries, and the limited extent of party-ticket voting all increase the likelihood that the death penalty will become a salient electoral issue that can be exploited for political gain.[16] Intensely competitive politics makes bipartisan reform unlikely and unpopular reform close to impossible. Locally elected representatives are under strong pressure to align themselves with majority sentiment, making it more likely that they will support death penalty retention, whatever their actual views on the issue. District attorneys function less as rule-following bureaucrats than as local *kadi* justices, intuiting the will of the community, gauging what will attract positive media headlines and what might convince a local jury. The intensely competitive nature of the American mass media increases the probability that the death penalty will be reported in a sensational manner and exploited for commercial gain.[17]

At a more fundamental level, the American state's historic failure fully to disarm the population and fully to monopolize violence continues to shape present-day events. This distinctive state formation, together with America's history of inter-racial hostilities, is the underlying source of several linked phenomena. These include high rates of homicide; widespread lynching and vigilantism; a masculine culture of honor-violence; widespread gun ownership; and a cultural fascination with violence.[18] Rather than view these phenomena in isolation we ought to think of them as elements in an adaptive pattern, a cultural complex formed around the nation's high rates of violence and victimization. In a society where this complex shapes public attitudes, a common-sense response to murderous violence is the counterviolence of the death penalty.

America's distinctive state formation left a legacy of extensive gun ownership and a collective experience of chronically high homicide rates.[19] This violent background, always more pronounced in some regions and communities than in others, gave rise to regional cultures of violence that persist to this day, most notably in Southern rural counties and Northern urban ghettoes. Even in regions where such patterns are less evident, there is an anxious awareness of this looming fact about American society, an emotional engagement which ensures that violence often forms the backdrop to everyday life. This cultural investment leads to various responses such as stern prohibition (in middle-class culture, in public institutions, in professional workplaces); romanticization (in movies, in youth culture, in "gangsta rap" music); and, in the most affected neighborhoods, acting out (habits of aggressive deportment, sensitivity to offense, and patterns of violent retaliation).[20]

A related legacy affects some of the frontier states and the cultural patterns established there. Thus in rural Western states such as Wyoming, Montana, and Colorado, support for the death penalty appears to be grounded in traditional practices of community self-help, a culture of masculine honor, and a relatively high tolerance of physical violence, all of which originated in the frontier experience and have been reproduced over time as "Western" cultural values.[21] Many people in these states support the death penalty for the same reasons they support the right to bear arms:

because until the late nineteenth century, incomplete pacification of these territories made armed self-defense the duty of every male householder. Violence was a fact of everyday life, and willingness to defend one's self and one's family became a necessary attribute and a valued mark of masculinity. Over time, self-help, self-defense, and private justice shifted from social necessities to cultural norms and symbolic markers of Westernness and masculinity. Once inscribed in the local culture, these traits could continue after their originating circumstances had receded. As a consequence guns, community justice, and lethal punishments have a greater salience for the rural inhabitants of Western states than for many urban dwellers elsewhere.[22] Many residents of these regions have a robust commitment to the death penalty, viewing it as one of a cluster of traditional values that define their local culture and identity.

Slavery in the Southern states had direct and continuing effects on the institution of capital punishment. It limited the impact of the humanitarian culture and revulsion at bodily suffering that liberal Protestant and evangelical groups developed in the antebellum North. It prevented abolitionist reform movements from taking hold in the South. It placed the police power in private hands. It retarded the development of state criminal justice institutions. It delayed the development of modern disciplinary prisons so that the institutions that made the death penalty unnecessary elsewhere were slower to develop in the South.[23] And following the abolition of slavery, Jim Crow institutions of lynching, racial violence, and racial segregation worked to preserve support for the death penalty, especially where black perpetrators were concerned.

Even after slavery, America's subsequent history of hostile race relations left a violent legacy. Historic practices of exclusion and subordination in housing, schooling, employment, and economic security—the traces of which continue today—together with the authorities' failure to provide equal protection against crime, have contributed to chronically high levels of violence within many poor African American communities. And though most crime and violence in America is intra-racial rather than inter-racial, the background threat that street crime represents helps justify harsh punishment and reinforce racial prejudice.[24]

Finally, the nature of the American legal process—for all its reformative potential—has worked to conserve the death penalty and even to entrench it more deeply in the nation's political culture. Given America's tendency to translate intractable political issues into judicial questions, it was no surprise that capital punishment eventually became a matter for the federal courts. And once it became a constitutional question, the culture of adversarial legalism ensured that it would be litigated and relitigated in state and federal courts with an energy and persistence that transformed the institution while preventing the issue from ever being finally settled.[25] Federal death penalty litigation—most often initiated on behalf of death row inmates facing execution—has aimed to restrict and restrain capital punishment and has succeeded in doing so in important respects. But an unintended effect of these court challenges and the Supreme Court rulings they have produced has been to enhance the perceived lawfulness and legitimacy of capital punishment and thus act as a force for its conservation.

Empowering Pro–Death Penalty Forces

These forces of conservation help explain why the death penalty has been more than usually difficult to eliminate from the American political landscape. These historical legacies and institutional patterns exert pressure toward retention and obstruct the road to abolition. Together they increase the resilience of the death penalty in the face of abolitionist pressure.

But more than resilience and conservation are at work here. There is also a periodic empowering and enlivening of the forces that propel death penalty use. The Supreme Court has on numerous occasions chosen to permit power over capital punishment to be exercised by local-level decision-makers who operate in a milieu in which death penalty sentiments are at their most raw and exposed. All societies are familiar with the vengeful passions and death demands aroused by atrocious murders.[26] But in other Western societies, national governments have ensured that these lethal, vengeful forces have been disarmed and disempowered. Whenever they threaten to emerge they are represented by officials as regrettably primitive, subjected to normative prohibition, and denied access to law-making processes. In these other societies, the issue of capital punishment has been settled, once and for all, at the national center of government, not decided on a discretionary, case-by-case basis by local actors at the periphery.

In a series of fateful decisions, the Supreme Court has repeatedly returned the power of life and death to the environment most prone to demand the execution of offenders. In doing so, the Court has chosen to align itself with the populist, localistic, democratic ethos of the American polity rather than take a stand against it.[27] The overall result—especially in states with high levels of violence and low levels of group solidarity—has been the sustained use of the death penalty, a racialized distribution of death penalty sentences, and the development of capital punishment practices designed to benefit the political and professional actors involved.[28]

Since the emergence of modern liberalism in the eighteenth century, every Western society has rendered the use of capital punishment politically problematic and culturally transgressive. The United States is no exception. American society exhibits strong political and cultural norms upholding the sanctity of human life, limiting state violence, and imposing civilized, humane restraints on the ill treatment of individuals. Every Western society also experiences public demands for harsh punishment and the expression, from time to time, of pro–death penalty sentiments. But the intensity of these sentiments differs from place to place, as does the probability of their expression in law and policy. America's political institutions have shaped that balance of forces and the means of their expression, making it more likely in America than in other Western nations that the death penalty will be retained.[29]

State-by-State Variation

America's institutional landscape may have made it difficult to abolish capital punishment on a national basis, but *within* the United States there is a great deal of state-by-state variation. Twenty-five states have, at one time or another, abolished capital punishment within their jurisdictions, and as of 2010, fifteen states and the District of Columbia have no capital punishment laws in force. Among the thirty-five states that have "retained" the death penalty—or, more precisely, re-enacted it by passing new capital punishment statutes in the wake of *Furman*—some never impose death sentences, some impose death sentences but rarely execute them, and others impose and execute death sentences with relative frequency. This variation is regionally patterned, with execution states concentrated in the South and abolitionist states in the Northeast.

In explaining these differences, our focus shifts from the institutional structures and constitutional restraints that affect the nation as a whole to the local politics, group relations, and legal arrangements that shape capital punishment at the state and county levels. Different states have had different policies at different times, ranging from the early and sustained abolitionism of Michigan, to the back-and-forth of repeal, reinstatement, and judicial invalidation of New York, to the sustained and enthusiastic retention of Texas. The death penalty's distribution and use within the United States is, like the international pattern, explained by the theoretical framework I outlined previously. The processes of transformation that caused the death penalty's long-term Western decline are the same ones that produced abolition, retention, and partial retention in the different parts of the United States.

The distribution being explained is a moving target, with the division between abolitionist and retention states changing over time. Three of the states that are currently in the abolitionist camp—New York, New Jersey, and New Mexico—were recently death penalty states, having come late to the abolitionist cause. But the movement is not all in this direction. Ten of the states that are currently "retentionist" had earlier periods of abolition: Colorado (1897–1901); Kansas (1907–1935); Washington (1913–1919); Oregon (1914–1920 and 1965–1978); South Dakota (1915–1939); Tennessee (1915–1916); Arizona (1916–1918); Missouri (1917–1919); Delaware (1958–1961); and California (1972–1974). The state of Connecticut, which had not executed anyone for more than forty years, recently put an offender to death (albeit one who "volunteered" for death by abandoning his appeals), thus moving the state from one group to another.

This back-and-forth movement reminds us that the differences separating the camps involve contingencies and events as well as structural determinants. It is striking, however, that only one of the former Confederate states (Tennessee) has ever abolished the death penalty for murder, and that for only one year (1915–1916), during which it retained the punishment for capital rape and for the black offenders usually charged with that offense.[30] If there is an unvarying feature of the American death penalty landscape it is the South's continuing embrace of the institution.

For more than two hundred years, the United States has experienced pressure for death penalty reform. In each of the states this has given rise to a long-term process of reduction, restraint, and refinement in the use of the death penalty, and twenty-five states have successfully enacted abolitionist legislation at some point or other, though ten of these subsequently enacted new capital statutes. Over the same period, there has also been ongoing pressure *against* reform exerted by the forces of conservation identified above—forces that make American states, in general, comparatively more resistant to abolitionist reform. We would expect that the transformative forces would be weaker and conservative forces stronger in those states where the death penalty has been retained, and that the reverse would be true in those states where it has been abolished.

Let us begin with temporal variation. Some of the states that are abolitionist today did away with capital punishment more than 150 years ago; others abolished during the last 5 years. The explanation for each abolition should focus on the social forces operating at the time and, since the abolition was sustained, on the circumstances that enabled abolitionists to resist subsequent attempts at re-enactment in the period since.

To take an important case in point, consider Michigan. In terms of its present-day levels of violent crime, urbanization, racial demographics,

Abolitionist states with dates of abolition

State	Prior abolition	Current abolition
Alaska		(1957–)
Hawaii		(1957–)
Iowa	(1872–1878)	(1965–)
Maine	(1876–1883)	(1887–)
Massachusetts		(1984–)*
Michigan		(1846–)
Minnesota		(1911–)
New Jersey	(1972–1982)	(2007–)
New Mexico	(1969–1979)	(2009–)
New York	(1955–1995)	(2004–)*
North Dakota		(1973–)
Rhode Island	(1852–1973)	(1984–)
Vermont		(1964–)
West Virginia		(1965–)
Wisconsin		(1853–)

* State courts invalidated the capital statutes.

and sentencing severity we would predict that Michigan would be a retentionist state. That it is not shows the importance of path dependency and
of the death penalty's place in the political history of a state, especially
where the state was one of the very first to repeal its capital laws and identify itself with the abolitionist cause.[31]

Michigan's political leaders used their autonomous powers to abolish
capital punishment at a time when the state had a small, homogeneous
population and low rates of violent crime. Opposition to the reform was
weakened by the case of a local man who had been executed by Canadian
authorities shortly before another man confessed to the crime.[32] At the
time, Michigan's population—like that of Wisconsin and Rhode Island,
the other vanguard abolitionists—was small enough to allow a determined
reform movement to push through its legislation. As Banner writes, "The
debate in Michigan was no different from that anywhere else. If the state
had any relevant distinguishing features, they were a relatively small political and economic elite and a correspondingly egalitarian distribution of
wealth and power, and a relatively small number of citizens who were
members of the more conservative religious denominations."[33]

In the period since 1846, Michigan's character has changed dramatically. Industrialization, urbanization, and migration altered the state's economic character and demographics, so that today, Detroit is an industrialized city of just under 1 million residents, home to the nation's automobile
industry and to a large African American community that, in 2000, made

up nearly 15 percent of the state's population. Over the same period, Michigan's murder rate has greatly increased and is now consistently above the national average.[34] The state's sentencing laws and imprisonment rates are relatively severe, as we might expect of a high-crime state. Public support for the death penalty has also shifted, so although a referendum on death penalty reintroduction was defeated in 1931, opinion polls since 1975 have consistently shown majority support for capital punishment running at a level close to the national average.[35]

These circumstances would lead us to expect a return to the death penalty. But the state's political leadership—which views Michigan's early abolition as a source of pride—has resolutely prevented this from occurring. This entrenched resistance was strengthened in 1963, when the state legislature enacted a constitutional provision requiring a supermajority for any reintroduction of capital punishment. These factors, together with vigorous anti–death penalty activism and a largely sympathetic press, have prevented new death penalty bills from being enacted into law.

Wisconsin, which also abolished in the mid-nineteenth century, has a contemporary profile closer to what we would expect of an abolitionist state: low homicide rates; a small, stable, homogeneous population; relative affluence; a developed system of state welfare; and a socially progressive identity. Since 1988 its courts have had the power to sentence murderers to "life without parole," which addresses concerns about public safety and demands for severe punishment. The state also has an active abolitionist movement, including religious, labor, and civil rights organizations, which receives support from local newspapers. Moreover, Wisconsin's constitution (unlike that of most death penalty states) has no provision for voter ballot initiatives and has a requirement that all new bills go through a fiscal analysis, both of which make the legislative process less open to popular sentiment. Between 1973 and 1990, twenty-four death penalty re-enactment bills were introduced in the Wisconsin legislature and all of them failed in committee.[36]

Several of the other abolitionist states—Maine, Minnesota, North Dakota, Iowa, Vermont, and West Virginia—share many characteristics with Wisconsin, each being small and rural, with stable, homogeneous populations and below-average murder rates. Massachusetts is more populous and urban, with a sizeable minority population (7 percent African American), but it too has a relatively low murder rate, a well-developed system of state welfare, a liberal-progressive political ethos, and a tradition of abolitionist activism. By contrast, Alaska and Washington, DC, both of which have no death penalty, have high murder rates, diverse demographics, and transient populations, making their abolitionism more puzzling. These two very different jurisdictions—like Hawaii, which also exhibits a high degree of population heterogeneity—appear to have refrained from capital punishment in part because their minority-dominated legislatures have tended to associate the death penalty with racial discrimination and the historic repression of minorities.[37]

Before leaving the question of timing we should note that eleven of fifteen currently abolitionist states repealed capital punishment in 1965 or before, so their abolitions preceded the marked rise in violent crime and urban disorder that helped shift American crime politics sharply to the right.[38] Of the four that abolished more recently, two of these—Massachusetts and New York—did so as a result of court decisions (though the absence of an effective political movement for restoration is significant), and the state of New Jersey, one of only two states to have passed abolitionist legislation since 1972, did so after several decades during which the state had the law on the books but never once carried out an execution.

Abolitionist and Death Penalty States Compared

Eleven of the fifteen abolitionist states have been abolitionist for more than forty years. These states might be thought of as settled, long-term abolitionist states, in which reintroduction has been successfully resisted over an extended period of time, including the backlash decade of the 1970s, when three dozen states enacted new capital statutes. We might properly ask, do these abolitionist states differ from death penalty states in any consistent ways?

International evidence has demonstrated that in nations where the governmental apparatus is highly rationalized and professionalized, use of the death penalty is less likely and abolition more likely. Conversely, low levels of state development are associated with death penalty retention and use. Across the United States there has always been considerable state-by-state variation in levels of governmental development and the rationalization of state agencies—with the Southern states being especially slow to professionalize government or develop formal-rational agencies to perform governmental functions.[39]

With respect to welfare, education, and social provision, the Southern states have tended to minimize expenditure, with the result that government agencies have been relatively less developed. The same is true with respect to law and criminal justice.[40] Long after the Northern states had developed penitentiaries and a professional, correctionalist approach to criminal justice, many Southern states refused to build prisons or develop correctional agencies, preferring to rely on convict lease systems that outsourced punishment to private employers.[41] The rehabilitative project that shaped criminal justice in the rest of the country—and which contributed to the decline of capital punishment—was never fully accepted in the South: "Southern chain gangs that built the roads and prison farms that cultivated cotton demonstrated little of the rehabilitative philosophy officially adopted elsewhere in the country."[42] A similar reluctance to raise taxes and build government—especially when expenditure would benefit the poor and minorities—resulted in a less developed legal bar and the absence of public defenders' systems in many of the states.[43] The South's comparative underdevelopment of government is also apparent in its expenditures on police and police training, which are substantially lower than in the rest of the country.[44]

Comparative studies of state variation in social welfare spending suggest that the underdevelopment of government in the South has persisted because many Southern states failed to form an effective multiparty democratic system. Single-party dominance, the absence of serious electoral competition, and the persistence of personalistic politics shaped by "friends and neighbors" localism have tended to exclude the poor and minorities from effective representation and have inhibited the development of institutions that benefit these groups. In the middle of the twentieth century, V. O. Keys demonstrated that the Southern states lagged behind the rest of the nation in the development of multiparty democracy and concluded that this disorganized, one-party politics was liable to disadvantage the "have nots." More recent studies have shown that this North/South differential persisted into the 1970s and beyond and has limited the local development of state welfare and policies that serve the poor.[45] Against this background of underdeveloped government power and the dominance of political elites less committed to addressing the problems of the poor, it is not surprising that the anti–death penalty movement has gained little traction.[46]

If democratic institutions and professional government are comparatively underdeveloped in the South, so too are the institutions of liberalism that curtailed capital punishment elsewhere. As Steiker observes, the American South was distinctive "in the strength and depth of its resistance to the civil rights movement of the 1950s and 1960s." This resistance to civil rights—largely driven by support for racial segregation—reinforced Southern opposition to liberal efforts to abolish the death penalty. As Steiker points out, in the 1960s, "death penalty abolition was being promoted by the very same institutional actors who had promoted the end of racial segregation in the South, and through the same means—federal constitutional imposition through litigation."[47]

In nations where the state has effectively pacified the population and secured a high level of social order, abolition is more likely. Conversely, high levels of interpersonal violence are associated with the retention of capital punishment. The evidence from the American states shows, quite clearly, that death penalty states generally have higher homicide rates. In particular, the South, where every state has the death penalty, is a high homicide region. In fact, with the brief exception of Florida in 2006, every Southern state consistently had murder rates above the national average.[48]

There are some exceptions to the general correlation between a state's high homicide rates and the presence of the death penalty: the abolitionist states of Michigan and Alaska, as well as Washington D.C., each have murder rates that are higher than the national average. But there are historical explanations for these unusual cases and the correlation is otherwise quite robust. As Leonard Beeghley shows, the South has consistently, throughout the twentieth century, had a higher homicide rate than the other regions, sometimes five or six times as high as the Northeast.[49]

Regions in which cultures of civility and humanism are well established are liable to abolish the death penalty. Conversely, regions where these sensibilities are limited are less likely to abolish it. Reliable evidence of cultural sentiment is difficult to obtain on a state-by-state or even a regional basis, especially if we avoid the question-begging device of inferring underlying sentiments from social practices. For example, one measure of the presence of ideas about civility and humanity might be the existence of anti–death penalty reform associations—which are fewer and less vocal in the South than elsewhere in the country. But the relative absence of such societies may indicate the specific lack of public support for abolition rather than the general absence of cultivated and humane sentiments. Similarly, there is evidence that death penalty states exhibit greater public support for capital punishment, but this could reflect policy preferences rather than cultural attitudes.[50]

One possible indicator of broad cultural attitudes in this region is, however, the position of the Southern Baptist Convention, which as recently as June 2000 "voted overwhelmingly in favor of a resolution affirming the use of capital punishment."[51] This position puts Southern Baptists at odds with most of the major Protestant denominations as well as with the Catholic Church.[52] And as America's largest denomination, with most of its members located in the South, the Southern Baptist Convention exerts a powerful cultural force for death penalty conservation. Generally, however, there is little solid evidence bearing on this question.

States with high levels of intergroup solidarity are more likely to abolish capital punishment. Conversely, states with high levels of intergroup hostilities and divisions are more likely to retain it. In an analysis comparing America's death penalty and abolitionist states, David Jacobs and Jason Carmichael produce a series of findings that lend support to this proposition. They find that death penalty laws are more likely in states that exhibit population instability, racial heterogeneity, and economic inequality, and they explain this finding by reference to communal solidarity and trust relations—or the lack thereof.[53] Their results show that "jurisdictions with the most residents born in state are less likely to have the death penalty," and that there is a correlation between the presence of high levels of economic inequality and the presence of death penalty laws. Most significantly, they find that "states with the largest black populations are more likely to retain capital punishment"—a correlation that persists even when controlling for rates of violent crime and other factors associated with the death penalty.[54]

The authors interpret their findings in terms of "communal solidarity," arguing that high migration rates and racial divisions disrupt interpersonal ties and create distrust between groups. Where hostility to strangers characterizes social relations to a greater extent than does solidarity between citizens, the death penalty becomes easier to impose. The link between the death penalty and racial hostilities is also given support in a 2003 study by Joe Soss which found that "white support for the death penalty in the United States has strong ties to anti-black prejudice."[55] Moreover, Lofquist observes that states in which social welfare provision is below average are more likely to have capital punishment: "Those states that are least generous in the provision of welfare—be it in the form of transfer payments to the poor, the provision of health care and education, or the taxation on which these and other services depend—are most committed to the death penalty."[56]

Variation among Death Penalty States

There is a great deal of variation *among* death penalty states with regard to capital punishment practice. Some states have the death penalty on the books but never impose death sentences; some impose death sentences but rarely execute them, and others execute offenders on a relatively frequent

basis.[57] These practices of *enactment, evocation,* and *execution* have been
described by other authors using different typologies. Steiker and Steiker
differentiate simply between "symbolic" and "executing" states, whereas
Culver presents a more elaborate fourfold typology of "non-users," "reluctant executioners," "occasional executioners," and "aggressive executioners"—a typology that is echoed in Lofquist's account of "non-users,"
"reluctant users," "users," and "enthusiastic users."[58]

In explaining this variation we must again consider the effect of change
over time. The regional differences separating the different types of death
penalty state are more distinct now than previously, with executions today
being more strongly concentrated in the South and above all in Texas.
Since 1976, the top-ten execution states have all been Southern ones, with
the exception of the border state of Missouri. By contrast, the top-ten execution states in most periods prior to *Furman* usually included California,
New York, and Ohio, with Pennsylvania not far behind.[59] And of course
the number of executions varies considerably from year to year, with very
few occurring in the late 1970s, rather more in the 1980s, a build-up to a
high of 98 per year in the late 1990s, and a steady decline in the annual
numbers since then.

Trends in the number of annual executions have been influenced by a
changing legal environment—the super due process restrictions between
1976 and 1983, the relaxation of procedural requirements after that, the
de facto moratorium pending legal challenges to the lethal injection in
2007, and so on—as well as by changes in the political environment and
public opinion.[60] But after the first few years of the post-*Furman* period,
when there was a tiny number of executions, the distribution of executions
across the states has been fairly stable, with the Southern states accounting
for about 80 percent of them and Texas consistently being the leading execution state.

Some of the variation in capital punishment practice between death penalty states can be explained by the same factors that explain the distinction
between death penalty and abolitionist states. We would expect, for example, that states exhibiting more evidence of underdeveloped government,
high homicide rates, large black minorities, and hostile group relations
would be likely to execute offenders more frequently than states that exhibit less. The research literature appears to bear this out.

According to Jacobs and Carmichael, the likelihood of death *sentences*
(as opposed to death penalty *statutes*) is greater where there are high rates
of violent crime, large numbers of fundamentalists, and political conservatism.[61] Keith Harries and Derral Cheatwood note, "States with historically
high rates of execution have generally been those with high rates of homi-

Death penalty states, by number of executions and death row inmates

Frequency of use	State	Executions since 1976	Death row populations
Low	Colorado	1	3
	Connecticut	1	10
	Idaho	1	18
	Kansas	0	10
	New Hampshire	0	1
	South Dakota	1	3
	Wyoming	1	1
	U.S. military	0	8
Medium	California	13	690
	Illinois	12	15
	Indiana	20	17
	Kentucky	3	36
	Maryland	5	5
	Mississippi	10	60
	Montana	3	2
	Nebraska	3	11
	Nevada	12	78
	Ohio	34	176
	Oregon	2	33
	Pennsylvania	3	225
	Tennessee	6	92
	Utah	6	10
	Washington	4	9
	U.S. government	3	58
High	Alabama	44	200
	Arizona	23	29
	Arkansas	27	43
	Delaware	14	19
	Florida	68	403
	Georgia	46	108
	Louisiana	28	84
	Missouri	67	52
	North Carolina	43	169
	Oklahoma	91	86
	South Carolina	42	63
	Texas	449	342
	Virginia	105	16

Source: Death Penalty Information Center.

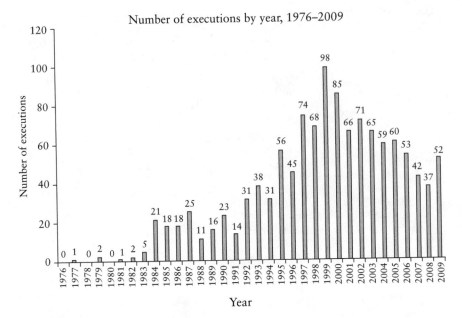

Number of executions by year, 1976–2009

Source: Death Penalty Information Center.

cide."[62] Similarly, Lofquist points to research that finds correlations between execution rates, "levels of racial threat," and "rates of white murder victimization," as well as to the steepness of "social hierarchies." Lofquist also notes that "one-party domination of the legislature and lower levels of African-Americans and women in the legislature" contribute to the ease with which executions proceed.[63]

As we would expect, then, the factors that differentiate death penalty states from abolitionist states also tend to differentiate high-execution states from death penalty states that rarely execute. But there are some further factors that determine whether capital statutes will or will not lead to death sentences and executions: factors that have to do with legal process variables and the different relationships between the branches of government in different states. These variables are important in their own right because the process of converting a death sentence into an execution is a complex one that involves a series of legal procedures and governmental decisions. Even where the political and social relations of the state press for the enactment and imposition of death penalties, the postconviction process can provide a number of opportunities to block their execution. Research on these legal variables is less quantitative and less reliable than the social science studies, but it provides some valuable insights nevertheless.

Let us start with legal process variables. Evidence exists that the presence of a strong, well-organized, and well-resourced defense bar in a state reduces the likelihood of executions taking place. California, Pennsylvania, New York, and New Jersey are, or were until very recently, death penalty states, but each of these states has a powerful capital defense bar that has been able to prevent death sentences from being translated into executions. It also seems likely that the expertise and activism of the Equal Justice Initiative in Montgomery and of the Southern Center for Human Rights in Atlanta have reduced the numbers of executions taking place in Alabama and Georgia respectively.

Carol and Jordan Steiker develop this point when they argue that states where a "due process culture" is well established tend to have fewer executions than those where it is not. In California, for example (which they classify as a "symbolic state" because relatively few death sentences are converted into executions), capital defense services are more likely to be well funded, "state appellate and post-conviction review of capital convictions is more likely to be intensive and demanding, federal habeas review of capital convictions is more likely to be intensive and demanding, and the appellate and post-conviction process is more likely to be drawn out." In "executing states," by contrast, the whole legal process is likely to be "nasty, brutish, and short." In states such as Texas, "counsel are less likely to file substantial briefs" and "reviewing courts are less likely to hold hearings," with the result that "the entire process moves much more quickly, often expedited by the early setting of execution dates." That due process cultures are less well developed in the South than elsewhere is consistent with the region's underdeveloped government and minimal social services. But, as the Steikers point out, it also reflects the historic resistance of Southern states to federal attempts to reform their criminal procedure: "It is no accident that so many of the executing states are concentrated in the South, as that region has a history of incomplete conversion to a due process culture of criminal adjudication."[64]

The other variable affecting capital punishment practice—and especially the conversion of death sentences into actual executions—is the level of conflict or agreement between the different decision-makers within state government. In New Jersey and New York, post-*Gregg* capital statutes were enacted only after a long period of conflict between the branches of government. Once enacted, the new statutes were enforced only sporadically owing to objections on the part of certain district attorneys—the Manhattan D.A., Robert Morgenthau, never brought a single capital indictment in the ten years the New York capital statute was in force. In the few cases where death sentences were imposed, the New York state's appellate courts—using a variety of safeguards and tests—effectively blocked each capital case, preventing every death sentence from being executed, until eventually the state abandoned its capital punishment efforts.[65] As Culver observes, "A governor can veto death penalty legislation favored by a majority of lawmakers, legislators can pass convoluted, difficult to implement death penalty statutes to mollify the governor and/or the public ... and the judiciary can strike down capital punishment legislation."[66] As a result, both New York and New Jersey had death penalty statutes for decades without being able to convert a single sentence into an execution.

The story in these two states is characteristic of death penalty states in the North and Northeast. It is also characteristic of states that are Democratic in political orientation. In the period since 1976, death penalty laws have been enacted in Democratic as well as Republican states, but the great majority of executions occur in states with a Republican leadership. Steiker and Steiker suggest an explanation for this when they note "the potentially higher costs and predictably lower benefits of proceeding with executions in blue states." In Democratic-dominated "blue" states, a preference for the death penalty on the part of state-wide public opinion is often combined with powerful "pockets of death penalty opposition" in certain parts of the state and in higher echelons of state government. The former can lead to the enactment of capital statutes, while the latter exerts powerful pressures to prevent these statutes from being fully enforced. Capital statutes are therefore easier (and more rewarding) for politicians to *enact* than to *execute*.[67] In predominantly Democratic states such as New York, New Jersey, and California—where death penalty skeptics and liberal Democrats are well represented in the legislatures, the bar, and the state courts—extensive legal safeguards and funding for capital defense have often been the *quid pro quo* that permitted death penalty legislation to be enacted.[68] These same safeguards then ensure that few capital cases are ever carried through to execution.

In contrast, in states such as Texas, Virginia, and Missouri, all the branches of government share a pro–capital punishment orientation, making the process of executing sentences much less conflictual. As Liptak observes of Texas, once a death sentence is imposed, "prosecutors, state and federal courts, the parole board and the governor are united in moving the process along."[69]

Ironically, the same separation of powers and multiple veto points that make it difficult to *abolish* the death penalty also make it difficult to *carry through* an execution. Only where there is political consensus on the issue, involving all the key actors and decision-makers, will capital statutes be unobstructed within a state. And even then, the federal courts can slow the process down.

THE standard forces of death penalty transformation—state formation and rationalization, liberalization and democratization, cultural refinement and humanitarian sensibilities—were operative in the United States just as they were elsewhere. But their impact in America was different, in certain respects, because of identifiable features of the American social field. The interaction between the general transformative processes and the peculiar features of the American landscape produced different outcomes at different times and in different parts of the country.

History matters. Aspects of the historical past are reproduced in the present. Constitutional rules, sectional divisions, and class and race relations give rise to institutional structures and power balances that persist over time. The effects of path dependency carry the past into the present and give history continuing force. But America is a dynamic social order, driven by capitalism, democracy, mobility, and migration. Power balances shift. Institutions adapt. Structures are modified and symbols change their meanings. In the end, contemporary events are determined by present-day processes and struggles, and it is on these that our explanatory account must ultimately rest.

EIGHT

An American Abolition

In striking down capital punishment . . . we achieve a major milestone in the long road up from barbarism.

JUSTICE THURGOOD MARSHALL, *FURMAN V GEORGIA*, 1972

D uring the last decades of the twentieth century, the Western nations
collectively and definitively abolished capital punishment. At precisely the same historical moment, America reinvented it. These two developments run in opposite directions, but in one respect they are intimately
linked: the processes that produced abolition throughout the liberal democratic world set the terms on which the new American institution would be
remade. To survive in an age of abolition America's death penalty has had
to adapt. In the period since 1972, the American capital punishment system has had to conform itself to a more demanding rule of law and to
"evolving standards of decency." This adaptation reformed the institution
from end to end, producing major changes to its legal forms, social functions, and cultural meanings.

At the heart of this process was a court-centered project of reinvention.
This began in the 1960s as a radical, abolitionist project led by a few reforming justices and a branch of the civil rights movement. It culminated
in the case of *Furman v Georgia* in 1972, when a majority of the Supreme
Court declared the nation's death penalty statutes unconstitutional as then
administered. Following the 1976 case of *Gregg v Georgia*—in which the
Court effectively reinstated capital punishment—this reinvention project
became a less radical undertaking. In effect, the Court sought to uphold
the states' right to impose capital punishment while simultaneously seek-

ing to rationalize and civilize its administration and distance it from the racial lynchings with which it had been associated.

A close study of this process reveals a great deal about the Court and about the American polity. It shows how the characteristic dynamics of Western reform—state rationalization and elite-driven change—came to operate in the American context. It demonstrates how the Court has variously functioned as a legal tribunal, a cultural elite, and an American political institution, struggling to undertake the reform work that other nations allocate to the political process. And it exhibits, in the Court's interaction with litigators, with state legislatures, and with the American public, the characteristic way in which America's governing institutions seek to manage contradictions and forge practical compromises, often leaving substantive issues unresolved in the process.[1]

When first presented with constitutional challenges to capital punishment, the Court could have ruled decisively in favor of national abolition and brought America into line with other Western democracies. Alternatively, it could have declined to become involved, leaving the death penalty in the control of the states and permitting each state legislature to retain or abolish as it saw fit. But rather than resolve the matter in one direction or the other, the Court has sought to regulate and reform the practice, developing a new Eighth and Fourteenth Amendment jurisprudence in the process. The result is that the Court has taken ownership of the issue, putting itself and the federal courts at the very heart of a vexed and ongoing conflict.[2]

The Political Background

In the second half of the twentieth century, Western countries experienced a grating conflict between the practice of capital punishment and the values of liberalism and humanitarianism. The conflict was heightened in these increasingly stable, affluent nations as liberalism and democracy expanded, class and racial inequalities lessened, government policy became more welfarist, and penal policy moved away from retributive rationales. In the United States, these underlying tensions were exacerbated by the shadow of racism. The American death penalty had long been associated with lynching or "legal lynching" and with discrimination against black people, especially in Southern states. Many Americans thought of it as a racially biased institution. In the aftermath of the Nazi Holocaust Western nations came to regard racism as a profound violation of human rights that had no place in a civilized society. Liberal opinion in the United States developed a similar antipathy, though it was not until the 1960s that the civil rights movement successfully challenged the openly racist institutions of the Jim Crow South and the more covert racism characterizing the rest of the country.[3] Residual patterns of discrimination continue in many parts of America today, but since the civil rights victories of the mid-1960s, racism has been subject to generalized and increasingly vigorous prohibition.

Most Americans now regard racism as disreputable. Wherever racist attitudes and behaviors continue to exist, therefore, they do so covertly and transgressively, risking social sanction if exposed. But precisely because the prohibition on racism is now taken for granted, it is important to realize just how recently this shift in social norms occurred, especially in the Southern states, where racism was openly and officially embraced until the 1960s. When *Brown v Board of Education* invalidated the "separate but equal" doctrine in 1954, the Court's decision met with widespread opposition, including in the U.S. Congress, where nearly every Southern state representative signed a "Manifesto" pledging "massive resistance" to the dismantling of school segregation. And when, a decade later, Governor George Wallace of Alabama stood in a schoolhouse doorway pledging "segregation forever," he could rely on a sizeable constituency of Southern whites who "thrilled to his message."[4]

In this racially charged context the National Association for the Advancement of Colored People's Legal Defense Fund launched its historic challenge to the death penalty, a challenge backed by the broad tide of Western history but facing powerful resistance from hostile groups and obstructive institutions. Behind the legal arguments and technical questions of constitutional interpretation, these were the real obstacles that the campaign would have to overcome.

The United States Supreme Court began its abolitionist project in 1963, when Justice Arthur Goldberg floated the idea that the death penalty might be open to constitutional challenge. It reached the high point of that venture a decade later, when its *Furman* decision invalidated all existing capital statutes on a variety of procedural grounds. In 1976, the Court that decided *Gregg v Georgia* turned decisively away from the abolitionist path, signaling that capital punishment would be lawful so long as states observed various procedural proprieties, the nature of which would be determined by a series of decisions in the following years. In 1983, the Court's direction shifted once more as it began to increase the procedural obstacles to be surmounted by the death row inmate; expedite post-conviction processes; and stress the importance of federalism, finality, and the need to execute sentences in a timely manner. That same decade saw the Court close the door on systemic challenges to the death penalty, most notably in the *McCleskey v Kemp* case of 1987, where it refused to invalidate Warren McCleskey's sentence despite evidence of racial discrimination in the allocation of death sentences by the state of Georgia. In the first decade of the twenty-first century, the Court sometimes resumed its reforming role, as when it prohibited the execution of the mentally retarded, of juvenile offenders, and of nonlethal rapists.[5] But a majority of the current justices clearly view the death penalty's constitutional validity as being beyond doubt.

The timing of these legal developments was not accidental. The Court's changing death penalty jurisprudence—most notably the shift from the radical *Furman* project to the more conservative aims of *Gregg*—was shaped by the broader politics of the time. In the 1960s, it was the politics of civil rights reform. In the 1970s, it was the politics of civil rights backlash.[6] In the 1980s and 1990s, the defining context was the politics of law and order. In the first decade of the twenty-first century, a new context was formed by declining homicide rates and growing public concerns about a "broken system" that is costly, unreliable, and prone to convict the innocent.[7]

These legal and political developments were played out on a distinctively American landscape marked by racial, regional, and cultural conflicts with roots reaching back to the Civil War, slavery, and before. And it is within these terms that the history of America's death penalty is usually narrated. But if we step back from the immediacies of these events and think comparatively about the broader sociological conditions that underpinned them, we notice that the Court's decisions—and the developments leading up to them—occurred within a familiar reformist context. In the United States, as elsewhere in the Western world, death penalty reform occurred in a context defined by processes of state building and state rationalization; by a politics of liberalization and democratization; by a culture of civilization and humanitarianism; and by concomitant shifts in group relations and levels of violence.

The decline and eventual abolition of capital punishment in the West were consequences of large-scale changes that reconstituted governmental power in ways that made death penalties less necessary and more problematic. In the second half of the twentieth century, similar processes transformed the character of the American state and the political and cultural context in which America's capital punishment operated. The New Deal and the Second World War greatly expanded the powers of America's central state, and the long postwar period of economic growth served to increase state revenues and facilitate the expansion of regulatory agencies, social programs, and administrative capacity. During the same period, economic transformations in the South, the emergent civil rights movement, and the politics of the Cold War all worked to weaken the hold of white supremacists and the Southern Democrats who sustained them.[8] These same social changes emboldened the Warren Court to pursue a reform agenda that expanded civil rights and imposed requirements of legality on local governments and police forces that had previously been a law unto themselves.

These state-building developments greatly expanded the power of America's national government *vis-à-vis* the states. By the mid-1960s, following the ending of the federal government's support for racial segregation, that power was being used to promote racial justice, social welfare, and full citizenship for African Americans.[9] The result was that the rule of law and national standards increasingly displaced the personalistic power of local authorities. This in turn increased the probability that the constitutional rights of individuals would be respected, including those of unpopular minorities in regions that had traditionally paid scant regard to the niceties of legal process wherever blacks were concerned.

Once it took the side of civil rights, the federal government became a powerful force for reform, enacting the Civil Rights and Voting Rights Acts, pressing for an end to segregation laws, curbing police malpractice, enforcing voting rights, and extending federal regulations well beyond their traditional limits. President Johnson's Great Society programs—Medicaid, urban reform, economic opportunity, transportation, and education reform—pushed to expand welfare, eliminate poverty, and build a more inclusive form of solidarity that would overcome historic divisions and racial hostilities.[10] This spurt of state building and rationalization expanded the reach of the new administrative state and produced important shifts in the balance of power—away from states toward federal government; away from police toward individual suspects; away from state prosecutors toward individual defendants; and away from the white majority toward African Americans.

This enhancement of the center's power came at the expense of the periphery. In extending new rights and entitlements to individual citizens, the federal government challenged local traditions and power relations, reducing the freedom of local states and counties to regulate the lives of their populations as they saw fit. This shift in the balance of power had ramifications throughout the social structure. Even the fate of the least individual—the condemned man on death row—was transformed. From now on, poor black men convicted of murder, despised by local communities and inadequately served by legal counsel, would be a matter of some concern to the federal government, to the federal law, and to the social forces supporting them.

These political circumstances, together with the rise of reform-oriented criminal justice and a long-term decline in homicide rates, made the early 1960s a propitious moment for the abolitionist movement.[11] News events and policy developments of the period largely reinforced this sense of possibility. Efforts to expand civil rights, integrate excluded groups, and raise up the poor created a liberal social climate in which criticisms of capital punishment resonated. At the same time, the forces that had traditionally propelled the death penalty—group hostilities, high homicide rates, faith in the deterrent effects of harsh punishment—were becoming less salient. Led by Chief Justice Earl Warren, the Supreme Court had since the 1950s been operating as an engine of liberal reform. President Johnson's landslide election victory in 1964 ensured that the other national institutions— the White House, the Congress, the Department of Justice—also moved in a more liberal direction. This leftward shift in American politics was echoed in Gallup Poll surveys that reported a marked drop in enthusiasm for the death penalty, with the number in favor decreasing by 26 percent between 1953 and 1966. In 1966, for the first time since polling began, more Americans were against the institution than for it.[12]

These shifts in public opinion were encouraged by a series of high-profile capital cases: Julius and Ethel Rosenberg, who were executed in 1953 for conspiring to pass information about the atom bomb to the Soviet Union; Barbara Graham, who was executed in 1955 for the murder of an elderly widow, despite doubts about her guilt; Caryl Chessman, convicted of multiple counts of robbery, kidnapping, and rape, whose case attracted worldwide attention; and Perry Smith and Dick Hickok, executed in 1965 for the murder of a Kansas farmer and his family, made famous by Truman Capote's book *In Cold Blood*. In each case, these defendants— some of them middle class, some female, all of them white—were executed amid intense publicity and widespread appeals for clemency. But the most important contributor to this changing climate of opinion was the growing consensus among liberal elites that the death penalty was unnecessary and unacceptable. By the early 1960s, this abolitionist viewpoint had become dominant within criminal justice, within the churches, and within the institutions of national government.[13]

Criminologists and penologists declared themselves against capital punishment, describing it as inimical to the reformative approach of modern penology. They backed their criticisms with empirical evidence casting doubt on its deterrent effect and showing that death penalty states were no more successful in preventing murders than were comparable abolitionist states.[14] In 1961, Donal E. J. MacNamara, president of the American Society of Criminology and dean of the New York Institute of Criminology, encapsulated the dominant criminological viewpoint in a ten-point critique that described capital punishment as "criminologically unsound . . . morally and ethically unacceptable . . . prejudicially and inconsistently applied . . . more costly than its alternatives . . . [and a barrier] in the way of penal reform."[15] That MacNamara had personally participated in several executions made his opinion all the more persuasive.

To these practical objections, America's churches added a more fundamental moral critique. The Methodist and Lutheran churches, each with millions of members, issued statements criticizing capital punishment, as did the American Baptist Convention, the Episcopal Church, and the United Presbyterian Church. Some smaller religious groups—the Quakers, the Mennonites, and the Union of American Hebrew Congregations—actively campaigned for abolition.[16] In 1968, the nation's largest ecumenical organization, the National Council of Churches, issued a joint statement calling for abolition, citing a belief in "the worth of human life and the dignity of the human personality as gifts of God."[17]

By the early 1960s, prominent figures in national politics were openly taking abolitionist positions and doing so without apparent political cost. Hubert Humphrey opposed the death penalty in 1960 when he sought the Democratic presidential nomination, as did Pat Brown in 1962 when he ran for governor of California. Humphrey lost and Brown won, but their stance on capital punishment did not appear to be a major factor in either outcome. In 1965, the U.S. Department of Justice issued a call for abolition, and three years later, Attorney General Ramsey Clark, on behalf of the Johnson administration, formally proposed to Congress that it abolish capital punishment.[18] In January 1971, President Johnson's Committee on the Reform of the Federal Laws reported that the federal death penalty ought to be abolished. Later that year, the judiciary committee of the Democrat-controlled House held hearings on a bill (of questionable constitutional validity) that would impose a nationwide moratorium on executions pending litigation on the question.[19]

By the spring of 1965, when Congress passed the Voting Rights Act—a high point of liberalism's ascendancy in the United States, immediately before the Newark riots and the political shift that they would herald—twenty state legislatures were considering abolitionist bills. Oregon repealed its death penalty law in 1964 following a referendum in which 60 percent voted for abolition. The next year, four other states would repeal their capital statutes—New York (which had been a leading execution state for most of the twentieth century), Iowa, Vermont, and West Virginia—making the total for 1965 the largest number of abolitions ever carried out in any year of American history.[20]

As this reform tide rose, America's capital punishment machinery slowly ground to a halt. From the 1940s onward, juries had been returning fewer and fewer death sentences, and execution chambers had been used less and less. The twentieth century's peak year for executions had been 1935, with 199 offenders put to death. Thereafter execution figures fell continuously, with each decade recording fewer executions than the one before. Of those death sentences that were imposed, more of them than ever before were being reviewed by the federal courts, a process that slowed the throughput of cases and created a growing population on death row.[21] In March 1960, *Time* magazine published an article under the headline, "Capital Punishment: A Fading Practice." By 1967, executions across the country had ceased altogether, the result of diminished enthusiasm on the part of juries and the legal uncertainty generated by abolitionist litigation.[22]

In important respects, this American scene looked remarkably similar to that of other Western nations. America in the 1960s stood on the verge of abolishing capital punishment, as did Britain, Ireland, Canada, Australia, New Zealand, and most of continental Europe. Its liberal elites were convinced that the institution was practically unnecessary and morally intolerable. Its legal system was introducing more and more obstacles to the process. And its political class was signaling that the institution's end was in sight. Given the peculiar structure of the American polity, the final-stage reform process in the United States would—if it were to be nationwide—have to take the form of constitutional litigation and judicial abolition rather than parliamentary legislation. If the institutional mechanisms differed, however, the underlying reform processes—state rationalization, liberalism and democracy, evolving elite sentiment—looked much the same.

But the mechanisms mattered. Unlike the absolute act of a powerful sovereign legislature, litigation is an instrument of change that takes time and generates resistance. As a means of reform it can retain a radical edge, but it suffers from a deficit of democratic authority and the legitimacy problems that entails. Above all, reform litigation invites challenge by further litigation, just as judicial abolition can be countered by competing political power—which, in the event, is exactly what would happen.[23]

The battle against capital punishment had historically been a political one, waged by local activists in state legislatures. But in 1965, after more than a century of campaigning, and at the height of the liberal ascendancy, the abolitionists could claim victory in only thirteen of the fifty states, none of them in the South.[24] Many state legislatures had repealed capital punishment only to re-enact it later under pressure of new events. In the face of this impasse, American liberals turned to the federal government to impose reforms that the states refused to adopt for themselves.

Such a move was hardly novel. The New Deal had shown how national government could rationalize state practices, overcome the personalistic power of local elites, and be a potent force for social justice.[25] More recently, the civil rights movement had discovered that, when the Congress and the executive branch were reluctant or unable to initiate reform, that other organ of national power—the Supreme Court—might be enlisted to do so, with transformative results.

With respect to death penalty politics, moreover, the federal courts held considerable appeal.[26] Because the Constitution allocated penal power to the states, neither the Congress nor the president had the capacity to prohibit state executions, short of a constitutional amendment—a proposition with no realistic hope of success even in the liberal 1960s. But the Supreme Court had the power to impose nationwide abolition at a stroke, if only it could be persuaded to find capital punishment unconstitutional. Such a prospect was encouraged by the fact that the Warren Court had been pushing ahead on civil rights and criminal procedure reform well in advance of the legislature and had developed expansive interpretations of the Constitution's implications for liberty and equality.

More to the point, the Supreme Court *invited* a litigation challenge. In cases such as *Fay v Noia* (1963)—where the Court granted a *habeas corpus* hearing to a New York state prisoner though his late appeal had already been ruled inadmissible by a New York court applying New York law—it had been creating law that made it easier for litigants to challenge state practices. And in 1963, Justice Arthur Goldberg, joined by Justices William Brennan and William Douglas, took the unusual step of publishing a dissent from the Court's refusal to hear the case of *Rudolph v Alabama,* in which a black defendant wished to challenge a death sentence imposed for the rape of a white woman.[27]

When Justice Goldberg issued his dissent in *Rudolph* he was signaling to the civil rights community that a constitutional challenge to capital punishment would find support on the Court. In doing so, he displeased Chief Justice Warren, who saw little likelihood that the Constitution could reasonably yield such an interpretation and every likelihood that a Court-imposed abolition would set off a barrage of political opposition. Despite the chief's objections, Goldberg's initiative was in keeping with the Warren Court's established pattern of intervening in state criminal justice processes to remedy rights violations and arbitrary uses of power. For much of its earlier history, the Supreme Court had refused to challenge state criminal decisions, preferring to construe the Fourteenth Amendment's due pro-

cess clause narrowly and to deny the applicability of the Fifth and Eighth
Amendments to the states. But from the 1920s onward, the Court had intervened in a series of Southern cases in which violence and intimidation
had produced death sentences that it regarded as a travesty of justice.[28]

In *Moore v Dempsey* (1923) the Court vacated the convictions of six
black men who had been sentenced to death following a race riot in Arkansas, finding that their due process rights had been violated by tortured
confessions and a mob-dominated trial.[29] In *Powell v Alabama* (1932) and
Norris v Alabama (1935), the Court overturned the death sentences of several black youths—popularly known as the Scottsboro Boys—convicted of
raping two white women, following a trial conducted amid mob violence
and intimidation. (In *Powell* the Court determined that the defendants
had been denied their Fourteenth Amendment right to counsel, and the
Norris convictions were reversed because black jurors had been illegally
excluded.) In *Brown v Mississippi* (1936) the Court reversed the death sentences of three black sharecroppers found guilty of murdering their white
landlord because the verdicts had been reached on the basis of confessions obtained by torture. As the deputy sheriff testified in court, he had
whipped the defendants and strung one of them up in a tree in order to obtain their statements of guilt. And in *Patton v Mississippi* (1947) the Court
overturned the capital conviction of a black petitioner who had been tried
by an all-white jury in a county where one-third of the residents were
black.[30]

All these cases shared one thing in common, as Michael Klarman points
out: they "revealed Jim Crow at its worst." In each one, "[i]mpoverished,
illiterate, black defendants, probably or certainly innocent of the charges
made against them, were railroaded to the death penalty in egregiously un-
fair trials." Each case was, in effect, a legal lynching—a hasty *pro forma*
proceeding, before an all-white Southern jury, utterly contemptuous of
the defendants' rights, where the verdict was never in question and the
sentence was designed to appease an angry, murderous mob. As Klarman notes, "Of the relatively few defendants who were acquitted in mob-
dominated trials, several were shot dead before they could leave the courthouse."[31]

The Court may have been reluctant to trespass on the jurisdiction of the
states. And it may have been inhibited from doing so by its previous interpretations of the relationship between federal constitutional rights and
state criminal procedure. But these Southern cases were an affront to the
Court's core values and to the credibility of American justice. In much the
same way that the public torture lynchings of the 1890s mobilized political
opposition and prompted the formation of the National Association for

the Advancement of Colored People (NAACP), these later "legal lynchings" outraged the nation's legal elites and provided opportunities for reinterpreting what the Constitution required. Mob lynchings that passed themselves off as legal trials were a violent sham and a disgrace to the American nation. But they were also a stinging insult to American law that, if left unanswered, threatened to bring the whole legal system into disrepute. Faced with this challenge to its reputation and integrity, the Supreme Court had little choice but to intervene.[32]

In its criminal procedure decisions of the 1960s—*Mapp v Ohio* (1961), *Brady v Maryland* (1963), *Gideon v Wainwright* (1963), *Miranda v Arizona* (1966), and *Terry v Ohio* (1968)—the Warren Court built on this legacy, intervening in capital and noncapital cases alike to provide new legal protections, such as informing suspects that they need not answer police questions without an attorney present, or excluding illegally obtained evidence.[33] In doing so, the Court created new laws curbing state powers and protecting individual liberty. But there was nothing in these Warren Court cases, nor in the earlier "legal lynching" cases, that directly challenged the death penalty *per se*.[34] Rather than raising questions about the punishment of death, the Court's concern was with the legal processes through which death was imposed. These were Fourteenth Amendment cases about procedure, not substance, about legal values, not moral ones. And in every previous case where the Court might have questioned capital punishment's constitutionality—in *Kemmler* (1889), where litigants challenged the legality of New York's new electric chair, or *Francis v Resweber* (1947), where Willie Francis appealed against a second electrocution after the first attempt failed—the Court had not raised any doubt that the penalty was lawful when carried out in a fair and civilized manner.[35]

In a separate series of Eighth Amendment cases, however, the Court developed a line of reasoning that would later prove crucial for the abolitionist challenge. In *Weems v United States* (1910), in which a federal employee was sentenced to fifteen years hard labor for falsifying a document, the Court established a proportionality test whereby certain punishments could be ruled unconstitutional if they were "cruelly disproportionate" to the offense in question. In *Trop v Dulles* (1958), where a U.S. soldier was denationalized as a penalty for deserting his post, Chief Justice Warren declared that the Eighth Amendment ought not to be understood as implying a fixed standard but must instead "draw its meaning from the evolving standards of decency that mark the progress of a maturing society." These two cases involved claims against the federal government, but in *Robinson v California* (1962) the Court held that it was also proper to apply the Eighth Amendment to the states, by way of the Fourteenth Amendment.[36]

So when Justice Goldberg raised doubts about the constitutionality of capital punishment in 1963, citing the "evolving standards" doctrine as his authority, the Court had already opened up the doctrinal and procedural paths down which this challenge might proceed.[37] The scene was now set for litigators to challenge the institution head on.

By 1963 the Court had developed a Fourteenth Amendment jurisprudence that invalidated "legal lynchings" and had established a set of precedents that used "proportionality" and "evolving standards" to test whether specific punishments were cruel and unusual under the Eighth Amendment. The case of *Rudolph v Alabama*—a *habeas* petition on behalf of Frank Lee Rudolph, a black man who claimed that his conviction for the capital rape of a white woman was based on a forced confession—brought these two developments together in a single case.

Earlier that year, Justice Goldberg, together with his clerk Alan Dershowitz, had written a memo setting forth the idea that capital punishment might be unconstitutional, at least in regard to nonlethal rape. The memo pointed to the Court's role "in articulating and establishing progressively civilized standards of behavior" and argued that capital rape might be unconstitutional on proportionality grounds. The memo also noted that the abolition of capital rape would "eliminate the well-recognized disparity in the imposition of the death penalty for sexual crimes committed by whites and non-whites."[38] The chief justice insisted that Goldberg's memo remain unpublished, but it was soon being circulated in civil rights circles.

When *Rudolph* was refused *certiorari* by a majority of the justices, Goldberg, together with Brennan and Douglas, made the unusual move of issuing a published dissent. Unlike the earlier memo, the dissent made no mention of the racial dimension of such cases. It was also silent on the "legal lynching" that Frank Lee Rudolph was alleged to have endured. Instead it simply argued that the death penalty was an unduly severe penalty for a nonlethal rape—a lack of proportion rendering it "cruel and unusual" and thus unconstitutional under the Eighth Amendment. That capital rape was everywhere disappearing—the dissenters noted that thirty-three American states had already abolished it, and only five of the world's nations retained it—added comparative weight to this claim.

Goldberg's dissent had the desired effect. Within a few months, a litigation campaign had been launched that would eventually challenge the constitutional foundations of American capital punishment. But it also set a pattern. In his public pronouncement Goldberg drew back from entering the treacherous currents of racial politics, preferring to characterize the issue in more neutral terms that might be less provocative to Southern audiences and so command wider support. In the struggles that raged throughout the 1960s and 1970s, explicit discussion of racial violence, racial discrimination, and racial lynching would be systematically suppressed in most legal proceedings. The specter of lynching would stay in the background, casting its shadow over legal discourse and decisions while the lawyers and judges took care to appear concerned with other things.

The Legal Challenge

The litigation campaign against capital punishment was spearheaded by the Legal Defense Fund (LDF) and its expert team of civil rights lawyers.[39] The LDF had originally been the legal department of the NAACP, an organization founded in 1909 for the promotion of civil rights and racial justice.[40] The NAACP aimed to challenge the disfranchisement of blacks and end racial violence in the South, and it pursued these aims by means of federal litigation as well as publicity campaigns and political mobilization.[41] As it pushed to end racial segregation in the postwar years, constitutional litigation moved to the center of its efforts. Following its victory in *Brown v Board of Education,* the NAACP—together with the Southern Christian Leadership Conference and the Student Non-Violent Coordinating Committee—went on to orchestrate a nationwide political campaign culminating in the civil rights legislation of the 1960s and the official abolition of Jim Crow.

Throughout the 1940s and 1950s, the LDF had mostly litigated segregation and voting rights issues, though it had occasionally taken on capital cases such as *Chambers v Florida* (1940) and *Patton v Mississippi* (1947), where racial issues were prominent. But it was a civil rights firm, not an anti–death penalty organization, and some LDF staffers were reluctant to become embroiled in capital punishment reform.[42] What convinced the organization to take up Justice Goldberg's challenge was the historic association of lynching with the American death penalty and the continuing role of race in determining which offenders lived and which died. "The charge of racism in the administration of the death penalty" was, as Robert Burt has noted, "often the text and always the subtext" of the LDF campaign.[43]

This antilynching orientation was apparent in the early phase of the campaign, when the LDF took on Southern rape cases, for instance, *Maxwell v Bishop,* in which black men were sentenced to death for the rape of white women. Such cases were part of an egregiously racist pattern in which the charge of capital rape was reserved for blacks. Indeed, in the one hundred years following the Civil War, "every single execution for a non-lethal crime in Mississippi—thirty three for rape and eight for armed robbery—involved an African American defendant and a white victim."[44] Outside the South, rape was no longer a capital offense, and the decision-making of Southern juries made it plain that they regarded inter-racial sexual assaults as especially atrocious and infuriating. The echoes of the classic lynching scene were unmistakable.

As the LDF's campaign developed, it broadened to challenge the death penalty in all its aspects—partly to serve its clients' interests, partly because the courts were proving unsympathetic to showings of racial bias, and partly because the lawyers came to regard capital punishment as an affront to civil rights that was inherently biased against unpopular minorities and the poor.[45]

The LDF campaign was a fateful development in American death penalty reform. The remarkable results that it would achieve—above all the *Furman* decision and a nationwide cessation of executions lasting from 1967 to 1977—meant that from this point on, and for a generation or more, the antigallows struggle would be predominantly a legal one. It would be led by lawyers. Its reform mode would be litigation, and its dominant meaning would be prodefendant, problack, civil rights reform. The moral, religious, and political arguments that had long been the staple of antigallows activism would now be displaced by constitutional claims, procedural arguments, and technical disputes about what the law required. It would remain that way for thirty years. And although the fruits of these litigation efforts were considerable, the "great displacement" that moved death from the political and moral arena to the constitutional realm would in subsequent decades come to have the effect of entrenching the institution rather than ending it.[46]

Once they decided to broaden their approach and mount a comprehensive attack on the death penalty, the LDF leaders formulated a strategy intended to maximize pressure on the Supreme Court. The "moratorium strategy," as it was known, involved litigating in all the nation's death penalty jurisdictions with the aim of producing a nationwide suspension of executions pending a decision by the Supreme Court. Lacking the resources to conduct its own litigation in every state, the LDF provided defense lawyers around the country with detailed drafts of legal arguments challenging the death penalty on multiple grounds, including racial bias, standardless jury sentencing, single-verdict procedures, and the exclusion of scrupled jurors. "The politics of abolition boiled down to this," one LDF lawyer would later write, "for each year the United States went without an execution, the more hollow would ring claims that the American people could not do without them; the longer death-row inmates waited, the greater their numbers, the more difficult it would be for the courts to permit the first execution."[47] Such were its results that by the time the Court decided to resolve the matter in *Furman,* five years had passed with no executions, and approximately 600 prisoners sat on the nation's death rows, awaiting the Court's decision.[48]

In their cases before the Supreme Court, the LDF lawyers developed a series of arguments attacking death penalty practices under the Eighth and the Fourteenth Amendments.[49] Building on the doctrinal possibilities offered by *Weems* and *Trop* they presented empirical evidence supporting the proposition that "evolving standards of decency" had rendered the death penalty cruel and unusual in contemporary America. The long-term decline in jury sentences and executions, the abandonment of the practice by fourteen states, the waning of public support, the fact that capital punishment was nowhere routinely used for any crime—all of these indicated, they argued, that the death penalty was a "dying institution" largely abandoned by the American people.[50]

In his argument to the Court in *Boykin v. Alabama* (in which a black defendant was sentenced to death for robbery), Anthony Amsterdam distinguished between "what the public conscience will allow the law to say" and "what it will allow the law to do." He argued that on those rare occasions when the death penalty was used, it was against "unhappy minorities, whose numbers are so few, whose plight so invisible and whose persons so unpopular" that their suffering passed unnoticed and largely unprotested. Were such penalties to be used more generally, against the ordinary populace, they "could not for a moment be acceptable" to the American public.[51] However valid it may once have been, America's death penalty had, he submitted, come to be in violation of the Eighth Amendment. It was now up to the Court to recognize this fact and interpret the law accordingly.

But the argument involved a further claim. If rarefaction was a sign of an Eighth Amendment violation, it was also the cause of a Fourteenth Amendment violation. The rarity with which death sentences were imposed, even in cases in which juries brought in murder convictions, inevitably made for a degree of arbitrariness in the system. There was nothing rule-governed or predictable about this pattern. Anyone unlucky enough to be selected for death was, *ipso facto,* being treated differently from the norm. As Justice Stewart later remarked, being sentenced to death was like "being struck by lightning."[52]

The Fourteenth Amendment claim that capital defendants were deprived of due process and equal protection was further evidenced by reference to several features of the states' capital trial procedures. The absolute discretion that most death penalty states gave jurors to choose between a life sentence and a death sentence was, according to the LDF, a lawless and arbitrary procedure.[53] So too was the unitary trial proceeding, which failed to separate the "guilt phase" of the trial, in which the defendant's guilt is determined, from the "penalty phase," in which the sentence is determined—with the result that defendants were forced to choose between contesting their innocence and presenting mitigating evidence that might save them from the electric chair.[54]

The final argument at the core of the LDF's pleadings was a claim about federalism and the Supreme Court's power to subject the states' capital processes to judicial review. As Amsterdam insisted in *Aikens v California*, "the central issue in this case, the real nub of the controversy, is the scope and indeed the propriety of judicial review of . . . State legislative determinations to use the penalty of death."[55] If local decision-makers persisted in a practice that necessarily imposed arbitrary suffering, violated civilized norms, and conflicted with the Constitution, it was, so the LDF argued, the Supreme Court's duty to require them to desist.

The Supreme Court's Predicament

These developments presented the Supreme Court with a dilemma. The Court was being urged—by dissenting justices as well as by reforming litigants—to resolve a deeply contested issue that had long divided the public and differentiated the states. The claims presented were legal ones, going to a number of constitutional issues. Moreover, the arguments so brilliantly presented by Amsterdam and the LDF team had sufficient legal force to be taken very seriously. But the substance of the challenge was inescapably political. Would the Court deprive the states of the power to put persons to death? Would it be willing to overturn the duly enacted statutes of nearly 40 jurisdictions and vacate the duly imposed sentences of nearly 600 murderers, rapists, and armed robbers? Would it constitute itself as a reforming elite and impose abolition in the name of civilized morals and individual liberty? The legal difficulty of these decisions stood in proportion to their political sensitivity.

The death penalty was a long-established law and state practice. As an institution it continued to command public support, though that support had softened and elite opinion had turned against it. The states were using it much less frequently, and it undoubtedly had serious procedural problems. But the question now before the Court was the death penalty's *constitutionality*, and this was something else altogether. The language of the Constitution implicitly acknowledged the power of the states to impose capital punishment.[56] And in the nearly two centuries since the Eighth Amendment was passed, no decision of the Supreme Court had, as Chief Justice Burger put it, "cast the slightest doubt on the constitutionality of capital punishment."[57] If the Court were now to declare the death penalty illegal it would have to set aside the letter of the law and reverse all the relevant precedents.[58]

The LDF challenge thus contained legal and political dangers for the Court, and it seriously discomfited several justices. Chief Justice Warren was hardly immune to the abolitionist appeal. On his retirement in 1968 he told a *New York Times* reporter that he was personally opposed to the death penalty: "there has always been something to me that was repulsive about having the government take a life." Nevertheless, Warren saw these dangers quite clearly, which is why he discouraged Goldberg's initiative in 1963. As Oshinsky writes, "The Chief saw Goldberg's memorandum as an unwelcome distraction from the more pressing matters before the Court," especially given the controversy generated by its decisions on school desegregation, reapportionment, and police interrogation.[59]

For liberal elite figures like Earl Warren—and for many judges all across the country—capital punishment generated role conflicts that were increasingly difficult to manage. These people had been raised in a culture of liberal democracy. Each was affected by the liberal norm that states ought not to take life unnecessarily and by the humanistic insistence that life is sacred. Each would have been familiar with the fate of capital punishment in the rest of the Western nations and with the reformers' view that the death penalty had no place in a civilized society. And each would have felt the burden of America's history of racial violence, the legacy of lynching, and the fact that capital punishment was still being used as a tool of race oppression.[60]

Supreme Court justices are members of the nation's highest legal and political elite and usually highly educated, cultured individuals. Over the years, many of them had made it clear that the moral problem of capital punishment weighed heavily on them, and several made no secret of the fact that they were personally opposed to it.[61] Aware that abolition occurred elsewhere only because governing elites imposed countermajoritarian repeal, the justices must surely have been tempted to do the same. They had the power to do so, after all. And they had already done something similar in *Brown* when they ruled that the sensibilities of a national elite ought to supersede regional laws and practices.

But the justices' power to effect reform is more tightly constrained than that of parliamentary rulers elsewhere. Their rulings must accord with the law, or at least a plausible interpretation of it, and they must act in ways that promote the efficient functioning of the federal law and the nation's courts. Whenever they reached beyond these constraints, as the Warren Court had done on earlier occasions, the Court paid a price in terms of diminished credibility and respect. Political outrage, hostile editorials, and even bumper stickers declaring, "Impeach Earl Warren" sent signals that the Court could not ignore. And as the Warren Court metamorphosed into the Burger Court, the liberal members such as Brennan, Douglas, and Marshall lost much of their capacity to form a majority and persuade their brethren to take such risks.

The LDF campaign had begun in 1963 at the height of the civil rights struggle and in the heyday of the Warren Court's progressive jurisprudence. The following year, 61 percent of the popular vote had gone to President Johnson and his promise of civil rights and social programs. But by the time the Court was deciding *Furman* in 1972, all of that had changed. The standing of civil rights, the dominant perceptions of race, the question of law and order—none of these retained their earlier meaning. In eight tempestuous years these issues had been transformed by urban riots, political assassinations, crime in the streets, violent conflict over Vietnam, and two Republican presidential election victories, the second by a landslide. The politics of backlash had emerged and America in 1972 was not the same country it had been in 1963. This changing political environment only served to deepen the predicament in which the Court found itself as it deliberated the fate of William Henry Furman, an African American sentenced to death by the state of Georgia for the murder of a white householder in the course of a burglary.

To some justices the issue was clear. Justice Hugo Black remarked in 1969 that in questioning capital punishment "[t]he Court is usurping the power of the legislature." According to Black, "The Constitution gives the states the power and we can't overrule."[62] But others were more conflicted. Justice Harry Blackmun confessed that "[c]ases such as these provide for me an excruciating agony of the spirit." His personal attitude toward capital punishment was, he said, one of "distaste, antipathy, and indeed abhorrence," and had he been a legislator, he would have voted for its abolition. But as a justice of the Court, charged with upholding the Constitution, he found abolition impossible to accept "as a matter of history, of law, or of constitutional pronouncement." Chief Justice Burger made much the same declaration: "If I were possessed of legislative power, I would [abolish] yet it is essential to our role as a court that we do not." With the exception of Justice William Rehnquist, a recent Nixon appointee who favored the death penalty and regarded it as good law, each of the justices expressed some degree of ambivalence.[63]

The Court's death penalty decisions in the run-up to *Furman* put this ambivalence on display. The holding in *Witherspoon v Illinois* (which restricted the state's power to select prodeath juries by excluding potential jurors who evinced misgivings about imposing a death sentence) gave encouragement to the reformers. The conference discussion in *Maxwell v Bishop* (an Arkansas capital rape case in which a jury, operating without guidance, found a black defendant guilty and sentenced him to death in the course of a single proceeding) would have encouraged them still more as the justices voted 8 to 1 to uphold the LDF's challenge to unguided sentencing and unitary trials. But in the *Boykin* decision of 1969 the Court drew back from declaring capital robbery unconstitutional and decided the case on other grounds, as it ultimately would do in *Maxwell*. And the *McGautha* and *Crampton* decisions of 1971 appeared to many, Justice Brennan included, to signal the end of the abolitionists' hopes when the Court decided by a 6–3 majority not to press further with the imposition of constitutional controls on state procedures in capital cases.[64] (*McGautha* involved a challenge to the practice of unguided sentencing by juries, while *Crampton* challenged the practice of finding guilt and imposing punishment in the course of a single proceeding. Both challenges failed.) Justice Harlan's opinion for the Court in *McGautha* was especially discouraging, declaring in forceful terms that neither unguided discretion nor unitary trials suffered from any constitutional infirmity—a position the exact opposite of the one he had held only three years before when the justices took a preliminary view on *Maxwell*.[65]

As the internal debates of the Court leaned this way and then that, moved by shifts in composition and sudden changes of heart, some of the justices felt the need to clear up the growing uncertainty that existed in the country, where states had suspended their executions and hundreds of condemned men awaited their fate. A month after *McGautha* was announced, Justice Douglas wrote his clerks to say that there was "a drive inside the Court to reach [an end] so that, to use the words of Justice Black, 'it may be disposed of once and for all.'"[66] Two of the justices were charged with going through the current capital petitions to select "clean" cases involving rape, robbery, and "run of the mill murders" so that each of these questions could be argued. The four cases selected were *Aikens v California, Furman v Georgia, Jackson v Georgia,* and *Branch v Texas*. The *Aikens* case, which concerned a multiple murderer sentenced to death for an especially atrocious, intentional killing, was mooted in April 1972 when the California Supreme Court declared the California capital punishment law unconstitutional.[67] The other cases—a capital murder and two capital rapes—were consolidated under *Furman,* argued in January 1972 and decided on June 29, 1972.

Hugo Black stepped down from the Court in September 1971 for reasons of ill health. He died a few days later, aged eighty-five. Had he lived to read the nine separate *Furman* case opinions, he would surely have revised his expectation that the question of capital punishment was about to be settled once and for all.

Furman

In a surprise reversal of the *McGautha* decision only a year before, the *Furman* Court held that "the imposition and carrying out of the death penalty" in the three cases before the Court "constitute cruel and unusual punishment in violation of the Eighth and Fourteenth Amendments."[68] The justices who made up the 5–4 majority (Brennan, Marshall, Douglas, Stewart, and White) differed among themselves as to the basis of the decision, and each published an individual opinion, as did the four dissenters (Burger, Blackmun, Powell, and Rehnquist).

Although there was no controlling opinion on which the majority could agree, there were nevertheless recurring themes running through their individual opinions. Each of them identified a problem of arbitrariness in the selection of those condemned to death and the absence of procedural safeguards that would guarantee fairness. Each pointed to the rarity with which death sentences were now imposed and the legal consequences of this development. Several expressed concern that racism and other prejudices were being allowed to determine who lived and who died.[69]

The Court's concern about the arbitrariness of the states' capital proceedings was most forcibly expressed by Justice Potter Stewart. Being sentenced to death was, he said, an arbitrary and inexplicable event that possessed neither rhyme nor reason. The American death penalty had become a "unique punishment" that was "wantonly and freakishly imposed." Accordingly it violated the Eighth Amendment prohibition on cruel and unusual punishments and the Fourteenth Amendment right to due process. Stewart went on to say that though racial discrimination had not been proven in the cases before the Court, there was reason to believe that it often played a role: "if any basis can be discerned for the selection of these few to be sentenced to die, it is the constitutionally impermissible basis of race."[70]

On the question of race, Justice Douglas was more emphatic. He ac-

cepted the petitioners' contention that the death penalty was disproportionately applied to "the Negro, and the members of unpopular groups,"
and he explicitly noted the race of the defendants (black) and the victims
(white) in the present cases, thereby disclosing a fact that remained *sub
rosa* in the opinions of the others.[71] Douglas insisted that a defendant's
Eighth Amendment rights are violated if his death sentence is imposed "by
reason of his race, religion, wealth, social position, or class" or even if it is
imposed "under a procedure that gives room for the play of such prejudices." Referring to a series of well-known murder cases involving affluent white defendants, he noted that "the Leopolds and Loebs, the Henry
Thaws, the Dr. Sheppards and the Dr. Finchs of our society are never executed." The death penalty was reserved instead for "members of an unpopular minority or the poor and despised."[72]

Justice Byron White was no great enemy of the death penalty, but for
him the declining use of death sentences and executions had undermined
the core rationale that made the practice permissible—its contribution
to public safety and crime control. To function as a deterrent, the death
penalty had to be imposed with frequency and certainty since "seldom-
enforced laws become ineffective measures for controlling human conduct." But as things stood, the threat of execution was so attenuated that
capital punishment could "make little contribution to deterring those
crimes for which it may be exacted."[73] In the absence of any special crime
control utility, there was no reason to impose death rather than some lesser
punishment. And absent a rational state purpose, it was cruel and unusual
to put a person to death. To execute an offender in such circumstances
would be a "pointless and needless extinction of life with only marginal
contributions to any discernible social or public purpose."[74]

For Justices Brennan and Marshall, the infrequency with which Americans now imposed capital punishment had a different constitutional significance. Juries were imposing fewer death sentences for the same reason
that legislatures were abolishing capital punishment and public support
for it was softening—these were all signs that the American nation was
growing more civilized. Building on the Eighth Amendment doctrines
enunciated in *Weems* and *Trop*, they argued that the "evolving standards
of decency" of the American people had rendered the death penalty cruel
and unusual. A once-tolerated punishment had become intolerable because of advances in moral sentiment and progress in the nation's culture—as evidenced by the marked ambivalence that now surrounded the
institution. The death penalty had come to seem inhumane and uncivilized, not just to members of the Court but to the American people. As
Brennan argued, "it is . . . 'We, the People' who are responsible for the rar-

ity of the imposition and the carrying out of this punishment." The juries that refrain from choosing death are thereby "expressing the conscience of the community on the ultimate question of life or death." In doing so, the American people had effectively transformed the constitutional status of the institution since the Eighth Amendment "prohibits the infliction of uncivilized and inhuman punishments."[75]

Marshall made a similar point when he characterized the death penalty as "morally unacceptable to the people of the United States at this time in their history" and "no longer consistent with our own self-respect." In light of evidence of the punishment's ineffective and excessive nature, the Court was obliged to find that the death penalty states had no rational basis for their actions. For the Court to strike down capital punishment was therefore to uphold the freedom of American society and recognize "the humanity of our fellow beings." In doing so, Marshall said, the Court's action would mark "'a major milestone in the long road up from barbarism,'" and the United States would "join the approximately 70 other jurisdictions in the world which celebrate their regard for civilization and humanity by shunning capital punishment."[76]

The *Furman* majority held the American death penalty unconstitutional on the grounds that it was lawless, pointless, uncivilized, and inhumane. What had once been an elementary particle of state power had come to appear inessential and inappropriate—in America as in the rest of the Western world. And five Supreme Court justices saw it as their duty to bring it to an end.

The dissenting justices did not necessarily disagree with the majority about the instrumental efficacy or moral standing of capital punishment. None of their opinions offered full-throated support for the institution, and one went so far as to characterize the practice as abhorrent. But they vehemently disagreed about the proper role the Court ought to play in relation to it. As Chief Justice Burger declared, "Our constitutional inquiry . . . must be divorced from personal feelings as to the morality and efficacy of the death penalty."[77] However problematic capital punishment had become, it was not the job of unelected judges to end it, not least because there was no legal basis upon which to do so. Instead of defenses of the death penalty, the four minority opinions offered legal disquisitions on the importance of federalism and states' rights, the separation of powers, and the principle of *stare decisis* that obliged judges to obey precedents established by prior decisions.

Justice Powell (joined by Burger, Blackmun, and Rehnquist) talked of the "shattering effect" the *Furman* judgment had "on the root principles of *stare decisis,* judicial restraint and—most importantly—the separation of powers." In reversing *McGautha* and *Crampton* from the previous year, together with a long line of earlier decisions, the majority had not only "departed from established precedent"; it had also "encroach[ed] upon an area squarely within the historical prerogative of the legislative branch." Referring to the "staggering number" of state and federal laws that the judgment invalidated, Powell declared that he could recall no case in which the Court had "subordinated national and local democratic processes to such an extent."[78] The effect, he said, was to remove from the states their sovereign power to make laws to protect their citizens and enact locally approved conceptions of justice.

Rehnquist described the effect of the Court's judgments as being to "strike down a penalty that our nation's legislatures have thought necessary since our nation was founded." In doing so, the Court had imposed a "judicial fiat" with no basis in the popular will and had violated "the right of the people to govern themselves."[79]

For Burger, too, the decision was a breach of America's governing principles. "In a democratic society," he declared, "legislatures, not courts, are constituted to respond to the will and . . . moral values of the people." With this in mind, the chief justice proceeded to offer the nation's legislators a recipe for bringing their capital statutes into line with the newly announced law—a recipe that disaggregated the majority opinions, separating the substantive arguments of Brennan and Marshall from the procedural arguments of the others. He noted that two of the opinions focused on the "random and unpredictable" way in which death sentences were meted out, suggesting that the constitutional infirmity affected "the sentencing system rather than the punishment itself." Consequently, "legislative bodies may seek to bring their laws into compliance" by providing "standards for juries and judges to follow in determining the sentence in capital cases" or else by "more narrowly defining the crimes for which the penalty is to be imposed."[80]

When other Western nations abolished capital punishment they did so by means of decisive acts of sovereign power. America's abolition came in the form of a mixed verdict that invited other political authorities to reverse its effect.

The *Furman* decision was a reform effort supported by America's national elites, argued by civil rights litigants, and mandated by liberal Supreme Court justices. It was, in many respects, the American equivalent of the elite-led abolition processes occurring at the same time elsewhere in the Western world. In America, as elsewhere, this abolitionist effort emerged at the end of a centuries-long process of death penalty reform and was made possible by underlying processes of state rationalization, political liberalization, and cultural change. In nullifying state laws that it deemed arbitrary and capricious, the Court aimed to rationalize state conduct at the local level, subjecting the use of state violence to the discipline of rules. By interposing itself between the punished and the punishers, the Court followed the example of the bureaucratic middlemen who had emerged in other nations to cool hot tempers and ensure more temperate punishments.[81] In effect, the U.S. Supreme Court was acting as a reforming elite, setting national standards, imposing its civilizing and humanizing norms, subjecting personalistic local power to regulation by rule. But the Court's capacity to play this role was tightly constrained. Unlike European political leaders, who could impose a forceful resolution to a highly charged social issue with the authority of sovereign legislators, the Court had to settle for case-based decision-making on the issues presented to it, always looking for external support and seeking public consensus. Moreover, it had to represent its interventions as interpretations of pre-existing legal texts, rules, and decisions. The result was a series of reforms that focused on breaches of legality—due process violations and procedural problems—rather than on substantive injustices or morally objectionable practices.

The impact of *Furman* was dramatic and far-reaching. It vacated the death sentences of William Henry Furman, Elmer Branch, Lucious Jackson, and all the other men and women on the nation's death rows. A total of 587 condemned men and 2 women were released from death row and given a new future of life in prison with the possibility of parole.[82] It invalidated all of the nation's death penalty statutes, nullifying the capital laws of 36 states and the District of Columbia. Overnight, capital punishment ceased to exist anywhere in the United States.[83] A more sudden and wide-ranging transformation had rarely occurred in criminal justice.

If the decision's impact was remarkable, so too was the form in which it was presented. Unable to agree among themselves, each justice filed a separate opinion, generating a judgment that ran to 230 pages and 50,000 words—more than the Court had written in any other case in the twentieth century.[84] The result was a monumental study in ambivalence. As a legal opinion it was conflicted and confused, offering little in the way of logic or lucidity.[85] As a juridical document, it exhibited an excess of discourse and an embarrassing lack of legal substance.

When it was first announced, *Furman* appeared to many to be a decisive act of abolition ending American capital punishment once and for all. Tony Amsterdam described it as "the biggest step forward criminal justice has taken in 1,000 years."[86] Warren Burger, for his part, privately expressed the belief that "[t]here will never be another execution in this country." But on closer inspection *Furman* turned out to be much less dispositive. In many respects it was a classically American outcome. It focused on procedure not substance, and on individual cases not general policies. It purported to follow public opinion rather than to lead it. And it ultimately avoided resolution in favor of further rounds of negotiation and compromise. Far from a decisive abolition imposed by a self-confident elite, it was more like a tentative test balloon, floated by the Court to see how the political winds were blowing.[87]

What had seemed at first to be a total abolition of capital punishment would turn out to be merely a condemnation of standardless sentencing in capital cases.[88] Death would require due process. Being "different," it might even require "super due process."[89] But it was not abolished. Rather than marking the end of capital punishment in America, *Furman* marked the beginning of the contemporary system that persists to this day.

NINE

New Political and
Cultural Meanings

I'm sick of crime everywhere. I'm sick of riots . . . I'm sick of the
U.S. Supreme Court ruling for the good of a very small part rather
than the whole of our society.

LETTER FROM A CONSTITUENT TO SENATOR SAM J. ERVIN, JR.,
OF NORTH CAROLINA, JUNE 1968

The immediate reactions to *Furman* were mixed. In the days following the decision, newspapers reported it as a human interest story,
highlighting the reaction of the men and women whose death sentences
had been overturned. Photographs of prisoners standing beside unplugged
electric chairs accompanied reports announcing, "Fifty-five inmates awaiting execution at the Ohio Penitentiary heard radio reports on the decision
and then 'broke out with cheers, shouts and yelling'"; and "At Florida's
Raiford Prison 96 men and 1 woman on death row engaged in 'considerable shouting and hilarity.'" But if the prisoners' reaction was straightforward, the political response was more conflicted. The *Washington Post*'s
June 30 headline read: "Joy on Death Row; Praise, Scorn on Capital
Hill."[1]

Liberal voices greeted the decision as enthusiastically as we would expect. Senator Edward Kennedy acclaimed it as "one of the great judicial
milestones in American history" and said that the Court had "ruled for
life" and thereby "given new life to our democracy and to the quality of
American justice." In the same vein, Pennsylvania Attorney General J.
Shane Creamer described the decision as "a triumph of reason and law
over fear and anxiety."[2] The Congressional Black Caucus described itself
as "relieved" by a "ruling that is of particular interest and importance to
Black Americans because of the high percentage of Black prisoners who
have been sentenced to death."[3]

But critical voices also formed part of that first day's story, many of them from Southern politicians and law enforcement officials. Police chiefs in Atlanta and Memphis complained that *Furman* had deprived them of an important deterrent at a time when crime was rising. Los Angeles Police Chief Edward M. Davis told a press conference that the decision was an "absurdity" and promised to lead a nationwide campaign to restore capital punishment.[4] Prison guards complained that the Court's decision took away "the only real protection we had."[5] Tennessee Governor Winfield Dunn professed "tremendous shock and disappointment," a sentiment echoed by Lieutenant Governor Jere Beasley of Alabama, who commented that the Court had evidently "lost touch with the real world." James O. Eastland, Democratic senator from Mississippi, raised the flag of states' rights when he accused the Supreme Court of "legislating" and "destroying our system of government," while Georgia's lieutenant governor, Lester Maddox—a firebrand white supremacist—called the decision "a license for anarchy, rape, and murder."[6]

It was to be expected that conservatives would push back against the Court's decision, but no one at first knew how or how hard. Initially there was some confusion about the meaning of the decision. Was the death penalty now completely unconstitutional? Would its reintroduction require a constitutional amendment? Republican leaders quickly took steps to clarify where things stood and to chart a way forward. The day after *Furman* was announced, President Nixon declared at a press conference that "the holding of the Court must not be taken . . . to rule out capital punishment," and Governor Ronald Reagan urged California voters to support an initiative on the November ballot to reinstate the death penalty.[7]

Before long, support for the death penalty was being mobilized all across the country. On July 2 the *New York Times* carried an article entitled "Banned—But for How Long?" describing the *Furman* precedent as "very vulnerable" and quoting legal experts to that effect. The article reported that a constitutional amendment had already been introduced into Congress permitting the death penalty for murder and treason and that "legislators in at least five states" had announced they would press for new state laws reintroducing capital punishment.[8] On July 6, only a week after *Furman*, Philadelphia District Attorney Arlen Specter was reported to have proposed a new bill to the Pennsylvania legislature that would provide the death penalty for eight different types of murder.[9] Within a few months activists were campaigning for reinstatement in every state in the country, supported by police chiefs, state attorneys general, local district attorneys, and assorted politicians.[10]

What this amounted to was the mobilization of pro–death penalty forces on a national scale for the first time in U.S. history. When the *Furman* case was argued in January 1972, dozens of *amicus* briefs had been attached to the LDF brief, but not a single organized group joined the states in defending capital punishment, not even the federal government. There had been no active, pro–death penalty lobby. Now a nationwide movement had been brought into existence. Instead of ending the death penalty, *Furman* had roused the nation's pro–death penalty forces and mobilized them as never before.

For 200 years, the activists in death penalty politics were chiefly antigallows abolitionists, challenging a settled, traditional practice and the embedded preference of a majority of Americans. Now the balance had changed. The Court's surprise decision and the accompanying publicity focused the issue of capital punishment and moved it up the political agenda.[11] Even before the decision was announced, public opinion was already moving in favor of capital punishment, and the new activism served to accelerate this shift.[12] Citizens expressed outrage at what they regarded as the Court's attack on their values. This in turn energized state legislators, who seized the opportunity to provide their constituents with the laws they demanded. In nullifying the death penalty statutes of so many states, the Court had created a gap between majority voter preferences and state law—a gap to which many politicians were immediately drawn. As Lee Epstein and Joseph Kobylka remark, in the summer of 1972, state legislatures "could barely wait to reconvene to pass new laws."[13]

Within two years, thirty-five states had enacted new capital statutes.[14] Re-enactment was rapid everywhere but faster in states where murder rates had increased and fastest in the South. Florida was the first to enact a new law, successfully passing a new statute in December 1972.[15] The month before, California voters had endorsed death penalty restoration, voting two to one for Governor Reagan's Proposition 17. In September 1973 Reagan signed the new act into law.

In every death penalty state the story was the same. Even Jimmy Carter, the liberal Democratic governor of Georgia, signed a new bill into law in 1973. Only Governor Michael Dukakis of Massachusetts stood against the tide, vetoing a capital punishment bill that the state legislature had approved—an abolitionist stance that would cost Dukakis dearly when he ran for president in 1988. Capital trials were soon under way across the country. By the end of 1974, despite serious doubts about their validity, new state statutes had been used to sentence some 231 people to death.[16]

So the death penalty re-emerged, with the enhanced support of public opinion and of newly mobilized activists. But the institution that resurfaced in the 1970s bore a new set of political and cultural meanings that had been forged in the course of the battles fought in the lead-up to *Furman* and in its aftermath.

The LDF litigation of the 1960s swept the death penalty up into the civil rights movement, rendering abolition as an NAACP-sponsored civil rights reform. In the same way, the *Furman* majority embodied the spirit of the Warren Court in offering a liberal reading of the Constitution, intended to heal racial divisions and expand the reach of liberty and equality.[17] The immediate effect was to alter the death penalty's connotations, associating it in the public's mind with civil rights, with liberal attitudes toward blacks, and with countermajoritarian federal reform. Then, in the process of reaction that followed *Furman,* the death penalty was inscribed into a very different politics—the politics of backlash—which gave the institution a whole new set of associations, linking it with "law and order," with "states' rights," and with what would later become known as "culture war" conservatism. These new associations clung to the death penalty for a generation, investing it with layers of meaning and depths of feeling that it had not previously had—both for conservatives who supported the institution and for liberals who opposed it. The death penalty as penal policy gave way to the death penalty as political and cultural symbol.

The Politics of Reaction

The reaction to *Furman* occurred within a definite context and had several distinct aspects. The LDF campaign that produced *Furman* was launched in 1963 at the height of the liberal ascendancy and the eve of President Johnson's Great Society project. By 1972 American liberalism had suffered a historic defeat and been displaced by a new conservative majority. In this new context, *Furman* was decried as an absurd, out-of-touch decision that undermined the fight against crime, infringed states' rights, and usurped the people's power. Each of these attacks was prefigured in the opinions of the four dissenting justices, all of whom had been appointed by President Nixon. And each of them sounded, in a minor key, the major themes of the political reaction against liberalism that Nixon and his Republican successors would undertake. Right from the start, the reaction against *Furman* was part of a wider backlash against civil rights, against Great Society liberalism, against the permissiveness and disorder of the 1960s, and against the elite-led, countermajoritarian power that liberals had wielded via the Court.

In the aftermath of *Furman* the American death penalty came to be narrated in three new frames, each of them retentionist in orientation, and each of them linked to the new politics of conservatism that dominated the national scene. From the mid-1970s onward, capital punishment came increasingly to be viewed as a law and order issue that treated support for the death penalty as crucial to the new war on crime; as a states' rights issue that treated support for the death penalty as a necessary response to an overreaching federal government; and as a culture wars issue that treated support for capital punishment as an expressive means of affirming belief in traditional values, fundamentalist religion, and the Southern way of life. All three were part of the more general backlash against civil rights, the Great Society, the Warren Court, liberal governance, and the cultural changes of the 1960s. All three had a prominent place in the "Southern strategy" of the Republican party. And all three worked to sustain the death penalty and increase its symbolic importance in the political and cultural life of the nation.

"Haven't we done enough for the Negro?" By 1966 white constituents were asking this question repeatedly, according to Democratic Congressman Lee Hamilton of Indiana.[18] Already in 1963 journalists had talked about a "backlash," referring to the countercurrent of resentment that the civil rights movement was creating, not just among white Southerners but also among ethnic white workers in Northern cities.[19] Reporting a survey about white backlash, the *New York Times* article that carried Congressman Hamilton's remarks noted that the politicians and commentators who had been surveyed all agreed on one point: "there seems to be growing white resentment to aspects of the civil rights movement, whether it be violence in the streets, the cry by militants of black power, or the question of open housing."

Those surveyed also agreed that the political beneficiaries of this backlash would be Republicans, since Democrats were the incumbents responsible for passing the major civil rights acts, though in some areas, such as Georgia, "the Democratic candidate is even more anti-Negro than his segregationist Republican opponent." The article went on to quote an anonymous White House source who described the backlash as "the number one issue," especially in the conflicts over busing that were breaking out in places such as Boston, Buffalo, and Long Island. As Lee Hamilton put it, "for Democrats it's as dangerous as any issue in the election in terms of changing votes."[20] In the language of the time, the civil rights revolution had been a "Negro revolution": now it was generating a countermovement among the working-class whites whose power it had allegedly diminished.

The backlash prompted countless letters to editors and complaints to congressmen. A letter sent to Sam J. Ervin, Jr., Democratic senator of

North Carolina, in June 1968 by Curt Furr, a white Southerner and the father of five, powerfully expressed its popular sentiments:

> I'm sick of crime everywhere. I'm sick of riots. I'm sick of "poor" people demonstrations (black, white, red, yellow, purple, green or any other color!) I'm sick of the U.S. Supreme Court ruling for the good of a very small part rather than the whole of our society . . . I'm sick of the lack of law enforcement . . . I'm sick of Vietnam . . . I'm sick of hippies, LSD, drugs, and all the promotion the news media give them . . . But most of all, I'm sick of constantly being kicked in the teeth for staying home, minding my own business, working steadily, paying my bills and taxes, raising my children to be decent citizens, managing my financial affairs so I will not become a ward of the City, County, or State and footing the bill for all the minuses mentioned herein.[21]

Progressive political change is normally followed by conservative reaction, and liberal reform achieved by court rulings may be especially susceptible to this backlash.[22] But the events of the mid-1960s fomented a remarkably potent reaction—one that rapidly gained ascendancy and then dominated U.S. politics for the next thirty years. Within the context of this political and cultural backlash the American death penalty was reinvented by the Supreme Court and the state legislatures, acquiring a new of set of forms and meanings in the process. To understand the death penalty's symbolism as it has come to operate over the last thirty years, we need to understand the politics of reaction.

The resistance of white Southerners to the civil rights movement was to be expected given the movement's assault on white supremacy and Jim Crow segregation. The reaction that was less predictable, and that transformed backlash from a regional to a national phenomenon, was the anger and resentment of working-class whites in Northern cities. Backlash politics had its roots in the demographic shifts of the Great Migration. The movement of large numbers of poor Southern blacks into Northern cities gave rise to ongoing conflicts with working-class whites over scarce resources, especially jobs, housing, and public schools. These tensions were manageable during postwar decades, when an expanding economy generated rising standards of living, but they became much more disruptive when adverse economic conditions set in and declines in entry-level industrial jobs devastated the lower sectors of the labor market in the urban North.[23]

By the 1950s, local elections in Northern working-class neighborhoods were showing signs of "simmering white discontent" and "antiliberal political organization" as ethnic whites objected to integration and miscegenation.[24] A decade later widespread deindustrialization, together with increased inflation and higher taxes, was causing a noticeable decline in real wages for working-class whites and an increase in opposition to civil rights legislation. Civil rights reforms in housing, schools, welfare, and political representation were widely viewed as a transfer of wealth, power, and status to blacks—a transfer ordained by well-to-do liberal Democrats but paid for by poorer and more conservative working-class whites.[25] The increased attention the media and government now paid to the problems of blacks made many working- and middle-class whites feel like a "forgotten majority." When urban crime rates began their dramatic rise (the murder rate doubled between 1963 and 1969 and overall crime rates increased by double digits nationwide) and the welfare rolls of large cities suddenly exploded—with blacks disproportionately involved in both developments—racial resentments were ready to spill over.[26]

These background tensions were roiled by a chain of disruptive events that unfolded during the second half of the decade. Noisy political demonstrations involving violent clashes with police; violent riots in one ghetto after another; more than 100 cities experiencing widespread looting, multiple deaths, and damages in the millions of dollars; the assassinations of the political leaders Robert Kennedy and Martin Luther King, Jr.—each of these events was captured on camera and screened on the evening news for the whole nation to see:

> On a hot August evening in 1965, days after Johnson had signed the Voting Rights Act into law, the Watts section of Los Angeles exploded in violence. Before the National Guard could restore order, 34 were dead, hundreds were injured, almost 4,000 were arrested, and roughly $35 million in damage was done.[27]

The "long hot summer" of 1967 saw riots in Newark, Detroit, and more than 100 other cities. In 1968, President Johnson ordered the U.S. army into position—tanks and all—after the burning and looting had come within two blocks of the White House. At the same time, the emergence of a more militant "black power" politics, the increased radicalism of the antiwar movement, and the cultural shock of feminists, hippies, and assorted countercultural forces all had a disturbing impact on the nation's psyche—not least on the lower-class whites who generally shunned radical politics but who were (after poor urban blacks) the chief victims of the violence and disruption that gripped their cities.[28]

In these years—the same years that the LDF litigation was slowly winding through the federal courts—the civil rights movement changed, becoming more controversial and generating more resistance. As Thomas and Mary Edsall observe, the civil rights agenda "shifted away from an initial, pre-1964 focus on government guarantees of fundamental citizenship rights for blacks" toward a new focus on a more radical set of goals "emphasizing equal outcomes . . . for blacks, often achieved through racial preferences." These new goals were vigorously opposed by conservatives and by the Republican party. The effect was to drive a wedge between the Democrats and their supporters, who were now identified with radical civil rights and the cause of African Americans, and Republicans, who became the party of opposition to the civil rights movement and the racial and social policies it entailed.[29] Among working-class whites, inflammatory issues such as busing, open housing, and affirmative action generated intense opposition, and Republicans soon positioned themselves to express this discontent, giving voice to the anger that many whites increasingly felt toward blacks and the liberal elites who were their chief allies.

The disruptive and racially charged upheavals of these years eventually produced a major realignment in American politics—a realignment defined by the collapse of liberalism, the resurgence of free-market economics and neoconservative social policy, the movement of white Southern voters from Democratic to Republican, and a decisive shift in race relations that brought a halt to the historic progress of black people and many of the policies that had facilitated it. This realignment, which would benefit the Republicans for more than a generation, was in large part the achievement of the party's "Southern strategy" and the racial and class divisions that it so successfully exploited. At the heart of this strategy was the popular appeal of "law and order," "states' rights," and "the social issue," together with all the unstated implications that these three slogans entailed.

The "Southern strategy"—first pursued by presidential candidate Barry Goldwater in 1964 and used to greatest effect by Richard Nixon in 1968 and 1972—fixed on the popular discontent generated in the wake of civil rights legislation. It developed these inchoate grievances and resentments into "wedge" issues that would define clear political divisions that worked to the Republican party's advantage. Running through all the strategy's issues was an increasingly hostile public perception of blacks and the claims being made on their behalf.

By the late 1960s, it was becoming apparent that there had been a marked shift in the dominant public perception of race issues. When it first got under way in the 1950s, the civil rights movement had presented an image of "the Negro" as an abused victim, a hard-working American who had been denied citizenship and subjected to violence and abuse but who was now patiently and lawfully struggling for justice. In the early 1960s, shocking televised images of white mobs and Southern sheriffs beating peaceful civil rights protesters, or unleashing dogs and water cannons on them, moved public opinion and generated a great deal of sympathy for the cause. By the late 1960s much of this support had disappeared. The events of the interim years—above all the urban riots and looting, the rise of black street crime, and the increasingly militant stance of black leaders—worked to reduce public sympathy and alter the way many people looked at the issues. As the decade came to a close, the meaning of the civil rights struggle for many Americans had been transformed. Instead of Dr. King and Rosa Parks, the figures who now came to mind were Malcolm X and Stokely Carmichael. Instead of peaceful, put-upon protesters, the figure of the African American was now the black mugger or urban rioter. As James Sundquist writes, "The image of the Negro in 1966 was no longer that of the praying, long-suffering nonviolent victim of southern sheriffs; it was a defiant young hoodlum shouting 'black power' and hurling 'Molotov Cocktails' in an urban slum."[30]

The association between civil rights and what conservatives decried as "violence in the streets" was always a tendentious one. But the worst riots had broken out immediately after the Voting Rights Act, forming an association in the public mind. Southern politicians such as George Wallace did their best to solidify the connection between rising crime and civil rights protest, depicting both as illegitimate challenges to law and traditional authority. Before long, the idea of "civil rights" was being used to attack the movement, with Richard Nixon repeating the refrain that "the first civil right of every American is to be free from . . . violence."[31] Soon a racial divide opened up over law enforcement, with blacks seeing police brutality as the cause of the riots, and whites seeing the need for firmer enforcement.[32]

An increasingly negative perception of blacks was reinforced by growing public concern about rising rates of crime and violence. Barry Goldwater picked up on this concern in 1964 when he talked about the need for "law and order" in a way that connected concrete fears of criminal victimization to more inchoate anxieties about shifting racial, class, and gender relations.[33] By 1968, more than 80 percent of Americans polled by the Gallup organization agreed with the statement, "Law and order has broken down in the country."[34] The same year, another poll showed "crime and lawlessness" ranking, for the first time since polls began, as the most important domestic problem in America.[35]

This new public concern about crime was grounded in a real collective experience of increased risk and victimization, and it was perfectly respectable for politicians to respond to this unease. But these concerns, however well founded, tended to be heavily imbued with racialized fears and overlaid by anxieties about the changing place of blacks in American society.

Against this background, crime control and support for law enforcement came to be understood, at least by some, as the reassertion of white power. The conservative insistence on "law and order" took on these additional meanings and began to function as a well-understood code. To declare oneself against "violence in the streets" and in favor of "law and order"— as Goldwater, Nixon, and their successors would do—was to communicate about public safety but also about much more besides. Indeed, "Crime became a short-hand *signal,* to crucial numbers of white voters, of broader issues of social disorder, tapping powerful ideas about authority, status, morality, self-control and race."[36]

The issue of race was rather closer to the surface in the second platform of the Southern strategy—the endorsement of "states' rights"—though it remained an unspoken implication rather than an explicit concern. The electoral prize that the Republicans so assiduously pursued was the Southern white vote. This had belonged to the Democrats ever since that party had brought about the end of Reconstruction and "redeemed" the region for its white population. Now, almost 100 years later, the Democrats' role in ending Jim Crow segregation had prompted millions of white voters to desert the party, destroying the "Solid South" and creating a floating voting bloc large enough to decide national elections.

The Republican leadership set out to secure the allegiance of that bloc, but they could hardly do so by disavowing civil rights or re-creating white supremacy. So rather than focus on substantive policies, the Republicans focused on constitutional interpretation. Echoing Strom Thurmond's claim that crime in the streets, communist agitation, and the breakdown of moral codes were all the fault of "the Supreme Court's assault on the Constitution" and a federal government that had "invaded the rights of the states," they took up a cause dear to the hearts of Southerners—that of "states' rights." Though it was 100 years before, many Southerners still felt the humiliation of defeat in the "War Between the States" and considered themselves victims of a cultural bigotry on the part of Northerners—a bigotry most recently expressed in the federal government's assault on racial practices that lay at the core of traditional Southern identity.[37] From Goldwater in 1964 to Reagan in 1980, "states' rights" was a Republican party slogan, signaling to the Southern states that under a Republican administration their "sovereignty" would be respected and they would be left to govern their own people in their own way.

The Republican embrace of states' rights could be represented to the nation as a principled belief that overreaching federal government was the problem and local control the solution. But to Southerners it said something more—namely, that President Nixon and a Republican Congress would seek to undo the gains of the civil rights movement and restore the "Southern way of life" with its racial inequalities and its religious commitments. And in this they were not mistaken. Several decades later, a top Republican adviser, Lee Atwater, explained to a researcher the political thinking behind the party's embrace of states' rights. "You start out in 1954 by saying, 'Nigger, nigger, nigger,'" said Atwater. "By 1968, you can't say 'nigger'—that hurts you. Backfires. So you say stuff like forced busing, states' rights, and all that stuff."[38] Atwater went on to say that even "cutting taxes" had racial appeal since "blacks get hurt worse than whites."[39] And the Republican tax revolt that began in these years, and was pressed further by Presidents Reagan and Bush, did indeed have a racially disparate impact, with blacks and Hispanics on the side of "tax recipients" and state beneficiaries and whites on the side of taxpayers, hostile to government programs. Being against tax increases and big government became, in some circles, a form of race politics.[40]

Anxiety about the course of social change was another discontent targeted by the Southern strategy. Many of the cultural changes that occurred in the 1960s—the spread of more relaxed, permissive attitudes; the birth control pill and casual sex; recreational drugs; feminism and "women's liberation"; the shift from rigid moral codes to "situational ethics"—had long generated disquiet on the part of "middle America." As statistics emerged about increasing rates of family breakdown, divorce, out-of-wedlock births, and welfare claims, this disquiet grew and became a palpable source of political energy. At stake in these cultural upheavals was not so much a specific objection to this or that practice, but instead a more general white middle-class fear that a whole way of life was being eroded, that tradition, morality, and order were breaking down, that "America was coming apart at the seams."[41]

For an anxious, onlooking public, "Ghetto riots, campus riots, street crime, anti-Vietnam marches, poor people's marches, drugs, pornography, welfarism, rising taxes" were all signs of the same underlying problem— the "breakdown of family and social discipline" and the collapse of "respect for law."[42] And though some of these cultural movements were led by white youths, college students, and professional women, the popular opposition that they engendered frequently took on a racial cast, focusing on the "urban black underclass" and its various "pathologies." As Dan Carter observes, it might be possible, in theory, to separate these issues from the question of race. But in reality, "fears of blackness and fears of disorder—interwoven by the subconscious connection many white Americans made between blackness and criminality, blackness and poverty, blackness and cultural degradation—were the warp and woof of the new social agenda."[43]

Southern communities were especially disturbed by the new social and cultural developments. The Southern white male was the biggest loser in the upheavals of the 1960s—the Jim Crow regime was dismantled, white supremacy denied, and the traditional values of family, female domesticity, and religious observance came under threat. To rail openly against these civil rights, once they were established, was to invite charges of racism and sexism and bigotry. But to press the issues of family, faith, and country— or indeed to demand a return to law and order—was perfectly respectable and could be openly and vigorously pursued.

The Republicans' Southern strategy embraced these discontents and offered slogans and policy proposals that appealed directly to them. Conservatives blamed liberals for the breakdown of law and order. They claimed that the civil rights movement had encouraged lawlessness and anarchy by popularizing civil disobedience. They accused the Supreme Court of undermining law enforcement by granting rights to suspects and being overly concerned about the civil rights of black murderers. They attacked the Great Society programs for rewarding urban rioters with undeserved benefits and with compassion instead of control.[44] From Nixon onward, the Republicans would become the party of law and order (and not of civil rights), the devotees of states' rights (and not of big federal government), and believers in conservative social values (and not in the "permissiveness" and "relativism" they associated with 1960s liberalism). De-emphasizing civil rights; waging war on crime; ending the war on poverty; ending busing; opposing "activist" judges; stepping back from desegregation; lowering taxes; rolling back the welfare state—these were the new populist politics of the "silent majority."

The "silent majority," the "forgotten Americans," people like North Carolinian Curt Furr with his five children and his list of "sick and tireds" —these were the people targeted by the Southern strategy. And these were the people on whose behalf Richard Nixon promised to govern in a 1968 speech that embraced these resentments and the political energy they supplied:

> Forgotten Americans, those who did not indulge in violence, those who did not break the law, people who pay their taxes and go to work, people who send their children to school, who go to their churches, people who are not haters, people who love this country, and because they love this country are angry about what has happened to America.[45]

In a speech the year before, George Wallace had made the same appeal, though his language was characteristically cruder and his racial allusions more explicit:

> You people work hard, you save your money, you teach your children to respect the law. Then when someone goes out and burns down half a city and murders someone, pseudo-intellectuals explain it away by saying the killer didn't get any watermelon to eat when he was ten years old ... The Supreme Court is fixing it so you can't do anything about people who set cities on fire.[46]

To all of this, the Democratic party was slow to respond. Its perceived "pro-black" stance and its commitment to civil rights ensured it was continually on the defensive whenever some new riot occurred or some controversial Court decision was announced. And its refusal to take a hard line on street crime and antiwar protesters put it on the losing side of these issues. Worse, the standard liberal response—that the crime statistics were not to be believed, that the problem was police brutality or institutional racism, or that crime was really a matter for local government—suggested to working-class whites that Democrats did not sufficiently care about their issues.

The result was a historic shift in the electorate that altogether restructured American politics. After nearly 100 years of loyal Democratic support, white Southern voters moved, *en masse,* to the Republican party, where they would stay for the next thirty years. Fundamentalist religion became a potent force in public life with the rise of the Christian Right. And Republican majorities in Congress (and eventually on the Supreme Court) began to undo the progressive changes of the previous decade. The transformation began in the 1968 election. Nixon won the presidency by a narrow margin from Hubert Humphrey—who was attacked from the left by the anti–Vietnam war movement and from the right by law and order enthusiasts—though the House and Senate remained under Democratic control. Nixon's narrow victory represented a historic defeat for liberalism, for no fewer than twelve million voters who had previously voted for President Johnson now either abstained or defected to Nixon or Wallace.[47] By 1972, Nixon and the Republicans were able to win in a landslide. In 1964, Lyndon B. Johnson had won 61.05 percent of the popular vote. In 1972, Richard Nixon won 60.67 percent. In eight years, the balance of power in the American nation had shifted decisively from liberal to conservative.

It would remain that way for more than thirty years, with a political landscape dominated by law and order politics, a "new federalism" that gave more power to the states, and the back and forth of the culture wars. Fully twenty years after Nixon's first presidential victory, Republican candidate George H. W. Bush ran a presidential campaign that accessed the same "submerged cluster of anxieties" and sounded all the same coded appeals to race and class division.[48] Only by this time, the death penalty had taken its place in the front and center of the campaign.

The Reinvention of Capital Punishment

In this postliberal, post–civil rights, law and order America the death penalty would be remade. Having been almost abolished in the liberal 1960s, it would be revived and reinvented in the more conservative decades that followed. The late-modern mode of capital punishment that emerged, jointly forged by the Supreme Court and the states, became a kind of masthead symbol for a new culture of control with its harsh sentencing laws, its mass imprisonment, and its risk-averse retributivism. The LDF litigation had represented the death penalty as a civil rights violation, a kind of legal lynching that ought to be abolished along with segregation and Southern racism. Now it became a populist crime-fighting measure, an emblem of states' rights democracy and a symbolic battleground in the emerging culture wars. In the process, death penalty discourse became infused with powerful currents of race and class resentment and with white fears of black violence.

From the late 1970s, the question of capital punishment functioned as a litmus test for law and order commitment in the same way that "abortion" tests for conservative commitment. To ascertain if a judicial nominee or an aspiring politician was sound on law and order, one asked if he or she supported the death penalty. If the answer was negative or even hesitant, his or her credentials were thereby shown to be suspect. The scene was played out on national television time and time again—most memorably when Michael Dukakis failed the test in 1988, a dramatic defining moment that marked the beginning of the end of his presidential campaign. But though this litmus test is familiar and taken for granted, it is actually quite peculiar.

The death penalty has always been a harsh punishment and a tool of law enforcement. And in its modern penal mode its function was to deter serious offenders and eliminate those who would not be deterred. But in post-1970s America it became not so much a policy or a penal sanction as a commitment, a symbolic badge that declared the wearer's position on "law and order" issues—and on much else besides. The paradox here is that, by the 1970s, the death penalty's deterrent effects had been shown to be uncertain at best, and the sanction had ceased to be used in a way that might make it an effective crime-fighting tool.

The idea of the death penalty as a key weapon in the war on crime became persuasive because conservatives chose to ignore doubts about its efficacy and endorse instead the popular attitude that favored the death penalty, either as a commonsense deterrent or as a harsh retributive response to hated criminals.[49] They did so, not because they were persuaded of capital punishment's penological efficacy, but because they were certain of its political benefits. Once they had made that political judgment, it became a shibboleth of the conservative movement that the equation between the death penalty and effective crime control be regarded as unquestionable.

These claims were helped by the fact that crime had been rising rapidly since 1963, and conservative figures made a point of blaming rising homicide rates on the death penalty moratorium that had been in place over the same years (though murder rates increased in death penalty and abolitionist states alike). As John Little McClellan, the Democratic senator from Arkansas, put it when he introduced death penalty bill S1401: "The last execution in this country took place in 1967 . . . In the five years between 1967 and 1971, the number of murders in this country rose 61%. . . . Can anyone argue that this was a mere coincidence?"[50] Southern newspapers made the same connection. The *Atlanta Constitution* carried articles tracing the supposedly negative impact of the suspension of executions: "Crimes punishable by death in the electric chair have increased 235 per cent in Atlanta since the chair was last used in 1964, a survey of police records showed."[51] "We are threatened people. And it is either them or us," the same newspaper said in a 1973 editorial entitled "Liberals and Crime."[52]

The conservative message went this way: the liberal elites and radical civil rights activists who had done so much to undermine the nation's social order, its traditional values, and its Southern way of life had also tried to abolish the death penalty. This message was a powerful one all across the nation but it resonated especially in the South, where Republicans were now focusing their electoral efforts. In that context, abolition of the death penalty was civil rights for black murderers. *Furman* was the work of an "activist" federal judiciary operating in concert with Northern liberal elites who disdained the Southern way of life. As Lester Maddox had declared, the decision "was a license for anarchy, rape and murder." Women were left unprotected in their homes. Order was undermined and

in danger of collapse. To a conservative white Southerner's way of thinking, the echoes of the hated Reconstruction were unmistakable. To demand the reintroduction of capital punishment was to do more than take a
position in penal policy: it was to reassert the old order and oppose the
changes wrought by liberal elites.

Republicans grasped that questions about capital punishment tended to
put liberals on the wrong side of the "law and order" issue. If support for
law and order was seen to require support for the death penalty—as Republicans now insisted—and the liberal establishment continued to oppose capital punishment (as it did for a decade and more), then Republicans won and liberals lost. However concerned Democrats might actually
feel about crime, however tough their stance on sentencing or policing or
crime-prevention might be, their opposition to capital punishment marked
them as definitively soft on crime and out of touch with popular feeling.
And in the 1970s, popular feeling was increasingly getting behind capital punishment. By November 1972, five months after *Furman* was announced, the *New York Times* reported that a Gallup poll had found a
sharp rise in the numbers supporting a death penalty. As the *Times* article
noted, "Despite the United States Supreme Court's ruling striking down
the death penalty, public support for capital punishment is currently at its
highest point in nearly two decades."[53]

Marked by fear of crime, racial hostility, and a growing gap between liberal elite sentiment and mass popular opinion, the death penalty came to
function as the epitome of an *expressive* punishment. Loud demands for
the death penalty were a kind of acting out, a means of communicating
rage and resentment as well as hatred of the criminal other. The sanction's
powerful capacity to convey emotion overwhelmed all doubts about its
ability actually to deter murderers. In the cut and thrust of electoral politics and rhetorical debate—especially in the sound-bite age of TV journal-
ism—the death penalty was the perfect leading edge for a harsher law and
order politics.

It was these circumstances, together with the rhetorical work of conservative commentators and party operatives, that transformed the American
death penalty into a powerful condensation metaphor, a synecdoche that
enabled a single position to stand for a whole law and order attitude.[54] Despite the death penalty's tenuous link to real crime control, despite its narrow application and the rarity of its use, despite the utter implausibility of
the idea, capital punishment became the "solution" to crime that dominated political debate. To voice unquestioning support for the death penalty was to communicate that one was for law and order. To raise doubts
about its efficacy or morality was to lose credibility and popular support.

A functioning litmus test had been devised, however unscientific its under-lying chemistry, and it worked time after time for the conservative cause.

The death penalty operated as a wedge issue benefiting Republicans for twenty years, from the early 1970s until the early 1990s. Presidents Nixon, Reagan, and George H. W. Bush would each use it to win popular support and to disparage liberal opponents—most notably in the 1988 Willie Horton campaign and the trouncing of Michael Dukakis.[55] As late as 1995, the Republican House majority leader, Newt Gingrich, was push-ing a platform of tax reductions and death penalty increases, and propos-ing mass executions ("27 or 30 or 35 people at one time") as a solution to the drug problem.[56] It was not until Bill Clinton embraced capital punish-ment and made it part of mainstream Democratic politics that the issue ceased to divide the parties.[57] In the mid-1990s congressional representa-tives of both parties competed to see who could introduce more new cap-ital statutes—by 1996, Democrats were claiming credit for enacting no fewer than sixty new federal capital offenses. Historians might see, in this spree of legislative *Thanatos,* an echo of the eighteenth-century process that produced England's Bloody Code. In both cases, lawmakers enacted penalties of death to further their political interests and those of their con-stituents—private property in eighteenth-century England, social values and racial hierarchies in twentieth-century America. In both cases, the practical result was a death penalty reinvigorated and reasserted—though more often on the books than on the scaffold.

The call by Southern politicians for a return to the gallows often con-tained distinct echoes of lynching. In its insistence on the punishment of death and the suppression of black civil rights, the Southern backlash against *Furman* echoed the backlash against Reconstruction and the lynching scenes that it created. On occasion it even produced explicit invo-cations of lynching imagery. Here, for example, is Georgia's lieutenant governor, Lester Maddox, invoking the lynching past when he enthuses about "the noose" and "court house square" hangings, even though Geor-gia was an electrocution state that had long since abolished hangings and public executions: "There should be more hangings. Put some more elec-tricity in the chair. Put more nooses on the gallows. We've got to make it safe on the street again . . . It wouldn't be too bad to hang some on the court house square, and let those who would plunder and destroy see."[58]

Maddox's evocation of public hangings outside the court house was not the only allusion to lynching voiced in these debates. Another Georgia leg-islator, State Representative Guy Hill of Atlanta, proposed a bill in the Georgia House Judiciary Committee that required hanging to take place "at or near the courthouse in the county in which the crime was committed."[59] The same debate included a remark from another death penalty enthusiast, Representative James H. (Sloppy) Floyd: "If people commit these crimes, they ought to burn."[60] No doubt Sloppy Floyd would insist, if asked, that he was referring to death in the electric chair. But the brutal language of "burning" offenders also evokes the worst kind of lynchings where black suspects were tortured and burned at the stake.[61] African Americans understood these coded messages. They, too, viewed the death penalty through a prism of race and saw that blacks were its chief targets. Little wonder, then, that black groups and black politicians were the main opponents of the new legislation as it swept through Southern state legislatures.[62]

States' Rights and Culture Wars

The *Furman* decision provoked bitter complaints about activist judges and overreaching federal government meddling in matters that fell within the autonomous scope of state authority. Herman E. Talmadge, the Democratic senator (and former governor) of Georgia greeted the decision by declaring, "Five of the nine members of the U.S. Supreme Court have once again amended by *judicial usurpation* the Constitution." His fellow Georgian, State Representative Sam Nunn, echoed Talmadge's sentiments by referring to a "dictatorship" of judges appointed for life. The chairman of the Senate Judiciary Committee, James O. Eastland, Democratic senator from Mississippi, accused the Court of "legislating" and, in doing so, "destroying our system of government." Robert List, the attorney general of Nevada, denounced the decision as "an insult to Nevada, to its laws, and to its people."[63] As the father of a murder victim said to the *Chicago Tribune,* "I guess it means nothing that the people of Illinois voted to keep the death penalty."[64] If elite-led countermajoritarian reform had been effective in ending the death penalty in Europe, in America it provoked only outrage and opposition.

Ironically—and by way of this outraged reaction—it was *Furman* that effectively forged the association between the death penalty and democracy that still prevails in America today. By denying "the people"—or at least the people of Georgia, Texas, and the other death penalty states—the punishment that they "willed," the *Furman* Court made capital punishment a symbol of that "will" and a token of popular democracy. Arguments for the death penalty, thereafter, became arguments for democracy.

Furman's invalidation of capital punishment was read in the South as an illegitimate attack on the region's cultural traditions by outside elites.

(As one poster outside an execution responded, "Texas Justice: Don't Like It? Leave!"[65]) It was seen as a continuation of the same assault on the Southern way of life—mounted by the Supreme Court and by Northern liberals—that had first dismantled segregation and racial hierarchies and more recently invalidated laws banning abortion. As on previous such occasions, the *Furman* decision unleashed a flood of popular resentment against the Court, its "activist judges," and the Northern liberal elites who supported them. But whereas the earlier fights against *Brown v Board of Education* had necessarily been openly racist in their commitments, and hence lacked support in the rest of the nation, the South's fight to retain capital punishment could be framed as a straightforward "law and order" issue that could generate support elsewhere with no thought of race. *Furman* thus gave the states, above all the Southern states, a means to assert their autonomy and push back against civil rights reform on an issue that was popular, respectable, and could be argued on grounds that were neither racial nor sectional. That the Southern states had very high homicide rates and a public that keenly supported capital punishment gave real force to this campaign, allowing local politicians to insist that Washington elites simply didn't understand "the way things are down here."[66]

Today, nearly forty years later, the claim of "states' rights" continues to resonate as a basis for opposing the Supreme Court's death penalty reforms. In 2005, when the Court ruled in *Roper v Simmons* that states may not execute offenders who were minors at the time of their offense, the decision provoked another furor. But it was not the substance of the decision that was attacked in the dozens of outraged editorials and *op eds* that followed. No one argued that executing minors makes for good policy or a higher standard of decency. That, its detractors said, wasn't the issue. The trouble with *Roper* was that in imposing its ruling the Supreme Court had usurped the power of the states and infringed their sovereign autonomy. The question was not, "what policy?" but, "who decides?"[67] A *CNN* commentator raged that "the majority's approach [is] anti-democratic, anti-states' rights, and anti-jury . . . A power that once belonged to state legislatures and local juries, now rests in the hands of the U.S. Supreme Court."[68] The decision "reeks of judicial arrogance," said the *Greenville News*, and showed what the *Omaha World Herald* called "an unhealthy disregard for the sovereignty of [our] homeland."[69] The following year a state judge in Alabama ran his election campaign on a platform of rejecting *Roper* and defying the Supreme Court on the grounds of states' rights.[70]

The same outpouring of states' rights outrage greeted *Kennedy v Louisiana* in June 2008, when the Supreme Court invalidated the capital child rape statutes of Louisiana and five other states.[71] As the *Chattanooga*

Times insisted to its readers, "The basic issue is not whether there should or should not be a death penalty law for child rapists. The basic question is who should decide."[72] A Texas prosecutor, Robert Etinger, accused the Court of seeking to "overthrow the will of the people."[73] Even Democratic presidential candidate Barack Obama was moved to take issue with the *Kennedy* Court, declaring that when it comes to the crime of child rape, "states have the right to consider for capital punishment."[74] The conservative culture warrior and one-time Nixon speechwriter Pat Buchanan responded to the decision by insisting that its chief author, Justice Stevens, "should be impeached." In his opinion Stevens had suggested that it was time to reconsider the "justification of the death penalty itself"—a remark that had Buchanan fulminating about democracy, states' rights, and the culture wars. "Stevens is not, or should not be, the decider," Buchanan wrote in his syndicated column. "In a democratic republic, that is the prerogative of the majority . . . It is just such usurpations of power by the Supreme Court justices that loosed the culture war that has torn us apart."[75]

When capital punishment was abolished in other Western nations, death penalty supporters often put up fierce opposition. But none of the reports of these struggles suggests that specific groups or regions felt that in being denied the use of capital punishment they had been deprived of their heritage, that their way of life, their ethnic identity had somehow been degraded. People objected strongly to abolition, but they did not regard it as a status slight. In America, following *Furman,* many Southerners did.

If Southern legislatures had proposed banning capital punishment, as the legislatures of a dozen non-Southern states had done before 1972, those objecting to abolition would have marshaled many arguments for rejecting the proposal. But it is unlikely that they would have claimed that the death penalty was an essential part of a Southern heritage that ought to be retained on that basis. The reason that many Southerners saw the *Furman* decision as an attack on their culture had less to do with the institution's cultural belonging and more to do with perceptions of the process that brought *Furman* about.

Furman "abolished" the states' death penalty, temporarily at least, at the prompting of the same NAACP civil rights litigators, in the same federal Court, in the same countermajoritarian fashion that segregation in schools had been abolished in 1954. (Southerners and others would later see school prayer, antiabortion laws, and antisodomy laws struck down in the same way, and have much the same reaction.) The LDF litigators—who specially targeted the capital punishment practices of the Southern states—viewed death penalty abolition as the abolition of modern-day lynching and an extension of the same civil rights movement that had abolished racial segregation, black disfranchisement, and Jim Crow. This attack on capital punishment more than anything else forged the institution's identity as part of "Southern culture." In the course of the litigation against capital punishment many white Southerners saw their culture and institutions being attacked by familiar enemies, and they determined to defend them accordingly. The death penalty was more Southern after *Furman* than it had been before.

Although the "culture wars" description did not become standard journalistic parlance until the 1990s, the underlying conflict between affluent, secular, liberal elites—located on the two coasts and especially in the Northeast—and religious, traditional conservatives, centered in the South and the Midwest, began much earlier, having been brought into focus by the Southern strategy and its emphasis on traditional, populist values.[76] Sparked into action by issues such as abortion, school prayer, flag burning, gun control, women's liberation, gay rights, and same-sex marriage, the "religious right" emerged as a potent political force in the 1980s and 1990s, using its influence to promote "faith, family, and country" and push back against what it saw as "permissiveness" and "secular progressivism" in public life.

The emergence of these cultural and religious divisions polarized death penalty debates still further. Support for capital punishment came to be seen as an integral part of the "traditionalist" worldview, just as opposition to it became standard for liberal "progressives." Depriving people of the right to impose capital punishment—like depriving them of their guns, or their right to school prayer, or their right to ban abortion—came to be viewed as a kind of elite contempt for common people, for their faith, and for their way of life. Alabama judge Tom Parker captured this sentiment when he protested that the Supreme Court's decision in *Roper v Simmons* had "usurped" Alabama's power to impose the death penalty on juveniles if it so chose. He noted that "the liberals on the U.S. Supreme Court already look down on the pro-family policies, Southern heritage, evangelical Christianity and other blessings of our great state. We Alabamians will never be able to sufficiently appease such establishment liberals, so we should stop trying and instead stand up for what we believe without apology."[77] Among groups primed by their class, their beliefs, or their regional identities to feel such slights, this contempt generated bitter opposition.

Christian fundamentalists and conservative evangelicals have a strong presence in the Southwest and the Midwest, too, but the culture wars mentality found its greatest resonance in the South. Why should this be? "Much of the dynamic in America's current culture war," one author suggests, comes from the fact that American liberalism destroyed "the culture of official racism in the South."[78] Not only did the South contain large numbers of religious and social conservatives but from Reconstruction on many white Southerners developed a sense of victimization, feeling themselves disdained by Northern liberal elites and discriminated against by a federal government intent on undermining the Southern way of life and destroying its cultural heritage.

The abolition of capital punishment did, of course, raise genuine questions of religious faith. And Christian leaders were among the political and cultural figures to whom the press turned for comment when *Furman* was first announced. On June 30, 1972, the *Los Angeles Times* quoted fundamentalist preacher Dr. Carl McIntire as saying, "The Supreme Court is taking the country further away from the moral law and the teachings of God."[79]

A week later, the letters column of the same paper carried five submissions about the Court's decision.[80] One said that it was characteristic of the four Nixon-appointed justices that they had all voted for the death penalty. Another remarked that the majority justices lacked wisdom. But each of the three others raised religious, "culture war" issues which, until that point, had been relatively absent from *Furman* debate. A letter from a reader in Long Beach objected that the death penalty was being abolished while abortion was still being permitted: "it staggers the imagination," the letter said, "that a vicious murderer will be spared while totally innocent potential human beings are being flushed into eternity via abortions." Keith Kearl of Los Angeles complained, "Without the death penalty we are changing our society from Christian to atheist," a sentiment echoed by Robert McConnell, who wrote, "The death penalty may no longer be man's law but it still is God's law . . . Let's get capital punishment into our Constitution."

So conservative religious objections emerged again, just as they had whenever abolition had been debated in the nineteenth century. But in the context of post-1970s America, the language of "tradition" and "faith"— like "law and order" and "states' rights"—could also be used to express racial and cultural attitudes that had become otherwise unsayable in respectable public settings. In these conflicts over culture, fundamentalist religion came to function less as a political theology than as a vehicle for lower-class resentments and the defense of traditional ways of life. In its insistence on literal readings of biblical texts and fundamentalist commitments unleavened by modernity and liberal tolerance, this old-time religion served as an affirmation of the worth of white Southern lower-class groups in the face of perceived condescension from secular progressives and liberal elites.

The biblical texts are ambivalent on the death penalty, and the various Christian churches are similarly divided on the issue. But cultural attitudes and a chain of historical events have made capital punishment a salient issue for religious conservatives. That the death penalty is seen as "traditional" rather than "modern," that it is viewed as an integral part of a valued way of life in which masculine honor codes, revenge, and Old Testament values remain strong—are part of the motivation. So is stern dislike of those who have offended against the laws of God and of man—righteous moralizing being a familiar trait of fundamentalists. To put a murderer to death—or merely to insist on the right to do so—is thus to uphold morality and deny solidarity in the most dramatic, profound way. The culture wars made it possible to express support for capital punishment in a way that conveyed a surface moral righteousness and a subterranean social animosity.

TODAY'S death penalty is deeply embedded in American political culture and casts a long shadow. The dramatic clash between federal courts and state legislatures—and, beyond that, the conflict between elite Northern liberalism and Southern popular conservatism—reshaped the meaning of American capital punishment and repositioned the issue in a new political and cultural context. *Furman*'s unintended effect was to mobilize a pro–death penalty backlash, give new salience to the issue of capital punishment, and transform its political connotations. After 1972, the death penalty ceased to be a matter of penal policy and became instead a symbolic battlefield—first in the "law and order" backlash against civil rights and later in the culture wars, functioning alongside issues like abortion, welfare rights, defendants' rights, and affirmative action as a litmus test of political affiliation and cultural belonging. Support for the death penalty became a marker of respect for states' rights and traditional authority; a respectable (that is to say, not openly racist) means of asserting that the civil rights movement had gone too far; and a vehicle for Southern resentment about interference by Northern liberals. It came to mean opposition to "moral decay," to the decline of personal responsibility, and to the erosion of traditional authority that was widely believed to be the social legacy of the 1960s.[81] Above all, support for the death penalty came to be a short-hand for a political position that was "tough on crime" and assumed to be in tune with popular attitudes.

After *Furman*, the death penalty became more than ever a Southern issue, first symbolically and then practically. After 1972, Northern states such as New York, Pennsylvania, and Ohio would no longer be among the leading executioners. Instead, the nation's executions would come to be concentrated in the South of the old Confederacy and Jim Crow. In the four decades since executions resumed in 1977, the Southern states have accounted for more than 80 percent of all executions.[82]

The reaction against *Furman* and America's subsequent shift to a "culture of control"—with its retributive revolution in sentencing law, the buildup of mass imprisonment, and the new politics of law and order—emerged out of the same political conflicts.[83] Indeed, the shift away from the progressive penal policy of the 1960s to the law and order politics of the 1990s began precisely at that moment, with the increase in prison population beginning in 1975 and continuing each year for more than thirty years thereafter. As retributivism and incapacitation displaced correctionalism as the core aims of penal policy, the death penalty ceased to stand in contradiction to general penal policy and became its symbolic leading edge. By politicizing the issue at a moment of rising anxiety about crime and disorder, and by mobilizing a wave of pro–death penalty activism, the *Furman* decision marked a watershed in public opinion trend lines. The steady erosion of public support for the institution that had been recorded throughout the 1950s and 1960s was reversed overnight, and majority opposition of the mid-1960s was transformed into majority support. This new pattern would continue for decades thereafter, peaking in the high-crime decade of the 1990s, when as many as 80 percent of Americans sometimes professed support for capital punishment.[84]

The decline of American liberalism in the late 1960s and 1970s is the fundamental cause of the failure of American "final-stage" abolition. That much is clear. It is also clear that the *Furman* episode was critical in transforming the political and cultural meaning of the American death penalty. The institution's new meanings were contingent—the product of a specific sequence of events, in a specific historical context. They were created by groups of actors who employed specific political rhetorics and strategies to forge semantic associations that resonated with parts of the public and eventually became embedded in the culture. But though they were contingent and event-driven, these new meanings also bear the marks of America's institutional structure. To that extent, they were overdetermined rather than chance outcomes. For this reason an analysis of America's institutions and social structures is vital to any explanation of America's peculiar institution.

These shifts in the death penalty's meaning were an emergent outcome of interaction sequences, not a fully controlled, deliberate recoding. That is how the political process works. Contingent, historical events, specific to a time and place, give rise to a sequence of actions and reactions. In that process, contingency counts, context counts, history counts. No one fully controlled what happened—not the LDF litigants, nor the Supreme Court justices, nor the right-wing commentators, nor the onlooking audience. The death penalty's meaning escaped the grasp of all who sought to control it. Instead, the underlying conflicts and fault lines of American society structured patterns of action and helped shape the eventual outcomes. The death penalty's new meanings were grounded in the raw materials of pre-existing conflicts and shaped by the structuring presence of an institutional landscape.

Reinventing the
Death Penalty

There exists in some parts of the world sanctimonious criticism of
America's death penalty as somehow unworthy of a civilized society. I say sanctimonious because most of the countries to which
these finger-waggers belong had the death penalty themselves until
recently—and indeed many of them would still have it if the democratic will prevailed.

JUSTICE ANTONIN SCALIA, *KANSAS V MARSH*, 2006

In the late 1960s, the U.S. Supreme Court was given a leading role in the
movement to secure abolition. In other Western nations, abolition had
come about because governing elites were able to pass laws prohibiting
the practice on a nationwide basis. Such legislative abolition was impossible in America, where the power to punish rests with individual states
rather than with the central government, but reformers hoped the federal
courts might bring about the same result by other means. The social forces
prompting abolition were much the same in America as they were elsewhere—the rationalization and softening of state power, the politics of liberal democracy and civil rights, the culture of humanism and civilized refinement. But the institutional mechanisms through which reform was
pursued were different, and different in ways that mattered.

From the 1960s onward, the death penalty reform movement directed
its efforts toward the nation's federal courts. Its new aim was to achieve
nationwide abolition by characterizing the death penalty not as a policy
matter for the individual states but as a constitutionally prohibited practice condemned by the U.S. Bill of Rights. By framing the issue in this way,
the reformers were, in effect, consolidating dozens of diverse jurisdictions
into a single practicable object to be addressed by the highest court of the
nation.

This, in itself, was a significant move. By the second half of the twentieth
century, the death penalties of other Western countries had long been sub-

ject to the reforming effects of a centralized, bureaucratized state that imposed national procedures and centralized control over the power to punish. In the United States, capital punishment practices remained radically localized and relatively unregulated, even as late as 1972. The constitutional litigation of the 1960s thus effected a structural change in the politics of the death penalty, shifting the issue from the local to the national level. And once the Court took up that challenge, it effectively federalized the system, locating the American death penalty in a complicated new system of local and national controls, and imposing new forms of procedure and review on every death penalty state.

Once it acknowledged that capital punishment raised questions of constitutional law, the Court became responsible for settling those questions. As LDF litigators made clear, the states' capital punishment processes raised issues of due process, equal protection, and cruel and unusual punishment. And by the 1960s, elite opinion in many parts of the United States had largely turned against the institution. But the death penalty was also a long-standing practice, popular with many Americans, and regarded as legitimate by the Constitution's Framers and the Supreme Court's prior case law. In taking up the question of capital punishment, the Court was entering a legal and political minefield. From the late 1960s to the present, the Court has sought to trace a route through that treacherous terrain while struggling to resolve a problem it has now made its own. In the hundreds of capital case decisions between then and now, we see the Court strive to reduce the gap between capital process and the rule of law; to reduce the friction between modern executions and civilized and humanitarian sensibilities; and to erase the association between capital punishment and the nation's history of lynching and racial violence.

Unlike the reforming parliaments of other nations, the Supreme Court could not act—or be seen to act—as an autonomous sovereign. Its authority was contained within the four corners of the Constitution, and the scope of its decision-making depended on the legal issues raised by the cases it heard. The Court's capital jurisprudence was affected by the need to maintain a proper balance between state and federal power and between judicial, legislative, and executive branches of government. It was affected, too, by changes in the Court's composition, shifts in the political environment, and practical problems of criminal justice administration, all of which hampered the Court's capacity for sustained and consistent policy formation. Most important, the Court operated in a legal context that was transformed every time it made a decision, the web of precedents growing each time denser and more constraining. The Court can ignore or reverse these, of course—and it has done so on several notable occasions.

But every time it does so, it risks paying a price in loss of perceived integrity and of popular trust.

The task of administering the death penalty also brought with it some uniquely grave burdens. From the late 1970s, the Court was obliged to decide last-minute appeals from prisoners facing imminent execution. Deciding, in emergency proceedings, whether a prisoner should live or die became an all-too-frequent task for the justices, bringing with it an unaccustomed moral burden that must have sometimes seemed insupportable.[1]

Overseeing the death penalties of three dozen states could never have proved to be an easy task, but its difficulty was increased by internal disagreements among the justices about the Court's role and the death penalty's constitutional validity. The results are plain for all to see. If commentators agree on one thing it is that the capital punishment case law developed by the Court over the last forty years is confused and contradictory.[2]

In the hundreds of decisions it has handed down on the topic, the Court has on several notable occasions reversed itself or abruptly switched directions. As a body of rules and principles, the constitutional law of capital punishment is notoriously hard to decipher.[3] But if these holdings are opaque when considered as doctrinal developments, their logic becomes clear when we attend to the strategic considerations motivating the Court's decisions.

Rationalize, Civilize, Democratize

Our story begins with *Gregg v Georgia* in 1976, the case that began the reconstruction of America's death penalty in its late-modern mode. In the years following *Furman,* dozens of capital statutes poured out of the state legislatures, each of them designed to overcome the constitutional infirmities that had troubled the Court. As early as 1973, offenders were once again being sentenced to death, though the legality of their sentences was in doubt pending a Court ruling on their validity. In 1976, the Court finally ruled on the issue, having chosen to hear five cases—*Gregg v Georgia, Jurek v Texas, Profitt v Florida, Woodson v North Carolina,* and *Roberts v Louisiana*—selected to represent each new type of capital statute passed since 1972.[4]

The climate in which the Court decided *Gregg* and the four associated cases was quite different from the one in which the *Furman* litigation had been launched in the 1960s—altered by the "law and order" backlash that swept the country in the Nixon years, by the post-*Furman* mobilization of death penalty support in the states, and more recently by criticism of the Court's decision on abortion in the 1973 case of *Roe v Wade*. Signs of this changed climate were everywhere in the 1976 cases: from the fact that thirty-five new state statutes were up for consideration, to the decision by the U.S. solicitor general to lodge an *amicus* brief supporting the states, to Justice Powell's pointed reference to the nation's rising murder rates and the need to deter "the slaughter of Americans."[5] If *Furman* had been viewed as a civil rights case, *Gregg* was decidedly about criminal justice.

The lawyers for convicted murderer Troy Leon Gregg argued that even under its new statutory regime Georgia's capital process remained constitutionally flawed. The state's attempts to channel discretion had, they claimed, neglected prosecutorial decisions and plea bargaining—key decisions in the capital process—and its statutory specification of aggravating and mitigating factors was too vague to be effective in guiding jury decisions. As a result, the selection of those sentenced to death remained arbitrary and often racist. The state responded that its reformed process—with separate hearings on guilt and penalty, statutory guidelines for the exercise of discretion, and mandatory appellate review—adequately met the *Furman* concerns about arbitrariness and discrimination and was therefore constitutional.

In his arguments to the Court, U.S. Solicitor General Robert Bork insisted that democratically elected legislators—and not the Supreme Court justices—should determine whether capital punishment is cruel and unusual. Noting that thirty-five states and the U.S. Congress had enacted new capital statutes, Bork submitted that "it is utterly implausible that so many legislatures can, time and again, fail to reflect the will of the people concerning capital punishment."[6] The American people had willed the death penalty, and it was no part of the Court's job to thwart that democratic will.

On July 2, 1976, the Court ruled seven to two that the Georgia statute was constitutionally valid and that Troy Leon Gregg had been properly sentenced to death. Presenting the plurality opinion, Justice Stewart said that the legislative response to *Furman* was a "marked indication of society's endorsement of the death penalty for murder"; that whether or not the death penalty deterred, retribution was a proper state purpose, it being "an expression of the community's belief" that some crimes are so grievous that only a death penalty is an "adequate response"; and that Georgia's new procedures "seem to satisfy the concerns of *Furman*" about arbitrariness and caprice. Stewart went on to say that "[c]onsiderations of federalism" and respect for a legislature's ability "to evaluate ... the moral consensus concerning the death penalty" led the Court to the conclusion

that "the infliction of death as a punishment for murder is not without justification and thus is not unconstitutionally severe."[7]

In the companion cases of *Jurek* and *Profitt* the Court upheld the Florida
and Texas statutes, which, though they differed in detail from the Georgia
law, also provided the due process safeguards of bifurcation, sentencing
guidelines, and appellate review. But in *Woodson* and *Roberts* the Court
struck down the North Carolina and Louisiana statutes on the grounds
that their mandatory sentencing structures provided no standards to guide
jury decision-making and failed to provide offenders with the individuated
sentencing process to which the Eighth Amendment entitled them.[8]

The *Gregg* majority decided, in effect, that *Furman*'s arbitrariness
concerns might be met by procedural arrangements that allowed for
guided discretion. In so doing, it contradicted Justice Harlan's argument in
McGautha that any such guidance would be impossibly vague and ineffective. By contrast, in declaring mandatory sentencing unconstitutional in
capital cases, the Court also insisted that the problem of discretion could
not be dealt with by abolishing it altogether. Henceforth, if a state wished
to employ the death penalty, it would have to design sentencing procedures
that steered between "the Charybdis of *Furman*," which gave too much
discretion, and "the Scylla of *Woodson*," which gave too little.[9]

Legally, the *Gregg* decision merely upheld a Georgia state statute and affirmed Gregg's death sentence. (As it turned out, Troy Gregg escaped the
state's executioner only to meet his death at the hands of a fellow capital
convict. In 1980 he and several other inmates escaped from Reidesville
Prison's death row. His dead body was discovered in a North Carolina
lake a day later; he had been stomped to death by one of his fellow escap-
ees.[10]) Practically, however, it determined the course of the next forty years
of America's death penalty history. In upholding Georgia's new law, the
Court declared that capital punishment could be constitutionally valid. Or,
more precisely, it declared that states were entitled to put people to death
so long as their processes for doing so conformed to procedural requirements that the Court deemed acceptable.

This was hardly a full-throated endorsement of the state's right to kill.
The double negative of the Court's formulation—"We hold that the death
penalty is not a form of punishment that may never be imposed"—made
its ambivalence perfectly apparent.[11] So, too, did the "death is different"
doctrine that the Court began to develop in *Gregg* and *Woodson,* a doctrine that treated the death penalty not as a regular criminal law sanction
but as a problematic undertaking that can be permitted only when accompanied by special safeguards and extraordinary procedures.[12]

The Court was saying, in effect, that the states could put people to death
so long as they did not stage anything that looked like a lynching. The

LDF's litigation had demonstrated to the Court that lynchlike processes—characterized by lack of due process, racial bias, and overweening community pressure—were still endemic in the Southern states. And the Court was in no doubt that "legal lynching" was anathema to constitutional law. But whereas the LDF insisted that the death penalty would always and inevitably resemble a lynching in its arbitrariness, lawlessness, and racialized selection, the Court eventually took the view that capital punishment could be cured of its association with racism and lawlessness. The Court's project then became to reform the death penalty by removing its offending elements and bringing it into line with the rule of law. The result was a reluctant, conditional permission: "*The state shalt not kill, unless . . .*" which is the commandment that has structured the American death penalty ever since.

Rather than outlaw capital punishment or declare it unproblematically legitimate, *Gregg* marked the start of an effort by the Court to rationalize and civilize the American death penalty. Over the next few years, most states crafted laws and processes that approximated those of the three state systems the Court had upheld. In the decades since, though with varying degrees of intensity, the Supreme Court has overseen the states' capital processes, engaging in an ongoing dialogue about the proper exercise of the states' power to put offenders to death.

For the LDF litigants who had won a great victory in *Furman* and closed down the nation's execution chambers for almost a decade, *Gregg* was a bitter defeat. The death penalty had been deemed constitutional and given the blessing of the Supreme Court. Indeed, for death penalty reformers everywhere, the Court's decision was a major setback. For all its ambivalence, the *Gregg* decision was the single most important affirmation that capital punishment had received anywhere in the Western world in recent times. America was back in the "retentionist" camp, and other retentionist nations across the globe would henceforth derive strength and legitimacy from its being there.

But the death penalty is never simply "on" or "off." If it is permitted at all it is practiced in accordance with specific legal, procedural, and evidentiary requirements that make sentences and executions more or less likely, more or less conditional, and more or less speedy—and its use is conditioned by a political and cultural environment that make it more or less legitimate, more or less transgressive. *Gregg* did not switch capital punishment back on, returning it to its earlier state. It inaugurated a whole new capital punishment complex—America's death penalty in a late-modern mode—with a distinctive set of legal rules, institutional forms, and cultural figures, the details of which would emerge over the ensuing decades.

The hundreds of capital case decisions made by the Court since *Gregg* are not reducible to any singular logic or unfolding pattern. Each line of legal reasoning has been contested by dissenting minorities on the Court, and many have been reversed or modified by subsequent decisions. The insistence on procedural propriety that characterized the Court's "super due process" phase later gave way to a stress on finality, on expediting postconviction processes, and on removing procedural obstacles that prevented the states from executing death sentences.[13] And in capital cases involving victim-impact statements, mentally retarded offenders, and juveniles, the Court ruled definitively on one occasion, only to reverse itself a few years later.[14]

Within the labyrinthine complexity of the Court's death penalty discourse we can identify three bright threads of jurisprudential reasoning that run through the texts from 1976 until the present. A *rationalizing* and *juridifying* jurisprudence grounded in the Fourteenth Amendment aims to rationalize the administration of capital punishment and subject it to the discipline of legal rules and procedures. A *civilizing* and *humanizing* jurisprudence based on the Eighth Amendment seeks to prohibit "cruel and unusual" practices and minimize the more disturbing elements of the death penalty process. Finally, a *democratizing* and *localizing* jurisprudence grounded in the Constitution's separation of powers insists on returning control of capital punishment to state legislators and to the discretionary decision-making of elected county prosecutors and judges and local community juries.

These three strategies, which often developed in tension with one another, emerged at different times, in changing legal and political climates, in reaction to different issues and events, in cases decided by different justices. Moreover, they do not describe all the characteristics of the Court's capital punishment jurisprudence. Concerns to uphold *stare decisis,* to ensure expediency and finality, to maintain public confidence in the legal system, to avoid disruption to criminal justice administration, and to uphold the Court's own authority and integrity—all of these also played a role. But the strategies of *rationalization, civilization,* and *democratization* have been absolutely fundamental to the body of law that the Court has devised to handle capital punishment, and America's late-modern death penalty law cannot be understood without reference to them.

These three approaches were developed to deal with the impossible predicament that capital punishment presented. Rather than decide the matter once and for all—as constitutional courts in South Africa and Hungary would subsequently do—the more divided, more deferential United States Supreme Court has developed a set of strategies that allow it to manage the death penalty problem, reform capital punishment's more egregious excesses, and shift responsibility for its continuing existence.[15] Some of the time the Court has sought to overhaul what Justice Blackmun called "the machinery of death" to align it more closely with norms of decency and justice. At other times, the Court has backed away from this ameliorative work, insisting that the death penalty is a creature not of law but of politics, to be determined by political processes and the preferences of local communities.

The Court's first two strategies—*rationalization* and *civilization*—are attempts to finesse the problems inherent in contemporary capital punishment. They aim to reduce the conflict between capital punishment and contemporary cultural norms by rationalizing state killing, subjecting it to the rule of law, and minimizing the extent to which it offends contemporary sensibilities. The third strategy—*democratization*—deals with the predicament by disowning it, denying the Court's responsibility for the issue, and pushing the death penalty back to the local political processes and crime scenes from which it emerged.

We should note that each of these strategies expresses concerns and arguments that are already familiar, either from the history of capital punishment reform or from the history of the American polity. This is because the Court, a paradigmatically American institution, wound up being the means through which the general transformative processes affecting capital punishment—the rationalizing, liberalizing, and civilizing of state power—took place in late twentieth-century America. Standing at the confluence of two large-scale historical processes—Western death penalty reform and American political development—the Court was in a position to determine the fate of capital punishment in the United States. In the event, the justices mostly backed away from this responsibility. They insisted instead that it was for "the people" to decide whether to retain lethal punishment and that, as a constitutional matter, the death penalty would be valid so long as it complied with those legal rules and civilized sensibilities that the Court deemed binding. In the thirty years since *Gregg*, the justices have assembled a complex legal scaffolding of procedures, prohibitions, and permissions. That elaborate scaffolding now frames America's peculiar practice of capital punishment.

Rationalizing

The line of cases that forms the Court's *rationalizing* jurisprudence attempts to regulate the individual states by means of national standards that subject their death penalties to the discipline of legal rules and procedural propriety—a project grounded in the due process and equal protection clauses of the Fourteenth Amendment. As Justice Stewart put it in *Woodson*, "rationalizing the sentencing process" is a recipe for reforming capital punishment, a cure that can be achieved "by replacing arbitrary and wanton jury discretion with objective standards to guide, regularize, and make [the process] rationally reviewable." In place of personalistic power, punitive passions, and arbitrary death sentences, this strategy aims to substitute the rule of law and rational decision-making. "It is," as Justice Stevens elsewhere insisted, "of vital importance to the defendant and to the community that any decision to impose the death sentence be, and appear to be, based on reason."[16]

The regulation of state power by reference to legal rules and procedures—*juridification*—is, of course, a familiar court activity.[17] But that juridifying activity runs into serious problems when it comes to regulating the death penalty, causing some justices to regard it as inappropriate and others as impossible.[18] The impulse to juridify capital punishment encounters political difficulty because considerations of "federalism" and "separation of powers" place limits on the Court's power to intrude on autonomous state practices. For some justices, such as Black, Burger, Rehnquist, Scalia, and Thomas, this is a central consideration that leads them to regard the Court's regulatory efforts as fundamentally misplaced. Then there is the jurisprudential difficulty of subjecting a discretionary, subjective, moral decision—who should live and who should die?—to the discipline of rules.[19] For some members of the Court, such as Justice Harlan, this was a practical impossibility that the Court should not even attempt, leading him to argue for a "hands-off" approach.[20] For others, such as Justice Brennan, the impossibility of juridifying juries' decisions about life or death led to the opposite conclusion. Since "the rule of law" and "the power of the States to kill" are in "irreconcilable conflict," the appropriate recourse for the Court is to abolish the institution altogether.[21]

Irreconcilable or not, the Court has made it its project to bring the practice of capital punishment within the purview of the rule of law, seeking to ensure, as Justice Blackmun put it, "a greater degree of equality and rationality in the administration of death." If the chief problem that *Furman* identified was the states' lawless capital processes, the chief solution would be the imposition of rules and procedures, developed on a nationwide basis and overseen by federal courts. Henceforth, and with the significant exception of prosecutorial discretion, every aspect of the capital process—jury selection, trial procedure, sentencing, appeals, and postconviction review—would be subject to more demanding substantive and procedural rules, backed up by the scrutiny of the federal courts. By these means, the

Court might fulfill what Justice Blackmun described as its "constitutionally imposed duty to provide meaningful judicial oversight to the administration of death by the States."[22]

In imposing these rules and undertaking to enforce them by allowing defendants access to the federal courts (by means of an expanded use of the *habeas corpus* writ), the Court was creating a new system of centralized control that allowed it to oversee the different capital processes of nearly forty death penalty jurisdictions. Compared with the more centralized, uniform, bureaucratically administered systems of criminal justice that characterized other Western nations, this was less than fully rational and systematic. Nevertheless, it was America's equivalent of the state rationalization that had occurred elsewhere. For the first time, a branch of the national government had developed a means to manage the diverse state systems from the center, allowing the Court to expand or contract the reach of the death penalty, and to speed up or slow down the rate of executions as it deemed appropriate.[23] At the same time, the juridification process enacted a liberal reform of capital punishment, using the values of liberalism (rule-based restraints on state power, respect for the individual, due process, legality) to reshape America's capital punishment practice.

The rationalizing and juridifying process began in earnest in 1976, when *Gregg* and its associated cases upheld state laws that mandated a bifurcated trial, guided jury discretion, and mandatory appeals. In *Woodson v North Carolina*, which reviewed the mandatory sentencing structure of a North Carolina capital statute, the Court identified a need for "objective standards to guide, regularize and make rationally reviewable the process for imposing a sentence of death" and deemed the statutes of Georgia, Texas, and Florida to have provided such standards.[24] On this reasoning, the *Woodson* decision invalidated the North Carolina statute on the grounds that its mandatory sentencing provision failed to provide an individuated sentencing process that could assess the death-worthiness of the particular defendant. As a result, today's death penalty sentencing involves a process of individuation that escapes the grip of general rules. In effect, the liberal value that requires respect for individuality has undermined the liberal value that requires uniform rules.

Of course, the juridification of capital punishment did not begin with *Gregg*. As early as the 1930s, the Court had begun to require legal counsel for capital defendants, to invalidate capital sentences imposed amid mob violence, and to limit the states' power to empanel all-white juries. Moreover, the Court's 1968 decision in *Witherspoon v Illinois* had placed limits on the state's power to exclude jurors who had qualms about capital punishment, while *Furman* had required that the sentencing authority in capital trials not be given unguided discretion.[25] But it was *Gregg* itself, and a series of decisions in the years immediately following, that gave real detail and substance to the notion that the capital process must be juridified, holding death to a higher standard of legality and procedural propriety.

In the period since 1976, that juridification project has waxed and waned, accounting for a greater or lesser number of the Court's decisions. Its high point was in the years immediately after *Gregg,* when the Court put in place a regime of enhanced procedural protections and safeguards that came to be known as "super due process." In 1977, *Gardner v Florida* extended due process requirements to the sentencing phase of the capital trial, and two years later *Green v Georgia* consolidated this development by declaring that the Sixth Amendment gave the capital defendant a right to present evidence at sentencing.[26]

Lockett v Ohio in 1978 concerned the validity of a death sentence imposed on Sandra Lockett, who had driven the getaway car in a robbery that had resulted in the murder of a pawnshop owner. Lockett had not been directly involved in the shooting, but because the Ohio statute did not permit the jury to consider mitigating circumstances in such cases, she was sentenced to death. The Supreme Court's seven-to-one decision in favor of Lockett significantly extended the rights of defendants during the "penalty" or "sentencing" phase of the trial, requiring that capital juries be allowed to consider any mitigating factor that the defense might present. In 1980, *Godfrey v Georgia* found one of Georgia's statutory aggravating factors to be unconstitutionally void for vagueness, thereby requiring greater precision in the guidance that states give to capital sentencers. Six years later, in *Ford v Wainwright,* the Court held that a death row prisoner claiming to be insane is entitled to a judicial evaluation of his claim before the state can execute his sentence.[27] These were all examples of juridification in its "super due process" phase, making it harder for states to secure a death sentence. In the seven years following *Gregg,* the Supreme Court vacated or reversed the death sentences in all but one of the fifteen capital cases argued before it.[28]

Juridification may have been the centerpiece of reforming efforts following *Gregg,* but it did not command a full consensus on the Court. At one extreme, the abolitionist justices Brennan and Marshall regarded it as a futile effort to reform an incorrigibly lawless institution. Justice Blackmun, after bitter experience, came to hold the same view: "Rather than continue to coddle the Court's delusion that the desired level of fairness has been achieved and the need for regulation eviscerated, I feel morally and intellectually obligated simply to concede that the death penalty experiment has failed."[29] At the other extreme, more conservative justices such as

Rehnquist (and later Scalia and Thomas) viewed much of the Court's juridifying effort as an illegitimate restraint on the powers of the states.

In the early 1980s, several justices expressed disquiet at the cumulative impact of the Court's juridifying decisions, pointing to the difficulties and delays that states now faced in executing properly imposed death sentences. In 1981, Justice Rehnquist lashed out at his more liberal colleagues, accusing them of having made "a mockery" of the nation's criminal justice system and of curtailing capital punishment until it was "virtually an illusion." In an exasperated dissent he declared, "Since 1976, hundreds of juries have sentenced hundreds of persons to death, presumably in the belief that the death penalty in those circumstances is warranted." Yet, he continued, "*virtually nothing happens* except endlessly drawn out legal proceedings."[30]

Two years later, this view was echoed by Justice Lewis Powell, who had come to believe that the juridifying reforms he had previously supported had now gone too far. In May 1983, Powell told a group of federal judges that the multiple appeals and *habeas* petitions that had become typical in capital cases represented "a malfunctioning of our system of justice" and threatened to undermine public confidence.[31] Evidently, this view came to find broader support because a series of cases on penalty-phase proceedings decided in 1983—*Zant v Stevens, Ramos v California, Barefoot v Estelle,* and *Barclay v Florida*—demonstrated that a majority of the Court had decided to pull back from "super due process" and refrain from further instructing the states on how they must administer death penalty trials.[32]

This turn away from juridification toward what Robert Weisberg called the "deregulation of death" was to recur periodically into the next decade.[33] In the mid-1990s, acting in concert with Congress, the Court again pressed the values of federalism, comity, and finality, stressing the need to speed up the capital process and permit the states to achieve their retributive purposes in a timelier manner.[34] In a series of decisions the Court relaxed standards on ineffective assistance of counsel and the prosecutorial duty to disclose exculpatory evidence, and also narrowed the availability of federal *habeas corpus* review. At the same time the Court made it clear that it would no longer examine case-specific proportionality, review capital sentencing patterns for evidence of disparity, nor require state appellate courts to conduct comparative proportionality review.[35] The predictable result was an increase in the flow of capital convicts into the nation's execution chambers. In 1999, the annual execution toll reached ninety-eight, the highest of the post-*Furman* period.

Despite these reversals, the Court continues sporadically to engage in this rationalizing project—as evidenced in recent cases where the Court pressured the states to provide better legal representation for defendants by making it easier for petitioners to sustain claims of ineffective assistance of counsel.[36] The cumulative impact of this whole line of rationalizing and juridifying decisions remains deeply controversial. Some commentators regard the new due process rights as a major limitation on the power of the states. Others view these supposed rights as a "Big Lie" because many defendants who lack good legal representation are unable to make use of them.[37] Whichever view one takes, it is nevertheless clear that the Court's rationalizing strategy has effectively transformed capital punishment, creating a late-modern modality quite distinct from the system that existed prior to *Furman*. And whether intended or not, the contemporary institution's characteristics of deferral and delay, death row confinement, reversal and exoneration, rarity of executions, and high-cost capital cases—together with the "capital punishment as law" narrative—all have their sources in these decisions.

Civilizing

The Court's second strategy has been to insist that the death penalty and its execution must accord with modern civilized norms, abjuring any elements that appear gruesome or inhumane. This jurisprudence is grounded in the Eighth Amendment and a reading of its prohibition on "cruel and unusual punishment" as requiring that capital punishment accord with "evolving standards of decency" and the civilized, humane sensibilities these entail.[38] As Justice Stewart put it, the Constitution requires "that the state's power to punish be exercised within the limits of civilized standards."[39]

According to the Court in *Furman* and since, American culture has come to embrace the values of human dignity, the uniqueness of the individual, and the standards of decency associated with "evolved," "mature," or "civilized" societies—and the death penalty must conform accordingly. In its Eighth Amendment opinions, the Court has frequently talked of "civilization" but it has not been careful to distinguish between "civilization" in the sense of aesthetics or appearances and "civilization" in the more moral, humane sense of empathy and compassion. As a consequence, the Court's commitment to "evolved standards" and to "decency" often invokes the language of humanitarianism interchangeably with the language of civilized propriety and refinement. But the decisions of the majority of justices have usually privileged the latter at the expense of the former and, as a result, the concealment of suffering in the capital process has taken priority over the aim of ending it altogether.

The language of civilization and humanity ("barbaric," "enormity," "civilized standards," "no man of right feeling and heart can refrain from shuddering," "conscience of mankind," and so on) is regularly invoked in the Supreme Court's capital case opinions. The rhetorical implication (if not exactly the doctrinal logic) is that any permissible capital punishment must be seen to be "civilized" and "humane" as well as lawful. In contemporary America, a constitutionally permissible death penalty has to satisfy aesthetic and moral standards as well as legal and procedural ones.[40]

Justice Brennan, for example, frequently insisted that the death penalty is inconsistent with the principles of "civilized treatment" and respect for "the dignity of man" that are guaranteed by the Eighth Amendment. As he put it, "The calculated killing of a human being by the State involves, by its very nature, a denial of the executed person's humanity."[41] Such a punishment, he said, has no place in a civilized society and violates our constitutional commitment to "life itself" and its "transcendent importance."[42]

More than any other justice, Brennan thought of "the civilized" and "the humane" as intertwined and explicitly invoked the values of humanism in his interpretation of the Eighth Amendment. On one occasion he wrote that the constitutional prohibition on "cruel and unusual punishments" is in fact a ban on "uncivilized and inhuman punishments."[43] On another he described the Eighth Amendment as prohibiting "inhuman and barbarous" methods. The state, he declared, must treat its members "with respect for their intrinsic worth as human beings"; "even the vilest criminal remains a human being possessed of common human dignity" and is entitled to be treated as a "fellow human being." On this reading of the Constitution, "The fatal constitutional infirmity in the punishment of death is that it treats 'members of the human race as nonhumans.'"[44]

But Brennan is hardly alone in invoking the values of humanism and civilization as bedrock principles of constitutional interpretation. A similarly humanistic concern for the uniqueness and value of individuals is apparent in *Woodson* and *Lockett,* where the Court held that capital juries must be permitted to consider the individuality of each defendant, viewing him or her as a unique person and hearing all claims in mitigation before deciding their fate.[45] Justice Stevens's dissent in *Stanford v Kentucky*—in which a majority held that there was no constitutional impediment to sentencing offenders to death who were sixteen or seventeen years old at the time of their crime—also invokes the language of humanizing change. As he wrote in a later memo decision about a rehearing of the case, "The practice of executing [juvenile] offenders is a relic of the past and is inconsistent with evolving standards of decency in a civilized society."[46]

If Brennan invoked the language of humanism, his fellow abolitionist Thurgood Marshall was more inclined to express himself in the idiom of "civilization" and invoke the progressive sweep of history as the basis for his position. Thus Marshall greeted the Court's decision in *Furman* as a triumph of the civilizing process, "a major milestone in the long road up from barbarism" that allowed the United States to join the other civilized nations that "celebrate their regard for civilization and humanity by shunning capital punishment."[47]

Similarly, the opinions in *Coker v Georgia, Enmund v Florida, Ford v Wainwright, Atkins v Virginia, Roper v Simmons,* and *Kennedy v Louisiana* insist that executing rapists, robbers, the insane, the mentally infirm, juvenile offenders, or child rapists is not appropriate in a civilized society.[48] The *Coker v Georgia* decision of 1977 ruled that the death penalty was a "grossly disproportionate" punishment for the crime of rape, given that nearly all the death penalty states now declined to make rape a capital offense, at least for the rape of an adult. (Ironically, given the historic use of capital rape laws to punish blacks, Erlich Coker was a white male. He had committed the rape after escaping from prison, where he was serving sentences for murder, rape, kidnapping, and assault.) The *Atkins* and *Roper* cases were major departures from precedent that show the influence of international opinion on Justices Kennedy and Breyer, the swing voters who helped form the majority. In these two cases the abolitionist opinions invoked a further type of civilization discourse, citing evidence of progressive historical trends—the shared direction of recent legislation in a number of states—and deeming these to be indicative of evolving standards.[49]

If the project of rationalization is reformative—fixing up the death penalty to conform to the rule of law—the civilizing and humanizing project tends toward the abolitionist, regarding capital punishment or particular forms of its application as offensive to civilized sensibilities and therefore unconstitutional. Given the orientation of the Court since *Gregg*—which has been reformist rather than abolitionist—this has meant that the trope of "civilization" is more often present in dissent than in the majority, but there have been numerous cases where the Court has prohibited a particular practice for being "cruel and unusual" or in violation of "evolved standards of decency."

Civilizing tropes shaped the abolitionist decisions of the *Coker, Enmund, Ford, Atkins, Roper,* and *Kennedy* cases just mentioned. But this should not blind us to those occasions when a "civilizing" reform works to *preserve* the death penalty, albeit in more aesthetically pleasing forms.

A civilized aesthetic is often invoked in cases concerned with execution methods and procedures—since executions are dangerously prone to generate the sights, sounds, and smells of physical violence and gruesome images of bodily distortion and disfigurement, all of which are disturbing to refined sensibilities. In a number of instances, state supreme courts and federal courts of appeal have ruled that certain execution technologies are "barbaric" and uncivilized, while allowing other methods to stand.[50] The first case to do so was *In Re Kemmler* in 1890, which deemed New York's new electrocution technique to be legal while noting in passing that punishments that were "manifestly cruel and unusual, such as burning at the stake, crucifixion, or hanging, drawing and quartering, or the like" would be constitutionally prohibited. One hundred years later, the Court of Appeals for the Ninth Circuit, discussing Washington state's practice of hanging, declared, "We reject barbaric forms of punishment . . . not merely because of the pain they inflict but because we pride ourselves on being a civilized society."[51] And the Georgia State Supreme Court, ruling the state's electric chair to be unconstitutional, declared a prohibition on punishments that "unnecessarily mutilate or disfigure" the condemned prisoner's body and held, accordingly, that "electrocution, with its specter of excruciating pain and its certainty of cooked brains and blistered bodies," is in violation of the prohibition against cruel and unusual punishment in the Georgia constitution.[52]

Lethal injection, by contrast, has been found to be lawful, since it generally puts the condemned to death without emitting the sights and sounds of suffering or defilement and does so in a context that suggests clinical care rather than lethal violence. When in 2008 a challenge was brought to Kentucky's execution protocol in *Baze v Rees,* alleging that a prisoner undergoing lethal injection may suffer extreme physical pain without showing signs of discomfort because of the prior administration of a paralyzing agent, the Court found that the protocol in question met the Constitution's standards. In concluding that Kentucky's execution protocol satisfies the Eighth Amendment, the Court refused to require the state to adopt an alternative means of administering the lethal drugs that expert witnesses had described as a more reliable means of avoiding pain. Although the proposed alternative promised to reduce the probability that the condemned would suffer pain, it would also have the effect of prolonging the time it would take for him to die and cause his body to writhe and spasm in a fashion liable to be disturbing to witnesses. In effect, the challengers offered the Court a choice between preventing a slight risk of suffering on the part of the condemned and protecting the witnesses from the sight of disturbing bodily movements. The Court chose the latter. Indeed, Chief Justice Roberts was quite explicit about the value the Court gave to "the procedure's dignity" and the importance of shielding witnesses from disturbing sights, even if that arrangement caused a risk of suffering to the condemned prisoner.[53]

The Court's civilizing decisions have established that if capital punishment is to be constitutional, the states must refine and sanitize their execution techniques until death comes to appear as the "mere extinguishment of life."[54] If persons are to be killed, their killing must involve a minimum of physical violence and visible unpleasantness. Today's lethal injection, the protocols that surround it, and the metaphor of medicine through which it represents itself have all been shaped by these civilizing concerns, as has the abolition of embarrassing practices such as the execution of juveniles and the mentally retarded.

These civilizing reforms did not go unopposed, on the Court or off, though in contrast to the rationalizing reforms, none of these developments has yet been reversed. Justices such as Rehnquist and Scalia, who vigorously objected to these decisions in the name of states' rights and strict constructionism, did not hesitate to describe them as elitist and antidemocratic. Thus in *Woodson,* Rehnquist criticized the Court for its "desire to save the people from themselves," and in *Atkins* Scalia accused the majority justices of imagining they have "moral sentiments superior to those of the common herd."[55] The major opposition, however, has stemmed from a majority of the American public, state legislatures, and the U.S. Congress, who repeatedly made it clear in the aftermath of *Furman* that American "standards of decency," as expressed through the political process, did not consider the death penalty so uncivilized or so inhumane that it ought not to be available as a punishment for murder and certain other offenses besides.

Democratizing

If *rationalizing* and *civilizing* were familiar processes, common throughout the Western world, the Court's third strategy—*democratizing* and *localizing*—was peculiarly American and changed the death penalty in ways that ran contrary to what occurred elsewhere. Grounded in—though never determined by—the institutional structure and ethos of the American polity (the separation of powers, the federalist commitment to sovereign states' rights, and the values of local democracy and populism), the Court's "democratizing" decisions declined to take over responsibility for capital punishment and instead returned the issue to "the people." This was not merely the deference typically shown by conservative justices to political majorities and legislators. It was a positive policy of devolving crucial decisions about the application of capital punishment to local communities and their political officials. The court has, on multiple occasions, chosen to empower fifty states to deploy capital punishment if *they* so choose, thereby forgoing the possibility of national abolition.

It was by means of this democratizing and localizing jurisprudence that the Court told state legislatures it was up to them to abolish or not as they saw fit, just as it was up to them to address evidence of systemic defects in their capital punishment systems—if they so chose. It was by dint of this same reasoning that the Court constituted local prosecutors, local judges, and local juries as the frontline arbiters of individual death-worthiness and the constitutional considerations involved. After a time the Court came to insist that justice—as shaped by the values of democracy and localism—required that juries alone might impose death sentences, since juries best understood the community sentiments that made such sentences justifiable. And finally, after having previously decided in the opposite direction, the Court ruled it permissible for victims' relatives to present "victim-impact" evidence in capital cases, in part because American public opinion appeared to favor such a development. In doing so, the Court strengthened the retributive forces at work in the capital trial while simultaneously giving voice to another group of local actors.

As a consequence of these holdings, the power to establish capital laws, to bring capital charges, and to impose death sentences was vested, once again, in local political actors and decision-makers. The Court systematically empowered local figures—governors, state legislators, district attorneys, state judges, and local juries: most of them elected, all of them responsive to community sentiment—to decide the questions of life and death that capital cases entailed. The result is that the most important decisions in death penalty proceedings are now made by locally elected officials and by juries selected from the local community. The radical localism and populism of the American polity continue to determine the practical administration of capital cases—not because impersonal structures dictate they must, but because the Supreme Court has repeatedly said they should.

In one Supreme Court case after another we hear the self-abnegating voice of the judicial democrat: "let the people decide." In *Furman,* where the majority took matters into its own hands and declared America's capital punishment unconstitutional, democracy was the favorite theme of the dissenters. Chief Justice Burger objected that it was not for the courts to decide that the death penalty violated the Eighth Amendment because in a democracy that is a matter for "legislative judgment" and not judicial decision. He wrote that "in a democratic society legislatures, not courts, are constituted to respond to the will and consequently the moral values of the people."[56] Justice Rehnquist's *Furman* dissent echoed the same sentiment: "Sovereignty resides ultimately in the people as a whole" and is not to be abrogated by the "fiat" of a judicial elite "whose connection with the popular will is remote at best."[57] And Justice Scalia put the point with his usual acerbity in 1994 when he wrote: "If the people conclude that . . . more brutal deaths may be deterred by capital punishment; indeed if they merely conclude that justice requires such brutal deaths to be avenged by capital punishment, the creation of false, untextual and unhistorical contradictions within the Court's Eighth Amendment jurisprudence should not prevent them."[58]

The charge that the Court was acting as a liberal elite usurping the sovereign power of the people has been a constant refrain of dissenting justices whenever a case threatened to restrict the states' death penalty powers. In 1980 Justice Byron White (joined by Justice Rehnquist) wrote that "our job is not to peer majestically over the lower court's shoulder," and he described the majority's *Godfrey* decision (holding that one of Georgia's statutory aggravators was unconstitutionally vague) as "an unwarranted invasion into the realm of state law."[59]

This respect for "states' rights" and reluctance to "invade" the "sovereign" realm of state law sometimes outweighed the constitutional claims of individual defendants. In the landmark case of *McCleskey v Kemp,* in which petitioners brought powerful statistical evidence that Georgia's capital punishment system discriminated on the basis of race, the Court drew back from evaluating the empirical evidence or addressing the racial disparities to which it pointed, insisting that the state legislature was the proper body to address such matters. Writing for the Court, Justice Powell said that McCleskey's arguments concerning race discrimination "are best presented to the legislative bodies." It is not the Court's responsibility, he said, to determine the appropriate punishment for particular crimes: "It is the legislatures, the elected representatives of the people, that are constituted to respond to the will and consequently the moral values of the people."[60] The same apparently self-denying preference for the legislature's view of what does or does not constitute "cruel and unusual punishment" is to be found in the majority opinions in *Atkins, Roper,* and *Kennedy,* where the majority of the Court engaged in "a crude headcount" of state legislatures that had abolished the practices in question "as a way of substituting the judgment of others for its own."[61]

Thirty years after *Furman*, Justice Clarence Thomas was still sounding the states' rights theme in the 2002 case of *Kelly v South Carolina*, a case in which the trial judge had refused to instruct the jury that Kelly would be ineligible for parole if sentenced to life imprisonment: "Today's decision allows the Court to meddle further in a State's sentencing proceedings under the guise that the Constitution requires us to do so . . . it is not this Court's job to micromanage state sentencing proceedings . . . these are matters that the Constitution leaves to the States." Justice Sandra O'Connor did the same in *Roper* when she wrote that "this Court should not substitute its own 'inevitably subjective judgment' on how best to resolve this difficult moral question for the judgments of the Nation's democratically elected legislatures."[62] In *Coleman v Thompson* (1991)—in which the petitioner was barred from having his claims heard because his attorneys had missed a state filing deadline by three days—O'Connor began her opinion with the declaration, "This is a case about federalism."[63]

For these justices, the power of capital punishment is a sovereign right possessed by "the people" and their local representatives that is not to be abrogated, even by the highest court in the land. In this respect, their attitude runs opposite to that of European parliamentary elites, who refuse to surrender control of such issues to the people. This strain of thinking shapes the Court's deference to state courts—in the principle of exhaustion, for example, which insists that all state remedies be exhausted before the federal courts intervene. It shapes its deference to the state legislature's understandings of rational state purposes, to the state preference for "death-qualified" juries, and to the local prosecutor's decision to indict.[64]

Once the Supreme Court embraced the task of regulating capital punishment, the most important issue it had to decide concerned the allocation of the power to punish. Who would determine if a defendant deserved to live or to be put to death? The Court arrogated some of that power for itself, in that it narrowed the punishment's scope, specified procedural rules, and undertook to oversee state processes. But these were framing decisions, stipulating a procedural framework within which the death penalty could be imposed. When it came to individual life or death decisions, the Court refused to take charge. Indeed, it refused even to provide detailed legal rules to determine the sentencing of individuals or to review jury decisions and their cumulative patterns. Instead, it devolved these decisions to local actors. It empowered the prosecutor—a local elected official whose discretion to bring capital charges and to plea-bargain were nowhere regulated by the Court and rarely even mentioned. And it empowered the local jury, which it permitted to be "death-qualified" as the states preferred. Until 2002, it also empowered state trial judges, most of whom were elected, in those states that gave sentencing authority to judges rather than to juries.

By devising a legal framework in which the ultimate decision about the defendant's fate would depend not on a concrete legal rule but on the subjective judgment of lay jurors, the Court divested itself of a crucial power. This power was given over to local juries; it was their verdicts—based on their individual consciences and reactions to the evidence and on their interpretations of the respective state penal codes—that became the constitutional measure of acceptable capital punishment. The jury's decision was, of course, subject to some appellate review, just as the prosecutor's decision was subject to restraints of the existing law and evidence. But in recognizing the discretion of prosecutor and sentencer in this way, and explicitly legitimizing them by reference to democratic considerations, the Court divested itself of a burdensome responsibility and set up local decision-makers as the arbiters of life and death.

The Court thus devised, as James Liebman puts it, "an imaginative scheme" for "sharing its justificatory burden with local democratic institutions." It did this by enlisting local juries (and elected state judges) as "provisional interpreters and implementers of the Constitution" subject to the Court's supervision and final say. As Liebman observes, the Court has long "recognized the need to set complex constitutional standards to govern frontline death penalty decision-making," yet it has refused to take responsibility for setting and applying these standards—for example, by applying a proportionality review to the decisions that they generate. Instead of taking responsibility for regulating sentencing decisions, it has engaged in a process of "shunting off that responsibility to the very actors the Court claims the constitutional need to regulate."[65]

Allowing juries to wield a discretionary power of life and death may seem surprising in light of *Furman*'s concerns about arbitrariness. But this delegation of power was already present in the 1976 *Woodson* case, which insisted that the jury's sentencing choice could not be mandated by law. Two years later, this discretionary power was further enhanced by the Court's decision in *Lockett v Ohio,* which held that a capital sentencer must be permitted to consider evidence of "any aspect of the defendant's character or record and any of the circumstances of the offense that the defendant proffers as a basis for a sentence less than death."[66] *Woodson* and *Lockett* were, in this way, *democratizing* judgments. They empowered jurors (one might say they also burdened them) by setting up the jury as the frontline agent of constitutional law, charged with applying the law's vague and indeterminate guidelines in order to decide the defendant's death-worthiness. As Liebman puts it, "*Lockett* turned every capital sentencing judge or jury into a miniature constitutional court," left to apply their own subjective judgment to the gravest of legal matters.[67]

In *Woodson* and *Lockett,* the jury's obligation to engage in individualized sentencing was understood as the corollary of the defendant's right to be treated as a unique individual. Eighth Amendment respect for the dignity of each human being required that defendants not be treated as "members of a faceless, undifferentiated mass" and instead be granted an individualized hearing before a jury that would hear mitigation and aggravation evidence before deciding on death-worthiness. But there is an additional reason for empowering the jury (as opposed to a judge) that concerns its special *vox populi* character, a reason to which Justice Harlan alluded in *McGautha* when he wrote that juries "do little more—and must do nothing less—than express the conscience of the community on the ultimate question of life or death."[68]

In 1984, only a few states still authorized judges to impose capital sentences or override jury recommendations, but in *Spaziano v Florida* the Court had upheld these arrangements.[69] On that occasion, Justice Stevens argued in dissent that only the jury ought to be entrusted with this "unique judgment" since the jury is "a more authentic voice of the community" and, unlike a judge, is not perceived as an instrument of state power. As Stevens puts it, "If the state wishes to execute a citizen, it must first persuade a jury of his peers."

In *Ring v Arizona* the Court held that the Sixth Amendment right to a jury trial required that capital juries—and not judges—find any aggravating factors that bear on the defendant's sentence, thereby establishing juries as the proper sentencing authority.[70] As Breyer stated in *Ring,* the Court had long interpreted the Eighth Amendment as requiring states to apply "special procedural safeguards" when they sought the death penalty. These safeguards were now deemed to include "a requirement that a *jury* impose any sentence of death."[71]

The importance of jury sentencing—and of the community wisdom and democratic imprimatur that it supposedly provides—has increased as the rationales for the death penalty have grown fewer. When the death penalty was a mandatory sentence routinely used for certain offenses, the jury did no special work in sentencing. When the death penalty was used to deter crime and incapacitate the dangerous, the jury had no special expertise to supply. Now that the death penalty is justified primarily because it is deemed "appropriate" by the community—as a way of expressing their view of the crime and the criminal—only a jury will do.[72]

A plurality of the Court has come to justify this awesome delegation of authority by means of a "democratic" account of capital punishment which states that only "the people" themselves can make this profoundly moral decision. Stevens set out this argument in *Spaziano v Florida* when he wrote that if capital punishment is justified because "it expresses the community's moral sensibility" and the community's demand for retribution, "it follows . . . that a representative cross-section of the community must be given the responsibility for making that decision." Breyer made the same point in *Ring* when he wrote that juries are more attuned than judges to "the community's moral sensibility" and are therefore more likely to "express the conscience of the community on the ultimate question of life or death."[73]

In constituting the jury as the democratically appropriate sentencer, the Court was making a virtue of a Sixth Amendment necessity. The jury had long been regarded as "the voice of the community" and "a body truly representative of the community" that allows "full community participation in capital sentencing."[74] In *Ring,* Justices Stevens and Breyer brought the requirement of a jury finding together with a democratic account of the jury's functioning to create a more fully democratic rationale for jury-imposed capital punishment. As Stevens had argued in dissent in the 1995 case *Harris v Alabama* (which upheld an Alabama statute giving trial judges power to impose a capital sentence though the jury recommends life imprisonment): "The most credible justification for the death penalty is its expression of the community's outrage." Indeed, this is now the institution's "only legitimate mooring." It therefore follows that the "community's undistorted judgment must decide a capital defendant's fate."[75] By the time of *Ring v Arizona* in 2002, the Court would come to the conclusion that "the Eighth Amendment requires individual jurors to make, and to take responsibility for, a decision to sentence a person to death."[76]

What the Court was saying, in this democratizing decision as in all the others, was that the power to impose capital punishment, and the responsibility for doing so, must rest with the American people and their local representatives. In American matters of life and death, *vox populi, vox dei.*

A final illustration of this democratizing approach is the Court decision in *Payne v Tennessee* in 1991 to permit the state to present "victim-impact" evidence in the penalty phase of capital trials. This holding allows a voice to murder victims' relatives, which is to say to people with a personal stake in sentencing who typically command community support and sympathy. Moreover, it permits the prosecution to enter evidence—in the form of a written or spoken statement, or even a video presentation—describing the crime's impact on the victim's family members, together with their characterization of the crime and the murderer.

Victim-impact evidence is a new development in American criminal justice, having emerged as part of the victim-centered "law and order" politics of the 1990s. And while such evidence was permitted in other noncapital criminal proceedings, the Court had ruled in *Booth v Maryland* (1987) that it ought not to be permitted in capital cases, since it "could serve no other purpose than to inflame the jury and divert it from deciding the case on the relevant evidence."[77] To admit victim-impact evidence, the *Booth* Court decided, would be "inconsistent with the reasoned decisionmaking required in capital cases." Why then, would the Court reverse its opinion and overrule *Booth* four years later?

The answer seems to lie in the Court's deference to shifting public sentiment and the increased value accorded to victims in political discourse—a development brought about by the powerful victims' movement that had emerged in the 1980s.[78] In his dissent in *Booth* Scalia noted, "Recent years have seen an outpouring of popular concerns for what has come to be known as 'victims' rights.'" And though such sentiments might be injudicious and fail to "sufficiently temper justice with mercy," it was not for the Court to dismiss them on this ground alone. The admissibility of such evidence was, declared Scalia, "a question to be decided through the democratic processes of a free people, and not by the decrees of this Court."

It is hard to imagine an opinion that runs more directly contrary to the Court's rationalizing reforms. But Scalia's dissenting opinion in *Booth,* which came to be the majority position in *Payne,* was grounded in the same democratic localism and populism that had shaped so many other decisions and which, in fact, allowed capital punishment to survive and flourish. What the Court did in *Payne* was, as Scalia put it, to "allow . . . the people to decide."[79] The same faith in "the people" that entrusted life or death decisions to an untrained, inexperienced jury was what justified the admission of inflammatory evidence from victims when a defendant's life was at stake. Both were gestures toward a localized, even personalized, form of justice in which the people most affected are empowered to determine the punishment imposed.

In responding to the predicament of capital punishment, the Supreme Court acted in accordance with its three institutional personas. It acted as a court of law, imposing rules on a lawless process; it acted as a governing elite, imposing a civilizing influence on culturally transgressive practices; and it acted as a branch of American government, recognizing the separation of powers and honoring the authority of "the people." In its first two modes it sought to tame the death penalty and render it less problematic. In its third, it sought to return the question to the political process to be decided by local actors and popular will. This democratizing response, like the jurisprudence it created, is distinctively American. It is what empowers the contemporary death penalty. No other nation responded to the predicament by democratizing or localizing the issue. In Europe and elsewhere, governing elites decided that the state ought not to kill its citizens, whatever the people thought. In the United States, the Court insisted that the people should decide.

The Specter of Lynching

How should we understand these strategies of the Court and the effects they have had? We can best grasp the logic of these decisions if we view them as having been shaped by the specter of lynching. Recall what we know about the American death penalty today. The bloody public lynchings of the Jim Crow South have long since ended, but the specter of lynching remains a presence in today's death penalty, a continuing historical force that imparts a peculiar shape to the contemporary institution. The official forms and administrative arrangements of contemporary capital punishment—which take great trouble to ensure extensive legal process, dispassionate administration, and dignified, humane execution—are a mirror image of the lynching process. They work to differentiate contemporary capital punishment from the arbitrary, summary, racist violence that too often characterized America's death penalty in the past. But the social dynamics and distributions of the institution tell a different story. The death penalty continues to be concentrated in the South. It continues to be driven by local politics and populist politicians. It continues to be imposed by lay people. It continues to give a special place to victims' kin. It continues to target blacks whose victims were white. It continues to produce false accusations and impose unwarranted punishments. And it continues to be an occasion for political mobilization around demands for local sovereignty, traditional values, and popular justice. Distinct echoes remain.

The specter of lynching has long haunted the way that the Supreme Court has looked at the death penalty. As early as the 1930s, legal lynchings moved the Court to action because the justices saw these summary proceedings as an affront to the values of American legality. In the 1960s it was the specter of lynching that mobilized the death penalty litigation of the LDF attorneys. They argued that the death penalty was often little more than a legal lynching—a racist punishment reserved for blacks alleged to have committed inter-racial atrocities—and must therefore be abolished.[80]

The LDF strategy was a smart one. Lynching had been the issue that had first persuaded the Court to set aside its federalist inhibitions and challenge the power of Southern states. Legal lynchings offended everything the Supreme Court stood for—violating legality, justice, due process, and the constitutional rights of individuals. It is no accident that the Court's first expression of doubt about the death penalty's constitutionality—Justice Goldberg's memo in *Rudolph v Alabama* in 1963—singled out the capital prosecution of a Southern black man for the alleged rape of a white woman, the classic instance of legal lynching. The Court's history of activism in legal lynching cases encouraged the LDF lawyers to mine this established seam. They sought to represent modern capital punishment as, essentially and necessarily, a legal lynching, and to persuade the Court that the modern death penalty was inexorably tied up with racial injustice and must therefore be abolished.

But the Court accepted this argument only in part. It agreed that the states' death penalty process was often summary, arbitrary, and perhaps even racist, but it insisted on drawing a distinction. Legal lynching was illegal and unconstitutional, but its constitutional flaws went to procedure and not to substance. Lynching was undoubtedly unlawful but the illegality did not extend to the death penalty as such—a punishment that had constitutional warrant and democratic support. This left the way open for a reformed death penalty that might leave the nightmare of lynching behind—or so a majority of justices believed.

The Court's central focus, from *Gregg* onward, has been process and the violation of due process rights, not the larger questions of the death penalty's value as a social practice or the pattern of its disparate impact.[81] The Court's chief concern has been a legalistic, procedural one—to eradicate arbitrariness and discrimination—not the substantive question of the death penalty itself. Breaches of due process and breaches of civilized decorum are the problems to which the Court has been most attuned. Above all, the Court has sought to invalidate capital punishment practices that seem reminiscent of the lynch mob and its summary justice.[82] In effect, it took legal lynching to be the central problem and devoted its energies to eradicating this legacy.[83] If the LDF began with lynching and broadened its concern to deal with the death penalty as such, the Supreme Court has done the opposite, beginning with the death penalty then narrowing its concern to focus on lynchlike practices. Ultimately, the Court distinguished between banning legal lynching, which it would do, and banning the death penalty, which it would not.

The LDF's attempt to demonstrate that America's death penalty was inextricably linked with lynching was ultimately defeated by the Court's refusal to engage with evidence of systematic racism. The key case here is *McCleskey v Kemp* in 1987, where the Court refused to consider statistical evidence showing that the state of Georgia routinely sentenced defendants to death on the basis of racial considerations.[84]

Warren McCleskey, who was black, was sentenced to death in 1978 in Fulton County, Georgia, for killing a white police officer in the course of a furniture store break-in.[85] A jury composed of eleven white people and one African American convicted him of murder and, having found that his crime was compounded by two aggravating circumstances (the murder was committed in the course of an armed robbery and the victim was a peace officer), elected to impose a death sentence rather than life imprisonment.

McCleskey's death sentence was the only one imposed in Fulton County between 1973 (when Georgia's homicide statute was passed) and 1980 (when LDF attorneys took up his appeal). During that period, the local prosecutors (who were predominantly white) brought murder charges against fifteen white defendants who had killed police killers but declined to seek the death penalty in any one of them. On the only other occasion when capital charges were brought in such a case, the defendant, like McCleskey, was black, as was his victim. All these other offenders had received sentences of life imprisonment. McCleskey, the only black defendant convicted of killing a white police officer, was also the only defendant sentenced to die.

The LDF attorneys brought evidence to show that McCleskey's death sentence was part of a statewide pattern of racially biased capital sentencing that violated the Eighth and Fourteenth Amendments. They presented, along with other evidence, two empirical studies of Georgia homicide cases between 1973 and 1979 conducted by Iowa law professor David Baldus and his colleagues—studies that were described by several of America's leading criminal justice researchers as "among the best empirical studies on criminal sentencing ever conducted."[86] The most striking finding of the study was that "[f]ewer than 40% of Georgia homicide cases involve white victims, but in 87% of cases in which a death sentence is imposed the victim is white. White-victim cases are roughly eleven times more likely than black-victim cases to result in a penalty of death."[87] After controlling for nonracial factors that might bear on sentencing, the study concluded that murderers of white victims were sentenced to death 4.3 times more frequently than murderers of black victims. The race discrimination that *Furman* had sought to abolish was evidently still in existence, albeit in a more subtle "race-of-victim" form.

In presenting its five-to-four majority decision, Justice Powell stated that the Court would "assume that the [Baldus] study is valid statistically." But the study's showing of systematic racial discrimination was nevertheless deemed to be irrelevant, since the Court required the petitioner to prove that "the decisionmakers in his case acted with discriminatory purpose"— a burden of proof that McCleskey could not meet.[88] Since McCleskey could not prove that purposeful discrimination had occurred in *his* particular trial and had produced a discriminatory effect on *him,* no constitutional violation had been shown. McCleskey's petition failed and he was subsequently put to death in Georgia's electric chair on September 28, 1991. That same year, Justice Powell, who had since retired from the Court, disclosed to his biographer that he would, in retrospect, have changed his vote in McCleskey's case and that he now believed that the death penalty ought to be barred because it can not be fairly enforced.[89]

If the Court's post-*Gregg* strategy was to permit the death penalty but to prohibit lynchlike procedures, *McCleskey* tested this approach by claiming that one of the characteristic elements of lynching—its racial targeting of black defendants who kill white victims—is an inevitable feature of the death penalty as practiced in certain regions. Faced with the disturbing implication that its two-pronged strategy was contradictory—that retaining death sentencing meant permitting legal lynching—the Court refused to countenance the evidence that displayed the contradiction. Rather than pursue an empirical inquiry that would show institutional racism to be endemic in Georgia's capital punishment process—and likely in other states and in noncapital proceedings as well—the Court retreated to a narrower test of race discrimination requiring direct evidence of specific discriminatory intent. In reality, evidence of such intent would rarely be available to the defense given the hidden and largely inscrutable nature of discretionary decision-making by prosecutors, juries, and judges.

The people's right to capital punishment thus trumped the rights of black defendants to a fair trial and equal protection. The Court refused to take its antilynching inquiries so far as to allow proportionality review or evidence of patterned racial disparity.[90] (In doing so, the Court also protected the rest of the criminal justice system from widespread challenges based on similar evidence of racial disparities, and resisted a shift in its jurisprudence from evidence of discriminatory intent to evidence of discriminatory impact.[91]) As its critics observed, the Court seemed willing to tolerate racism so long as it stayed hidden and avoided explicit expression. As with its civilizing jurisprudence, its chief concern focused on appearances rather than on outcomes.

The *Furman* decision was not a victory for the abolitionists so much as the opening move in a classic American dialogue between central and local powers, elite and popular opinion, and liberal and conservative politics. Whereas other liberal democracies abolished capital punishment in a countermajoritarian reform, in the United States the issue was put into play as a question of federalism, becoming part of an ongoing struggle between the federal courts and the state legislatures with an aroused public and a "law and order" politics supplying much of the political energy.

America's reinvented death penalty came to bear the marks of the conflicts and compromises that produced it. Once capital punishment became a matter of federal constitutional law, a vigorous adversarial legalism and an equally determined states' rights conservatism ensured that capital cases would be the focus of continuous legal and political struggle, pushing the Supreme Court's rulings to the limits of whatever interpretations they would bear. The system that has resulted is a peculiar one—a Rube Goldberg contraption pushed in one direction by local prosecutors, state legislators, and national politicians, pulled in another by a dedicated community of capital defense attorneys mounting postconviction challenges in one case after another, and presided over with weary resignation by a Supreme Court that no longer seems interested in the issue but that retains responsibility nevertheless.

In the course of these struggles, the American death penalty has been largely transformed, both as an institutional structure and as a legal and cultural practice. Before the LDF litigation began, capital punishment was a matter of state policy, determined by state legislatures, imposed by state trial courts, and moderated by the clemency decisions of state governors. Appellate and federal courts played little part in the process. Since *Furman* the architecture of the system has undergone a structural change. State appellate courts are now involved in every case, as are the federal courts, while governors have mostly retreated from the scene, exercising their prerogative of mercy only in the rarest of cases or when they cease to run for office.[92]

American capital punishment has become a complex federated system: legislated, enforced, and administered at the state and county levels but subject to supervision by the federal courts and the constraints of federal constitutional law. Three dozen diverse and formerly independent death penalty jurisdictions have been corralled into a loosely regulated national system, governed by newly imposed national standards, and subject to federal oversight and review. Enabled by this new structure and the regulatory powers it provides, the Supreme Court has used its juridifying, civilizing, and democratizing jurisprudence to develop a new case law in which the states' power to kill has been alternately abridged and affirmed.

ELEVEN

Death and Its Uses

For those of us who believe justice is served by the most severe
sanction available for the most heinous crime, the death penalty is
a tremendous benefit.

DUDLEY SHARP, VICE PRESIDENT OF JUSTICE FOR ALL, 1998

Critics frequently allege that the American capital punishment system
lacks purpose and coherence. As a system, they claim, it serves no
functions, obeys no logic, and has no redeeming rationale.[1] As one writer
recently noted, "the dominant attitude within social science . . . rejects
capital punishment and questions any alleged positive returns from adopting it."[2] This idea of a wholly dysfunctional death penalty may work well
as critical rhetoric, but it fails to explain how the system survives and why
it is continually supplied with fresh energy and resources. If today's death
penalty is so devoid of function, why does it persist in the face of challenge
and controversy?

In *Discipline and Punish,* Michel Foucault sets out a methodological
prescription: "Do not concentrate the study of the punitive mechanisms on
their 'repressive' effects alone, on their 'punishment' aspects alone, but sit-
uate them in a whole series of their possible positive effects, even if these
seem marginal at first." We should, he contends, "[r]egard punishment as
a complex social function."[3] If we insist, with Foucault, on a positive account of capital punishment's uses and utilities, even those that at first
seem marginal or unimportant, then a picture emerges that turns the conventional wisdom upside down. What becomes apparent is that the state's
power to kill is actually productive, performative, and generative—that it
makes things happen—even if much of what happens is in the cultural

realm of death penalty discourse rather than in the biological realm of life and death.

Critics are right to argue that the classic criminal justice purposes are not well served by contemporary capital punishment. America's capital punishment arrangements tend to undermine these purposes rather than advance them.[4] Form does not follow these functions—it defeats them. But this critique misses its mark. Today's death penalty system is no longer oriented toward crime control and criminal justice: it has its own forms, its own functions, and its own rationality. The conventional wisdom views today's practices as so many deviations from the logic of deterrence and retribution. A better approach is to insist that its practices have a logic of their own, an intrinsic rationality that might be understood if we pay attention to what gets said as well as what gets done.

In the absolutist systems of early-modern Europe, the death penalty was a necessary element of state formation and maintenance, an elementary particle of state power. In the modernist system of the nineteenth and early twentieth centuries, it was a fundamental element of crime control and criminal justice, the special punishment reserved for the most serious crime. In late-modern America, the death penalty has ceased to be governmentally or penologically necessary in these ways. It no longer performs any grand social functions for state maintenance or for society as a whole. Instead, its uses are more petty and more partisan, serving the private or professional purposes of specific actors and sectarian interests rather than more general social ends.

The distinctive forms of today's capital punishment complex, far from being irrational or dysfunctional, are, in fact, oriented toward the distinctive purposes for which the American death penalty now exists. The discursive death penalty, the imaginary death penalty, the virtual death penalty: these are some of the forms in which late-modern American capital punishment is now enacted. We should not be surprised, therefore, if these specific forms enable some of its contemporary uses as well. But these uses, like the institution itself, have narrowed over time. Today's capital punishment complex is, in fact, functional, meaningful, and effective. But instead of serving broad governmental or social purposes, it is now put to work for the more partisan and private purposes of specific professional and political users, of the mass media, and of its public audience. Late-modern capital punishment is, in fact, reasonably well adapted to the purposes that it serves, but deterrent crime control and retributive justice are not prominent among them.

Social Dynamics of Capital Punishment

America's capital punishment complex meets needs, provides benefits, and generates value for specific groups and actors. The gratifications it produces become sources of energy that drive and sustain the system. The specific character of these gratifications helps explain why the system produces such an excess of talk about death but is comparatively economical with actual deaths. From where does the capital punishment complex derive its emotional power, its popular interest, and its perennial appeal?

One source of energy was the Supreme Court's decision in *Furman v Georgia,* which invalidated all the states' death penalty statutes and thereby mobilized policy entrepreneurs across the country. By creating a gap between majority opinion and state law, *Furman* provided legislators with easy opportunities to pass popular laws. Lawmakers exploited these opportunities as soon as they appeared, rapidly passing legislation in thirty-five states. In states where such efforts were blocked, as they were in New York, lawmakers pressed the issue year after year. In some states the impact of *Furman* continued for decades.

A second source of energy is adversarial legalism. Every Supreme Court capital case decision angers and inflames the losing side, mobilizing the death penalty's supporters or else its opponents. Every new capital statute does the same thing. Some court decisions prompt waves of legislative action. Others prompt new litigation strategies. Either way, the adversarial response is triggered and more legal action results. Fueling this legal dynamic is a more diffuse but more fundamental source of energy: namely, the cultural tension between capital punishment and liberal humanism. This tension ensures that the death penalty is always scandalous to a degree and that anti–death penalty sentiment is always already mobilized. Liberal opposition, in turn, reactivates prodeath opinion, and so it goes in an unending process.

There is also a dynamic of political entailment. That American capital punishment has come to be associated with larger political and cultural issues (civil rights, states' rights, race relations, culture wars, and law and order politics) means that death penalty events and developments now have a resonance that goes beyond the case at issue. These events activate a base and mobilize support.

And then there is the revenge dynamic. Each capital case begins with an atrocious crime that ignites community anger and demands a retributive response.[5] The punitive passions aroused by heinous murders are what prompt capital indictments in the first place and what invest these cases with their moral force, emotional interest, and collective involvement.

These four dynamics—the *Furman* effect, cultural conflict, political entailment, and the passion of crime and punishment—are already familiar. But there is a further source of energy that, though rarely discussed, may be the most important of all: namely, the emotional power of killing and death. The crime of murder and its capital punishment put death into play, giving capital cases a distinctive emotional charge. Death—and the collective capacity to impose it—has, for human beings everywhere, a special power or sacred energy. It commands our attention, especially when the killing is done in our name and at our behest.[6] In late-modern America, this power is enhanced by death's cultural status as the last great taboo. Despite our efforts to understand and prevent it, death continually escapes our grasp, remaining unknowable, unmanageable, beyond our control. This uncontrollable fate hovers in the background of our lives, obeying no laws, respecting no persons, evoking fear and loathing. Murder narratives focus these anxieties and arouse our innermost fears. In such a context, the prospect of killing the killer is an empowering and liberating one with widespread appeal, if only as a fantasy. In today's death-denying, Thanatophobic culture, it can be liberating to talk of death in a positive way and pleasurable to exert some control over its imposition. Social actors who use the death penalty are able to draw on these diffuse public emotions and put them to productive use.

Certain groups of social actors routinely succeed in aligning their interests with capital punishment and harnessing its practices for their own use. It is not that they have needs that can only be satisfied by capital punishment. Nor has America's death penalty system been specifically designed to meet these needs. But given that the death penalty continues to exist, various individuals adapt to its possibilities and take advantage of the opportunities it makes available. Over time, the cumulative effect is to anchor the death penalty in networks of interest and routine which then act as obstacles to abolition.

These functional alignments may be encapsulated as follows: For criminal justice professionals, capital punishment is a practical instrument that allows them to harness the power of death in the pursuit of professional objectives.[7] For politicians and elected officials, the death penalty is a commodity, an exchange value, a political token in an electoral game that is played before a viewing audience. For the mass media, each capital case promises a suspenseful, dramatic narrative, a classic human interest story that is constantly renewed. And for the onlooking public, the death penalty is variously an edifying morality play, a vehicle for moral outrage, a prurient entertainment, or an opportunity for the expression of hatreds and aggressions otherwise prohibited.

In American death penalty politics, among the most reliable and most active supporters of capital punishment are police officers, prison guards, and local district attorneys. And for good reason. For each of these groups, the death penalty is a practical tool with which to leverage power and secure professional objectives. Its continued existence provides them with a powerful, irreplaceable instrument they can use in various ways.

Prison officials use the threat of a death sentence to control long-term, life-sentenced prisoners who, in the absence of capital punishment, sometimes have nothing to lose.[8] In such a context, where disincentives are few and the risk of violence is high, capital punishment provides a tool that many prison staff in the United States regard as vital for the efficient administration of the institution and for their own protection. Many police officers similarly view the death penalty as a deterrent that enhances on-the-job safety, even if police chiefs are less confident.[9] Police union officials demand death sentences for "cop killers" and regard the issue as a test of any politician's support. During the 1988 presidential campaign the "wild cheers that greeted calls for death to cop killers" left little doubt about the appeal of death sentences to the law enforcement community.[10] When in 2004 the Staten Island district attorney held a press conference to announce that he would seek the death penalty for a defendant charged with the murder of two undercover detectives, "applause erupted from the roughly 40 police officers, detectives and family members who had gathered to pay witness."[11] When, in 2006, that case (now conducted by federal prosecutors) produced a death sentence, a New York Police Department union official said, "I think the government pursuing the penalty of death and being able to attain the death penalty sends a very much needed message to the law enforcement community." That message was one of support and retribution: "If we're going to be gunned down in cold blood performing our jobs, then the just punishment should be the death penalty."[12]

Whereas law enforcement officers value capital punishment as a measure of self-protection and a symbol of political support, many prosecutors see it in more instrumental terms, using it as a means to crack cases, as a platform for gaining media attention, and as an issue for mobilizing political support. Prosecutors use the threat of lethal punishment to secure confessions or guilty pleas and to persuade codefendants to give evidence against one another. In 2007, prosecutors in Washington state promised a man suspected of abducting and murdering a twelve-year-old girl that they would not pursue death penalty charges if he told detectives her whereabouts. As the prosecutor stated after being led to the girl's body, without the death penalty, "We would have no leverage in some instances . . . It's nice to have that tool in your kit."[13]

In the conduct of litigation, definite legal and political dividends accrue to prosecutors who bring capital charges. As a legal tactic, the American capital indictment has a number of advantages. It ensures that the jury pool will be "death qualified," making it more likely that jurors will be proconviction.[14] Capital charges increase the defense's burden without increasing that of the state: having to prove innocence while also taking care to avoid the death penalty make defense counsel more risk averse, which is a definite advantage for the state.

Because capital cases are difficult to mount and to win, prosecutors see them as a pinnacle of professional achievement and a path to enhanced status and advancement.[15] The availability of the death penalty also provides prosecutors with opportunities to mount capital charges that are popular with constituents and likely to bring media attention.[16] Recall that prosecutors are elected officials who serve specific constituencies and make decisions in light of local opinion; as a Texas district attorney remarked, "we spend a lot more time with victims' families who are criticizing us for not seeking the death penalty than we ever do for seeking it too much."[17] Elected state judges who hear capital cases at the trial and appellate stages have similar political incentives and use capital punishment in similar ways.[18]

Capital cases are extraordinarily difficult for defense counsel. Funds are scarce, workloads heavy, and stakes high. To conduct a proper trial defense, mount an appeal, or draft an effective *habeas* petition requires considerable expertise. It also requires considerable personal fortitude, as lawyers who defend individuals accused of heinous murders must be "willing to be loathed" by outraged members of the public.[19] But even for defense attorneys, capital cases bring tangible benefits. Like their opponents on the prosecution side, defense counsel may enjoy the high visibility of capital trials and the professional and psychological rewards they bring. State-appointed attorneys earn little for their trouble—and many vow never to represent a capital defendant again—but even they can sometimes earn publicity and professional kudos. And for the public-interest lawyers who dedicate themselves to this work—among whom are some of the most admired and charismatic individuals in the American legal community—there is the attraction of a heroic role and the psychic rewards that flow from it. For the full-time defense bar, as well as for the many corporate litigators and Ivy League law students who provide *pro bono* services to indigent clients, the death penalty provides not just "something to believe in" but also "extraordinary rewards."[20] Perhaps as a result, the extent of dedicated, time-consuming, emotionally draining volunteer work in this field is remarkable. And although defense lawyers point to the deficiencies of public provision and the likelihood of injustice as the main reasons for their involvement, there is also an intensity and excitement—even a hint of glamour—that comes from personal involvement in these dramas of life and death.[21]

For the jury, the power to impose a death sentence on a convicted, aggravated murderer provides a mode of expression and moral judgment that is not otherwise possible. The availability of a death sentence extends the penal lexicon, allowing the jury to communicate beyond the limited vocabulary of the prison sentence. To announce a capital sentence is to make a distinct and powerful statement, signaling the heinous nature of the crime and the evil nature of the criminal. It is to mark the murderer as among the worst of the worst, distinguishing his crime from run-of-the-mill felonies sanctioned by prison terms and life sentences.[22] In the context of America's mass incarceration, where the currency of imprisonment has been devalued by overuse, the imposition of capital punishment dramatizes the sentence and raises it out of the ordinary.[23] Death sentences permit a satisfying moral symmetry, a like-for-like, life-for-a-life reckoning that many find intuitively appropriate.[24] In the same way, a death sentence may carry special meaning for the murder victim's relatives, providing them with the satisfaction of (what they regard as) just punishment and a vindication of their loved one's worth.[25] Wherever the death penalty is the ultimate punishment permitted by law, any lesser sentence—even one of life imprisonment without parole—can appear grievously lacking to those who hope for proper retribution following a heinous crime. As one relative whose wife and daughters had been brutally raped and murdered put it, "My family got the death penalty and you want to give murderers life? That is not justice."[26]

The most prominent "users" of capital punishment in recent decades have been actors on the political stage. For candidates running for office, for legislators, and for government officials, the death penalty offers a highly visible opportunity to demonstrate popular "tough on crime" credentials and to discredit the positions of more liberal opponents.

Legislators enact capital statutes—including many that will never be executed—as a means to raise public morale and demonstrate resolve in the "war against crime." In places where the public distrusts the criminal justice system or regards it as soft on crime, death penalty statutes provide a way of signaling toughness and determination. Support for death penalty laws allows politicians to show that they support law enforcement and will supply them with the necessary means to do their job.[27] *Congressional Quarterly* reports and the transcripts of floor debates in state assemblies provide many examples. California Senator Barbara Boxer bragged that she voted 100 times for the death penalty. And George W. Bush first ran for president in a year when, as governor of Texas, he had presided over the largest number of state executions ever carried out in a single twelve-month period—a total of forty in the year 2000.[28]

During the 1980s and 1990s, the death penalty allowed conservative politicians and commentators to condense racial fears, states' rights, and fundamentalist values in a single coded issue. After the civil rights movement of the 1950s and 1960s, openly expressed racial prejudice ceased to be acceptable in American politics. But the death penalty—with its cultural associations and racial implications—provided opportunities to talk in coded terms about unspeakable topics. In the context of America's "war on crime" a strong stance on the death penalty connoted masculine resolve, a determined, warriorlike commitment to face down murderous criminals and protect the lives of citizens.[29] Its historic connotations of absolutist sovereign power reinforced this strong symbolism reassuring the public that they would be protected by powerful and resolute leaders.[30] In a campaign advertisement during the Texas gubernatorial election of 1990, former governor Mark White was shown walking down a hallway adorned with oversized photographs of men put to death during his 1983–1986 administration. "Only a governor can make executions happen," White declared to a background of ominous music. "I did, and I will."[31]

The death penalty provides an opportunity for conservative supporters to make liberal opponents seem incapable of protecting the public or understanding how victims feel. So powerful is this symbolism that it undid the Democratic nominee Michael Dukakis in the 1988 presidential race and set the tone for death penalty politics for a decade thereafter. Asked, in the course of a televised debate, if he would favor the death penalty if someone were to rape and murder his wife, Kitty, the hapless Dukakis responded by explaining that he had always been opposed to the death penalty and that research showed it to be a suboptimal policy option. This turned out to be a disastrous response. His failure to express impassioned outrage made him appear weak and unmanly to many viewers. Dukakis had been presented with the classic lynching scenario—his white wife raped and murdered, presumably by a black rapist like Willie Horton— but he had failed even to gesture toward the vengeful response that honor traditions and popular opinion expected of him.[32]

The death penalty also functions as a token of political exchange between elected representatives and their constituents. Hence the popularity among lawmakers of "aggravating factor" laws that increase the likelihood of a murderer's facing death if he kills a particular kind of victim—a police officer, a senior citizen, a child, a federal officer, and so on. As a New York assemblywoman put it, "We're saying to the families of victims, 'your daughter's life was important. Your husband's life was important.'" Capital penalties are made to operate as "tokens of esteem," allocating an enhanced status to selected constituents. And though victims' relatives sometimes resist the suggestion that they are honored by having the wrongdoer killed—just as they sometimes dispute the glib notion that a death sentence provides them with "closure"—these ideas have become elements of political common sense and now function as rationales for capital punishment.[33]

In the democratic process, candidates pursue votes by promising to give voters something in exchange for their support. The death penalty operates in this context as a political commodity that can be given and received in the process of political bargaining. The intended beneficiaries of this gift are victims groups and members of the public who support capital punishment—and of course the politicians who are rewarded for their gesture with electoral support. Here the death penalty acts not just as a signal, communicating a message from political representatives to their constituents. It also constitutes a gift, in return for which the politician can expect the gratitude—and the support—of the group in question.

In his classic study of capital punishment in eighteenth-century England, Douglas Hay identified the private power to secure pardons as an important collateral benefit of the death penalty. The pardon system—with its letters and petitions and influence peddling—was, he explains, a way of putting the power of life and death into private hands. If a landowner or employer could intercede on behalf of a convicted laborer and have the sentence commuted, the result benefited them both. The prisoner's life was spared, and the noble's standing was enhanced. As Hay explains, patronage was a two-way street: "the power of gentlemen and peers to punish or to forgive worked to maintain the fabric of obedience, gratitude and deference."[34]

The circuits of exchange are different in America today, and the operative mechanism is one of democratic representation, not hierarchical deference. But capital punishment still functions as a valued commodity that can be given and received. The power to determine if a person lives or dies, and the power to influence that determination, is still a resource, a form of property, a kind of capital. And this value—produced by, and dependent on, capital punishment—ceases to exist wherever the death penalty disappears.

The death penalty is also news. It is an exciting drama that grabs attention, a spectator sport full of tension, uncertainty, and life-or-death outcomes. And though the authorities now refuse to provide the public with the actual spectacle, the controversial, transgressive practice of killing offenders remains one of perennial interest. Journalists and their editors know that capital trials, death penalty verdicts, and execution stories create interest, excitement, and emotional release among their readers, and their reporting and writing reflect this fact.[35]

Cases are reported as episodic dramas, punctuated by moments of high tension, suspense, and revelation. Will the sentence be life or death? How will the defendant react? Will the last-minute appeal succeed? Will the execution go smoothly or be botched? How did the condemned person react? How did the victim's relatives feel? Reading or hearing about these moments brings gratification. For some vulnerable members of the public, worn down by crime and violence, there can be a pleasure in punishing, a thrill in defeating hated enemies, a satisfaction in seeing the tables turned against those who have humiliated them or put them in fear of their lives. For those committed to retributive justice, who view capital punishment as a murderer's just deserts, it is satisfying to see justice done and to have the courts affirm their beliefs. For others, the merely curious, the controversy and uncertainty that surround capital cases make them stand out from run-of-the mill crime stories, adding dramatic intensity and interest.

Media writers understand the entertainment value of a death threat, which is why reports of murder cases routinely mention the possibility of a death sentence even when its likelihood is actually quite remote. Crime news, trial reports, jury verdicts, legislative debates, constitutional cases, moral arguments for and against, and media coverage of high-profile executions—all of these put judicial death into cultural discourse, sometimes with seriousness and solemnity, more often as one more story on the evening news.

As an executed sanction, the American death penalty has become a relatively rare occurrence. But as an enunciated "sentence," a discursive statement, a communicated idea or image, the death penalty is much more pervasive, thanks in large part to its appeal for the mass media. In late-modern, mass-mediated America, crime and punishment are news but they are also part of "the entertainment zone."[36] Narratives of crime and punishment are constantly played out before a viewing audience, and the possibility of death deepens the play for all involved. Capital punishment raises the stakes of criminal justice and "sexes up" the story, imparting to murder trials "a dramatic quality that is lacking . . . where a life sentence is the heaviest possible punishment."[37] A life hangs in the balance—and unlike other stories involving killing and death (on the roads, in war, in natural disasters) this death is known in advance, is under control, and carries the official imprimatur of a legal order.

The mass media deal in feeling, in sensation, in heightened emotion—and trials where defendants face the prospect of death are perfect for media purposes. The capital trial is the most intense and suspenseful of criminal justice rituals, in part for the verdict, but more especially for the decision on sentence. In other criminal trials, the moment of sentencing offers little drama or uncertainty since lengthy prison sentences are ubiquitous in the United States and sentencing guidelines proclaim in advance the likely term that will be imposed. But in trials where the death penalty is in play, the jury's discretionary sentencing decision provides a moment of heightened emotion, uncertainty, and excitement. What will the jury decide? How will the defendant react? How will the victim's family feel? A tightly focused drama is set up that will climax with a life or death pronouncement. "Yes!" cries the victim's partner when the death sentence is announced. "And the Lord Rejoices!"[38]

This is a key moment in the contemporary capital trial: a moment of climactic seriousness and intensity whose theatrical impact is undiminished by the fact that most death sentences are never carried out. When a death penalty is imposed on a defendant, the ordeal is understood as revelatory, allowing us to glimpse the man's soul and character. We want to know how the defendant will take the news that he is to be put to death. His reaction is a moment of truth that journalists take care to record and report for their readers.[39]

Because today's death penalty proceeds amid normative anxiety and in violation of cultural taboos, it remains full of narrative potential. The death penalty is always good to talk about, even if it is bad to execute. To readers or viewers who are skeptical about the institution, each new imposition is a scandal, a cause for moral outrage. To the institution's supporters, death penalty stories elicit an equally powerful and opposite response. And precisely because of the element of transgression involved—an authorized killing in a world where killing is the worst sin—unconscious sentiments become a resource for journalists to tap into. Real life stories of killing and death subliminally connect with emotional responses that lie just below the surface, triggering a release of violent, vengeful sentiment and the pleasure that comes with disinhibition. It is this process that occurs when readers take in a newspaper headline and silently intone, "Yeah! Serves you right!"[40]

Tough talk here is liberating and empowering. Just for a moment, the reader may throw off the constraints of civilized propriety and enjoy the pleasures of uninhibited violence. The pleasure this entails is what tough-talking politicians seek to get at when they invoke the sentiments of vengeance and of war. Their hot-headed appeals set aside the prudent consideration of costs and benefits and connect instead with the pleasure of righteous aggression. And though this righteous violence is mostly enjoyed at the level of fantasy, of discourse, and of the imaginary, it is altogether real in its effects. It helps sustain the popular mandate for capital punishment and energizes a system that, on forty or fifty occasions in America each year, puts living, breathing men and women to death.

Capital cases, with their tales of wrongful killing and righteous death, are a news and entertainment classic of which the media never tires. As Leigh Bienen notes, "Murder mysteries, fantasies of murder, sanitized representations of killings, and dramatizations of capital punishment have long been staples of popular literature and entertainment . . . Capital cases dominate the newspaper headlines and evening news not just because journalists are ghoulish or exploitative, but because people want to know about them."[41] The reasons for the morality play's continuing appeal and for its repetitive structure lie in the emotional investment people have in these dramas. And people desire capital punishment for any number of reasons. These desires are grounded in the fascination with the death of others, in the wish for narrative closure following the disruption of a murderous act, in the socially sanctioned enjoyment of vengeful violence, and in the uncertainty and excitement produced by the trial and jury sentence.

Although there is a formulaic sameness in the basic repertoire, the details of each story (a different killer, a different victim, a different motive, or weapon, or set of circumstances) are sufficiently novel that audiences can be drawn in repeatedly. In the stock drama of judicial death, journalists work to find new angles to explore and new issues to investigate. Karla Faye Tucker's case raised issues of redemption, religion, and gender. Stanley "Tookie" Williams posed the problem of the inmate as reformed citizen and a force for good. Timothy McVeigh opened up a new focus on America's home-grown terrorists and the execution as martyrdom. Danny Rolling returned Americans to their fascination with sex murder and the allure of the serial killer. Other cases raise questions of discrimination (think of Warren McCleskey), or innocence (Cameron Todd Willingham), or prosecutorial misconduct (Delma Banks, Jr.), or botched execution (Pedro Medina). And so it goes on. The capital case narrative continually renews itself, each time putting death into discourse for edification and entertainment.[42]

Of course the death penalty's news and entertainment value might be so much greater if only the authorities would open up access to executions and relax their restrictions on photographs and images. From the mass media's point of view, the actual execution is a lost opportunity, a story deliberately spoiled.[43] But even today's closed-off, sanitized, uneventful executions provide some journalistic possibilities. The last words of the condemned are dutifully reported, as is his response to the flow of "execution medications" through his veins: "Zimmerman started praying before stopping suddenly in mid-sentence as the lethal dose of drugs began flowing through his body." "Busby remarked as the lethal drugs begin to flow, 'Here it comes. I can feel it.' He took a couple of breaths, closed his eyes and then slipped into unconsciousness."[44]

For more spectacle and excitement, the media turn to the revelers in the parking lot outside the prison where the execution is taking place. The Saturnalian celebrations and bad-taste festivities of these rowdies appear at the margins of the event, like the return of the repressed in an otherwise civilized procedure. On those rare occasions when executions become large-scale media events, the crowds and the cameras feed off each other. Reporters and TV crews show up for the execution of notorious killers, expecting to find crowds of celebrants and protesters. And, sure enough, the crowds appear—the presence of the TV cameras ensures that the usual small gatherings of death penalty activists are joined by revelers, publicity-seekers, and crowds of curious sightseers. The result is a carnival of sorts, occasioned by the execution and fostered by the floodlights. The execution of serial killer Ted Bundy in Florida in 1995 took exactly this form:

> In the predawn hours outside the prison, a macabre carnival assembled in the pasture. [C]ars disgorged people from across the state—police officers carrying sparklers, fraternity boys swigging from hip flasks, parents with their babies. They carried homemade signs, almost all of them in dubious taste. *Chi O, Chi O, its off to hell we go,* said one, making a pun at the expense of the murdered and beaten women of the Chi Omega house. Another listed the ingredients for "Bundy BBQ." An entrepreneur had commissioned tiny electric-chair lapel pins, which sold quickly at five dollars apiece. Two women strolled the pasture wearing homemade versions of Old Sparky's headpiece, which they had fashioned from Christmas gift boxes and lead stripped from a stained-glass window. An hour before the execution, a fourteen-car caravan pulled up, led by a flatbed truck bearing an illuminated sign: *Burn Bundy, Burn in Hell.* In the bed of another truck was a life-size effigy: A handcrafted mannequin seated on a wired kitchen chair, a crown of sparklers on its head. The cameras, it was clear, were the reasons so many people had spent so much energy on their signs and costumes—they wanted to be on television. The Zeta Tau brothers whooped and waved their frying pans whenever a cameraman ambled close. "The only one I'm talking to is Ted Koppel!" someone shouted above the noise.[45]

For the mass media, the death penalty is a controversy that is always fresh, a familiar story that can be constantly retold, a narrative gift that keeps on giving. And what is true of the mass media is true more generally of the world of literature, art, and popular culture. It is no surprise, then, that the death penalty is a recurring theme in modern film and novels. It lends depth and drama to crime stories, giving writers and filmmakers a "serious" subject that is also sensational—as viewers saw in *In Cold Blood, The Executioner's Song,* and *Dead Man Walking*—all of which transformed an actual capital case first into a best-selling book and then into a popular film.[46] The death penalty forms a theme in modern art, from Andy Warhol's electric chair screen prints to Ian Hamilton Findlay's guillotines. And it features as a recurring interest—solemn or ghoulish or pornographic by turn—on countless Internet sites and blogs. It exists, as I have said, in the entertainment zone.

How do ordinary members of the public engage with these deaths that proceed in their name? The question is a complicated one, but important nevertheless. Public attitudes toward the death penalty are various and differentiated, and individuals engage with the issue on a variety of levels and in different contexts. At either extreme are groups and individuals with strongly defined views and commitments—the fervent supporters at one end ranged against the committed abolitionists at the other. Unruly enthusiasts take all-too-evident pleasure in the prospect of an execution, celebrating with tailgate parties, souvenir T-shirts, and cheering encouragement. More sober supporters regard the practice as an unpleasant duty that morality demands or a harsh public policy that ultimately saves lives. Many people who oppose the institution do so not out of moral principle but because they doubt the system can be fairly or reliably administered. Yet others draw back in horror at the idea of putting a fellow human being to death. We know that most Americans have formed an opinion on the issue—comparatively few respond to surveys that they "don't know"—but we also know that few of them take part in campaigns, belong to activist movements, or are especially well informed about the issue.[47] It seems likely, too, that the majority of Americans today are neither horrified nor delighted by the prospect of executing someone by lethal injection. Nor are they especially interested in the institution. Instead they are drawn to capital punishment as casual, curious spectators, interested to follow the course of a capital trial, to see justice done, and to learn the fate of the condemned when an execution takes place.

Americans actively engage with the death penalty in many ways—by voting, responding to opinion polls, writing letters to editors, arguing with friends and family, writing middle school essays, and taking part in civics class debates. If a capital case takes place in their county they may become directly involved as jurors and witnesses or follow the case as members of a concerned community. (Capital punishment is, in practice, a local affair, administered by local political actors who play to a local public gallery. Whatever expressive purposes it serves are primarily realized in this local context.) For most Americans, however, that direct involvement never occurs. By far the most common form of engagement is, instead, that of the newspaper reader, the TV viewer, the Internet user. The relationship that most Americans have to the death penalty today is that of distantiated *consumers* of its narratives and images.

We should be careful in characterizing this involvement. We might think, for instance, that interest in capital punishment entails some elements of voyeurism or even sadism, but it is hardly appropriate to classify a majority of the population in the language of psychopathology.[48] Supporters of the death penalty see themselves as taking a hard line, perhaps, but few think of themselves as brutal or sadistic.[49] And even those who take the trouble to attend executions may be motivated less by sadism than by curiosity and a thirst for excitement: as John McManners says of the eighteenth-century execution crowd, we understand the appeal better if we view executions as public theater rather than as human slaughters.[50] But for all that, there is considerable evidence that many people do take pleasure in punishment, and especially pleasure in the death of demonized others.[51]

Vengefulness and pleasure in the pain of others are not especially primitive emotions, nor are they necessarily asocial. The demand for retaliation is rooted less in instinctive aggression than in the practices of exchange and reciprocity on which all human societies are built. The urge to strike back against wrongdoers is a social and contemporary desire, even if modern culture and state institutions strive mightily to contain it.[52] In warrior societies, retaliatory violence is a sacred duty required by masculine codes of honor, but even in peaceable, commercial cultures, individuals are inclined to strike back and take pleasure in the suffering of those who have harmed or humiliated them—which is why we need powerful norms to prevent them from doing so. People everywhere respond to stories of murder and mayhem with the urge to avenge the wrongdoing and humble the perpetrator: what varies is the probability that they (or their representatives) will act on these impulses. The tension between vengeful aggression and civilized restraint remains a vital one, particularly where group relations are fraught and fears of violence intense.

Stories of heinous crime followed by righteous punishment contain, for their audiences, a source of vicarious aggression and pleasure. When a murderer of others is murdered in his turn, these violent pleasures are intensified accordingly. As Elias Canetti remarks, "A murder shared with many others, which is not only safe and permitted, but indeed recommended is irresistible to the great majority of men."[53] The civilized culture of contemporary liberal-democratic America represses and sublimates these violent drives but does not make them entirely disappear. The pleasures of righteous, lethal violence are psychic facts that still play a role in the culture. Capital punishment allows ordinary Americans to collude in killing. It permits a subterranean violence to surface, even if only in private imagination or on the allusive margins of public discourse.

Traces of this conflict become visible here and there in the capital punishment complex, even though officials strive to keep them hidden. In contemporary America there is a deep seam of gallows humor and of lascivious enjoyment—a whole pornography of pain and death—surrounding the death penalty. We see these sentiments vividly expressed in the tailgate parties outside prisons when executions take place; in local bars where drinkers toast the executioners; and in news stories about champagne receptions in prosecutors' offices following the announcement of a death sentence. These unruly behaviors are regarded by respectable people as vulgar and scandalous, but they occur regularly enough to be symptomatic rather than aberrant.[54]

To take pleasure in the act of state killing involves, nonetheless, an element of transgression. It violates the civilized values and sensibilities that urge respect for life and the abhorrence of violence. It breaches the moral norms of proper conduct and embarrasses morally serious supporters of the institution. It is, strictly speaking, obscene. But this impulse undoubtedly exists as an undercurrent in the culture, and it is by no means limited to revelers in the prison parking lot. Recall, for example, the statements of the Florida attorney general, Bob Butterworth, who reacted to news of a horribly botched electrocution by cheerfully warning that murderers should avoid Florida, because its electric chair doesn't work too well.[55] Or consider the Georgia state legislators who repeatedly resisted shifting from electrocution to lethal injection because they wanted "to keep it gruesome."[56]

Media representations play to their audiences in different ways. The *New York Times* stories address concerned, liberal readers while the *New York Post* headline assumes a readership more openly enthusiastic about "frying" bad guys. One begins by engaging the intellect while the other goes straight to the visceral. One elicits aggression, catharsis, triumph at the vanquishing of a hated enemy—*"Fry Baby!"*—while another prompts serious reflection on normative dilemmas and human tragedy.[57] But both engage in the production of pleasure. And members of the public who engage with this death penalty discourse, who identify with its force and enjoy its fantasy, thereby become complicit in the process—as consumers of capital punishment's proffered identities, its psychic gratifications, and its cheap thrills.

If this is true then there is a terrible disjunction between the moral seriousness of the system's life or death decisions and the moral shallowness of the public's typically casual engagement with the issue. Popular culture and media transform a grave issue with which democratic citizens might be expected to engage in a serious way into a cheap entertainment and an occasion for ribaldry and easy prejudice.[58] Sound-bite comments and gallows humor often set the standard for public discussion, and capital punishment is routinely regarded as a casual badge of political and cultural identity rather than a somber matter requiring deep moral reflection. Surveys and opinion polls enumerate these superficial attitudes and lend them the false gravity of "public opinion" and "democratic will," thus mistaking stereotypical fantasy for rational opinion. Unlike those few individuals who directly experience the process, the vast majority engages with an imaginary abstraction, a death penalty that floats free in the ether of media narrative, political ideology, and popular fantasy, untroubled by the living, breathing, terrified individuals about to killed.[59]

Elias Canetti once remarked, "Disgust at collective killing is of very recent origin and should not be overestimated." The morbid curiosity that led masses of people to join the hanging-day crowd or the Southern lynch mob has not disappeared from the modern soul.[60] We are still, many of us, spectators at the scaffold and viewers in the public gallery, though the norms that shape our conduct are certainly more civilized. One hundred years ago, lynch mobs demanded to see burning and blood and broken bodies. Today's public settles for death sentences that are painlessly and privately executed. Indeed, they often settle for virtual death sentences that are never executed at all. But there is continuity between one event and the other—a common interest in making death work to create power, profit, and pleasure: a collective effervescence that still thrills to the prospect of a killing.

The Idea of Death

The idea of death is at the core of America's cultural and psychological engagement with capital punishment. The death penalty is not a form of punishment that happens to involve death, but rather a death that comes in the form of a punishment. Death is what exerts the gravitational pull, the cultural and psychic force that sparks anxiety and energizes action.[61] This is more than ever true in America today, when state executions have become rare in much of the country and death penalties are always controversial. The prospect of death has a terrifying, mysterious power that finds its way at some time or other into the imagination of each and every one of us. So even when official threats of death do not deter criminals who kill, they command the attention of others. There is a power released by death, a sacred, irresistible energy—and the institutions of capital punishment are employed to exploit it.

As with all emotionally powerful subjects, the individual's relationship to death is an ambivalent, paradoxical one. Death horrifies but it also attracts. It engenders fear but also fascination, exerting what Charles Dickens termed the "attraction of repulsion."[62] It is "in our secret nature," he wrote, "to have a dark and dreadful interest in the subject." Many writers, not all of them Freudians, have made the same point. Arlette Farge talks of the "paradoxical and contradictory co-existence" between the "fear and horror of death and a real taste for it." And Elizabeth Bronfen has written of our capacity to "delight at, be fascinated, morally educated, emotionally elevated and psychologically reassured . . . by the depiction of a horrible event in the life of another."

This death fascination was, as V. A. C. Gatrell has shown, a powerful motivation for the crowds who gathered to watch a death unfold on the scaffold.[63] "Scaffold death offered witnesses [an encounter with] danger, pleasure and desire," he wrote. No wonder, then, that "people were (and are) capable of the most elemental excitement—and thence curiosity— about what happened on scaffolds." The spectator's delight in death is premised on the fact that it is the death of another. The witness to an execution "experiences" death but as a vicarious encounter at the end of which is an "affirmation of self." As Bronfen puts it, "Even as we are forced to acknowledge the ubiquitous presence of death in our own lives, our belief in immortality is confirmed. There is death but it is not our own."[64]

This capacity to take pleasure in the death of others greatly depends on who these others are. Attitudes to death are heavily conditioned by perspectives and relationships: the deaths of friends and the deaths of enemies affect us very differently.[65] If those on death row are marginalized individuals from disreputable minorities or are regarded as monstrous, their deaths may be contemplated by many with little concern. The special appeal of the scaffold death is that it releases viewers from the anxiety of identification and the obligations of compassion. The death of a convicted capital murderer is the death of a certified social enemy, deemed dangerous and beyond human fellowship. It is a death that can prompt pleasure and righteous affirmation.

The interest that human beings take in death and the attraction it sometimes holds for them are paradoxical phenomena. They become more paradoxical still when we recall that contemporary America is predominantly a "death-denying" culture that goes to great lengths to suppress the facts of death and dying.[66] In contrast to other times and other cultures that give death a more public, more ritualized, more conscious place in everyday life, the disposition of American culture today is to deny death, to minimize the relation to it, to put it "behind the scenes" and keep its acknowledgment to a minimum.[67] Daily lives are lived in accordance with health and fitness regimes designed to stave off aging, ill health, and death. Youthfulness, vitality, the minimization of aging, and the banishment of death are the more prominent cultural traits that shape action and attitude.[68]

In this social setting, death is a profound anxiety. It is a fear that lingers at the margins of consciousness but resists being put into speech, an unknowable mystery that eludes attempts to give it meaning. In the United States—as in contemporary Western culture more generally—human life is sacred and human individuals sacralized. At the same time, and correspondingly, the subjects of death and dying have become increasingly taboo, surrounded by tension and rules of avoidance: "We speak of death when we don't mean it, and when we do mean it, we use euphemisms."[69] It is in this context that Western societies came to regard *murder*—and not treason, or heresy, or blasphemy, or *lèse-majesté*—as the ultimate crime and simple *death* as the ultimate punishment. Death is the great taboo and killing the great prohibition, which is why only murderers are now eligible for capital punishment. The ultimate punishment is reserved for the ultimate crime. And herein lies the source of much of the conflict and ambivalence that surround the death penalty. Killing is prohibited and death is taboo: if it is permissible to put killers to death it is because the transgression of their crime licenses the transgression of their punishment.

Human beings are by nature fascinated by that which is denied to them. Strict rules of repression, of prudery, and of Puritanism are a recipe for intensifying the pleasure of transgression. And so it is with death. George Gorer pointed out half a century ago that "while natural death has become more and more smothered in prudery violent death has played an ever-growing part in the fantasies offered to mass audiences."[70] Gorer had in mind the fantasies of film and literature—"detective stories, thriller, war stories" and so on—but it seems clear that one of the fantasies offered to mass audiences in the United States today is the death of murderers promised by the institutions of capital punishment.

Death is neurotically charged and hypersignificant in American culture, but in the normal course of events, Americans are inhibited and restrained from talking about it. Death is on our minds but not in our conversations. The institution of capital punishment relaxes these restraints, allowing the possibility of talking about death in a way that is free of the usual anxieties. It allows capital punishment's supporters to talk, in an uninhibited way, about the deaths of demonized others. Hence the extraordinary amount of talk about the death penalty, much of which involves imagined deaths that will never happen—capital laws that won't be enforced, death sentences that won't be executed, executions that will never take place. Like death itself, the death penalty has become hypersignificant in contemporary America, owing to its conflicted cultural status, historical associations, and contemporary political resonance. But above all, the death penalty is hypersignificant because it talks of killing and death and makes that talk pleasurable and empowering.

In the day-to-day life of most late-modern Western societies, people strive to keep death hidden, placing it behind the scenes of social life. They avoid talking about it in front of the children and do their best to put it out of mind. It has, for Americans today, the kind of status that sex had for the Victorians. When they are obliged to talk of it, their speech comes freighted with emotion and anxiety. Discourse about death is discourse burdened with devastating, often unbearable, implications for the self— except when the death in question is the controlled, socially approved, legally authorized death of a demonized other. The existence of a death penalty for convicted murderers prompts people to talk of death and contemplate killing, permitting the guilty pleasures of taboo violation. This permission functions as a kind of liberation, a release from repression. It licenses new and productive relationships to death. It opens the way for the righteous enjoyment of prohibited wishes and fantasies.

Putting death into discourse in this way transforms it, creating new sensations, new pleasures of stimulation and projection, new possibilities of mastery and detachment. It allows a displacement but also an excitation, prompting spirals of discourse, power, and pleasure. The millions of citizens who consume death penalty discourse for interest, gratification. and pleasure are certainly not sadists in any proper sense of the term. But it is not inaccurate to describe them as the casual consumers of a quietly sadistic pornography that uses the death of a criminal as a transgressive source of pleasure.

Consider, for example, the enthusiasm with which hundreds of Californians donated money to ensure that the serial killer Gerald Gallego would be put to death rather than languish on death row. Gallego had been convicted of murder and sentenced to death in California, but, given that state's postconviction processes, it was thought unlikely that he would ever be executed. In 1984, California's governor agreed to extradite Gallego to face murder charges in Nevada, since he would be more likely to be executed if tried and convicted in that state. When it emerged that the Nevada county where the murders had occurred could not afford the $60,000 cost of a capital trial, the journalist Stan Gillian of the *Sacramento Bee* wrote a column urging Californians to send money to the county treasurer: "There must be 59,999 other Californians besides me happy enough to see Gallego in the clutches of no-nonsense Nevada to send a dollar to help the cause. My buck's on the way." In the weeks that followed, almost 1,800 donations were sent, totaling more than $26,000. Was this a morally serious effort by concerned citizens to ensure proper retribution? Perhaps. But it more closely resembles a fusion of popular outrage and sensationalist news-making that occasioned an outpouring of private revenge fantasies. In the event, Gallego was sentenced to death by a Nevada court, but no execution had occurred by the time of his death from cancer in 2002.[71]

In late-modern Western society, the death penalty is a cultural contradiction, a source of disruption. It inflames, causing irritation and prompting reaction. The result is an outbreak of discourse—criticism, legitimation, argument, and commentary. Everyone has an opinion on the matter, and for every opinion there is a counter-opinion waiting to provide a response. Hence the repetitive character of death penalty debate. There is a pleasurable familiarity, a formulaic litany of *pro* and *con* that helps us bring this difficult issue under control. The unfathomable mystery of death and the evil of killing are transformed into the reassuring experience of a moral debate. We moderns may have lost the public ritual of execution, but we have substituted the ritual of the capital punishment debate.

The enactment of death penalty statutes, the bringing of capital indictments, the pronouncement of death sentences, the evocation of death's imaginary—these and other declarations of lethal intent allow local groups of people to imagine themselves sovereign, to overcome their usual impotence and take control over life and death. And these effects of power and pleasure are sustained even when death remains virtual rather than real. Critics of capital punishment insist that we ought not to put people to death because it is not our place to "play God." But playing God in this way constitutes a large part of the penalty's appeal.

In dealing death, American voters and viewers usurp God's role, taming and controlling death's "natural terror," putting it to their use, directing lethal violence against their enemies. But they do this safely, from the sidelines, without fear of retaliation and without the "agonies of the spirit" that affect those obliged to administer the penalty or to see it up close. When they put death into discourse in this way they take a taboo—an unspeakable object of anxiety—and make it an instrument of power and pleasure.

The murder story is a disruptive, anxiety-producing narrative, prompting fear as well as fascination in the onlookers. To impose a sentence of death on the murderer is a psychically satisfying resolution. We get to talk about, and to imagine, the killer's death in a way that produces pleasure rather than anxiety, a sense of moral order rather than amoral chaos. His is a deserved death, a controlled killing, a legally approved sacrifice that may, in any case, never even happen. The death sentence brings death within the reach of power. It tames death and puts it to work.

In releasing people from the prohibition on killing, the murder and its punishment put them into a new relation to death. Death loses none of its dread and its anxiety, but instead of being an unknowable calamity imposed on people from without, it becomes a fate over which they exert control. The power of life and death, once the distinguishing mark of kings, the stamp and signature of sovereign might, now becomes a public utility, available to "we, the people" to impose on our most hated enemies. To be able to speak, righteously and unanxiously, about the death of demonized others, to have the power to impose death on another individual, and to do so legally, without fear of retaliation, is to be in possession of a power that is unique in modern society. Is it hardly surprising that so many people—in America and elsewhere—are unwilling to give it up.

The dubious pleasures that derive from the death of demonized others are not an exclusively American vice. The people of other Western nations no doubt experienced the same thrills when they witnessed the state's righteous killings, either as early-modern spectators or as modern newspaper readers.[72] But elsewhere in the West, governing elites have insisted that these pleasures be relinquished in the name of liberal democracy and civilization. In America, by contrast, this is a pleasure that groups of "the People" have repeatedly permitted themselves.

AMERICA'S death penalty has adapted to the late-modern context in which it operates. That context is one in which death has become taboo; violence is subject to heavy prohibition; individuals are regarded as sacred; and government is expected to enhance the welfare and happiness of its citizens. These background facts render the state's deliberate killing of offenders somewhat transgressive. But contemporary America is also a context in which powerful social currents press to avenge heinous crimes, vanquish hated enemies, express sovereign power, and enjoy the deaths of demonized others. In this context these transgressive currents are empowered by specific institutional structures and by recurring legal and political choices. Above all, these lethal urges are empowered by the Supreme Court's insistence on devolving decisions about death to local political actors—state legislators, district attorneys, state judges, and local juries.

The urgent demand for vengeance, the pent-up hatreds of race and class, the righteous absolutes of retaliation, in short, the myriad pleasures of punishment—these are emotions that well up in American communities traumatized by vicious murders, especially when the perpetrator is a low-status black and the victim a high-status white.[73] Primitive, unruly, and disruptive, these sentiments are suppressed much of the time by norms of civilized propriety and the institutional controls that back them up. But in the wake of heinous murders these restraints are relaxed and the expression of passionate outrage becomes culturally required.

The American capital punishment complex works to hold these competing forces together, to manage the conflicting pressures of prohibition and aggression, restraint and revenge in a manner that comports with the law, respects cultural boundaries, and moves with the changing tides of public sentiment. It does so by projecting the potent and pleasurable fantasy of the collective killing of a convicted killer. This fantasy is sustained up until the moment of execution, at which point the system shifts gears, stifling rather than encouraging communication, and striving to obscure the brute fact of death beneath layers of legal bureaucracy and medical solicitude. This arrangement functions to maximize public enjoyment of death penalty discourse while minimizing public exposure to actual state killing.

Epilogue

Discourse and Death

We have little more than an illusion of a death penalty in this country.

ALEX KOZINSKI, CHIEF JUDGE OF THE U.S. COURT OF APPEALS
FOR THE NINTH CIRCUIT, 1995

A merica's death penalty presents us with two compelling questions: Why does it survive in an age of abolition? And why is it enacted through such peculiar, seemingly dysfunctional forms?

Earlier explanations, framed in terms of American Exceptionalism or cultural essentialism, have been shown to be inadequate and misleading. Instead of regarding America as an exception to broader Western patterns, this account has shown that American history has been in the mainstream of death penalty developments and that its capital punishment practices have been affected by the same broad processes that have produced reform and abolition elsewhere in the Western world. These same processes make the U.S. death penalty today an ever-more marginal institution, constantly grating against liberal and humanitarian sentiments and appearing increasingly transgressive whenever it is actually carried through to an execution.

Instead of assuming that America's retention of capital punishment is a consequence of an underlying culture that is more punitive than that of other Western nations, this book has shown that the survival of American capital punishment is the outcome of developments that were shaped not by "culture" alone but by the distinctive history and social structure of American society—above all, its process of state formation, its political and legal institutions, and its group dynamics and cultural commitments.

That America's deployment of death has varied in certain respects from that of other Western nations is in keeping with the rule, rather than an exception to it. All nations exhibit a distinctive national pattern of death penalty use and transformation, though this variation is now concealed by an abolitionist present that makes all other Western nations appear alike. That America's deployment of capital punishment is distinctive in various ways—both in the present, where it persists in a regionalized, attenuated form three decades after abolition elsewhere, and in the past, when it was more local, more communal, and more prone to abuse by popular mobs— has been explained by reference to the structure of the country's institutional terrain and the political and cultural struggles that have taken place on it.

America's death penalty may not be "exceptional" but it is certainly distinctive. Today's capital punishment complex carries traces of the institutional structures and cultural practices that dominate the American social landscape, together with the marks of the national and local histories that have shaped its changing forms. Far from being the essential expression of an unchanging culture, the current American system is the outcome of historical events that unfolded within a distinctive set of institutional structures and social processes. The peculiar forms of the late-modern institution contain the story of their historical production and display the traces of the political and cultural terrain on which they were built. Capital punishment today is an assemblage of constructed forms and compromise formations that embody a whole history, a whole culture, and a whole governmental structure, all of which are distinctively American. By examining capital punishment up close, we have been able to see in some detail the peculiar ways in which the American state and society are put together and the characteristic processes whereby American institutions and culture combine to shape social action and legal outcomes.

The institutional forms and cultural practices of today's death penalty articulate the social field from which they emerged. They embody its forces and its fault lines, its cultural commitments and its political compromises, its ethos and its ideologies. And these forms *function*. They are used to meet needs, to serve purposes, and to affirm values in ways that draw them back into the social field from which they emerged, reconnecting them with ongoing political and cultural struggles and advancing the interests of specific groups and individuals.

Why does America retain the death penalty? The short answer does not point to Puritanism, or punitiveness, or violent vigilantism, as conventional commentaries would have it. It points instead to one of America's chief values and virtues—a radically local version of democracy—which is the primary cause of capital punishment's persistence into the twenty-first century. If the death penalty is a particle of state power, in America that power has never been so concentrated or so centrally controlled as it has been elsewhere, being instead devolved to the local level and copossessed by a local electorate. In America, as we have seen, all politics are local and democracy can kill. The annual execution tolls of places like Harris County, Texas, are proof enough of that.

But this same characteristic, local democracy, also provides an answer to the opposite question: Why was an American state the first Western jurisdiction to *abolish* the death penalty? The explanation for this paradox—the same cause explaining two opposing effects—is that "democracy" only partly explains historical outcomes. It describes the locus and process of decision-making and the power of local majorities to shape political outcomes. But it tells us nothing about the interests of these majorities, their relationships to minority groups, and their attitudes to death penalty policy. Capital punishment policy is always shaped by state interests, group relations, cultural values, and levels of violence control—and these have varied over time and across the vast continental landmass of the American nation.

American capital punishment persists, despite its conflict with contemporary liberal and humanitarian norms, because of the structure of the American polity. That structure makes it difficult to abolish the death penalty in the face of majority public opinion and deprives governing elites of the opportunity for top-down, countermajoritarian reform of the kind that has led to abolition elsewhere. (That same structure helps shape the political attitudes of these elites, which is why America's national leaders are so much less abolitionist than their equivalents elsewhere.) America's pluralist state, its popular local democracy, and the Supreme Court's constitutional decisions have empowered local majorities that support the death penalty, while simultaneously restraining, refining, and restricting its implementation.

But even in the face of these institutional conditions, the death penalty could have been abolished: indeed it has been, at various times, in about half of the states. That it has been so widely retained is a consequence, at base, of group relations and their political expression. Stark inequalities and enmities between groups, limited solidarity, and fear of crime and violence—these are what allow this punishment to persist. The degradations of capital punishment are not the result of an American disregard for status and dignity, as some have claimed, but a consequence of a deep-rooted inequality of status and respect that shapes race relations and permits the dehumanization of offenders from the bottom of the social hierarchy. For hundreds of years of its history, America's democracy enslaved, segregated, and excluded African Americans, a social (and racial and regional) division that has had major consequences for the course of capital punishment's history. Despite the Supreme Court's effort to eliminate that heritage and bring the death penalty into line with the rule of law and civilized culture, the specter of lynching continues to haunt the system right up to the present day.

And then there is violence. America's death penalty cannot be viewed apart from the striking social fact of America's extraordinary rates of homicide. The same processes of state formation and group relations that explain capital punishment's persistence lie at the base of America's continuing problem of deadly criminal violence. It is thus no surprise that the states that carry out executions today are mostly states with chronically high murder rates—places where capital punishment is more realistically regarded not as deterrence but as retaliation in kind.

The American capital punishment system has not survived into the twenty-first century because death sentences are more necessary or more functional in the United States than elsewhere. Capital punishment's capacity to serve the conventional ends of crime control and criminal justice is no greater here than it was elsewhere in the modern West—indeed, the convoluted, restricted, and restrained forms of today's American death penalty make it even less well adapted to these purposes. Its survival has little to do with its instrumental value for governmental or penal purposes and everything to do with the institutional difficulty of securing abolition in the face of majority public opinion. But having continued in existence in this peculiar configuration, the institution has been used by groups and actors who have seized the opportunities that it provides to advance their interests or meet their needs. These actors have taken the death penalty and made it work for them, using it sometimes to express their sense of justice, sometimes to enhance their power, their profit, and their casual pleasure.

IF CAPITAL punishment's early-modern mode was shaped by the overriding state purpose of maintaining rule, and its modern mode by the rationalized state purpose of governing crime, the late-modern mode is shaped not by any grand state purpose but by the partisan interests of political actors and their constituents. The day-to-day uses of the American death penalty are grounded in the microphysics of local politics—of group relations and status competition, professional rivalry and ambition, and the venal give-and-take of political exchange—rather than being connected to the great ends of state. Petty functions have replaced grand ones, private uses have largely replaced public ones. In late-modern America, capital punishment has ceased to be an instrument of state rule or penal purpose and has become, instead, a resource for political exchange and cultural consumption.

In the course of the last half century, the American death penalty has been transformed from a penal instrument that puts persons to death to a peculiar institution that puts death into discourse for political and cultural purposes. Over this period, the capital punishment complex has become increasingly discursive in nature. A legislative act is announced, an indictment read, a sentence declared, a verdict upheld. Even the killing of the condemned is transformed into words, since the general public sees and hears nothing of the event, except in the form of pictureless published reports. Today's system—especially in death penalty states outside of the South—is primarily about enactment and evocation, rather than execution. It revolves around the utterance of words, not the breaking of bones or the spilling of blood. In the morality play that is staged today, the body in pain recedes from view, while the promise, the power, and the pleasure of death are put center stage to become the major focus of audience attention.

The system of capital punishment that exists in America today is primarily a communication system. For the most part the system is not about executions, which, outside of Texas and a few Southern states, are relatively rare—more people are killed each year by lightning. It is about mounting campaigns, taking polls, passing laws, bringing charges, bargaining pleas, imposing sentences, and rehearing cases. It is about threats rather than deeds, anticipated deaths rather than actual executions. What gets performed, for the most part, is discourse and debate. From the point of view of the system, the discreet violence of the execution is a necessary underpinning, but not the thing itself. Capital punishment is like a credit system with a high volume of circulating value underwritten by a gold standard—actual executions—that enables all of the system's exchanges but is less often cashed out.

Capital punishment in America today operates primarily on the plane of the imaginary, and the great majority of its deaths are imagined ones. But the political and economic effects of these grim fantasies are no less real for being imagined. In American criminal sentencing, the availability of the death penalty permits very lengthy sentences of imprisonment, even life imprisonment without parole, to appear comparatively humane, thereby contributing to the nation's extraordinary rates of imprisonment. In the American political system and in the entertainment zone of popular culture, talk about death permits symbolic acts, exchanges, and representations that are used by groups and individuals in their pursuit of power, profit, and pleasure. That the death penalty is increasingly declaratory and discursive makes it no less powerful in its political, legal, and cultural effects. Nor is it any less lethal for the more than twelve hundred men and women who have been put to their deaths since executions resumed three decades ago.

Notes

Prologue

1. Quoted in *Orlando News*, October 25, 2006.
2. The defender description is from Fiona Steel, "Grisly Gainesville," available at www.clarkprosecutor.org/html/death/US/rolling1051.htm (accessed 1/6/10). The account of Rolling's death is from Dianna Hoyt, a witness to the execution, quoted in the *Miami Herald* report available at www.clarkprosecutor.org/html/death/US/rolling1051.htm (accessed 1/6/10).
3. The victims' families ran an advertisement in the *Gainesville Sun,* thanking the community for its support: "We hope you will remember August 1990 and the years that followed without any sense of community shame for what has happened here. You turned a blemish into a rose." See Ron Word, "16 Years Later, Rolling Executed," available at www.clarkprosecutor.org/html/death/US/rolling1051.htm (accessed 1/6/10).
4. The full quotations can be read at www.clarkprosecutor.org/html/death/US/rolling1051.htm.
5. For books on Rolling see Danny Rolling and Sondra London, *The Making of a Serial Killer* (Portland, OR: Feral House, 1996); James Fox and Jack Levin, *Killer on Campus* (New York: Avon Books, 1996); Mary S. Ryzuk, *Gainesville Ripper: A Summer's Madness, Five Young Victims—The Arrest and the Trial* (New York: D. I. Fine, 1994); and John Philpin and John Donnelly, *Beyond Murder: The Inside Account of the Gainesville Student Murders* (Memphis, TN: Onyx, 1994). Several television shows, including *The Forensic Factor; American Justice with Bill Kurtis;* and *Body of Evidence: From the Case*

Files of Dayle Hinman, aired episodes about Rolling. *The Gainesville Ripper,* a film directed by Josh Townsend, was released in 2007.

1. A Peculiar Institution

1. "The Cabinet, No. LXXV," *Philadelphia Repertory* 2 (1812), quoted in Stuart Banner, *The Death Penalty: An American History* (Cambridge, MA: Harvard University Press, 2002), 112. Roger Hood, *The Death Penalty: A World-Wide Perspective* (Oxford, England: Oxford University Press, 1989), writes at 6 that "no one can embark on a study of the death penalty without making the commonplace remark that from a philosophical and policy standpoint there appears to be nothing new to be said."
2. Dan Kahan, "The Secret Ambition of Deterrence," 113 *Harvard Law Review* (1999): 413–500 at 436.
3. Robert Badinter notes the same repetitious discourse in France. Talking of the public meetings he attended on the death penalty, he writes, "The sessions would unfold with little variation. The same arguments provoked the same questions that called for the same answers." Robert Badinter, *Abolition: One Man's Battle against the Death Penalty* (Boston, MA: Northeastern University Press, 2008), 11.
4. The Michigan law of 1846 abolished the death penalty for all ordinary crimes, retaining it only for treason. In the period since, no person has been capitally indicted, sentenced, or executed in the state.
5. Discussing the case of *Furman v Georgia* (1972), which suspended the use of capital punishment throughout the United States, and *Gregg v Georgia* (1976), which reactivated it, Zimring and Hawkins say, "*Furman* was the culmination of a historical movement of long duration, whereas *Gregg* signaled a sharp departure from trends in the United States and the development of capital punishment policy in the rest of the West." Franklin Zimring and Gordon Hawkins, *Capital Punishment and the American Agenda* (New York: Cambridge University Press, 1986), 46.
6. According to FBI reports, there were more than 14,000 murders in the United States in 2008. In that year a total of 111 sentences of capital punishment were imposed.
7. Alex Kosinski and Sean Gallagher, "For an Honest Death Penalty," *New York Times,* March 8, 1995, A21.
8. David Baldus and George Woodworth, "Race Discrimination and the Death Penalty: An Empirical and Legal Overview," in James Acker, Robert Bohm, and Charles Lanier, eds., *America's Experiment with Capital Punishment,* 2nd ed. (Durham, NC: Carolina Academic Press, 2003). The authors observe that "a controlled pre- and post-*Furman* . . . study showed a marked decline in the evidence of race-of-defendant discrimination, although race-of-victim effects were the same in both periods" (517).
9. Thomas Laqueur, "Festivals of Punishment," *London Review of Books,* October 5, 2000, 17–24.
10. See David Garland, "Penal Excess and Surplus Meaning: Public Torture

Lynchings in Twentieth-Century America," *Law & Society Review* 39 (2005): 793–834.

11. Franklin Zimring, *The Contradictions of American Capital Punishment* (Oxford, England: Oxford University Press, 2003). On the "peculiar institution" of slavery in the antebellum South, see Kenneth Stampp, *The Peculiar Institution: Slavery in the Ante-Bellum South* (New York: Vintage Books, 1956).

12. Stuart Banner, "Traces of Slavery: Race and the Death Penalty in Historical Perspective," in Austin Sarat and Charles Ogletree, eds., *From Lynch Mobs to the Killing State: Race and the Death Penalty in America* (New York: New York University Press, 2006), 97. See also Judith Kay, *Murdering Myths: The Story behind the Death Penalty* (New York: Rowman and Littlefield, 2005); James Marquart, Sheldon Ekland-Olson, and Jonathan Sorensen, *The Rope, the Chair and the Needle: Capital Punishment in Texas, 1923–1990* (Austin: University of Texas Press, 1994); Stephen Bright, "Discrimination, Death and Denial: Race and the Death Penalty," in David Dow and Mark Dow, eds., *Machinery of Death: The Reality of America's Death Penalty Regime* (New York: Routledge, 2002), 47; Zimring, *Contradictions;* Margaret Vandiver, *Lethal Punishment: Lynchings and Legal Executions in the South* (New Brunswick, NJ: Rutgers University Press, 2006).

13. According to the Death Penalty Information Center, the race of those executed between 1976 and the end of 2009 is as follows: 56 percent white; 35 percent black; 7 percent Hispanic; 2 percent other. Today racial bias is most egregious in terms of race of victim. In executions since 1976, the racial breakdown of murder victims is 79 percent white; 14 percent black; 5 percent Hispanic; and 2 percent other.

14. Stampp, *Peculiar Institution.*

15. The phrase is from Philippe Buc, *The Dangers of Ritual: Between Medieval Texts and Social Scientific Theory* (Princeton, NJ: Princeton University Press, 2001), 259.

16. Michel Foucault, *Discipline and Punish: The Birth of the Prison* (New York: Allen Lane, 1977), 30–31.

17. The quotations are from Stevens in *Baze v Rees* 128 SCt 1520 (2008); Charles Black, *Capital Punishment: The Inevitability of Caprice and Mistake* (New York: Norton, 1981), 20; Hugo Bedau, *The Courts, the Constitution and Capital Punishment* (Lexington, MA: Lexington Books, 1977), 80; Sunil Dutta, "Kill the Death Penalty," *The Nation,* February 26, 2007, 8; Thorsten Sellin, ed., *Capital Punishment* (New York: Harper & Row, 1967); and Thomas Laqueur, "Festivals of Punishment," *London Review of Books,* October 5, 2000, 20. See also Robert Johnson, *Death Work: A Study of the Modern Execution Process* (Belmont, CA: Wadsworth, 1998) ("the death penalty is an anachronism"); Jesse Jackson, Sr., Jesse Jackson, Jr., and Bruce Shapiro, *Legal Lynching: The Death Penalty and America's Future* (New York: New Press, 2001) ("We have inherited a death penalty that is a relic, in so many ways, of the worst of the American past.").

18. Sellin, *Capital Punishment;* Gary Wills, "The Dramaturgy of Death," *New York Review of Books,* June 21, 2001, 6–10. See also Jack Greenberg: "the

318 Notes to Pages 19–21

system . . . looks irrational . . . and serves no purpose." Jack Greenberg, "Capital Punishment as a System," *Yale Law Journal* 91 (1981–1982): 927. And see Johnson, *Death Work,* 9 ("Capital punishment has . . . become a commodity dispensed without any redeeming social or communal purpose.").

19. Despite periodic claims that correlations have been discovered between death penalty use and homicide rate declines, the settled view of most experts is that there is no persuasive empirical evidence to show that the deterrent effect of the death penalty for murder is any—or is not—more effective than that of life imprisonment. For an overview, see Ruth Peterson and William Bailey, "Is the Death Penalty an Effective Deterrent for Murder? An Examination of Social Science Research," in James Acker, Robert Bohm, and Charles Lanier, eds., *America's Experiment with Capital Punishment,* 2nd ed. (Durham: University of North Carolina Press, 2003). For an account of recent debates, see Adam Liptak, "Does Death Penalty Save Lives? A New Debate," *New York Times,* November 18, 2007. As for retribution, the decades-long delays associated with a capital sentence generally dilute the retributive effect, as does the tendency to sympathize with death row inmates, who are often portrayed as victims of a cruel and unusual system.

20. See, for example, William Bowers quoted in Robert Lifton and Greg Mitchell, *Who Owns Death: Capital Punishment, the American Conscience and the End of Executions* (New York: Perennial, 2000), 248–249; Phoebe Ellsworth and Samuel Gross, "Hardening of Attitudes: Americans' Views on the Death Penalty," in Hugo Bedau, *The Death Penalty in America: Current Controversies* (New York: Oxford University Press, 1997), 384; Richard Dieter, "Sentencing for Life: Americans Embrace Alternatives to the Death Penalty," in Bedau, *Death Penalty in America,* 124; G. L. Pierce and M. Radelet, "The Role and Consequences of the Death Penalty in American Politics," *New York University Review of Law and Social Change,* 15 (1990–1991).

21. See Zimring, *Contradictions;* Tony Poveda, "American Exceptionalism and the Death Penalty," *Social Justice* 27 (2000): 252–267; Brian Jarvis, *Cruel and Unusual: A Cultural History of Punishment in America* (London: Pluto Press, 2004); Antonin Scalia, "God's Justice and Ours," *First Things* 123 (2002): 17–21.

22. See Roger Hood and Carolyn Holye, *The Death Penalty: A Worldwide Perspective* (Oxford, England: Oxford University Press, 2008). Although it remained abolitionist for ordinary crimes, Portugal carried out military executions between 1916 and 1918. Venezuela was the first country in the world permanently to abolish the death penalty for all crimes, whether committed in peacetime or in war. Spain's last execution was in 1975; it abolished the death penalty in 1978. France's last execution was in 1977; it abolished in 1981.

23. Badinter, *Abolition,* 3. On the day the *Furman* decision was announced, the *Los Angeles Times* reported that George Campbell Chalwell was put to death in the British Virgin Islands after the queen of England rejected a plea for clemency. "Queen Rejects Plea, Murderer Executed," *Los Angeles Times,* June 29, 1972, A4.

24. See Chapter 4.

25. Some "retentionist" countries, such as India and Japan, are relatively sparing in their use of the penalty. Others, like Iran and Saudi Arabia (which use public executions to deal with moral and sexual offenses), and China (which executes thousands of offenders each year), are at the other end of the spectrum.

26. See David Garland, *The Culture of Control: Crime and Social Order in Contemporary Society* (Chicago: University of Chicago Press, 2001); Garland, ed., *Mass Imprisonment: Social Causes and Consequences* (London: Sage, 2001); James Whitman, *Harsh Justice: Criminal Punishment and the Widening Divide between America and Europe* (New York: Oxford University Press, 2003); Bruce Western, *Punishment and Inequality in America* (New York: Russell Sage Foundation, 2006). By focusing on the differences that mark off America from other Western nations, the present book addresses a problem that was deliberately bracketed off in my earlier work *Culture of Control*, namely, the comparative intensity of American punishment.

27. David Garland, "Capital Punishment and American Culture," *Punishment & Society* 7 (2005): 347–376.

28. Banner, *Death Penalty;* Richard Evans, *Rituals of Retribution: Capital Punishment in Germany, 1600–1987* (Oxford, England: Oxford University Press, 1996).

29. See Seymour Martin Lipset, *American Exceptionalism: A Double-Edged Sword* (New York: Norton, 1997); Byron Shafer, ed., *Is America Different? A New Look at American Exceptionalism* (New York: Oxford University Press, 1991); Charles Lockhart, *The Roots of American Exceptionalism: Institutions, Culture and Policies* (New York: Palgrave, 2003); Deborah Madsen, *American Exceptionalism* (Jackson: University of Mississippi Press, 1998). This sociological conception is distinct from the related idea of Americans as the new chosen people. The term is sometimes used today with a critical implication, as in discussions of U.S. penal exceptionalism, human rights exceptionalism, and welfare state exceptionalism. See Godfrey Hodgson, *The Myth of American Exceptionalism* (New Haven, CT: Yale University Press, 2009).

30. Most writers simply invoke Foucault without much discussion. For more extended and more thoughtful treatments, see Austin Sarat, *When the State Kills* (Princeton, NJ: Princeton University Press, 2001); Timothy Kaufman-Osborn, *From Noose to Needle: Capital Punishment and the Late Liberal State* (Ann Arbor: University of Michigan Press, 2002); and Michael Meranze, "Michel Foucault, the Death Penalty, and the Crisis of Historical Understanding," *Historical Reflections* 29 (2003): 191–209; Meranze, "The Death Penalty between Law, Sovereignty and Biopolitics," in David Garland, Randall McGowen, and Michael Meranze, *America's Death Penalty: Between Past and Present* (New York: New York University Press, 2010).

31. Foucault, *Discipline and Punish,* 3.

32. Ibid., 48–49.

33. Ibid., 59.

34. Foucault himself applied it to the late-modern death penalty that existed in France until 1981: "If death figured at the apex of the criminal justice system for so many centuries," he explains, "this was not because the lawmakers

and judges were especially sanguinary people. The reason was that justice was the exercise of sovereignty." Michel Foucault, "Against Replacement Punishments," in James Faubion, ed., *Michel Foucault: Power* (New York: New Press, 1994), 459–461; originally published in *Liberation* (September 1981).

35. Elias and Foucault tend to view the development of the French state as their model, but French absolutism was not the only developmental path. See Pieter Spierenburg, *The Spectacle of Suffering: Executions and the Evolution of Repression: From a Preindustrial Metropolis to the European Experience* (Cambridge, England: Cambridge University Press, 1984); Perry Anderson, *Lineages of the Absolutist State* (London: New Left Books, 1974); Charles Tilly, *Coercion, Capital and European States, 1660–1990* (New York: Wiley, 1990).

36. The U.S. government response to the U.N. Sixth Quinquennial Survey, quoted in Roger Hood, *The Death Penalty: A World-wide Perspective*, 3rd ed. (New York: Oxford University Press, 2002), 67.

37. Several Caribbean nations have used their power to impose death penalties as a marker of their sovereign autonomy in the face of what they regard as "neocolonialist" pressure to abolish capital punishment. See Meranze, "Law, Sovereignty and Biopolitics." As I argue in Chapter 9, many American states did something similar in the wake of *Furman v Georgia*.

38. Foucault, *Discipline and Punish*, 23.

39. A different aspect of Foucault's work, quite unrelated to his account of punishment, will prove suggestive later in this book. See Michel Foucault, *The History of Sexuality*, vol. 1 (New York: Allen Lane, 1978), where he develops the idea of "putting sex into discourse" and its role in producing power and pleasure.

40. Reprinted from *ProQuest Historical Newspapers*. The original report contains some even more disturbing passages that I have omitted here.

41. W. Fitzhugh Brundage, *Lynching in the New South: Georgia and Virginia, 1880–1930* (Urbana: University of Illinois Press, 1993); David Garland, "Penal Excess."

42. Michael Pfeifer, *Rough Justice: Lynching and American Society, 1874–1947* (Urbana: University of Illinois Press, 2004), 3.

43. James Allen, ed., *Without Sanctuary: Lynching Photographs in America* (Santa Fe, NM: Twin Palms, 2000); Garland, "Penal Excess."

44. Allen, *Without Sanctuary*, reproduces the texts and images of these and other postcards.

45. Joel Williamson, *The Crucible of Race: Black-White Relations in the American South since Emancipation* (New York: Oxford University Press, 2002); Brundage, *Lynching in the New South*; W. Fitzhugh Brundage, ed., *Under Sentence of Death: Lynching in the South* (Chapel Hill: University of North Carolina Press, 1997); Garland, "Penal Excess."

46. Pfeifer, *Rough Justice*, 67. William Miller and John Gardner discuss how private revenge can re-emerge as a supplement to state justice if the state's punishments are perceived as inadequate. William Miller, "Clint Eastwood and Equity: Popular Culture's Theory of Revenge," in Austin Sarat and Thomas

Kearns, eds., *Law in the Domains of Culture* (Ann Arbor: University of Michigan Press, 1998); John Gardner, "Crime: In Proportion and in Perspective," in Andrew Ashworth and Martin Wasik, eds., *Fundamentals of Sentencing Theory* (Oxford, England: Oxford University Press, 1998), 31–52.

47. The first phrase is from Eduardo Bonilla-Silva, *White Supremacy and Racism in the Post–Civil Rights Era* (Boulder, CO: Lynne Reinner Publishers, 2001), 106; the second from Jackson et al., *Legal Lynching.* For other accounts of the relationship between lynchings and contemporary capital punishment, see Zimring, *Contradictions;* Kaufman-Osborn, *Noose to Needle;* and Margaret Vandiver, *Lethal Punishment: Lynchings and Legal Executions in the South* (New Brunswick, NJ: Rutgers University Press, 2006). The term "legal lynching" is often used today to describe capital proceedings that lack due process, are swayed by popular sentiment, or are racially biased.

48. George Herbert Mead, "The Psychology of Punitive Justice," *American Journal of Sociology* 23 (1918): 577–602.

49. Zimring, *Contradictions,* and Pfeiffer, *Rough Justice,* independently set out important arguments in this respect that have helped shape the thesis argued here.

50. U.S. General Accounting Office, *Death Penalty Sentencing: Research Indicates Pattern of Racial Disparities* (February 1990); David Baldus and George Woodworth, "Race Discrimination and the Death Penalty: An Empirical and Legal Overview," in James Acker, Robert Bohm, and Charles Lanier, eds., *America's Experiment with Capital Punishment* (Durham, NC: Carolina Academic Press, 2003); Sarat and Ogletree, eds., *From Lynch Mobs to the Killing State;* David Cole, *No Equal Justice: Race and Class in the American Criminal Justice System* (New York: New Press, 1999); Scott Phillips, "Racial Disparities in the Capital of Capital Punishment," 45 *Houston Law Review* 3 (Fall 2008): 807–840.

51. Sarat and Ogletree, eds., *From Lynch Mobs to the Killing State.* Though black killers of white victims have the highest likelihood of being sentenced, we should remember that the death penalty is not reserved for blacks and minorities. As of January 2010, 44 percent of death row inmates are white, 42 percent black, 12 percent Hispanic, and 2 percent other. Since 1976, 56 percent of those executed have been white, 35 percent black, 7 percent Hispanic, and 2 percent other. In the cases that resulted in executions, 77 percent of the victims were white; 15 percent black; 6 percent Hispanic, and 2 percent other. Eleven women have been executed since 1976, and currently fifty-three women are on death row. Death Penalty Information Center: http://www.deathpenaltyinfo.org/.

52. Albert Post, "Michigan Abolishes Capital Punishment," *Michigan History Magazine* (January–March 1945): 49.

53. Michigan Legislature, *Majority Report of the Select Committee on the Abolishment of Capital Punishment* (Detroit: State of Michigan, 1844).

54. Larry Wayne Koch, "Michigan's Continuing Abolition of the Death Penalty: A Matter of Life and Death" (Ph.D. Dissertation, University of Missouri-Columbia, May 1987); Thomas Coffey and Jerry Morton, "Trial, Error and

the Abolition of the Death Penalty," *Journal of Contemporary Criminal Justice* 5 (1989): 249.

55. Post, "Michigan Abolishes Capital Punishment," 49.

56. Michigan Legislature, *Report of the Proceedings and Debates in the Convention to Revise the Constitution of the State of Michigan* (Detroit: State of Michigan, 1850), 1.

57. On the background of the reformers, see John Galliher et al., *America without the Death Penalty: States Leading the Way* (Boston, MA: Northeastern University Press, 2002), 11.

58. The quotation is from Michigan Legislature, *Report of the Proceedings and Debates*. For an account of the history of abolition in Michigan, see Koch, "Michigan's Continuing Abolition."

59. Wisconsin and Rhode Island followed Michigan's example in 1852 and 1853, respectively.

2. The American Way of Death

1. Alex Kozinski and Sean Gallagher, "Death: The Ultimate Run-On Sentence," *Case Western Reserve Law Review* 46 (1995): 4.

2. Steve Dunleavy, "Seeking the Death Penalty Is a Cruel Hoax," *New York Post,* December 19, 2006.

3. New Hampshire moved from the first category into the second category in December 2008, when a jury imposed a death sentence on Michael Addison for the murder of a police officer. It was the first capital sentence in New Hampshire in almost fifty years—the previous sentence having been imposed in 1959. New Jersey and South Dakota were states of the second type until 2007, when New Jersey abolished the death penalty and South Dakota executed Elijah Page. The United States Military remains in that category.

4. William Lofquist, "Putting Them There, Keeping Them There, and Killing Them: An Analysis of State-Level Variations in Death Penalty Intensity," *Iowa Law Review* 87 (2001–2002): 1508.

5. Carol Steiker, "Capital Punishment and American Exceptionalism," *Oregon Law Review* 81/1 (2002): 97–130 at 119; Sara Beale, "Federal Criminal Jurisdiction," in Joshua Dressler, ed., *Encyclopedia of Crime and Justice* (New York: Macmillan, 2002); Sangmin Bae, "The Death Penalty and the Peculiarity of American Political Institutions," *Human Rights Review* 9 (2008): 233–240.

6. Lofquist, "Putting Them There"; Keith Harries and Derral Cheatwood, *The Geography of Execution: The Capital Punishment Quagmire in America* (Lanham, MD: Rowman and Littlefield, 1997).

7. Critics Carol and Jordan Steiker describe capital punishment law as "a confusing morass of hyper-technical rules." Carol Steiker and Jordan Steiker, "Sober Second Thoughts: Reflections on Two Decades of Constitutional Regulation of Capital Punishment," *Harvard Law Review* 109 (1995): 402. Justice

Clarence Thomas refers to the Court's "Byzantine death penalty jurisprudence" (*Knight v Florida* 528 U.S. 990 [1999]).

8. Carol Steiker and Jordan Steiker, "A Tale of Two Nations: Implementation of
the Death Penalty in 'Executing' versus 'Symbolic' States in the United States,"
84 *Texas Law Review,* 1869–1927 at 1876.

9. The writ of *habeas corpus* is a procedural device that permits prisoners to ask
a court to review the constitutionality of their convictions and sentences. The
writ can be lodged in state courts—where it refers to the state constitution—or
in federal courts with respect to the U.S. Constitution. The courts have discretion to grant or deny such petitions. If a court decides to grant review (and in
fact such petitions are most often denied) it issues a writ of *certiorari* directing
the lower court to send the case record for review.

10. John T. Noonan, Jr., "Horses of the Night: Harris v Vasquez," *Stanford Law
Review* 45 (1993): 1017–1018.

11. Gina Holland, "Supreme Court Lawyer Makes Full Time Job out of Death
Business," *Daily Courier,* June 17, 2002.

12. On average delays, see Tracy Snell, *Capital Punishment, 2005* (Washington,
DC: Bureau of Justice Statistics, 2006). In *Thompson v McNeil* 556 US (2009)
the Supreme Court declined to review a Florida case in which a death row inmate had spent more than thirty-two years awaiting execution.

13. Samuel Gross, "The Romance of Revenge: Capital Punishment in America,"
Studies in Law, Politics and Society 13 (1993): 71–104.

14. Robert Johnson, *Death Work: A Study of the Modern Execution Process*
(Belmont, CA: Wadsworth, 1998), 71. On state-by-state variation, see Lofquist, "Putting Them There." Courts outside the United States have declared
lengthy death row confinement to be cruel and inhumane. See *Pratt v Attorney
General for Jamaica* [1993] 4 All E.R. 769 and *Soering v the United Kingdom*
11 Eur. Ct. H. R. (ser. A) (1989).

15. Stuart Banner, *The Death Penalty: An American History* (Cambridge, MA:
Harvard University Press, 2002), 216. The United Nations Capital Punishment Report (1968) notes that, in 1960, the interval between a death sentence
and its execution was as follows: Canada, 2 to 3 months; France, 5 months,
12 days; United Kingdom, 18 to 25 days; South Australia, 1 month; other
Australian states and territories, between 28 days and 9 months; New Zealand, 4 to 5 weeks. U.N. Department of Economic and Social Affairs, *Capital
Punishment: Part I. Report 1960; Part II. Developments, 1961–1965* (New
York: United Nations, 1968). On delays in contemporary Japan, see David
Johnson, "Where the State Kills in Secret: Capital Punishment in Japan," *Pun-
ishment & Society* 8 (2006).

16. Kozinski and Gallagher, "Death," 21; Stephen Bright, "Counsel for the Poor:
The Death Penalty Not for the Worst Crime but for the Worst Lawyer,"
Yale Law Journal 103 (1994): 1835–1866; White Welsh, *Litigating in the
Shadow of Death: Defense Attorneys in Capital Cases* (Ann Arbor: University
of Michigan Press, 2005); Justice Ruth Ginsburg, quoted in "Death Penalty
Moratorium Backed," *Houston Chronicle,* April 10, 2001, 10. See generally

Death Penalty Information Center (DPIC), *With Justice for Few: The Growing Crisis in Death Penalty Representation* (Washington, DC: DPIC, 1995).

17. James Liebman, "The Overproduction of Death," *Columbia Law Review* 100 (2000): 2030–2156; Lofquist, "Putting Them There," 1513; *Thompson v McNeil* 556 U.S. (2009): 3; DPIC, *With Justice for Few.*

18. *Kansas v Marsh* 548 U.S. 163 (2006) at 193, Justice Scalia concurring.

19. Richard Dieter, *Smart on Crime: Reconsidering the Death Penalty in a Time of Economic Crisis* (Washington, DC: DPIC, 2009); L. Carver, "Death Penalty Cases More Expensive Than Life Imprisonment," *Lubbock Avalanche Journal,* December 13, 2009. Kozinsky and Gallaher, "Death," note that some state supreme courts spend one-third of their time on capital appeals. On costs generally, see Robert Bohm, "The Economic Costs of Capital Punishment," in James Acker, Robert Bohm, and Charles Lanier, eds., *America's Experiment with Capital Punishment* (Durham, NC: Carolina Academic Press, 2003).

20. See Richard Dieter, *Killing for Votes: The Dangers of Politicizing the Death Penalty Process* (Washington, DC: DPIC, 1996). The state attorneys general in forty-three states are elected directly by the people. In Alaska, Hawaii, New Hampshire, New Jersey, and Wyoming, they are appointed by the governor. In Maine they are elected by the state legislature; in Tennessee they are appointed by the state supreme court. Only in a few states (Alaska, Connecticut, Delaware, New Hampshire, and Rhode Island) does the state attorney general have any supervisory control over local prosecutorial decisions.

21. Jeffrey Pokorak, "Probing the Capital Prosecutor's Perspective: Race of the Discretionary Actors," *Cornell Law Review* 83 (1997–1998): 1811–1820. For evidence that prosecutorial discretion may lead to racial bias in capital charging, see Leigh B. Bienen et al., "The Reimposition of Capital Punishment in New Jersey: The Role of Prosecutorial Discretion," 41 *Rutgers Law Review* 27 (1988).

22. David Dow, "How the Death Penalty Really Works," in David Dow and Mark Dow, eds., *Machinery of Death: The Reality of America's Death Penalty Regime* (New York: Routledge, 2002), 14; John Culver, "Capital Punishment Politics and Policies in the States, 1977–1997," *Crime, Law and Social Change* 32 (2000): 287–300; and Dieter, *Killing for Votes,* 8. Chief Justice Rose Bird and two of her colleagues on the California Supreme Court were recalled following public criticism that they were too prone to reverse capital convictions. In subsequent years, the court's capital appeal record went from a reversal rate of 80 percent to one of 20 percent. See Stephen Bright and Patrick Keenan, "Judges and the Politics of Death: Deciding the Bill of Rights and the Next Election in Capital Cases," 75 *Boston University Law Review* (1995): 759–813, at 779; Robert Bohm, *Deathquest: An Introduction to the Theory and Practice of Capital Punishment in the United States* (Cincinnati, OH: Anderson Publishing Co., 1999).

23. Jeffrey Kubik and John Moran, "Lethal Elections: Gubernatorial Politics and the Timing of Executions," *Journal of Law and Economics* 46 (2003): 1. See also Jonathan Rauch, "Death by Mistake," *National Journal,* May 30, 1998, 10; Dieter, *Killing for Votes;* and Culver, "Capital Punishment Politics." Gov-

ernor George Ryan, who famously commuted the sentences of more than 100 capital prisoners on Illinois's death row, was then facing federal corruption charges of which he was subsequently convicted.

24. Jed Shugerman, "The People's Courts: Elected Judges and Judicial Independence in America" (Unpublished book prospectus, 2004), 2.

25. Prior to *Ring v Arizona* 536 U.S. (2002), twenty-nine of thirty-eight states committed sentencing decisions to juries. Arizona, Colorado, Idaho, and Montana committed capital sentencing fact-finding and the ultimate sentencing decision to judges. A number of other states—Alabama, Delaware, Florida, and Indiana—retained a sentencing jury but only to render an advisory "recommendation" of the proper sentence, which was then reviewed by the court and might be overturned. See U.S. Courts (2006), Section 4.6. *Ring v Arizona* 536 U.S. (2002)—which followed on *Apprendi v New Jersey* 530 U.S. 466 (2000)—stipulated the right of capital defendants to jury determination of any fact leading to an increase in maximum punishment.

26. The quotation is from Judge Patrick Higginbotham, "Juries and the Death Penalty," *Case Western Law Review* 41 (1991): 1048. Morris Hoffman notes that only five states permit juries to make sentencing decisions in noncapital felony cases. The states are Arkansas, Missouri, Oklahoma, Texas, and Virginia—all of them Southern death penalty states. Morris Hoffman, "The Case for Jury Sentencing," *Duke Law Journal* 52 (2003): 953, n1. On the history of felony jury sentencing in the United States see Nancy J. King, "The Origins of Felony Jury Sentencing in the United States," *Chicago-Kent Law Review* 78 (2003): 937.

   Badinter indicates that the nine-person French capital jury decided on guilt, premeditation, and extenuating circumstances, so in effect, it brought in a death penalty or not. But the jury decides together with three judges. A majority of eight of the twelve jury members is needed. Robert Badinter, *Abolition: One Man's Battle against the Death Penalty* (Boston, MA: Northeastern University Press, 2008). Steiker, "American Exceptionalism," writes that "no other country authorizes such a large role for criminal trial juries as does the United States" (118).

27. J. Christoph, *Capital Punishment and British Politics: The British Movement to Abolish the Death Penalty, 1945–1957* (Chicago: University of Chicago Press, 1962), 89, 91. The *Daily Mirror* columnist Cassandra told readers, "The Noose is Passed to You." Chuter Ede, the former home secretary, called the proposal "absurd." Elizabeth Tuttle, *The Crusade against Capital Punishment in Great Britain* (London: Stevens & Sons, 1961), 96.

28. *Ring v. Arizona* 536 U.S. 584 (2002) requires that a jury be responsible for any fact-finding that bears on the penalty to be imposed. (The Court's earlier decision in *Apprendi v New Jersey* 530 US 466 [2000] had made the same finding for noncapital criminal cases.) In the capital context, where the sentencing decision involves weighing mitigating against aggravating factors, this effectively gives the jury the power to decide on a sentence. Judicial overrides continue in both Alabama and Florida, though the validity of this practice is now questionable.

In a few states, such as Virginia, a murder is only capital, and therefore eligible for the death penalty, if it is an aggravated murder. Once convicted of this capital murder, the jury need not find further aggravation in order to impose a death sentence.

29. Scott Sundby, *A Life and Death Decision: A Jury Weighs the Death Penalty* (New York: Palgrave, 2005), 177; Elicka Peterson and Kimberley Kempf-Leonard, "A Matter of Life and Death: The Failure of Juror Instructions in Capital Cases," *The Justice Professional* 12 (1999): 173; Richard L. Wiener, Christine C. Pritchard, and Minda Weston, "Comprehensibility of Approved Jury Instructions in Capital Murder Cases," *Journal of Applied Psychology* 80 (1995): 455. Justice Stevens in dissent in *Spaziano v Florida* 468 U.S. 447 (1984), at 481.

30. Stevens in *Spaziano v. Florida* 468 U.S. 447 (1984), at 487.

31. "Death qualified" is a term used to describe juries composed only of jurors who indicate that they are willing to apply the death penalty should it be necessary. The leading cases are *Witherspoon v Illinois* 391 U.S. 510 (1968) and *Lockhart v McCree* 476 U.S. 162 (1986).

32. As of 2005, "thirty-five of the thirty-eight states with the death penalty, as well as the federal government and the military, permit the use of victim-impact evidence in capital trials." Kenji Yoshino, "The City and the Poet," *Yale Law Journal* 114 (2005): 1868.

33. On capital punishment as "closure," see Franklin Zimring, *The Contradictions of American Capital Punishment* (New York: Oxford University Press, 2003). On Islamic punishment, see Edward Peters, *Torture* (Philadelphia: University of Pennsylvania Press, 1996); on the Norsemen, see William Miller, *Bloodtaking and Peacemaking: Feud, Law and Society in Saga Iceland* (Chicago: University of Chicago Press, 1997); on lynching, see David Garland, "Penal Excess and Surplus Meaning: Public Torture Lynchings in Twentieth-Century America," *Law & Society Review* 39 (2005): 793–834.

34. Badinter notes that, in French capital cases prior to abolition in 1981, the family of the deceased could make a statement to the court, through a lawyer, about the crime's impact. They could also write to the president to urge him not to use his clemency power. Badinter, *Abolition*, 47.

35. U.S. General Accounting Office, *Death Penalty Sentencing: Research Indicates Pattern of Racial Disparities* (Washington, DC, 1990); American Bar Association, *Toward Greater Awareness: The American Bar Association Call for a Moratorium on Executions Gains Ground* (Washington, 2001). See also David Baldus, George Woodworth, and Charles Pulaski, *Equal Justice and the Death Penalty* (Boston, MA: Northeastern University Press, 1990).

36. Bright, "Counsel for the Poor"; Austin Sarat and Charles Ogletree, eds., *From Lynch Mobs to the Killing State: Race and the Death Penalty in America* (New York: New York University Press, 2006). A recent study focusing on five of the most active death penalty states—Texas, Virginia, Oklahoma, Missouri, and Florida—from 1972 to 1999 found that death sentences in the 504 cases studied were more likely to be imposed on black defendants and more likely to be imposed in cases involving white victims. Scott Phillips, "Racial Disparities in

the Capital of Capital Punishment," 45 *Houston Law Review* 3 (Fall 2008): 807–840. There is also evidence that wrongful conviction for capital crimes is disproportionately frequent in cases involving black defendants and white victims. See Jim Dwyer, Peter Neufeld, and Barry Scheck, *Actual Innocence: When Justice Goes Wrong and How to Make It Right* (New York: NAL Trade, 2003).

37. Charles Black, *Capital Punishment: The Inevitability of Caprice and Mistake* (New York: Norton, 1981), 101. See also David Baldus and George Woodworth, "Race Discrimination and the Death Penalty: An Empirical and Legal Overview," in James Acker, Robert Bohm, and Charles Lanier, eds., *America's Experiment with Capital Punishment,* 2nd ed. (Durham, NC: Carolina Academic Press, 2003); Jesse Jackson, Sr., Jesse Jackson, Jr., and Bruce Shapiro, *Legal Lynching: The Death Penalty and America's Future* (New York: New Press, 2001).

38. Smith, *Punishment and Culture;* Austin Sarat and Christian Boulanger, eds., *The Cultural Lives of Capital Punishment: Comparative Perspectives* (Stanford, CA: Stanford University Press, 2005).

39. John Lofland, "The Dramaturgy of State Executions," in H. Bleakley and J. Lofland, *State Executions, Viewed Historically and Sociologically* (Montclair, NJ: Patterson Smith, 1977), 318.

40. David Kertzer, *Ritual, Politics and Power* (New Haven, CT: Yale University Press, 1988), 9; Phillip Smith, *Punishment and Culture* (Chicago: University of Chicago Press, 2008).

41. Thirty-five states, the U.S. government, and the U.S. military employ lethal injection. Nine states retain the electric chair as an alternative to lethal injection, two allow death by hanging, another three by firing squad, and five by lethal gas. Death Penalty Information Center and Deborah Denno, "When Legislatures Delegate Death," *Ohio State Law Journal* 63 (2002): 63–261. New Jersey's capital punishment statute—repealed in 2007—referred to the lethal chemicals as "execution medications." Jamie Fellner and Michel Tofte, "So Long as They Die: Lethal Injections in the United States," in Council of Europe, *Death Penalty: Beyond Abolition* (Strasbourg: Council of Europe Publishing, 2004), 39.

42. Robert Lifton and Greg Mitchell, *Who Owns Death: Capital Punishment, the American Conscience and the End of Executions* (New York: Perennial, 2000), 64; *Campbell v Wood* 18 F.3d 662 C.A. 9 (1994) at 702. The American Medical Association prohibits its members from taking part in execution procedures, and the American Nurses Association considers such participation a breach of professional ethics. David Rothman, "Physicians and the Death Penalty," *Journal of Law and Policy* 4 (1995): 151–160.

43. Quoted in Elizabeth Weil, "The Needle and the Damage Done," *New York Times Magazine,* February 11, 2007, 51. Some victims' relatives have made similar complaints—see reports in *Ocala Star-Banner,* October 9, 2002, and *St. Petersburg Times,* August 26, 2000.

44. Richard Perez-Pena, "One Reporter's Lonely Beat: Witnessing Executions," *New York Times,* October 21, 2009, A1.

45. Excerpted with omissions from the Federal Bureau of Prisons *Execution Protocol* (2001).

46. See "Arkansas Puts 3 to Death after Flurry of Appeals," *New York Times,* August 4, 1994, A14. See also "Arkansas Carries Out Nation's First Triple Execution in 32 Years," *New York Times,* August 5, 1994, A23.

47. It is now standard to permit the murder victim's family to attend the execution, but it was not always thus. Seth Kotch, "Unduly Harsh and Unworkably Rigid: The Death Penalty in North Carolina, 1910–1961" (Ph.D. dissertation, University of North Carolina-Chapel Hill, 2008), 62.

48. Federal Bureau of Prisons, *Execution Protocol,* 9, 2. State execution protocols vary, and some are not so well defined as the federal one cited here.

49. Paul Farhi, "Networks' Quiet Coverage; Commercials Only Jarring Note in Reports on McVeigh," *Washington Post,* June 12, 2001, C1. A *New York Times* article, Sam Howe Verhovek, "As Texas Executions Mount, They Grow Routine," May 25, 1997, 11, discusses the problems faced by TV reporters at executions. As the reporter explains, there are "no visuals."

50. C. J. Drake, Florida Department of Corrections quoted in the *Sarasota Herald-Tribune,* March 3, 2000. See also Timothy Kaufman-Osborn, *From Noose to Needle: Capital Punishment and the Late Liberal State* (Ann Arbor: University of Michigan Press, 2002), 179. Warden John Whitley, director of executions at Louisiana's Angola State Prison, is quoted in Ivan Solotaroff, *The Last Face You'll Ever See: The Private Life of the American Death Penalty* (New York: Harper Collins, 2001), 34. Michael Madow, "Forbidden Spectacle: Executions, the Public and the Press in Nineteenth Century New York," 43 *Buffalo Law Review* (1995): 461–562; Johnson, *Death Work;* Stephen Trombley, *The Execution Protocol* (New York: Crown Publishers, 1997); Austin Sarat, *When the State Kills: Capital Punishment and the American Condition* (Princeton, NJ: Princeton University Press, 2001).

51. Sarat, *When the State Kills;* Wendy Lesser, *Pictures at an Execution: An Inquiry into the Subject of Murder* (Cambridge, MA: Harvard University Press, 1998). Bentham is quoted in Basil Montagu, *The Opinions of Different Authors upon the Punishment of Death,* 3 vols. (London: Longman, Hurst, Rees, and Orme, 1816), 217. The passage continues, "the great art consists in augmenting the apparent punishment without augmenting the real punishment."

52. As Banner observes, "The execution itself has been hidden from public view, but the issue of capital punishment has grown extraordinarily visible." Banner, *Death Penalty,* 3.

53. The phrases are from Madow, "Forbidden Spectacle," and Gary Wills, "The Dramaturgy of Death," *New York Review of Books,* June 21, 2001, 8. There have been (unsuccessful) efforts to televise executions: see Lesser, *Pictures at an Execution.*

54. Official transcript, New York State Assembly debate on the death penalty, March 6, 1995, 441.

55. Quoted in Thomas Laqueur, "Festivals of Punishment," *London Review of Books,* October 5, 2000, 17–24.

56. Samuel Gross, "The Romance of Revenge: Capital Punishment in America," *Studies in Law, Politics and Society* 13 (1993): 83.

57. See, for example, Sarat, *When the State Kills;* William Miller, "Clint Eastwood and Equity: Popular Culture's Theory of Revenge," in Austin Sarat and Thomas Kearns, eds., *Law in the Domains of Culture* (Ann Arbor: University of Michigan Press, 1998), and the remarks of Solicitor General Bork quoted above.

58. State Assemblyman Stringer, New York State Assembly debate, March 6, 1995, official transcript, p. 278.

59. Statements of Ohio Attorney General Jim Petro on the execution of Adremy Dennis, October 13, 2004, and in a press release dated February 7, 2006.

60. Remarks made by a prison warden to an inmate about to be executed, quoted in Johnson, *Death Work,* 174.

61. Prison officer, a member of the death work team, quoted in Johnson, *Death Work,* 174; Kenneth Dean, head of execution team, Huntsville, Texas, quoted in the *Austin American-Statesman,* April 1, 2001.

62. First quote, Governor Phil Bredesen of Tennessee, cited in Erik Schelzig, "Tennessee Execution Manual Full of Errors," ABC News, February 9, 2007; second, Arkansas Governor Mike Huckabee, Governor's Radio Address, August 8, 1996; the third is from Mike Huckabee, *From Hope to Higher Ground* (Washington, DC: Center Street, 2007).

63. Philip Hager, "Plans for Harris Execution Renew National Debate on Capital Punishment," *LA Times,* April 16, 1992, A3, quoted in James Marquart, Sheldon Ekland-Olson, and Jonathan Sorensen, *The Rope, the Chair and the Needle: Capital Punishment in Texas, 1923–1990* (Austin: University of Texas Press, 1994), 190.

64. Stephanie Cohen, "Fry Baby," *New York Post,* January 31, 2007, 1; Attorney General Bob Butterworth, quoted in "Condemned Man's Mask Bursts into Flame During Execution," *New York Times,* March 26, 1997, B9.

65. Craig Dezern and Donna Blanton, "Ted Bundy Executed," *Orlando Sentinel,* January 24, 1989, A1.

66. Adam C. Smith, "Stano Executed with No Glitch," *St. Petersburg Times,* March 24, 1998, A1.

67. V. A. C. Gatrell, *The Hanging Tree: Executions and the English People, 1770–1868* (Oxford, England: Oxford University Press, 1994).

68. An exception is Republican Majority Leader Newt Gingrich, who suggested in 1995 that mass executions might serve to deter drug dealers. Robert Singh, *Governing America: The Politics of a Divided Democracy* (New York: Oxford University Press, 2003). Gallup poll research finds that nearly half of Americans say that the death penalty is not imposed often enough, but the poll does not inquire further. Frank Newport, "In U.S., Two-Thirds Continue to Support Death Penalty," www.gallup.com, October 13, 2009, p. 2: http://www .gallup.com/poll/123638/in-u.s.-two-thirds-continue-support-death-penalty .aspx (accessed 1/12/10).

69. See the reports in *Hartford Courant,* May 13, 2005, and the *New York Post,* May 13, 2005.

70. See James Liebman, "Slow Dancing with Death: The Supreme Court and Capital Punishment, 1963–2006," *Columbia Law Review* 107 (2007): 1–130;

Anthony Amsterdam, "Selling a Quick Fix for Boot Hill," in Austin Sarat, ed., *The Killing State: Capital Punishment in Law, Politics and Culture* (New York: Oxford University Press, 1999); and Dow, "How the Death Penalty Really Works."

71. Kenneth Burke, *A Rhetoric of Motives* (Berkeley: University of California Press, 1969).

72. In her analysis of execution reports, Erin Braatz notes a shift in the format of American newspaper articles between the mid-nineteenth and the late twentieth centuries: "The earlier execution accounts focused on the moments leading up to the execution in terms of the individual's spiritual preparation, whereas the later accounts all focus on legal battles that were waged up until the very last minute." Erin Braatz, unpublished paper on history of execution reports in Illinois, 26. On file with the author.

73. Craig Haney, *Death by Design: Capital Punishment as a Social Psychological System* (New York: Oxford University Press, 2005), 7.

74. Quoted in "Execution was 'Justice,'" *USA Today,* June 12, 2001, D7. See also Joshua Marquis, "Keep the Debate Honest," *National Law Journal,* February 28, 2005, 1; Clark County Prosecuting Attorney Steven Stewart, http://www.clarkprosecutor.org/html/death/death.htm (last accessed January 30, 2010).

75. Robert Weisberg, "Deregulating Death," *Supreme Court Review* (1983): 305–395; Jackson, Jackson, and Shapiro, *Legal Lynching;* Stephen Bright, "Discrimination, Death and Denial: Race and the Death Penalty," in D. Dow and M. Dow, eds., *Machinery of Death: The Reality of America's Death Penalty Regime* (New York: Routledge, 2002): 45–78; Sarat and Ogletree, eds., *From Lynch Mobs to the Killing State;* and Eliza Steelwater, *The Hangman's Knot: Lynching, Legal Execution and America's Struggle with the Death Penalty* (New York: Basic Books, 2003).

76. Cass Sunstein and Adrian Vermeule, "Is Capital Punishment Morally Required? Acts, Omissions, and Life-Life Tradeoffs," 58 *Stanford Law Review* 703 (2005); "Bush Asked to Cease Executions," *Victoria Advocate,* February 18, 2000, B1; Jeb Bush, "Justice Is Working in Florida," http://www.prodeathpenalty.com/Liebman/FloridaBush.htm (accessed 1/12/10); memorandum by Governor George Pataki, state of New York executive chamber, Albany, March 7, 1995.

77. See the speech by Justice Lewis F. Powell, Jr., "Commentary: Capital Punishment," *Harvard Law Review* 102 (1989): 1044.

78. "Presidential Rivals Wage Battle in Blue in Boston," *Boston Globe,* September 23, 1988. See also U.S. Representative George W. Gekas, R-Pennsylvania, arguing for capital punishment for drug traffickers, quoted in Julie Rovner, "House Passes $6 Billion Anti-Drug Package," *CQ Weekly,* September 13, 1986, 2125. Governor George Pataki, "Memorandum Filed with Senate Bill Number 2850," March 7, 1995, 6. See also Governor George Pataki, "Death Penalty Is a Deterrent," *USA Today Magazine,* March 1997, 52–53.

79. Georgia District Attorney E. Mullins Whisnant, charging the jury in the penalty phase of William Brooks's trial, quoted in William McFeely, *Proximity to Death* (New York: Norton, 2000), 100.

80. Kozinski and Gallagher, "Death," 22–23.

81. Justice Stewart, writing for the court, in *Gregg v Georgia*. See also Antonin Scalia, "God's Justice and Ours," *First Things* 123 (2002): 17–20.

82. "A. G. King Will Petition Court for Death Penalty for Mass Murderer of Crenshaw County Family," press release, Alabama Attorney General's Office, June 17, 2005.

83. Statement from Governor Jeb Bush regarding the U.S. Supreme Court's decision in the death penalty cases of Linroy Bottoson and Amos King, June 28, 2002.

84. President Bush's statement on Timothy McVeigh's execution, in *USA Today*, "Execution Was 'Justice.'"

85. Scott Turow, *Ultimate Punishment: A Lawyer's Reflections on Dealing with the Death Penalty* (New York: Picador, 2003), 63–64; Dudley Sharp, "Death Penalty and Sentencing Information," http://www.prodeathpenalty.com/DP .html, p. 1 (accessed 1/10/02).

86. Kozinski, "Tinkering with Death," 14.

87. David Gelernter, "What Do Murderers Deserve?" *Commentary* (1998): 21–24. Gelernter nearly lost his life in a Unabomber attack.

88. June 14, 2000, statement from Texas Attorney General John Cornyn regarding the execution of Gary Graham scheduled for June 22. Ashcroft quoted in Mike Dorning, "Hundreds Will Watch McVeigh Die," *Chicago Tribune*, April 13, 2001, 20. See Zimring, *Contradictions*, on "closure" in recent death penalty politics.

89. Quoted in Ellen Goodman, "What the Execution Did to Us," *Boston Globe*, June 14, 2001, A19. For a report on the viewing victims' comments, see "Federal Execution Brings Little Relief to Survivors Watching in Okla. City," *Denver Post*, June 12, 2001, A1.

90. Attributed to Harris County District Attorney John H. Holmes in *Houston Chronicle*, February 4, 2001.

91. "Bush Abroad: Unity Is Security," *Atlanta Journal-Constitution*, June 13, 2001, A1; New York State Assemblyman Seminerio, official transcript, New York State Assembly debate, March 6, 1995, p. 304.

92. Assistant District Attorney Kelly Siegler, who has prosecuted fourteen death penalty cases, quoted in "Harris County Is a Pipeline to Death Row. A Four-Part Series Examines Why, and Explores Whether Justice Is Served. A Deadly Distinction," *Houston Chronicle*, February 5, 2001, A1. See also Indiana prosecuting attorney Stephen Stewart: http://www.clarkprosecutor.org/html/ death/death.htm (last accessed, January 30, 2010).

93. See Brennan and Marshall in *Furman*.

94. Norbert Elias, *The Civilizing Process: Sociogenetic and Psychogenetic Explorations* (London: Blackwell, 2000), 59; Paul Q. Hirst, *Law, Socialism and Democracy* (London: Allen & Unwin, 1986), 152.

3. Historical Modes of Capital Punishment

1. Keith Otterbein, *The Ultimate Coercive Sanction: A Cross-Cultural Study of Capital Punishment* (New Haven, CT: HRAF Press, 1986). On the place of the death penalty in the ancient world, see Emile Durkheim, "Two Laws of Pe-

nal Evolution," *Economy and Society* 2 (1973); Eva Cantarella, *Les Supplices Capitaux en Grèce et à Rome* (Paris: Albin Michel, 2001); Robert Lifton and Greg Mitchell, *Who Owns Death: Capital Punishment, the American Conscience and the End of Executions* (New York: Perennial, 2000), 20–21; and William Miller, *Bloodtaking and Peacemaking: Feud, Law and Society in Saga Iceland* (Chicago: University of Chicago Press, 1997).

2. Roger Hood and Carolyn Hoyle, *The Death Penalty: A Worldwide Perspective* (Oxford, England: Oxford University Press, 2008); and David Greenberg and Valerie West, "Siting the Death Penalty Internationally," *Law & Social Inquiry* 33 (2008): 295–343.

3. For Elias's "civilizing process" theory, see Norbert Elias, *The Civilizing Process: Sociogenetic and Psychogenetic Explorations* (London: Blackwell, 2000).

4. Evans gives several examples of such reversals in nineteenth- and twentieth-century Germany. Richard Evans, *Rituals of Retribution: Capital Punishment in Germany, 1600–1987* (Oxford, England: Oxford University Press, 1996). See also Charles Duff, *A Handbook on Hanging* (New York: New York Review Books, 2001), 41.

5. My evidence comes chiefly from the United States, the United Kingdom, Canada, Australia, New Zealand, and the continental European nations, especially France, Germany, and the Netherlands. The pattern of change in the rest of the world is not addressed here. On the death penalty in Asia, see David Johnson and Franklin Zimring, *The Next Frontier: National Development, Political Change and the Death Penalty in Asia* (New York: Oxford University Press, 2009).

6. Otterbein, *Ultimate Coercive Sanction*. See also the U.N. Department of Economic and Social Affairs: "There are practically no countries where the death penalty has never existed," in *Capital Punishment: Part I: Report 1960. Part II: Developments, 1961–1965* (New York: United Nations, 1968), 31.

7. Hood and Hoyle report that as of 2007, forty-eight nations retain the death penalty; eight more retain it for extraordinary crimes; and forty-five have capital punishment laws that have not recently been enforced. Hood and Hoyle, *Death Penalty*.

8. Samuel Johnson, *The Rambler*, 114, April 20, 1751.

9. The phrase in quotations is from Friedrich Nietzsche, *The Genealogy of Morals*, trans. Walter Kaufman (New York: Vintage Books, 1967), 214. Charles Tilly, *Coercion, Capital and European States, AD 990–1992* (Cambridge, England: Blackwell, 1992), makes a similar point in his discussion of why wars occur: "The central, tragic fact is simple: coercion *works:* those who apply substantial force to their fellows get compliance, and from that compliance draw the multiple advantages of money, goods, deference, access to pleasures denied to less powerful people" (70).

10. Evans, *Rituals of Retribution*, 894–895.

11. A *mode* or *modality* of capital punishment is an ideal type that groups together the institutional arrangements characteristic of a particular period—institutions that have more in common with each other than with institutions in

later or earlier modes. Grouping them together in this way does not deny the specificity of particular institutions in particular places at particular times, but it highlights the shared characteristics of these institutional forms and their roots in certain kinds of social organization. The concern here is not with variation—of which there was no doubt a great deal. It is with the generic form, or ideal type, insofar as we can specify it. The primary purpose is not to understand the details of capital punishment in the past but to produce contrastive types that help us better understand capital punishment in the present.

12. For an analysis of patterns of punishment and crime control in late-modern America and Britain, see David Garland, *The Culture of Control* (Chicago: University of Chicago Press, 2001).

13. Evans, *Rituals of Retribution*, 50; James Sharpe, *Judicial Punishment in England* (London: Faber and Faber, 1990), 31; Otterbein, *Ultimate Coercive Sanction*.

14. Pieter Spierenburg, *The Spectacle of Suffering: Executions and the Evolution of Repression* (Cambridge, England: Cambridge University Press, 1984), 1; Katherine Royer, "The Body in Parts: Reading the Execution in Late Medieval England," *Historical Reflections/Réflexions Historiques* 29 (2003): 323.

15. Absolutist monarchs—relatively unrestrained by other institutions, such as churches, legislatures, or social elites—ruled in Europe from the seventeenth to the nineteenth century. Absolutism was a political system in which the monarch's power was concentrated and consolidated, state laws unified, and the power of the nobles decreased. The classic example is King Louis XIV of France, but the monarchies of Austria, Spain, Italy, Poland, Prussia, Russia, Denmark, and Sweden were also absolutist in form. Peter Wilson, *Absolutism in Central Europe* (London: Routledge, 2000); Perry Anderson, *Lineages of the Absolutist State* (London: New Left Books, 1974).

16. Radzinowicz, *English Criminal Law,* 28, 32; Esther Cohen, "Symbols of Culpability and the Universal Language of Justice: The Ritual of Public Execution in Late Medieval Europe," *History of European Ideas* 11 (1989): 407.

17. The history of abolition in Europe and South America shows a tendency to abolish first for "ordinary" crime while retaining for "extraordinary crime"— that is, for political offenses, crimes in wartime, offenses against the security of the state, treason, and so on. Hood and Hoyle, *Death Penalty*. This retention of death for crimes against the state harks back to capital punishment's original purpose.

18. Cesare Beccaria, *An Essay on Crimes and Punishments* (Brookline, MA: Branden Press, 1983), 45.

19. The last phrase is taken from Clifford Geertz, "Centers, Kings and Charisma: Symbolics of Power," in *Local Knowledge* (New York: Basic Books, 1983).

20. Douglas Hay, "Property, Authority and the Criminal Law," in Douglas Hay et al., eds., *Albion's Fatal Tree: Crime and Society in Eighteenth Century England* (New York: Pantheon Books, 1975); Spierenburg, *Spectacle of Suffering*; Evans, *Rituals of Retribution*; Mitchell Merback, *The Thief, the Cross and the Wheel: Pain and the Spectacle of Punishment in Medieval and Renaissance Europe* (Chicago: University of Chicago Press, 1999); Randall

McGowen, "The Body and Punishment in the Eighteenth Century," *Journal of Modern History* 59 (1987).

21. Joseph de Maistre, from the St. Petersburg dialogues of 1821. Joseph de Maistre, *The Works of Joseph de Maistre,* ed. Jack Lively (New York: Macmillan, 1965), 192.

22. Evans, *Rituals of Retribution,* 50.

23. Anton Blok, "The Symbolic Vocabulary of Public Executions," in June Starr and Jane F. Collier, eds., *History and Power in the Study of Law: New Directions in Legal Anthropology* (Ithaca, NY: Cornell University Press, 1989), 47; Richard Van Dulmen, *Theatre of Horror: Crime and Punishment in Early Modern Germany* (Oxford, England: Polity Press, 1990); Spierenburg, *Spectacle of Suffering;* Merback, *The Thief, the Cross and the Wheel;* John Langbein, *Torture and the Law of Proof* (Chicago: University of Chicago Press, 1976). Hay, "Hanging and the English Judges," in David Garland et al., eds., *The American Death Penalty: Between Past and Present* (New York University Press, 2010), notes the extraordinary severity of the executions staged for the Jacobin rebels and the Cato Street conspirators.

24. V. A. C. Gatrell, *The Hanging Tree: Executions and the English People, 1770–1868* (Oxford, England: Oxford University Press, 1994), 2 and 32; Hay, "Property," 17, 56. See also John McManners, *Death and the Enlightenment: Changing Attitudes to Death among Christians and Unbelievers in Eighteenth Century France* (New York: Oxford University Press, 1981), 379–380.

25. Gatrell, *The Hanging Tree,* 2 and 32; Hay, "Hanging," 10.

26. See Hay, "Property," and E. P. Thompson, *Whigs and Hunters: The Origins of the Black Act* (Harmondsworth: Penguin, 1975).

27. Randall McGowen, "Punishing Violence, Sentencing Crime," in Nancy Armstrong and Leonard Tennenhouse, eds., *The Violence of Representation: Literature and the History of Violence* (London: Routledge, 1989), 92.

28. Evans, *Rituals of Retribution,* 65 and 66.

29. Michel Foucault, *Society Must Be Defended: Lectures at the College de France, 1975–1976* (New York: Picador, 2003), 247. See also McGowen, "Punishing Violence," 143; Stuart Banner, *The Death Penalty: An American History* (Cambridge, MA: Harvard University Press, 2002), 14; Masur, *Rites of Execution,* 5 and 26.

30. Keith Thomas, *Religion and the Decline of Magic* (Harmondsworth: Penguin, 1991); Evans, *Rituals of Retribution,* 93–96; Philip Smith, *Punishment and Culture* (University of Chicago Press, 2008); Banner, *The Death Penalty.*

31. McGowen, "Body and Punishment," 665.

32. Hay, "Hanging," 24.

33. Cohen, "Public Execution," 409.

34. See the 1752 *Act for Better Preventing the Horrid Crime of Murder* (25 Geo. 2, c.37), quoted in *Pratt v Att Gen for Jamaica,* Privy Council Appeals No. 10 of 1993, appendix, p. 10. This regime of immediate execution was relaxed after 1836 to allow time for postconviction review.

35. Randall McGowen, "Cruel Inflictions and the Claims of Humanity in Early Nineteenth Century England," in Katherine Watson and Eric Chelstrom, eds.,

Assaulting the Past: Violence and Civilization in Historical Context (Newcastle: Cambridge Scholars Publishing, 2007), 38–57.

36. Hay, "Property," 18, 21. See also Radzinowicz, *English Criminal Law*, 4; and Thompson, *Whigs and Hunters*.

37. Hay, "Property," 48, 42.

38. Dwight Conquergood, "Lethal Theatre: Performance, Punishment and the Death Penalty," *Theatre Journal* 54 (2002): 343.

39. John Lofland, "The Dramaturgy of State Executions," in Horace Bleakley and John Lofland, eds., *State Executions Viewed Historically and Sociologically* (Montclair, NJ: Patterson Smith, 1977), 316.

40. Gene Ogle, "Slaves of Justice: Saint Domingue's Executioners and the Production of Shame," *Historical Reflections* 29 (2003): 283; James Whitman, *Harsh Justice: Criminal Punishment and the Widening Gap between America and Europe* (New York: Oxford University Press, 2003), 103.

41. Lynn Hunt, *Inventing Human Rights: A History* (New York: Norton, 2007), 80.

42. Blok, "Symbolic Vocabulary," 47; Merback, *The Thief, the Cross and the Wheel*, 141.

43. A trace of this distinction persisted into the modern period. According to the U.N. Department of Economic and Social Affairs, "in the great majority of countries there are two methods of carrying out a death sentence: one for crimes tried by the ordinary courts and the other in military cases; the latter is nearly always carried out by firing squad." U.N. Department of Economic and Social Affairs, *Capital Punishment*, 24.

44. Hunt, *Inventing Human Rights*, 94.

45. David Cooper, *The Lesson of the Scaffold: The Public Execution Controversy in Victorian England* (Athens: Ohio State University Press, 1974), 5. See also Blok, "Symbolic Vocabulary," 47.

46. Spierenburg, *Spectacle of Suffering*, 63.

47. Sharpe, *Judicial Punishment in England*, 36; Evans, *Rituals of Retribution*, 105. Andrea McKenzie suggests that theological themes continued to be a prominent part of London's Tyburn executions until the end of the eighteenth century at least. Andrea McKenzie, *Tyburn's Martyrs: Execution in England, 1675–1775* (London: Hambledon Continuum, 2007).

48. For a detailed discussion of this development, see Simon Devereaux, "Recasting the Theatre of Execution: The Abolition of the Tyburn Ritual," *Past and Present* 202 (2009): 127–174.

49. On the first interpretation see Hay, "Property"; Michel Foucault, *Discipline and Punish: The Birth of the Prison* (New York: Allen Lane, 1977); and Spierenburg, *Spectacle of Suffering*. On the second, see McGowen, "Body and Punishment"; and Banner, *The Death Penalty*. On the third, see Thomas Laqueur, "Crowds, Carnival and the State in English Executions, 1604–1868," in A. L. Beier, David Cannadine, and James Rosenheim, eds., *The First Modern Society: Essays in Honor of Lawrence Stone* (New York: Cambridge University Press, 1989); and Gatrell, *The Hanging Tree*.

50. Cohen, "Public Execution." The same symbols could mean different things in

different cultures. Cohen suggests that, in early modern Europe, women were rarely hanged for reasons of modesty. In ancient Greece and Rome, hanging was a punishment specifically reserved for women. Cantarella, *Les Supplices Capitaux*.

51. Sir Edward Coke, quoted in Radzinowicz, *English Criminal Law,* 221–222.

52. Merback, *The Thief, the Cross and the Wheel,* 157; McGowen, "Punishing Violence," 143.

53. On gallows literature, see James Sharpe, "Last Dying Speeches: Religion, Ideology and Public Execution in Seventeenth Century England," *Past and Present* 107 (1985): 144–167; Karen Halttunen, *Murder Most Foul: The Killer and the American Gothic Imagination* (Cambridge, MA: Harvard University Press, 1998); McGowen, "Body and Punishment"; Louis Masur, *Rites of Execution: Capital Punishment and the Transformation of American Culture, 1776–1865* (New York: Oxford University Press, 1989).

54. Gatrell, *The Hanging Tree,* 2.

55. Evans, *Rituals of Retribution,* 99; James Farrell, *Inventing the American Way of Death, 1830–1920* (Philadelphia, PA: Temple University Press, 1980).

56. McGowen, "Body and Punishment."

57. Norbert Elias, *The Loneliness of the Dying* (New York: Continuum, 2001), 23.

58. Lofland, "The Dramaturgy of State Executions."

59. Durkheim, "Two Laws of Penal Evolution."

60. John Beattie, *Crime and the Courts in England, 1660–1800* (Princeton, NJ: Princeton University Press, 1986), 453.

61. Radzinowicz, *English Criminal Law,* 35; Banner, *The Death Penalty,* 23.

62. McGowen, "Punishing Violence," 142; Spierenburg, *Spectacle of Suffering,* 98.

63. Bentham (1799) quoted in Basil Montagu, *The Opinions of Different Authors upon the Punishment of Death,* 3 vols. (London: Longman, Hurst, Rees, and Orme, 1816), 221–222.

64. On Robert Damiens's execution, see Foucault, *Discipline and Punish;* and McManners, *Death and the Enlightenment.* For an account of Ravaillac's execution, see Orest Ranum, "The French Ritual of Tyrannicide in the Late Sixteenth Century," *Sixteenth Century Journal* 11 (1980): 63–82.

65. David Garland, *Punishment and Welfare: A History of Penal Strategies* (Aldershot [Hampshire]: Gower, 1985); and David Garland, *The Culture of Control: Crime and Social Order in Contemporary Society* (Chicago: University of Chicago Press, 2001).

66. Alphonse de Lamartine, quoted in James Megivern, *The Death Penalty: An Historical and Theological Survey* (New York: Paulist Press, 1997), 236. See also Beccaria, *Crimes and Punishments,* 45: "[I]n peace-time, in a form of government approved by the united wishes of the nation; in a state well fortified from enemies without and supported by strength within . . . there can be no *necessity* for taking away the life of a subject."

67. Evans, *Rituals of Retribution,* 231.

68. Halttunen, *Murder Most Foul,* 10. See also Durkheim, "Two Laws of Penal Evolution."

69. Evans, *Rituals of Retribution,* 146.

70. In 1854, the Bavarian ministry of justice complained about the conduct of clerics at the execution. Ministry officials objected that "the clergymen often take a different point of view in these admonitory sermons from that which is required in the interests of the state . . . [I]t can happen that a man condemned to death for a terrible crime is portrayed as a penitent and remorseful converted sinner, who is sure of God's forgiveness. This is not the way to achieve fear of the death penalty and deterrence from crime." Evans, *Rituals of Retribution,* 310. See also Hunt, *Inventing Human Rights,* 95–96, 93; McGowen, "Body and Punishment"; and Halttunen, *Murder Most Foul.*

71. Timothy Kaufman-Osborn, *From Noose to Needle: Capital Punishment and the Late Liberal State* (Ann Arbor: University of Michigan Press, 2002), 92.

72. Ibid., 142, quoting Michael Madow, "Forbidden Spectacle: Executions, the Public and the Press in Nineteenth Century New York," *Buffalo Law Review* 43 (1995): 486.

73. Evans, *Rituals of Retribution,* 246.

74. Ibid.; Simon Schama, *Citizens: A Chronicle of the French Revolution* (New York: Vintage, 1989), 619.

75. The "defensive/demonstrative" distinction is from Herb Haines, quoted in Kaufman-Osborn, *Noose to Needle,* 108.

76. Madow, "Forbidden Spectacle."

77. McGowen, "Body and Punishment," 673; Madow, "Forbidden Spectacle," 482.

78. Masur, *Rites of Execution.*

79. Ibid., 52. Paley quoted in Gatrell, *The Hanging Tree,* 263.

80. Albert Camus, "Reflections on the Guillotine," in *Resistance, Rebellion and Death: Essays* (New York: Knopf, 1961), 176.

81. Evans, *Rituals of Retribution,* 367; Michel Foucault, *The History of Sexuality,* vol. 1 (New York: Allen Lane, 1978), 138ff.

82. Halttunen, *Murder Most Foul,* 57; Gatrell, *The Hanging Tree,* 263; Evans, *Rituals of Retribution;* Karen Halttunen, "Humanitarianism and the Pornography of Pain in Anglo-American Culture," *American Historical Review* 100 (1995): 303–334.

83. On the "politics of life," see Foucault, *History of Sexuality;* and Nikolas Rose, *The Politics of Life Itself: Biomedicine, Power, and Subjectivity in the Twenty-First Century* (Princeton, NJ: Princeton University Press, 2007).

84. Banner, *The Death Penalty;* Robert Badinter, *Abolition: One Man's Battle against the Death Penalty* (Boston, MA: Northeastern University Press, 2008); Terence Morris, *Crime and Criminal Justice since 1945* (Oxford, England: Blackwell, 1989).

85. "Learning to have an opinion about capital punishment was becoming part of public education. . . . Similar debates were taking place all over the world." Banner, *The Death Penalty,* 242.

86. Banner, *The Death Penalty;* Badinter, *Abolition;* Morris, *Crime and Criminal Justice.*

87. The non-Western retentionist democracies, India and Japan, both use the punishment rarely and after much delay. Hood and Hoyle, *Death Penalty.*

88. Badinter, *Abolition;* Morris, *Crime and Criminal Justice.*

89. Outside of Europe, New Zealand abolished the death penalty for ordinary crime in 1961, Canada in 1976, and the last state in Australia in 1984.

4. The Death Penalty's Decline

1. Strictly speaking, judicial torture was not a punishment but an investigative method used prior to a finding of guilt and was distinct from torture on the scaffold (the French term for which is "supplice"), which was an aggravated method of execution. But the reform of one was intimately linked to the reform of the other.

2. Lynn Hunt, *Inventing Human Rights: A History* (New York: Norton, 2007), 75–76; Robert Nye, "Two Capital Punishment Debates in France: 1908 and 1981," *Historical Reflections/Réflexions Historiques* 29 (2003): 211; John Langbein, *Torture and the Law of Proof* (Chicago: University of Chicago Press, 1976); Pieter Spierenburg, *The Spectacle of Suffering: Executions and the Evolution of Repression: From a Preindustrial Metropolis to the European Experience* (Cambridge, England: Cambridge University Press, 1984); Richard Evans, *Rituals of Retribution: Capital Punishment in Germany, 1600–1987* (Oxford, England: Oxford University Press, 1996), 115.

3. Spierenburg, *Spectacle of Suffering,* 184; Anton Blok, "The Symbolic Vocabulary of Public Executions," in June Starr and Jane F. Collier, eds., *History and Power in the Study of Law: New Directions in Legal Anthropology* (Ithaca, NY: Cornell University Press, 1989).

4. By 12 Geo III, c 20—see Simon Devereaux, "Imposing the Royal Pardon: Execution, Transportation and Convict Resistance in London, 1789," *Law and History Review* 25, 1 (2007): 1–50; David Cooper, *The Lesson of the Scaffold: The Public Execution Controversy in Victorian England* (Athens: Ohio State University Press, 1974), 4; Leon Radzinowicz, *A History of the English Criminal Law,* vol. 1: *The Movement for Reform* (London: Stevens & Sons, 1948), 212.

5. Leon Radzinowicz, *Adventures in Criminology* (London: Routledge, 1999), 278; V. A. C. Gatrell, *The Hanging Tree: Executions and the English People, 1770–1868* (Oxford, England: Oxford University Press, 1994), 298.

6. Radzinowicz, *English Criminal Law,* vol. 1, 294; Hunt, *Inventing Human Rights,* 102.

7. Personal communication from Dr. Raquel Vaz-Pinto.

8. Jose Diez-Ripolles, *Derecho penal español. Parte general. En esquemas* (Valencia: Tirant lo Blanch, 2007); Evans, *Rituals of Retribution,* 238.

9. Spierenburg, *Spectacle of Suffering,* 197.

10. Ibid., 190; Gatrell, *The Hanging Tree,* 268. The last hanging in chains in the British colonies took place in Australia five years later.

11. Gatrell, *The Hanging Tree,* 84. Cooper places the abolition two years later, in 1834. Cooper, *Lesson of the Scaffold,* 48.

12. Evans, *Rituals of Retribution,* 225ff.

13. M. Mougins de Roquefort, to the National Assembly in 1791, quoted in Philip Smith, *Punishment and Culture* (Chicago: University of Chicago Press, 2008), 122; Diez-Ripolles, *Derecho;* Evans, *Rituals of Retribution,* 47–48.

14. Douglas Hay, "Hanging and the English Judges," in Garland et al., eds., *America's Death Penalty: Between Past and Present* (New York: New York University Press, 2010), notes that in early nineteenth-century England, the judges "were more willing to accept repeal with respect to thefts because imprisonment was now much more widely available."

15. All the American death penalty states now have "life imprisonment without parole" laws. Texas was the last to adopt it in 2005.

16. Langbein, *Torture.*

17. Ibid., 40; John Beattie, *Crime and the Courts in England, 1660–1800* (Princeton, NJ: Princeton University Press, 1986), 519; Evans, *Rituals of Retribution,* 117.

18. Pieter Spierenburg, "Punishment, Power and History," *Social Science History* 28 (2004): 621; Diez-Ripolles, *Derecho.*

19. J. Christoph, *Capital Punishment and British Politics: The British Movement to Abolish the Death Penalty, 1945–57* (Chicago: University of Chicago Press, 1962), 17.

20. Elizabeth Tuttle, *The Crusade against Capital Punishment in Great Britain* (London: Stevens & Sons, 1961), 25; Leon Radzinowicz, quoted in Langbein, *Torture,* 40.

21. Gordon Wright, *Between the Guillotine and Liberty: Two Centuries of the Crime Problem in France* (New York: Oxford University Press, 1983), 39, 168.

22. Evans, *Rituals of Retribution,* 282.

23. Offenses against the state—treason, desertion in time of war, political assassination, etc.—often survived on the books but were rarely invoked. European nations finally repealed these remaining political capital offenses in the 1990s.

24. Benefit of belly spared female offenders by deeming them to be pregnant. Benefit of clergy spared first offenders by treating them as if they were clergymen—if they could read or recite a biblical passage. The traditional "neck verse" was Psalm 51: "Have mercy upon me, O God, according to thy loving kindness: according to the multitude of thy tender mercies, blot out my transgressions." Lawrence Friedman, *Crime and Punishment in American History* (New York: Basic Books, 1993), 43.

25. Tuttle, *Crusade,* 27, 50, 28.

26. Spierenburg, *Spectacle of Suffering,* 186; Cooper, *The Lesson of the Scaffold,* 6–7.

27. Cooper, *The Lesson of the Scaffold,* 7. See also Spierenburg, *Spectacle of Suffering,* 197; John Pratt, *Punishment and Civilization: Penal Tolerance and Intolerance in Modern Society* (London: Sage Press, 2002); Gatrell, *The Hanging Tree;* Stuart Banner, *The Death Penalty: An American History* (Cam-

bridge, MA: Harvard University Press, 2002); Evans, *Rituals of Retribution;* and Wright, *Guillotine and Liberty.*

28. Gatrell, *The Hanging Tree,* 52. According to Cooper, "The Newgate mob yelled and hissed at the innovation of black cloth draping on the scaffold, designed to hide all but the 'heads of the culprits after the bolt is drawn'" (*The Lesson of the Scaffold,* 3).

29. Wright, *Guillotine and Liberty,* 169–170; Spierenburg, *Spectacle of Suffering,* 198; Daniel Arasse, *The Guillotine and the Terror* (London: Allen Lane, 1989), 95 and 109; Robert Badinter, *Abolition: One Man's Battle against the Death Penalty* (Boston, MA: Northeastern University Press, 2008), 55; Michel Foucault, *Discipline and Punish* (New York: Allen Lane, 1977), 15. Reformers in France's Senate succeeded on more than one occasion in passing bills that would move the guillotine within prison walls, only to see these bills defeated by radicals and socialists in the Chamber of Deputies who objected that ending public executions was a means of preserving the death penalty, which they would prefer to see abolished. See Wright, *Guillotine and Liberty,* 170.

30. Pratt, *Punishment and Civilization,* 26–27.

31. English Royal Commission on Capital Punishment, *Report, 1949–53* (London: H. M. Stationery Office, 1953), 242–243.

32. Evans, *Rituals of Retribution,* 419.

33. Ibid., 315, 316; Spierenburg, *Spectacle of Suffering;* Gatrell, *The Hanging Tree.* See also Anulla Linders, "The Execution Spectacle and State Legitimacy: The Changing Nature of the American Execution Audience, 1833–1937," *Law & Society Review* 36 (2002): 616, n7.

34. Cooper, *The Lesson of the Scaffold,* 133; John Bessler, *Death in the Dark: Midnight Executions in America* (Boston, MA: Northeastern University Press, 1997), 37.

35. The term "delocalization" is from William Bowers, *Legal Homicide: Death as a Punishment in America, 1864–1982* (Boston, MA: Northeastern University Press, 1984). Banner notes that the introduction of electric chairs and gas chambers furthered the shift from local to central control. But this is an American story. Most European nations continued to use traditional methods that could have been administered locally if permitted. *The Death Penalty,* 204.

36. Spierenburg, *Spectacle of Suffering,* 45. See also James Sharpe, *Judicial Punishment in England* (London: Faber and Faber, 1990), 5.

37. Evans, *Rituals of Retribution,* gives examples from the Nazi era in Germany. Dieter Reicher, "Bureaucracy, 'Domesticated' Elites, and the Abolition of Capital Punishment: Processes of State-Formation and Numbers of Executions in England and Habsburg Austria between 1700 and 1914," *Crime, Law and Social Change* (2010).

38. Daniel Gordon, "The Theater of Terror: The Jacobin Execution in Comparative and Theoretical Perspective," *Historical Reflections* 29 (2003): 253, n7; Smith, *Punishment and Culture,* 125. Guillotin's contraption (actually invented by Dr. Antoin Louis, permanent secretary of the Academy of Surgery) was by no means the first mechanical axe of this type to be used in European

executions: see Arasse, *Guillotine;* and Daniel Gerould, *Guillotine: Its Legend and Lore* (New York: Blast Books, 1992).

39. Foucault, *Discipline and Punish,* 38.

40. John Lofland, "The Dramaturgy of State Executions," in Horace Bleakley and John Lofland, eds., *State Executions Viewed Historically and Sociologically* (Montclair, NJ: Patterson Smith, 1977), 290.

41. Royal Commission, *Report,* 247; Gatrell, *The Hanging Tree,* 54 and 46. Banner presents evidence suggesting that most persons who were hanged died by strangulation *(The Death Penalty).*

42. Royal Commission, *Report,* 250.

43. Royal Commission, *Report,* 247, 248, and 253–255.

44. U.N. Department of Economic and Social Affairs, *Capital Punishment: Part I. Report 1960. Part II. Developments, 1961–1965* (New York: United Nations, 1968), 101.

45. Langbein, *Torture,* 28.

46. Evans, *Rituals of Retribution,* 275, 329–340. Mussolini reintroduced the death penalty to Italy in 1926. It was subsequently abolished again by the Constitution of 1948 (Personal communication, Claudio Giusti).

47. On Portugal, see Guilherme Braga da Cruz, "O Movimento Abolicionista e a Abolição Death Penalty Pena de Morte em Portugal-Resenha Historica," in *Pena de Morte, Coloquio Internacional Comemorativo Death Penalty Centerario da Abolição da Pena de Morte em Portugal,* vol. 2 (Coimbra: Facultade de Direito da Universidade de Coimbra, 1967), 423–457.

48. Leon Radzinowicz and Roger Hood, *A History of the English Criminal Law,* vol. 5: *The Emergence of Penal Policy* (Oxford, England: Clarendon Press, 1985), 672.

49. Randall McGowen, "History, Culture and the Death Penalty: The British Debates, 1840–70," *Historical Reflections* 29 (2003): 229.

50. Roger Hood and Carolyn Holye, *The Death Penalty: A Worldwide Perspective* (Oxford, England: Oxford University Press, 2008); Robert Nye, "Two Capital Punishment Debates in France: 1908 and 1981," *Historical Reflections* 29 (2003): 211–228; and Badinter, *Abolition.*

51. Hood and Hoyle, *Death Penalty;* William Schabas, *The Abolition of the Death Penalty in International Law* (Cambridge, England: Cambridge University Press, 2002).

52. See Hood and Hoyle, *Death Penalty.*

53. Banner, *The Death Penalty,* 76, 151, 234. Dissection continued in some Southern states into the twentieth century, though not as a court-ordered punishment. As Kotch explains, in North Carolina "the bodies of executed criminals, white and black, ordinary and extraordinary, were treated the same way as anyone who died in state custody. If relatives claimed the body within twenty-four hours of death, the state provided $50 for transportation costs and burial expenses. If not, the prison gave the body to one of the medical schools in the area." Seth Kotch, "Unduly Harsh and Unworkably Rigid: The Death Penalty in North Carolina, 1910–1961" (Ph.D. Dissertation, University of North Carolina-Chapel Hill), 107.

54. Louis Masur, *Rites of Execution: Capital Punishment and the Transformation of American Culture, 1776–1865* (New York: Oxford University Press, 1989), 5; Banner, *The Death Penalty,* 99.

55. Tocqueville, quoted in Banner, *The Death Penalty,* 99.

56. Banner, *The Death Penalty,* 99.

57. Justice James Wilson, quoted in Banner, *The Death Penalty,* 99.

58. David Brion Davis, "The Movement to Abolish Capital Punishment in America, 1787–1861," *American Historical Review* 63 (October 1957): 28.

59. Bowers, *Legal Homicide,* 4, 7; Masur, *Rites of Execution,* 71. See also Banner, *The Death Penalty,* 97; and Roger Lane, *Murder in America: A History* (Columbus: Ohio State University Press, 1997), 253.

60. Banner, *The Death Penalty,* 131; Louis Filler, "Movements to Abolish the Death Penalty in the United States," *Annals of the American Academy of Political and Social Science,* vol. 284, *Murder and the Penalty of Death* (November 1952); and Craig Haney, *Death by Design: Capital Punishment as a Social Psychological System* (New York: Oxford University Press, 2005), provide details of similar developments in federal law and California law.

61. Thorsten Sellin, *Slavery and the Penal System* (New York: Elsevier, 1976), 141.

62. Davis, "Movement to Abolish," 27; Christopher Mooney and Mei-Hsein Lee, "The Temporal Diffusion of Morality Policy: The Case of the Death Penalty Legislation in the American States," *Policy Studies Journal* 27 (1999): 766–780; Bowers, *Legal Homicide,* 11.

63. Linders, "The Execution Spectacle," 616; Hugo Bedau, *The Death Penalty in America: Current Controversies* (New York: Oxford University Press, 1997), 5. In the 1860s, America's experience was invoked to persuade doubtful members of the British Parliament that privatization was a practicable policy. Cooper, *The Lesson of the Scaffold,* 123–124.

64. Negley Teeters, *Hang by the Neck* (Springfield, IL: C. C. Thomas, 1967), at 152–153; Banner, *The Death Penalty,* 154. Linders gives a slightly different account in "The Execution Spectacle," 616 n7. See also Masur, *Rites of Execution.*

65. Banner, *The Death Penalty,* 163.

66. Bowers, *Legal Homicide,* 13–14, 46–47. See Kotch, "Unduly Harsh," 37.

67. Bowers, *Legal Homicide,* 14: "In 1890, local executions accounted for 87.3% of the total: in 1920, state-administered executions accounted for 88.3% of the total." See also William McFeely, *Proximity to Death* (New York: Norton, 2000), 44.

68. Gas chambers were adopted in Nevada in 1921, then Colorado and Arizona in 1933, North Carolina in 1935, California, Missouri, and Oregon in 1937, Mississippi in 1954, and Maryland and New Mexico in 1955. The original Nevada statute provided that the condemned person be executed by means of lethal gas "without warning and while asleep in his cell," but this proved impractical (Bowers, *Legal Homicide*).

69. Masur, *Rites of Execution,* reports the chloroform proposal, made in 1848 (20). The guillotine proposal was made in the *New York Times* in 1880 (Banner, *The Death Penalty,* 175; see also 171).

70. Banner, *The Death Penalty,* 169.
71. Bedau, *Death Penalty in America,* 11; Bowers, *Legal Homicide,* 12.
72. Deborah Denno, "Is Electrocution an Unconstitutional Method of Execution?" *William and Mary Law Review* 35 (1993/1994): 551–692, 566–567.
73. New York State Commission on Capital Punishment, *Report of the Commission to Investigate and Report the Most Humane and Practical Methods of Carrying into Effect the Sentence of Death* (Albany, NY: The Argus Company, Printers, 1888).
74. W. Fitzhugh Brundage, *Lynching in the New South: Georgia and Virginia 1880–1930* (Urbana: University of Illinois Press, 1993); Edward Ayers, *Vengeance and Justice: Crime and Punishment in the 19th Century American South* (New York: Oxford University Press, 1984); David Garland, "Penal Excess and Surplus Meaning: Public Torture Lynchings in 20th Century America," *Law & Society Review* 39 (2005): 793–834.
75. New York State Commission on Capital Punishment, *Report* at 55.
76. *Campbell v Wood* 18 F.3d 662 701 (9th Cir. 1994).
77. Bowers, *Legal Homicide,* 8; Davis, "Movement to Abolish," 33. The Maine Law prefigures today's system in which procedural delays and postconviction decision-making operate to reduce the likelihood of executions.
78. Bowers, *Legal Homicide,* 9. Michigan for a time retained the death penalty for treason. Rhode Island, in 1882, restored the death penalty for any life-term convict who committed a murder.
79. Banner, *The Death Penalty,* 208.
80. Karen Halttunen, *Murder Most Foul: The Killer and the American Gothic Imagination* (Cambridge, MA: Harvard University Press, 1998), 23.
81. Halttunen, *Murder Most Foul,* 22–24; Banner, *The Death Penalty.* See Foucault, *Discipline and Punish;* Gatrell, *The Hanging Tree;* Evans, *Rituals of Retribution.*
82. Banner, *The Death Penalty,* 193. Oshinsky describes the Louisiana electric chair known as Gruesome Gertie: "Strapped to a pick-up truck, the contraption, outfitted by International Harvester, contained a switchboard, a generator, several hundred feet of cable wire, and a heavy wooden chair with three straps to keep a body in place." David Oshinsky, *Capital Punishment on Trial: "Furman v Georgia" and the Death Penalty in Modern America* (Lawrence, KS: University Press of Kansas, 2010), 22.
83. Banner, *The Death Penalty,* 155.
84. Samuel Walker, *Popular Justice: A History of American Criminal Justice* (New York: Oxford University Press, 1998), 92.
85. Banner notes: "As of 1954 rape was punished by death in eighteen states, sixteen in the South . . . Five states, all southern, still retained the death penalty for arson . . . Burglary was still capital in four . . . While northerners were vigorously debating whether to abolish capital punishment even for murder, most of the southern states barely changed their capital codes." Banner, *The Death Penalty,* 228. As late as 1972, several Southern states retained a list of nonlethal capital offenses, none of which was capital in the North. Judith Randle, "The Cultural Lives of Capital Punishment in the United States," in Austin

Sarat and Christian Boulanger, eds., *The Cultural Lives of Capital Punishment* (Stanford, CA: Stanford University Press, 2005), 107. Southern states were also slow to build prisons. Kotch, "Unduly Harsh," 14; Michael Hindus, *Prison and Plantation: Crime, Justice and Authority in Massachusetts and South Carolina, 1767–1878* (Chapel Hill: University of North Carolina Press, 1980).

86. See Kenneth Stampp, *The Peculiar Institution: Slavery in the Ante-Bellum South* (New York: Vintage Books, 1956), 210. In 1836, Alabama abolished the death penalty for burglary, robbery, arson, counterfeiting, and forgery—but only for whites. Thorsten Sellin, *Slavery and the Penal System* (New York: Elsevier, 1976), 141.

87. Banner, *The Death Penalty*, 155.

88. See ibid., 215; and Bedau, *Death Penalty in America*, 5.

89. Michael Tonry, *Sentencing Matters* (New York: Oxford University Press, 1998).

90. Brundage, *Lynching*, estimates that between 1882 and 1930 a total of 3,220 blacks and some 723 whites were lynched in the South. See also Stewart Tolnay and E. M. Beck, *Festival of Violence* (Urbana: University of Illinois Press, 1995).

91. Garland, "Penal Excess."

92. Banner, *The Death Penalty*, 229.

93. Tony Judt, *Postwar: A History of Europe since 1945* (New York: Penguin, 2006).

5. Processes of Transformation

1. David Greenberg and Valerie West, "Siting the Death Penalty Internationally," *Law & Social Inquiry* 33 (2008): 295–343.

2. Anton Blok, "The Symbolic Vocabulary of Public Executions," in June Starr and Jane F. Collier, eds., *History and Power in the Study of Law: New Directions in Legal Anthropology* (Ithaca, NY: Cornell University Press, 1989), 52.

3. Pieter Spierenburg, *The Spectacle of Suffering: Executions and the Evolution of Repression: From a Preindustrial Metropolis to the European Experience* (Cambridge, England: Cambridge University Press, 1984), 109.

4. Stephen Mennell, *The American Civilizing Process* (Cambridge, England: Polity, 2007), 16, 17.

5. Theda Skocpol, "The Origins of Social Policy in the United States: A Polity-Centered Analysis," in Lawrence Dodd and Calvin Jilson, eds., *The Dynamics of American Politics* (Boulder, CO: Westview Press, 1994); Charles Tilly, *Coercion, Capital and European States, AD 990–1992* (Cambridge, England: Blackwell, 1992).

6. James Whitman, "The Comparative Study of Criminal Punishment," *Annual Review of Law and Social Science* 1 (2005): 26.

7. Roberta Senechal de la Roche, "The Sociogenesis of Lynching," in W. Fitzhugh Brundage, ed., *Under Sentence of Death: Lynching in the South* (Durham: University of North Carolina Press, 2001); Greenberg and West, "Siting

the Death Penalty Internationally"; Rick Ruddell and Martin Urbina, "Minority Threat and Punishment: A Cross-National Analysis," *Justice Quarterly* 21 (2004): 931.

8. Spierenburg, *Spectacle of Suffering,* 80–84; James Sharpe, *Judicial Punishment in England* (London: Faber and Faber, 1990), 33; Richard van Dulman, *Theatre of Horror: Crime and Punishment in Early Modern Germany* (Oxford, England: Polity, 1990); Mitchell Merback, *The Thief, the Cross and the Wheel: Pain and the Spectacle of Punishment in Medieval and Renaissance Europe* (Chicago: University of Chicago Press, 1999).

9. Merback, *The Thief;* Katherine Royer, "The Body in Parts: Reading the Execution in Late Medieval England," *Historical Reflections/Réflexions Historiques* 29 (2003): 327.

10. Merback, *The Thief,* 134; Maneul Eisner, "Long Term Historical Trends in Violent Crime," *Crime and Justice* 30 (2003): 126; Spierenburg, *Spectacle of Suffering,* 8.

11. As Tilly observes, "Weber's definition of the state began to become a reality." *Coercion,* 69.

12. Manuel Eisner, "Modernization, Self-Control and Lethal Violence: The Longterm Dynamics of European Homicide Rates in Theoretical Perspective," *British Journal of Criminology* 41 (2001): 628. Eisner reports the results of "a systematic meta-analysis of more than ninety publications on pre-modern homicide rates in Europe as well as on a comprehensive collection of modern homicide time series in ten countries." See Eisner, "Long Term Historical Trends," 88; Ted Gurr, *Violence in America,* vol. 2 (Newbury Park, CA: Sage, 1989); Richard Evans, *Rituals of Retribution: Capital Punishment in Germany, 1600–1987* (Oxford, England: Oxford University Press, 1996), 118; Pieter Spierenburg, "Violence and the Civilization Process: Does It Work?" *Crime, Histories and Societies* 5, 2 (2001): 101; and Pieter Spierenburg, *A History of Murder: Personal Violence in Europe from the Middle Ages to the Present* (Cambridge, England: Polity, 2008).

13. Eisner, "European Homicide Rates," 630–631. See also Tilly, *Coercion,* 76.

14. The phrase is from Beccaria's 4th edition of 1775. Cesare Beccaria, *An Essay on Crimes and Punishments* (Brookline, MA: Branden Press, 1983), 44.

15. Anton Blok, "Symbolic Vocabulary," 52.

16. Reicher writes that "the introduction of a modern police organization went hand in hand with the reduction of capital punishment." Dieter Reicher, "Weak States and Brutal Punishment: State Building Processes and the Death Penalty" (unpublished manuscript, n.d.). In England, the reduction of capital offenses began only after Prime Minister Robert Peel created the modern police force. See J. Christoph, *Capital Punishment and British Politics: The British Movement to Abolish the Death Penalty, 1945–57* (Chicago: University of Chicago Press, 1962).

17. John Beattie, *Crime and the Courts in England, 1660–1800* (Princeton, NJ: Princeton University Press, 1986), 506.

18. Reicher, "Weak States and Brutal Punishment," 27.

19. Victor Bailey, "The Death Penalty in British History," *Punishment & Society* 2

(2001): 106–113; Stuart Banner, *The Death Penalty: An American History* (Cambridge, MA: Harvard University Press, 2002).

20. David Garland, *Punishment and Modern Society: A Study in Social Theory* (Oxford, England: Oxford University Press, 1990), Chapter 8.

21. Philip Smith, *Punishment and Culture* (Chicago: University of Chicago Press, 2008); Dwight Conquergood, "Lethal Theatre: Performance, Punishment and the Death Penalty," *Theatre Journal* 54 (2002): 362.

22. V. A. C. Gatrell, *The Hanging Tree: Executions and the English People, 1770–1868* (Oxford, England: Oxford University Press, 1994); Thomas Laqueur, "Festivals of Punishment," *London Review of Books,* October 5, 2000, 17–24; Louis Masur, *Rites of Execution: Capital Punishment and the Transformation of American Culture, 1776–1865* (New York: Oxford University Press, 1989); Evans, *Rituals of Retribution,* 315; Smith, *Punishment and Culture;* and Michel Foucault, *Discipline and Punish: The Birth of the Prison* (New York: Allen Lane, 1977).

23. *Baze v Rees* 553 U.S. 35 (2008). See also Wendy Lesser, *Pictures at an Execution: An Inquiry into the Subject of Murder* (Cambridge, MA: Harvard University Press, 1998).

24. Paul Starr, *Freedom's Power: The True Force of Liberalism* (New York: Basic Books, 2007), 77–78 and 87–88.

25. Eric Neumayer, "Death Penalty: The Political Foundations of the Global Trend Toward Abolition" (unpublished manuscript, 2006), 9.

26. Starr, *Freedom's Power,* 2; John Gray, *Liberalism* (Minneapolis: University of Minnesota Press, 1992); and Stephen Holmes, *Passions and Constraints: On the Theory of Liberal Democracy* (Chicago: University of Chicago Press, 1995). Alan Grimes usefully distinguishes several forms of liberalism: Lockean liberalism, Jeffersonian liberalism, Manchester liberalism, Pragmatic Deweyian liberalism, etc. Alan Grimes, "The Pragmatic Course of Liberalism," *Western Political Quarterly* 9 (1956): 633–640.

27. Starr, *Freedom's Power,* 3.

28. On the Enlightenment liberals, see Peter Gay, *The Enlightenment: The Science of Freedom* (New York: Norton, 1996).

29. John McManners, *Death and the Enlightenment: Changing Attitudes to Death among Christians and Unbelievers in Eighteenth Century France* (New York: Oxford University Press, 1981).

30. These rights were embodied in the English Bill of Rights of 1689 and the Treason Trials Act of 1696. Later they featured in most of the new constitutions of the late eighteenth and nineteenth centuries.

31. William Bowers, *Legal Homicide: Death as a Punishment in America, 1864–1982* (Boston, MA: Northeastern University Press, 1984), 40.

32. Lynn Hunt, *Inventing Human Rights: A History* (N.Y.: Norton, 2007), 20.

33. Discussing recent developments in Eastern Europe, Zimring says that abolition is now considered "an integral part of liberalization." Franklin Zimring, *The Contradictions of American Capital Punishment* (New York: Oxford University Press, 2003), 37.

34. Evans, *Rituals of Retribution,* 897. Sarat and Boulanger write, "The more authoritarian a country is, the more it is likely to have the death penalty." Austin

Sarat and Christian Boulanger, eds., *The Cultural Lives of Capital Punishment: Comparative Perspectives* (Stanford: Stanford University Press, 2005).

35. Evans, *Rituals of Retribution,* 626.
36. Emile Durkheim, "Individualism and the Intellectuals," *Emile Durkheim on Morality and Society,* ed. Robert Bellah (Chicago: University of Chicago Press, 1973), 46–47. See also Steven Lukes, "Liberal Democratic Torture," *British Journal of Political Science* 36 (2005): 14.
37. Beccaria, *On Crimes and Punishments,* 45 and 49.
38. Michigan Legislature, *Majority Report of the Select Committee on the Abolishment of Capital Punishment* (Detroit: State of Michigan, 1844), 2.
39. On liberalism and the death penalty in Germany, see Evans, *Rituals of Retribution,* 248; on France, see James Whitman, *Harsh Justice: Criminal Punishment and the Widening Gap between America and Europe* (New York: Oxford University Press, 2003); and on Britain, see Christoph, *Capital Punishment and British Politics,* 15ff, and Randall McGowen, "History, Culture and the Death Penalty: The British Debates, 1840–70," *Historical Reflections* 29 (2003): 231.
40. On opposition to death penalty reform, see Hay, "Hanging and the English Judges," in David Garland et al., eds., *America's Death Penalty: Between Past and Present* (New York University Press, 2010); Philip Mackey, *Hanging in the Balance: The Anti-Capital Punishment Movement in New York State, 1776–1861* (New York: Garland Publishing, 1982); Christoph, *Capital Punishment and British Politics,* 15ff; Michigan Legislature, *Abolishment of Capital Punishment,* 3.
41. Peter Hodgkinson, "Capital Punishment: Improve It or Remove It," in Peter Hodgkinson and William Schabas, eds., *Capital Punishment: Strategies for Abolition* (Cambridge, England: Cambridge University Press, 2004), 1; Council of Europe, *Death Is Not Justice: The Council of Europe and the Death Penalty* (Strasbourg: Council of Europe Publishing, 2001), 10.
42. Justice Black in *In re Winship* 397 U.S. 358 (1970), 385.
43. Gary Wills, *Lincoln at Gettysburg* (New York: Simon and Schuster, 1992).
44. Richard Pildes, "The Constitutionalization of Democratic Politics," *Harvard Law Review* 118 (2004): 43; Dietrich Rueschemeyer, Evelyne Stephens, and John Stephens, *Capitalist Development and Democracy* (Chicago: University of Chicago Press, 1992), 10; Charles Tilly, *Democracy* (New York: Cambridge University Press, 2007), 13.
45. Issacharoff notes, "War is often the midwife to democracy" and quotes John Keegan's phrase "no conscription without representation." Samuel Issacharoff, "Political Safeguards in Democracies at War," *Oxford Journal of Legal Studies* 29 (2) (2009): at 194, 204; See also Tilly, *Coercion,* 63.
46. Rueschemeyer et al., *Capitalist Development and Democracy,* 5.
47. Benjamin Rush, *Considerations on the Injustice and Impolicy of Punishing Murder by Death* (Philadelphia, PA: Matthew Carey, 1792). The French revolutionaries viewed the guillotine as a democratic machine in that it provided the same death for all—and that death a noble one. See Foucault, *Discipline and Punish,* 12–13.
48. Reginald Paget MP, quoted in Brian Block and John Hostettler, *Hanging in the*

Balance: A History of the Abolition of Capital Punishment in Britain (Winchester: Waterside Press, 1997), 110.

49. John Paton, MP, quoted in John Pratt, *Punishment and Civilization: Penal Tolerance and Intolerance in Modern Society* (London: Sage Press, 2002), 28.

50. Quoted in Christopher Hitchens, "Slouching toward Abolition," D. Dow and M. Dow, eds., *Machinery of Death: The Reality of America's Death Penalty Regime* (New York: Routledge, 2001). Badinter says that "in a democracy founded on human rights there is no place for a justice that kills." Robert Badinter, *Abolition: One Man's Battle against the Death Penalty* (Boston, MA: Northeastern University Press, 2008), xviii. See also Gary LaFree, "Too Much Democracy or Too Much Crime? Lessons from California's Three-Strikes Law," *Law & Social Inquiry* 27 (2002): 875–902.

51. Though the United States was one of the earliest nations to install partial democracy, having established full white male suffrage by the 1830s, it did not become a full democracy until the 1960s, when the Voting Rights Act ensured that African Americans might vote. Social science studies of death penalty policies provide strong evidence of a correlation between the presence of liberal-democratic institutions and the absence of capital punishment. See Greenberg and West, "Siting the Death Penalty Internationally"; Jerome Neopolitan, "An Examination of Cross-National Variation in Punitiveness," *International Journal of Offender Therapy and Comparative Criminology* 45 (2000): 691–710; Martin Killias, "Power Concentration, Legitimation Crisis and Penal Severity: A Comparative Perspective," *International Annals of Criminology* 24 (1986): 181–211; and Andrew Moravcsik, "The New Abolitionism: Why Does the U.S. Practice the Death Penalty While Europe Does Not?" *European Studies* (September 2001). A time-series study by Neumayer finds that capital punishment abolition coincided with the rise of democracy and that the widespread abolition after World War II was a fundamentally political process. Eric Neumayer, "Death Penalty: The Political Foundations of the Global Trend Toward Abolition" (unpublished manuscript, 2006).

52. See Pildes, "Constitutionalization," 29. See also Rueschemeyer et al., *Capitalist Development and Democracy*, 2.

53. William Schabas, *The Abolition of the Death Penalty in International Law* (Cambridge, England: Cambridge University Press, 2002), 363.

54. The Philippines abolished capital punishment in 1987 but revived it thereafter. Zimring and Johnson describe the timing and political circumstances of postwar abolition in Europe: "Italy, 1944, fall of Mussolini; West Germany, 1949, Constitution for new state; Austria, 1950, Socialists join governing coalition; Great Britain, 1965/1969, Election of Labour government; Portugal, 1976, Transition from Salazar regime; Spain, 1978, Transition from Franco regime; France, 1981, Election of Left government." Franklin Zimring and David Johnson, *The Next Frontier: National Development, Political Change and the Death Penalty in Asia* (New York: Oxford University Press, 2009).

55. See Greenberg and West, "Siting the Death Penalty Internationally," 331; and Neumayer, "Death Penalty: Political Foundations," 5. The *Economist*'s De-

mocracy Index, which ranks the degree of democracy present in 153 of the world's countries, reveals that the top 10 most democratic nations are all abolitionist, and the bottom 10 are all retentionist. See http://www.economist .com/images/rankings/Democracy.jpg, accessed 1/21/10.

56. In 1981, several other European nations such as Belgium and the United Kingdom had residual capital codes that were not abolished until the 1990s. And the subsequent expansion of Europe to include several formerly communist states means that there are now European Union nations that introduced abolition after 1981.

57. I take this Beccarian phrase from the frontispiece of the book by Robert Badinter, the minister of justice who led the campaign to abolish the death penalty in France. That Badinter's memoir uses this as its opening epigraph makes my point.

58. The *New York Times* commented in 1886 that the introduction of the electric chair would substitute a "civilized for a barbarous method." Quoted in Smith, *Punishment and Culture*, 144. And when the chair was used for the first time to electrocute William Kemmler, state commission member Alfred Southwick declared, "We live in a higher civilization today." Ibid., 151.

59. Spierenburg argues the former position, Foucault the latter. Spierenburg, *Spectacle of Suffering*; and Foucault, *Discipline and Punish*. The "civilizing process" account has been taken up by Pratt, *Punishment and Civilization*; and Garland, *Punishment and Modern Society*. Smith makes a strong case for a "culturalist" account of punishment and penal change. Smith, *Punishment and Culture*. The skeptical view of humanitarian sentiment can be found in Georg Rusche and Otto Kirchheimer, *Punishment and Social Structure* (New York: Russell and Russell, 1968), and, in a more sophisticated form, in Gatrell, *The Hanging Tree*.

60. Thomas Haskell, "Capitalism and the Origins of Humanitarian Sensibility," in Tom Bender, ed., *The Antislavery Debate: Capitalism and Abolitionism as a Problem in Historical Interpretation* (Berkeley: University of California Press, 1992); John Bender, *Imagining the Penitentiary: Fiction and the Architecture of Mind in 18th Century England* (Chicago: University of Chicago Press, 1989); Karen Halttunen, *Murder Most Foul: The Killer and the American Gothic Imagination* (Cambridge, MA: Harvard University Press, 1998); Evans, *Rituals of Retribution*; Norbert Elias, *The Civilizing Process: Sociogenetic and Psychogenetic Explorations* (London: Blackwell, 2000); Spierenburg, *Spectacle of Suffering*.

61. Spierenburg, *Spectacle of Suffering*, 187.

62. Haskell, "Humanitarian Sensibility"; Bender, *Imagining the Penitentiary*. In the United States, the contrasting cultures of honor (in the South) and dignity (in the North) produced differential effects. Edward Ayers, *Vengeance and Justice: Crime and Punishment in the 19th Century American South* (New York: Oxford University Press, 1984).

63. John Stuart Mill, "Civilization," *London and Westminster Review* 25 (April 1836): 160–205. On the disappearance of death from the public sphere, see Philippe Aries, "The Reversal of Death: Changes in Attitudes Toward

Death in Western Societies," *American Quarterly* 26 (1974): 536–560; Norbert Elias, *The Loneliness of the Dying* (New York: Continuum, 2001); and Michel Foucault, *Society Must Be Defended: Lectures at the College de France, 1975–1976* (New York: Picador, 2003), 247.

64. See Evans, *Rituals of Retribution,* 227, for evidence of this in Germany; and Masur, *Rites of Execution,* 102–103 for the United States.

65. Mill, "Civilization," 160.

66. See Beattie, *Crime and the Courts in England;* Hunt, *Inventing Human Rights;* Garland, *Punishment and Modern Society;* John Langbein, *Torture and the Law of Proof* (Chicago: University of Chicago Press, 1976); and Edward Peters, *Torture* (Philadelphia: University of Pennsylvania Press, 1996).

67. On the decline of corporal punishment in the United States, see Mayra Glenn, *Campaigns Against Corporal Punishment: Prisoners, Sailors, Women and Children in Antebellum America* (Albany: State University of New York Press, 1984).

68. Middle- and upper-class critics of public executions talked of the "demoralizing and degrading" effect that these hangings had on the public, claiming that they "did debase, and lower, and brutalize the public morals and the public mind." William Ewart MP and Sir Samuel Lushington, quoted in McGowen, "British Debates," 236. Laqueur describes the "stereotypical middle-class reaction" to execution crowds as being one of disturbance and disapproval. Thomas Laqueur, "Crowds, Carnival and the State in English Executions, 1604–1868," in A. L. Beier, David Cannadine, and James Rosenheim, eds., *The First Modern Society: Essays in Honor of Lawrence Stone* (New York: Cambridge University Press, 1989), 330. Similar sentiments were being expressed by social elites all across Europe and America. See Banner, *The Death Penalty,* 153; Evans, *Rituals of Retribution,* 148; and Gatrell, *The Hanging Tree.*

69. Gatrell, *The Hanging Tree;* Blok, "Symbolic Vocabulary," 51; Spierenburg, *Spectacle of Suffering,* 190; Banner, *The Death Penalty,* 177; Smith, *Punishment and Culture,* 35.

70. See also Gatrell, *The Hanging Tree;* Masur, *Rites of Execution;* Spierenburg, *Spectacle of Suffering.*

71. Banner, *The Death Penalty,* 174.

72. John Lofland, "The Dramaturgy of State Executions," H. Bleakley and J. Lofland, *State Executions Viewed Historically and Sociologically* (Montclair, NJ: Patterson Smith, 1977), 281.

73. Lesser, *Pictures at an Execution.*

74. See William Wollaston in 1724: "It is grievous to see or hear (and almost to hear of) any man, or even any animal whatever, in torment" (quoted in Karen Halttunen, *Murder Most Foul,* 62). On the emergence of an eighteenth-century culture of humanism in religion, philosophy, literature, and social reform, see Halttunen, *Murder Most Foul;* Thomas Haskell, "Capitalism and the Origins of Humanitarian Sensibility," in Bender, *The Antislavery Debate;* and Keith Thomas, *Religion and the Decline of Magic* (Harmondsworth: Penguin, 1991).

75. The "motive force of penal reform" is, according to Morris, "Decency, empathy, the ability to feel at least to a degree the lash on another's back, the removal occasionally of our customary blinkers to human suffering, a respect for each individual springing from religious or humanitarian beliefs." Norval Morris, "Impediments to Penal Reform," *University of Chicago Law Review* 33 (1966): 627.

76. David Brion Davis, "The Movement to Abolish Capital Punishment in America, 1787–1861," *American Historical Review* 63 (October 1957): 29; Halttunen, *Murder Most Foul*, 63–65; and Hunt, *Inventing Human Rights*. The British Society for the Abolition of Capital Punishment was led chiefly by Quakers. Christoph, *Capital Punishment and British Politics*, 27.

77. Chief Justice Warren wrote in *Trop v Dulles* 356 U.S. 86 (1958), 100: "The basic concept underlying the Eighth Amendment [and its prohibition on "cruel and unusual punishments"] is nothing less than the dignity of man."

78. See Haskell, "Humanitarian Sensibility"; Halttunen, *Murder Most Foul*; Laqueur, "English Executions"; Hunt, *Inventing Human Rights*.

79. McGowen, "British Debates," 237. Hunt points to the impact of Enlightenment ideas in expanding empathy and evincing a new concern for the human body. She argues that this affected capital and corporal punishments. Hunt, *Inventing Human Rights*, 94.

80. Halttunen, *Murder Most Foul*.

81. Karen Halttunen, "Humanitarianism and the Pornography of Pain in Anglo-American Culture," *American Historical Review* 100 (1995): 303–304.

82. Abram de Swaan, "Widening Circles of Disidentification: On the Psycho- and Sociogenesis of the Hatred of Distant Strangers—Reflections on Rwanda," *Theory, Culture and Society* 14 (May 1997): 106.

83. I borrow this "conductivity" metaphor from my colleague Moshe Halberthal.

84. Spierenburg, *Spectacle of Suffering*; Randall McGowen, "The Body and Punishment in the Eighteenth Century," *Journal of Modern History* 59 (1987): 651–679.

85. Markus Dubber, "The Pain of Punishment," *Buffalo Law Review* 44 (1996): 553–554.

86. Rush, *Considerations on the Injustice and Impolicy of Punishing Murder by Death*; Hunt, *Inventing Human Rights*, 76.

87. Randall McGowen, "Cruel Inflictions and the Claims of Humanity in Early Nineteenth Century England," in Katherine Watson and Eric Chelstrom, eds., *Assaulting the Past: Violence and Civilization in Historical Context* (Newcastle: Cambridge Scholars Publishing, 2007), 38–57.

88. Quoted in McGowen, "British Debates," 239. Spierenburg writes: "In the middle of the nineteenth century sensitivity towards executions is taken so much for granted that, just as with torture three generations before, the defenders feel obliged to show their revulsion too." In effect, the predominant cultural tropes are folded into the debate and come to be used by both sides. Spierenburg, *Spectacle of Suffering*, 196.

89. See Gatrell, *The Hanging Tree*, 267: "Some historians interested in the relationship between punishment and sensibility have confused squeamishness

with sympathy or empathy . . . [Squeamishness] is a colder, more distanced, more aesthetic emotion [than empathy], defensively fastidious in the face of the rude and the unsightly."

6. State and Society in America

1. Carol Steiker, "Capital Punishment and American Exceptionalism," *Oregon Law Review* 81 (2002): 97–130; David Garland, "Capital Punishment and American Culture," *Punishment & Society* 7(4) (2005): 347–376.

2. For overviews, see Russell Duncan and Joseph Goddard, *Contemporary America* (New York: Palgrave, 2005); Stephen Mennell, *The American Civilizing Process* (Cambridge, England: Polity Press, 2007); and Peter Schuck and James Wilson, *Understanding America: The Anatomy of an Exceptional Nation* (New York: Public Affairs, 2008).

3. John Sutton, "Imprisonment and Social Classification in Five Common-Law Countries, 1955–85," *American Journal of Sociology* 106 (2000): 364. See also Seymour Lipset, *Continental Divide: The Values and Institutions of the United States and Canada* (New York: Routledge, 1990), 21; J. P. Nettl, "The State as a Conceptual Variable," *World Politics* 20 (1986): 559–592; Stephen Skowronek, *Building a New American State: The Expansion of National Administrative Capacities, 1877—1920* (New York: Cambridge University Press, 1982), 3; and Ronald Jepperson, "Political Modernities: Disentangling Two Underlying Dimensions of Institutional Differentiation," *Sociological Theory* 20 (2002): 71.

4. Theda Skocpol, "The Origins of Social Policy in the United States: A Polity-Centered Analysis," in Lawrence Dodd and Calvin Jilson, eds., *The Dynamics of American Politics* (Boulder, CO: Westview Press, 1994), 192.

5. For a critique of the "weak state" thesis, see William Novak, "The Myth of the 'Weak' American State," *American Historical Review* 113 (2008): 752–772.

6. In *Chisholm v Georgia*, 1793, quoted in Sheldon Wolin, "The Idea of the State in America," John Diggins and Mark Kann, eds., *The Problem of Authority in America* (Philadelphia: Temple University Press, 1981), 42. See also David Robertson, *The Constitution and America's Destiny* (New York: Cambridge University Press, 2005), xiii; and John Higham, "Hanging Together: Divergent Unities in American History," *Journal of American History* 61 (1974): 28.

7. Robertson, *The Constitution and America's Destiny,* 182.

8. Robin Einhorn, *American Taxation, American Slavery* (Chicago: University of Chicago Press, 2006).

9. Julian Zelizer, "The Uneasy Relationship: Democracy, Taxation and State Building Since the New Deal," in Meg Jacobs, William Novak, and Julian Zelizer, eds., *The Democratic Experiment* (Princeton, NJ: Princeton University Press, 2003).

10. Alex Keysarr, *The Right to Vote: The Contested History of Democracy in the*

United States (New York: Basic Books, 2001); Paul Starr, *Freedom's Power: The True Force of Liberalism* (New York: Basic Books, 2007), 80, 90.

11. New Jersey's 1776 constitution gave the vote to all "inhabitants" who were otherwise qualified, but a state law of 1807 disfranchised women.

12. Keysarr, *The Right to Vote;* Jill Quadagno, *The Color of Welfare: How Racism Undermined the War on Poverty* (New York: Oxford University Press, 1994), 191.

13. Richard Bensel, *Sectionalism and American Political Development: 1880–1980* (Madison: University of Wisconsin Press, 1984), 239, 229.

14. Richard Bensel, *Yankee Leviathan: The Origins of Central State Authority in America, 1859–1877* (New York: Cambridge University Press, 1990). See also Quadagno, *The Color of Welfare,* 189; Skowronek, *Building the New American State,* viii; and Skocpol, "The Origins of Social Policy," 193–194.

15. Robert Kagan, *Adversarial Legalism: The American Way of Law* (Cambridge, MA: Harvard University Press, 2001), 15.

16. Lipset, *Continental Divide,* 20–1.

17. William Novak, *The People's Welfare: Law and Regulation in Nineteenth-Century America* (Chapel Hill: North Carolina University Press, 1996); Bensel, *Yankee Leviathan.* See also Skowronek, *Building the New American State,* 15; and Thomas Sugrue, "All Politics Is Local: The Persistence of Localism in Twentieth Century America," in Jacobs et al., *The Democratic Experiment.*

18. Bensel, *Yankee Leviathan;* Skowronek, *Building the New American State;* Eric Monkkonen, "Homicide: Explaining America's Exceptionalism," *American Historical Review* 114 (2006): 91. The meaning of federalism, and the balance of power that it implies among central, state, and local government, are ongoing debates over which the Supreme Court presides. See Malcolm Feeley and Edward Rubin, *Federalism: Political Identity and Tragic Compromise* (Ann Arbor: University of Michigan Press, 2008); and Erwin Chemerinsky, *Enhancing Government: Federalism for the 21st Century* (Palo Alto, CA: Stanford Law Books, 2008).

19. Sugrue, "All Politics Is Local," 301, 302, 319.

20. Anne Harris, Raymond Paternoster, and Bobby Brame, "Deterrence and Capital Punishment: A Within-State Analysis," paper presented at the annual meeting of the American Society of Criminology, St. Louis, November 11, 2008.

21. James Liebman, "Slow Dancing with Death: The Supreme Court and Capital Punishment, 1963–2006," *Columbia Law Review* 107 (2007): 16; Tim Newburn, "Contrasts of Intolerance: Cultures of Control in the United States and Britain," in Tim Newburn and Paul Rock, eds., *The Politics of Crime Control* (Oxford, England: Oxford University Press, 2006), 227–270, at 234.

22. Quoted in Anthony Giddens, *Capitalism and Modern Social Theory* (Cambridge, England: Cambridge University Press, 1973), 62.

23. V. O. Keys, *Southern Politics in State and Nation* (New York: Knopf, 1949); William Stuntz, "Unequal Justice," 121 *Harvard Law Review* (2008): 1969–2040; Einhorn, *Taxation, Slavery,* 7.

24. According to Stuntz in "Unequal Justice," the Southern states remain comparatively underprovided in terms of police resources. He suggests that this deficiency reduces deterrence and contributes to the harsh sentencing and high rates of imprisonment that characterize the region.

25. Austin Sarat and Christian Boulanger, eds., *The Cultural Lives of Capital Punishment: Comparative Perspectives* (Stanford, CA: Stanford University Press, 2005), 8. For a comparative discussion, see Franklin Zimring, Gordon Hawkins, and Sam Kamin, *Punishment and Democracy: Three Strikes and You're Out in California* (New York: Oxford University Press, 2001).

26. Michael Hindus, *Prison and Plantation: Crime, Justice and Authority in Massachusetts and South Carolina, 1767–1878* (Chapel Hill: University of North Carolina Press, 1980); David Oshinsky, *"Worse Than Slavery": Parchman Farm and the Ordeal of Jim Crow* (New York: Free Press, 1996); Mark Colvin, *Penitentiaries, Reformatories and Chain Gangs* (New York: St. Martin's Press, 1997); Edward Ayers, *Vengeance and Justice: Crime and Punishment in the 19th Century American South* (New York: Oxford University Press, 1984); Samuel Walker, *Popular Justice: A History of American Criminal Justice* (New York: Oxford University Press, 1998).

27. Alexis de Tocqueville, *Democracy in America* (New York: Vintage, 1990; original French edition, 1835), 290; John Kingdon, *America the Unusual* (Belmont: Thomson/Wadsworth, 1999), 47; Kagan, *Adversarial Legalism,* 7; Lipset, *Continental Divide,* xii.

28. As a *New York Times* headline declared on April 16, 2008, the day after the decision, "Litigation Assured in Wake of Decision." The article reported, "Opponents of the death penalty said the decision was little more than a road map for more litigation."

29. Lipset, *Continental Divide,* 34; Edward Banfield and James Wilson, *City Politics* (Cambridge, MA: Harvard University Press, 1963), 1. See also Nicholas Lehman, "Rovian Ways," *New Yorker,* August 27, 2007, 30.

30. On the weakness of U.S. political parties, see Zakaria, *The Future of Freedom,* 181; Pildes, "Constitutionalization"; and Kingdon, *America the Unusual.* This may be changing. In recent years, the Republican party in particular has become a much more disciplined organization that operates increasingly like a European political party.

31. Introduced in the Progressive era, party primaries are unique to the United States. They have the effect of broadening popular participation in the process of nomination and thereby depriving party leaders of significant power.

32. Anthony King, *Running Scared: Why America's Politicians Campaign Too Much and Govern Too Little* (New York: Free Press, 1997), 3; Robertson, *The Constitution and America's Destiny,* 257–258; Sven Steinmo, "American Exceptionalism Reconsidered: Culture or Institutions?" in Lawrence Dodd and Calvin Jilson, eds., *The Dynamics of American Politics* (Boulder: Westview Press, 1994), 106–131, at 117. See also Zakaria, *The Future of Freedom,* 166; and Joachim Savelsberg, "Punitiveness in Cross-national Comparison: Toward a Historically and Institutionally Founded Multi-Factorial Approach,"

in Helmut Kury and Theodore N. Ferdinand, eds., *International Perspectives on Punitivity* (Bochum, Germany: Brockmeyer, 2008), 13–31.

33. Wolin, "The Idea of the State," 42.

34. Morris Fiorina, Samuel Abrams, and Jeremy Pope, *Culture War: The Myth of a Polarized America* (New York: Longman, 2005), 14.

35. Richard Pildes, "The Constitutionalization of Democratic Politics," *Harvard Law Review* 118 (2004): 29–154, at 78. See also Stephen Powers and Stanley Rothman, *The Least Dangerous Branch? Consequences of Judicial Activism* (Westport: Praeger, 2002), 186. Americans' distrust of expert bureaucracy has varied over time. During the Progressive era and the New Deal, such agencies were given considerable power. For much of the twentieth century, state parole boards operated as relatively apolitical agencies that moderated the length of the prison sentences imposed by the courts. In the 1980s, the powers of parole boards were sharply curtailed and key sentencing decisions were lodged in the political process.

36. Lipset, *Continental Divide*, 132; Kagan, *Adversarial Legalism*. The United States Senate was opened up to popular election in 1913. Before that time, senators were selected by state legislatures.

37. Fareed Zakaria, *The Future of Freedom: Illiberal Democracy at Home and Abroad* (New York: Norton, 2004). On the more limited role of nonpolitical expertise in the United States, see Kagan, *Adversarial Legalism*.

38. See Robert Lieberman, *Shifting the Color Line: Race and the American Welfare State* (Cambridge, MA: Harvard University Press, 1998); Ira Katznelson, *When Affirmative Action Was White* (New York: Norton, 2005); and Sutton, "Imprisonment and Social Classification," 378.

39. Zimring, Hawkins, and Kamin note that only the United States allows sentencing law to be shaped by direct democracy. The other seven nations discussed by the authors have various forms of "insulated discretion." Zimring, Hawkins and Kamin, *Punishment and Democracy*.

40. Carol Steiker, "Capital Punishment and American Exceptionalism," *Oregon Law Review* 81, 1 (2002): 97–130, at 119, notes that "some of the most 'active' counties [in the use of the death penalty] have been those with a District Attorney highly and vocally committed to the use of capital punishment." For details of the various judicial selection processes in the fifty states, see Henry Glick, "Courts: Politics and the Judicial Process," in Virginia Gray and Russell Hanson, eds., *Politics in the American States: A Comparative Analysis* (Washington, DC: C. Q. Press, 2004), 232–261. See also Sarat and Boulanger, eds., *Cultural Lives of Capital Punishment*, 9.

41. Joachim Savelsberg, "Knowledge, Domination, and Criminal Punishment," *American Journal of Sociology* 99 (1994): 911–943; Dieter Reicher, "Bureaucracy, 'Domesticated' Elites, and the Abolition of Capital Punishment," *Crime, Law and Social Change* 52, 1 (2010).

42. See Savelsberg, "Knowledge"; and James Whitman, *Harsh Justice: Criminal Punishment and the Widening Gap between America and Europe* (New York: Oxford University Press, 2003), 199–201.

43. Lieberman, *Shifting the Color Line;* Katznelson, *Affirmative Action.*

44. For cross-national evidence about American inequality, see Seymour Lipset, "American Exceptionalism Reaffirmed," in Byron Shafer, ed., *Is America Different? A New Look at American Exceptionalism* (New York: Oxford University Press, 1991), 1–45 at 43; Kingdon, *America the Unusual;* Timothy Smeeding, "Public Policy, Economic Inequality and Poverty: The United States in Comparative Perspective," *Social Science Quarterly* 86 (2005): 955–984; and Jonas Pontusson, *Inequality and Prosperity: Social Europe v Liberal America* (Ithaca, NY: Cornell University Press, 2005).

45. Kingdon, *America the Unusual,* 17.

46. William J. Wilson, *The Truly Disadvantaged: The Inner City, the Underclass, and Public Policy* (Chicago: University of Chicago Press, 1990); Loic Wacquant, *Punishing the Poor: The Neoliberal Government of Social Insecurity* (Durham, NC: Duke University Press, 2009).

47. On relations between the early Republic and Native Americans, see Frederick Hoxie, ed., *Native Americans and the Early Republic* (Charlottesville: University of Virginia Press, 1999).

48. On free blacks and their rights after the founding, see Keysarr, *The Right to Vote.*

49. On population heterogeneity as a cause of punitiveness, see Pitrim Sorokin, *Social and Cultural Dynamics* (New Brunswick, NJ: Transaction Books, 1985). For data suggesting that demographic heterogeneity correlates with murder rates, see Henry Hannsman and John Quigley, "Population Heterogeneity and the Sociogenesis of Homicide," *Social Forces* 61 (1982): 206–225.

50. Andrew Hacker, *Two Nations: Black and White, Separate, Hostile, Unequal* (New York: Scribner, 2003).

51. Ibid.

52. Kenneth Stampp, *The Peculiar Institution: Slavery in the Ante-Bellum South* (New York: Vintage Books, 1956), 426.

53. Ian Haney Lopez, "Post-Racial Racism: Policing Race in the Age of Obama," *California Law Review* (Fall 2009) at 112, argues that the American state has come to be seen by some as a "racial state" dominated by African American interests and personnel. On the role of race in limiting working-class solidarity and welfare programs in the United States, see Quadagno, *The Color of Welfare;* Ira Katznelson, "Working Class Formation: Constructing Cases and Comparisons," in Ira Katznelson and Aristide Zolberg, eds., *Working Class Formation* (San Francisco, CA: Jossey-Bass, 1986); and Martin Gilens, *Why Americans Hate Welfare* (Chicago: University of Chicago Press, 2000). For a comparative study, see Alberto Alesina and Edward Glaeser, *Fighting Poverty in the US and Europe* (New York: Oxford University Press, 2004).

54. Gilens, *Why Americans Hate Welfare;* Mark Peffley and Jon Hurwitz, "The Racial Components of 'Race-Neutral' Crime Policy Attitudes," *Political Psychology* 23, 1 (2002): 59–75; Amanda Abraham, "Racial Attitudes and the Structural Determinants of White Americans' Support for Crime Policy," paper presented at the annual meeting of the American Sociological Association, Philadelphia, August 2005.

55. Katherine Beckett and Bruce Western, "Governing Social Marginality," in David Garland, ed., *Mass Imprisonment* (London: Sage, 2001), 35–50; Vanessa Barker, *The Politics of Imprisonment* (New York: Oxford University Press, 2009); David Greenberg and Valerie West, "Siting the Death Penalty Internationally," *Law & Social Inquiry* 33 (2008): 295–343.

56. Randolph Roth, *American Homicide* (Cambridge, MA: Harvard University Press, 2009), 384; Pieter Spierenburg, "Masculinity, Violence and Honor: An Introduction," in Pieter Spierenburg, ed., *Men and Violence* (Columbus: Ohio University Press, 1998), 25. America's violence rates—as measured by homicide statistics—are high compared with those of the other Western liberal democracies. For details and data, see Richard Brown, *Strains of Violence: Historical Studies of American Violence and Vigilantism* (New York: Oxford University Press, 1975); Ted Gurr, *Violence in America*, vol. 2 (Newbury Park, CA: Sage, 1989); Leonard Beeghley, *Homicide: A Sociological Explanation* (Lanham, MD: Rowman and Littlefield, 2003); and Ira Leonard and Christopher Leonard, "The Historiography of American Violence," *Homicide Studies* 7 (2003): 99–153.

57. Spierenburg writes: "Local elites and, increasingly, common people, equated democracy with the right of armed protection of their own property and interests." Pieter Spierenburg, "Democracy Came Too Early: A Tentative Explanation for the Problem of American Homicide," *American Historical Review* 114 (2006): 104–114, at 109–110. For the spread of gun culture and the rise in homicide rates in the United States after the mass production of handguns began in the 1840s, see Roger Lane, *Murder in America: A History* (Columbus: Ohio State University Press, 1997), 344.

58. John Phillip Reid, *Policing the Elephant: Crime, Punishment and Social Behavior on the Overland Trail* (San Marino, CA: Huntington Library Press, 1996); Michael Pfeifer, *Rough Justice: Lynching and American Society, 1874–1947* (Urbana: University of Illinois Press, 2004); Brown, *Strains of Violence*; Edward Ayers, *Vengeance and Justice: Crime and Punishment in the 19th Century American South* (New York: Oxford University Press, 1984); Spierenburg, "Democracy Came Too Early," 111. Spierenburg notes, "In an unpacified society, these excuses had a measure of reality."

59. Mennell, *The American Civilizing Process* (154), and and Wendy Kaminer, *It's All the Rage: Crime and Culture* (New York: Addison Wesley, 1995) (63–64), suggest that this Southern culture of violence may have been transmitted, first to the blacks who were subjected to it, and then to the Northern cities to which Southern blacks subsequently migrated.

60. Spierenburg, "Democracy Came Too Early," 111; Garland, "Penal Excess"; W. Fitzhugh Brundage, *Lynching in the New South: Georgia and Virginia, 1880–1930* (Urbana: University of Illinois Press, 1993); Brown, *Strains of Violence*.

61. On the army, see Mennell, *American Civilizing Process;* on police, see Lane, *Murder in America;* Walker, *Popular Justice;* and Monkkonen, "Homicide."

62. Roth, *American Homicide;* Mennell, *American Civilizing Process,* 134; Beeghley, *Homicide,* 49; and Franklin Zimring and Gordon Hawkins, *Crime*

Is Not the Problem: Lethal Violence in America (New York: Oxford University Press, 1997), 52.

63. The first quote is from Leonard and Leonard, "The Historiography of American Violence," 99; the second is from Monkkonen, "Homicide," 82; and the third is from Douglas Eckberg, "Estimates of Early Twentieth Century U.S. Homicide Rates," *Demography* 32 (1995): 14. Roth, *American Homicide,* argues that the differential between the United States and the rest of the Western world is more recent, having opened up in the mid-nineteenth century, as a result of the relative failure of state building in the former.

64. Mennell, *American Civilizing Process,* 123: "the *trends* in the long-term graph of violence have been similar in the USA and other Western nations, but actual *rates* of at least some forms of violent crime have tended to be higher in America."

65. Roth, *American Homicide,* 384; Mennell, *American Civilizing Process.*

66. Beeghley, *Homicide,* 49. The rate for England and Wales was 0.9.

67. Ibid., p. 49.

68. Charles Tilly, *Coercion, Capital and European States, AD 990–1992* (Cambridge, England: Blackwell, 1992), 69. At present, there are an estimated 250 million firearms in circulation in the United States, with 40 percent of American households having a firearm in the home. See Toni Locy, "States with High Crime See More Guns Stolen," *USA Today,* December 18, 2002, A3.

69. Roth, *American Homicide,* 418; Beeghley, *Homicide,* 66; Keith Harries and Derral Cheatwood, *The Geography of Execution: The Capital Punishment Quagmire in America* (Lanham, MD: Rowman and Littlefield, 1997), 61.

70. Cas Wouters, "Etiquette Books and Emotion Management in the Twentieth Century: American Habitus in International Comparison," Peter Stearns and Jan Lewis, eds., *An Emotional History of the United States* (New York: New York University Press, 1998,) 283–304. See also Richard Slotkin, *Regeneration through Violence: The Mythology of the American Frontier, 1600–1860* (Norman: University of Oklahoma Press, 1973).

71. Wouters, "Etiquette Books and Emotion Management," 300.

72. See Lipset, *Continental Divide,* 26: "the American creed can be subsumed in four words: anti-statism, individualism, populism and egalitarianism." Six years later, the same author had a different version: "The American Creed can be described in five terms: liberty, egalitarianism, individualism, populism, and laissez-faire." Lipset, *American Exceptionalism,* 19. Samuel Huntington, *American Politics* (Cambridge, MA: Harvard University Press, 1981), describes the "American Creed" as including constitutionalism, liberalism, democracy, and egalitarianism (14). McCloskey and Zaller say, "Two major traditions of belief, capitalism and democracy, have dominated the life of the American nation from its inception" (quoted in Kingdon, *America the Unusual,* 25). See also Vann Woodward, "Over the centuries, American character has probably presented to the world as . . . a variety of conflicting images . . . puritanic and hedonistic, idealistic and materialistic, peaceful and war-like, conformist and individualistic, consensus-minded and conflict-prone." Vann

Woodward, "Race Prejudice Is Itself a Form of Violence," *New York Times Magazine,* April 28, 1968, 114.

73. See Walt Whitman's *Song of Myself,* section 51.

74. See Lipset, *Continental Divide,* 30; and Byron Schafer, ed., *Is America Different? A New Look at American Exceptionalism* (New York: Oxford University Press, 2001), x and 234.

75. Lipset points out that these populist, egalitarian values were reinforced by America's congregational Protestant sects and the absence of an established church. Lipset, *Continental Divide,* 75.

76. Savelsberg, "Knowledge," 913; Crevecoeur quoted in Seymour Lipset, "American Exceptionalism Reaffirmed," 4.

77. William Langewiesche, "Towers of Strength," *New York Times,* December 26, 2009, WK12. Pildes talks of America's "hyperdemocratic culture and history." Pildes, "Constitutionalization," 82. See also James Marone, *Hellfire Nation: The Politics of Sin in American History* (New Haven, CT: Yale University Press, 2003), 1. As Kingdon notes, the Founders were more skeptical of the idea of direct popular control: only the House was directly representative. Kingdon, *America the Unusual,* 28. On the rather different relationship of European politicians to public opinion, see Raymond Forni and John Townend, "Two Views of Capital Punishment," *Europe* 40 (2000): 14 and 15.

78. Mennell, *American Civilizing Process;* Richard Hofstadter, *Anti-Intellectualism in American Life* (New York: Vintage, 1966).

79. Kingdon, *America the Unusual,* 64; Andrew Moravcsik, "The Paradox of U.S. Human Rights Policy," in Michael Ignatieff, ed., *American Exceptionalism and Human Rights* (Princeton, NJ: Princeton University Press, 2005), 160; Lipset, "American Exceptionalism Reaffirmed," 8.

80. Vermont citizens protested when federal authorities brought capital prosecutions in their state, which had long been abolitionist. See Katie Zezima, "US Case Draws Vermont into Debate on Death Penalty," *New York Times,* May 29, 2005.

81. Kingdon, *America the Unusual,* 66; David Barron, "Reclaiming Home Rule," 116 *Harvard Law Review* 2255 (2003); Nathan Newman and J. J. Gass, "A New Birth of Freedom: The Forgotten History of the 13th, 14th and 15th Amendments" (New York: Brennan Center for Justice, NYU Law, 2004), 8. Today, death penalty supporters have little to fear from national government intrusion, since strong majorities in the U.S. Congress and on the Supreme Court are supportive of capital punishment.

82. Hartz, quoted in Lipset, "American Exceptionalism Reaffirmed," 7; Franklin Zimring, *The Contradictions of American Capital Punishment* (New York: Oxford University Press, 2003); Einhorn, *Taxation, Slavery;* Garry Wills, *A Necessary Evil: A History of American Mistrust of Government* (New York: Simon & Schuster, 1999), 17; Zelizer, "The Uneasy Relationship," 281–282.

83. Zimring, *The Contradictions of American Capital Punishment.*

84. See Steven Lukes, *Individualism* (New York: Harper & Row, 1973), for a discussion of the different meanings of "individualism." These include (i) the dig-

nity of man—the supreme and intrinsic value, or dignity, of the individual human being; (ii) autonomy or self-direction; (iii) privacy—the right to a sphere
of private existence within a public world; (iv) self-development—the cultivation of individuality and uniqueness. Individualism may also refer to the thesis
that individuals are (or ought to be) the atomic basis of society, which is
viewed as the outcome of individual wills.

85. Quoted in Ibid. See also Walter McDougall, *Freedom Just Around the Corner:
A New American History* (New York: Harper Collins, 2004).
86. Lipset, *Continental Divide,* 170.
87. Marone, *Hellfire Nation,* 22; Lipset, "American Exceptionalism Reaffirmed,"
20.
88. Marone, *Hellfire Nation,* 3; Lipset, "American Exceptionalism Reaffirmed,"
19.
89. As Tocqueville wrote: "Religion never intervened directly in the government
of American society," but it "should be considered the first of their political
institutions" (quoted in Marone, *Hellfire Nation,* 4).
90. Antonin Scalia, "God's Justice and Ours," *First Things* 123 (2002): 20.
91. Ibid., 19. See also Whitman, *Harsh Justice,* 217, n56. Justice Scalia's views are
not necessarily shared by his Catholic coreligionists: Vatican officials recently
described the death penalty as "not just a negation of the right to life, but also
an affront to human dignity." Quoted in Hood and Hoyle, *The Death Penalty,*
65, n102.
92. Wills, *A Necessary Evil,* 169.
93. Marone, *Hellfire Nation,* 4; Lipset, *Continental Divide,* 77.
94. David Garland, "Criminology, Crime Control, and 'The American Difference,'" *University of Colorado Law Review* 69 (1998): 1–23.
95. A version of this conflict gets played out in Southern capital cases when Ivy
League–trained, *pro bono* capital defense lawyers from silk-stocking firms in
Northern cities show up to do battle with local prosecutors.
96. Pfeifer, *Rough Justice.*
97. Kaminer, *All the Rage,* 17.
98. Marone, *Hellfire Nation,* Conclusion.

7. Capital Punishment in America

1. Herbert Haines, *Against Capital Punishment: The Anti-Death Penalty Move-
ment in America, 1872–1994* (New York: Oxford University Press, 1996);
Louis Filler, "Movements to Abolish the Death Penalty in the United States,"
Annals, AAPSS 284 (1952): 124–136; David Brion Davis, "The Movement to
Abolish Capital Punishment in America, 1787–1861," *American Historical
Review* 63 (October 1957): 23–46; Elizabeth Clark, "Sacred Rights of the
Weak: Pain, Sympathy, and the Culture of Individual Rights in Antebellum
America," *Journal of American History* 82 (1995): 463–493.
2. The New Deal might appear to be an exception, since the twentieth century's
highest yearly total of executions (199) occurred in 1935 and there were no
state abolitions during the 1930s. But it would seem more appropriate to asso-

ciate the reform hiatus and record execution numbers of these years with the Great Depression, and to note that, after 1935, the annual number of executions trended downward.

3. See Roger Hood and Carolyn Holye, *The Death Penalty: A Worldwide Perspective* (Oxford, England: Oxford University Press, 2008); Franklin Zimring, *The Contradictions of American Capital Punishment* (New York: Oxford University Press, 2003); and Andrew Moravcsik, "The New Abolitionism: Why Does the U.S. Practice the Death Penalty While Europe Does Not?" *European Studies* (September 2001).

4. Robert Badinter, *Abolition: One Man's Battle against the Death Penalty* (Boston, MA: Northeastern University Press, 2008).

5. Hood and Hoyle, *Death Penalty*; Zimring, *Contradictions*.

6. We can imagine scenarios whereby this constitutional limitation might be circumvented, but as a political matter, they are mostly implausible. Theoretically, Congress might declare that the death penalty infringes on the equal protection clause of the Fourteenth Amendment and use the powers granted by Section 5 of that amendment to abolish capital punishment throughout the nation. Or the president, with the Senate's advice and consent, could bring about a nationwide end to the death penalty using the treaty-making powers granted by the Constitution. Or Congress might do so by threatening to withdraw federal subsidies to death penalty states. But such measures are inconceivable without a supermajority of senators and representatives supporting abolition. And such support is unlikely so long as a majority of American voters and state legislatures wish to retain capital punishment.

7. Elizabeth Bazan, *Capital Punishment: An Overview of Federal Death Penalty Statutes* (Washington, DC: Congressional Research Service, Library of Congress, 2005).

8. Joachim Savelsberg, "Knowledge, Domination, and Criminal Punishment," *American Journal of Sociology* 99 (1994): 911–943; Zimring, *Contradictions*.

9. Lieberman demonstrates these points with respect to American welfare policy. Robert Lieberman, *Shifting the Color Line: Race and the American Welfare State* (Cambridge, MA: Harvard University Press, 1998). Carol Steiker and Jordan Steiker, "A Tale of Two Nations: Implementation of the Death Penalty in 'Executing' versus 'Symbolic' States in the United States," *Texas Law Review* 84 (2005–2006): 1914.

10. Stuart Banner, *The Death Penalty: An American History* (Cambridge, MA: Harvard University Press, 2002).

11. Michael Meranze, "Penality and the Colonial Project: Crime, Punishment and the Regulation of Morals in Early America," in Christopher Tomlins and Michael Grossberg, eds., *The Cambridge History of Law in America* (New York: Cambridge University Press, 2008).

12. Zimring, *Contradictions*.

13. Hugo Bedau, quoted in Lee Epstein and Joseph Koblyka, *The Supreme Court and Legal Change: Abortion and the Death Penalty* (Chapel Hill: University of North Carolina Press, 1992), 330, n12. Bedau refers to white Americans. Collective memories of murderous Southern lynch mobs and law officers who

assisted them likely explain why African Americans are less supportive of the death penalty than are white Americans.

14. Philip Dray, *At the Hands of Persons Unknown: The Lynching of Black America* (New York: Random House, 2002).

15. See Chapter 9 below.

16. Christopher Mooney and Mei-Hsein Lee, "Morality Policy Reinvention: State Death Penalties," *Annals, AAPSS* 566 (1999): 80–92.

17. Savelsberg argues that the U.S. media are more market-driven and less public than European equivalents, and thus more prone to sensationalism. Savelsberg, "Knowledge."

18. For data, see Randolph Roth, *American Homicide* (Cambridge, MA: Harvard University Press, 2009).

19. Charles Tilly, *Coercion, Capital and the European States, AD 990–1992* (New York: Wiley, 1992).

20. Denis Duclos, *The Werewolf Complex: America's Fascination with Violence* (New York: Berg, 1998); Roger Lane, *Murder in America: A History* (Columbus: Ohio State University Press, 1997); Carol Stearns and Peter Stearns, *Anger: The Struggle for Emotional Control in America's History* (Chicago: University of Chicago Press, 1986); Roth, *American Homicide*.

21. Michael Pfeifer, *Rough Justice: Lynching and American Society, 1874–1947* (Urbana: University of Illinois Press, 2004).

22. Zimring, *Contradictions;* Eric Baumer, Steven Messner, and Richard Rosenfeld, "Explaining Spatial Variation in Support for Capital Punishment: A Multilevel Analysis," *American Journal of Sociology* 108, 4 (2003): 844–875.

23. Elizabeth Clark, "The Sacred Rights of the Weak: Pain, Sympathy and the Culture of Individual Rights in Antebellum America," *Journal of American History* 82, 2 (1995): 463–493; David Oshinsky, *"Worse Than Slavery": Parchman Farm and the Ordeal of Jim Crow* (New York: Free Press, 1996); Mark Colvin, *Penitentiaries, Reformatories and Chain Gangs* (New York: St. Martin's Press, 1997); Michael Hindus, *Prison and Plantation: Crime, Justice and Authority in Massachusetts and South Carolina, 1767–1878* (Chapel Hill: University of North Carolina Press, 1980); Edward Ayers, *Vengeance and Justice: Crime and Punishment in the 19th Century American South* (New York: Oxford University Press, 1984).

24. Baumer et al., "Explaining Spatial Variation."

25. Drehle writes: "This is the way a good death penalty lawyer works. Run all the traps, fight every issue, hit every court. Go to the state supreme court, to the federal district court, the federal appeals court, the Supreme Court of the United States. Fight an issue on broad terms, and if you lose, fight it again on narrow terms. Turn every stone, poke into every mushy spot in the law. Read every opinion rendered by every court, and when some other death row inmate wins his case, shoehorn his issue into your own client's appeal. Make the law do what it promises. Make it be perfect." David Don Drehle, *Among the Lowest of the Dead: The Culture of Capital Punishment* (Ann Arbor: University of Michigan Press, 2006), 196.

26. For examples from France, see Badinter, *Abolition* (Boston: Northeastern Uni-

versity Press, 2008); from Britain, see Terence Morris, *Crime and Criminal Justice since 1945* (Oxford, England: Blackwell, 1989); and from the Netherlands, see Ian Baruma, *Murder in Amsterdam: Liberal Europe, Islam, and the Limits of Tolerance* (New York: Penguin, 2007).

27. See Chapter 10.

28. Steiker and Steiker, "Tale of Two Nations," 1914.

29. Federalism, as such, has no necessary consequence for death penalty politics. In Germany, for example, far from being a mark of local autonomy, the death penalty became a symbol of national unification (uniform law and administration being crucial ingredients of a proper nation state), and the power to kill was lodged in the national government. Richard Evans, *Rituals of Retribution* (New York: Oxford University Press, 1996). It is the radical democratic localism so prominent in the American polity that is most consequential.

30. Margaret Vandiver, *Lethal Punishment: Lynchings and Legal Executions in the South* (New Brunswick, NJ: Rutgers University Press, 2006), 162; Banner, *The Death Penalty*.

31. William Lofquist, "Putting Them There, Keeping Them There, and Killing Them: An Analysis of State-Level Variations in Death Penalty Intensity," *Iowa Law Review* 87 (2001–2002): 1539. On "path dependency" see Rudolf Klein and Theodode Marmor, "Reflections on Policy Analysis," *Oxford Handbook of Public Policy* (New York: Oxford University Press, 2006), 900.

32. John Galliher et al., *America Without the Death Penalty: States Leading the Way* (Boston, MA: Northeastern University Press, 2002), 12.

33. Banner, *The Death Penalty*, 134.

34. In 2007 Michigan's murder rate was 6.7 per 100,000. The U.S. national average was 5.6.

35. Galliher, *America Without the Death Penalty*, 25.

36. Ibid., 33–51.

37. Ibid., chapters 7, 8, and 11. Averil Lerman, "Capital Punishment in Territorial Alaska," *Frame of Reference*, Alaska Humanities Forum 9, 1 (1998), writes that prior to abolition in 1957, the death penalty had, in practice, been reserved for minority offenders—chiefly Alaskan natives and African Americans. When the territorial legislature abolished its death penalty in 1957, concern about race discrimination was a motivating factor. In Washington, DC, a 1992 referendum proposing to reintroduce capital punishment was rejected by 68 percent of DC voters, a majority of whom were African Americans. In the period prior to *Furman*, 80 of the 118 prisoners executed had been black.

38. See Chapter 9.

39. V. O. Keys, *Southern Politics in State and Nation* (New York: Knopf, 1949); Edwin Amenta, *Bold Relief: Institutional Politics and the Origins of Modern American Social Policy* (Princeton, NJ: Princeton University Press, 1998).

40. Samuel Walker, *Popular Justice: A History of American Criminal Justice* (New York: Oxford University Press, 1998), 23.

41. Hindus, *Prison and Plantation*; Colvin, *Penitentiaries*; Oshinsky, *Parchman Farm*.

42. Bruce Western, *Punishment and Inequality in America* (New York: Russell Sage Foundation, 2006), 58.

43. Larry Yackle, "Capital Punishment, Federal Courts, and the Writ of Habeas Corpus," in Stephen Garvey, ed., *Beyond Repair: America's Death Penalty* (Durham, NC: Duke University Press, 2003), 58–93, at 70.

44. William Stuntz, "Unequal Justice," 121 *Harvard Law Review* (June 2008).

45. Keys, *Southern Politics;* Amenta, *Bold Relief;* Lieberman, *Shifting the Color Line.*

46. Baumer et al., "Explaining Spatial Variation," 849.

47. Carol Steiker, "Capital Punishment and American Exceptionalism," *Oregon Law Review* 81 (2002): 97–130, at 125.

48. James Liebman, "The Overproduction of Death," *Columbia Law Review* 100 (2000): 2074.

49. Leonard Beeghley, *Homicide: A Sociological Explanation* (Lanham, MD: Rowman and Littlefield, 2003), 66.

50. Baumer et al., "Explaining Spatial Variation"; Borg, quoted in Steiker, "American Exceptionalism."

51. An association between Southern fundamentalism and popular support for the death penalty has been observed by several sociological studies. See Steiker, "American Exceptionalism," which cites a number of sources. The Southern Baptist Convention originally broke with national Baptist organizations over the issue of slavery and was for much of the twentieth century associated with segregationist sentiment. In 1995, the convention publicly renounced its racist roots and apologized for its past defense of slavery.

52. David Greenberg and Valerie West, "Siting the Death Penalty Internationally," *Law & Social Inquiry* 33 (2008): 295–343. Bedau points out that several of America's evangelical, Pentecostal, and fundamentalist Protestant denominations have also supported capital punishment. Hugo Bedau, *The Death Penalty in America: Current Controversies* (New York: Oxford University Press, 1997).

53. David Jacobs and Jason Carmichael, "The Political Sociology of the Death Penalty: A Pooled Time-Series Analysis," *American Sociological Review* 67 (2002): 109–31.

54. Ibid., 126.

55. Soss, Langbein, and Metelko note: "For white people living in an all-white county, racial prejudice emerges as the strongest predictor of white death penalty support in our analysis. For their counterparts in more integrated counties, this effect is more than doubled." Joe Soss, Laura Langbein, Alan Metelko, "Why Do White Americans Support the Death Penalty?" *Journal of Politics* 65 (2003): 416.

56. Lofquist, "Putting Them There," 1532, citing data from Raymond Michalowski and Michael Pearson, "Punishment and Social Structure at the State Level: A Cross-Sectional Comparison of 1970 and 1980," *Journal of Research in Crime and Delinquency* 7 (1990): 52–75. On the inverse relation of welfare and punishment more generally, see Katherine Beckett and Bruce Western, "Governing Social Marginality," in David Garland, ed., *Mass Imprisonment* (London: Sage, 2001).

57. The laws and procedures contained in capital statutes vary from state to state. See Keith Harries and Derral Cheatwood, *The Geography of Execution: The Capital Punishment Quagmire in America* (Lanham, MD: Rowman and Littlefield, 1997), 13. The most salient difference is that some statutes set out a capital offense and then require the addition of an aggravating factor before a death penalty can be imposed, while others specify the capital offense itself in a manner that already includes aggravation.

58. Steiker and Steiker, "Tale of Two Nations"; Lofquist, "Putting Them There"; John Culver, "Capital Punishment Politics and Policies in the States, 1977–1997," *Crime, Law and Social Change* 32 (2000): 287–300. As Vandiver reminds us, the *county* is the locus for death penalty indictments, trials, and sentences, while death penalty laws and executions occur at the *state* level. Different counties within the same state can vary widely in the frequency with which they pursue and impose death sentences. Vandiver, *Lethal Punishment*, 4.

59. Thomas Laqueur, "Festivals of Punishment," *London Review of Books,* October 5, 2000, 19.

60. Savelsberg notes that there is a close correlation between rates of execution and trends in public opinion. Joachim Savelsberg, "Punitiveness in Cross-National Comparison: Toward a Historically and Institutionally Founded Multi-Factorial Approach," in Helmut Kury and Theodore N. Ferdinand, eds., *International Perspectives on Punitivity* (Bochum, Germany: Brockmeyer, 2008), 13–31.

61. David Jacobs and Jason Carmichael, "Ideology, Social Threat, and the Death Sentence: Capital Sentences across Time and Space," *Social Forces* 83 (2004): 249–278.

62. Harries and Cheatwood, *Geography of Execution,* 34.

63. Lofquist, "Putting Them There," 1548. See also Tony Poveda, "American Exceptionalism and the Death Penalty," *Social Justice* 27 (2000): 261.

64. Steiker and Steiker, "Tale of Two Nations," 1915–1916. See also Michael Klarman, *From Jim Crow to Civil Rights: The Supreme Court and the Struggle for Racial Equality* (New York: Oxford University Press, 2004).

65. Leigh Bienen, "Not Wiser After 35 Years of Contemplating the Death Penalty," *Corrections and Sentencing Law and Policy* 3 (2007).

66. Culver, "Capital Punishment Politics and Policies," 287. For more on variation between death penalty states, see Lofquist, "Putting Them There"; Bienen, "Not Wiser"; Stephen Bright, "Counsel for the Poor: The Death Penalty Not for the Worst Crime but for the Worst Lawyer," *Yale Law Journal* 103 (1994): 1835–1866; Stephen Bright, "The Politics of Crime and the Death Penalty: Not 'Soft on Crime' but Hard on the Bill of Rights," *St. Louis University Law Journal* 39 (1995): 479–498; and Stephen Bright and Patrick Keenan, "Judges and the Politics of Death: Deciding Between the Bill of Rights and the Next Election in Capital Cases," *Boston University Law Review* 75 (1995): 759–813.

67. Steiker and Steiker, "Tale of Two Nations," 1911–1912.

68. See the comments made by Senator DeFrancisco during the New York Senate debate on capital punishment in 1995: "unless there were procedural safeguards, I couldn't support this bill, and I believe there are ample procedural

safeguards" (New York State Senate debate, March 6, 1995, p. 1946). Lofquist notes that few executions occur in states that "make larger investments
in capital defense, generally as part of a compromise with anti–death penalty
legislators or as a concession to judicially-imposed higher standards." Lofquist, "Putting Them There," 1542.

69. Adam Liptak, "At 60% of Total, Texas Is Bucking Execution Trend," *New
York Times,* December 26, 2007, A22.

8. An American Abolition

1. On the Supreme Court's relation to public opinion and political forces, see
Mark Tushnet, "Is Judicial Review Good for the Left?" *Dissent* (Winter
1998): 65–70; and Barry Friedman, *The Will of the People: How Public Opinion Has Influenced the Supreme Court and Shaped the Meaning of the Constitution* (New York: Farrar, Strauss and Girard, 2009).

2. One indicator is the increased number of capital cases it now hears. Liebman
notes that the Court issued two capital case decisions between 1937 and 1967.
Between 1972 and 2006 it issued at least 209. James Liebman, "Slow Dancing
With Death: The Supreme Court and Capital Punishment, 1963–2006," *Columbia Law Review* 107 (2007): 14.

3. On Northern racism in the 1940s and 1950s, see Thomas Sugrue, *The Origins
of the Urban Crisis: Race and Inequality in Postwar Detroit* (Princeton, NJ:
Princeton University Press, 2005); and Thomas Sugrue, *Sweet Land of Liberty: The Forgotten Struggle for Civil Rights in the North* (New York: Random House, 2008).

4. Tali Mendelberg, *The Race Card: Campaign Strategy, Implicit Messages, and
the Norm of Equality* (Princeton, NJ: Princeton University Press, 2001);
Brown v Board of Education 347 U.S. 483 (1954); Jeremy Rabkin, "The
Supreme Court in the Culture Wars," *Public Interest* 125 (1996): 8–9. On
George Wallace and the "politics of rage" see Dan Carter, *The Politics of
Rage: George Wallace, the Origins of the New Conservatism, and the Trans-
formation of American Politics* (New York: Simon and Schuster, 1995).

5. According to Toobin the Court moved to the left in the 2000s because Justices Breyer and Kennedy grew more international in orientation, a development that had consequences for their death penalty jurisprudence. In *Knight v
Florida* (1999) and in *Roper v Simmons* (2005) these two justices introduced a
discussion of European and foreign law into their opinions about American
capital punishment, each time pushing the Court in a more abolitionist direction. Jeffrey Toobin, *The Nine: Inside the Secret World of the Supreme Court*
(New York: Doubleday, 2007).

6. If the Court's push for death penalty abolition in *Furman* was part of the expansion of the regulatory powers of national government, the return to the
death penalty was part of the effort to reduce the power of the federal government and reallocate power to the states. President Nixon's "New Federalism"
was intended to limit the power of national government in this way. Justice
William Rehnquist, Nixon's first appointee to the Supreme Court and a for-

mer assistant attorney general in the Nixon administration, was a forceful advocate of this position. See Rick Perlstein, *Nixonland: The Rise of a President and the Fracturing of America* (New York: Scribner, 2008).

7. David Garland, *The Culture of Control: Crime and Social Order in Contemporary Society* (Chicago: University of Chicago Press, 2001); Jonathan Simon, *Governing Through Crime* (New York: Oxford University Press, 2007); Frank Baumgartner, Suzanna De Boef, and Amber Boydstun, *The Decline of the Death Penalty and the Discovery of Innocence* (New York: Cambridge University Press, 2008).

8. Mary Dudziak, *Cold War Civil Rights: Race and the Image of American Democracy* (Princeton, NJ: Princeton University Press, 2000).

9. Desmond King, *Separate and Unequal: Black Americans and the U.S. Federal Government* (Oxford, England: Oxford University Press, 1995).

10. Robert Lieberman, *Shifting the Color Line: Race and the American Welfare State* (Cambridge, MA: Harvard University Press, 1998), 3.

11. In 1930, the murder rate was 8.2 per 100,000. In 1935, its high point, it was 9.6. By 1962 and 1963 that rate had fallen by 50 percent to a new low of 4.6 per 100,000 in both years (with a total of 8,530 in 1962 and 8,640 in 1963). James Alan Fox and Marianne W. Zawitz, *Homicide Trends in the United States* (Washington, DC: Bureau of Justice Statistics, 2007), available at http://bjs.ojp.usdoj.gov/content/pub/pdf/htius.pdf (accessed January 26, 2010).

12. Thomas Edsall and Mary Edsall, *Chain Reaction: The Impact of Race, Rights and Taxes on American Politics* (New York: Norton, 1992), 46; Perlstein, *Nixonland,* 1; Lee Epstein and Joseph Koblyka, *The Supreme Court and Legal Change: Abortion and the Death Penalty* (Chapel Hill: University of North Carolina Press, 1992), 46.

13. David Oshinsky, *Capital Punishment on Trial: "Furman v Georgia" and the Death Penalty in Modern America* (Lawrence, KS: University of Kansas Press, 2010), chapter 2; Stuart Banner, *The Death Penalty: An American History* (Cambridge, MA: Harvard University Press, 2002), 224.

14. Thorsten Sellin, *The Death Penalty: A Report for the Model Penal Code Project* (Philadelphia, PA: American Law Institute, 1959); Banner, *The Death Penalty.*

15. Quoted in James Megivern, *The Death Penalty: An Historical and Theological Survey* (New York: Paulist Press, 1997), 323.

16. Banner, *The Death Penalty,* 241. Southern Baptists opposed this movement. The Assembly of Baptist Church representatives rejected an abolitionist proposal at the annual Southern Baptist Convention meeting in 1964. Tom Strode, "Baptists Support Capital Punishment, Adopt 6 Resolutions in Morning Session," *Baptist Press,* June 24, 2000, http://www.bpnews.net/bpnews.asp?ld=6002 (accessed April 26, 2010).

17. Megivern, *The Death Penalty,* 333. This wording echoed Pope John XXIII's encyclical *Pacem in Terris* of 1963.

18. Banner, *The Death Penalty,* 240–241. Epstein and Kobylka, *Abortion and the Death Penalty,* 58. The legislature declined to act on the attorney general's proposal.

19. U.S. House of Representatives, *Capital Punishment: Hearings Before Subcommittee 3 of the Committee on the Judiciary* (Washington, DC: U.S. Government Printing Office, 1971).
20. Banner, *The Death Penalty,* 244; William Bowers, *Legal Homicide: Death as a Punishment in America, 1864–1982* (Boston: Northeastern University Press, 1984), 9. The territories of Alaska and Hawaii had abolished in 1957; Delaware abolished in 1958, only to bring back capital punishment in 1961. New Mexico's legislature abolished the death penalty in 1969.
21. Banner, *The Death Penalty,* 246–247. On the development of *habeas corpus* as a means to seek relief in the federal courts, see Larry Yackle, "Capital Punishment, Federal Courts, and the Writ of Habeas Corpus," in Stephen Garvey, ed., *Beyond Repair: America's Death Penalty* (Durham, NC: Duke University Press, 2003), 58–93.
22. Oshinsky, *Capital Punishment on Trial,* 17. The last person to be put to death before the 1967 moratorium was Luis Monge of Colorado, executed on June 2, 1967. No further executions occurred until that of Gary Gilmore in Utah on January 17, 1977. Joan Cheever, *Back from the Dead: One Woman's Search for the Men Who Walked off America's Death Row* (New York: Wiley, 2006).
23. Steven Teles, *Whose Welfare? AFDC and Elite Politics* (Topeka: University of Kansas Press, 1998), 117. See Michael Meltsner, *Cruel and Unusual: The Supreme Court and Capital Punishment* (New York: Random House, 1973), 25; Gerald Rosenberg, *The Hollow Hope: Can Courts Bring about Social Change?* (Chicago: University of Chicago Press, 1993).
24. Four years later, in 1969, New Mexico would make it fourteen.
25. Lieberman, *Shifting the Color Line.*
26. The Court had not always looked kindly on "liberal" or progressive causes. As Burns recounts, for a long period following its decision in *Lochner v New York* (1905), the Court struck down social legislation in the name of property rights and freedom of contract. James MacGregor Burns, *Packing the Court: The Rise of Judicial Power and the Coming Crisis of the Supreme Court* (New York: Penguin Press, 2009).
27. *Fay v Noia* 372 U.S. 391 (1963); *Rudolph v Alabama* 375 U.S. 889 (1963).
28. Michael Klarman, *From Jim Crow to Civil Rights: The Supreme Court and the Struggle for Racial Equality* (New York: Oxford University Press, 2004); Marie Gottschalk, *The Prison and the Gallows* (New York: Cambridge University Press, 2006), 206–210.
29. *Moore v Dempsey* 261 U.S. 86 (1923). See Klarman, *From Jim Crow to Civil Rights,* 120.
30. *Powell v Alabama* 287 U.S. 45 (1932); *Norris v Alabama* 294 U.S. 587 (1935); *Brown v Mississippi* 297 U.S. 278 (1936); Klarman, *From Jim Crow to Civil Rights,* 128; *Patton v Mississippi* 332 U.S. 463 (1947).
31. Klarman, *From Jim Crow to Civil Rights,* 117–118, 120.
32. Ibid., 118.
33. *Mapp v Ohio* 367 U.S. 643 (1961); *Brady v Maryland* 373 U.S. 83 (1963);

Gideon v Wainwright 372 U.S. 335 (1963); *Miranda v Arizona* 384 U.S. 436 (1966); and *Terry v Ohio* 392 U.S. 1 (1968).

34. Epstein and Kobylka note that members of the American Law Institute (ALI) and the legal academy had begun to question the death penalty's constitutionality earlier. In the late 1950s, an ALI advisory committee supported abolition, but the institute's council voted against taking any policy position. In 1961, Gerald Gottlieb published an article (which had previously been a memo to the ACLU) in the *Southern California Law Review* that suggested that capital punishment could be challenged on Eighth Amendment grounds. Around the same time, Walter Oberer, a University of Texas law professor, published an article in the *Texas Law Review,* arguing that the practice of death-qualifying juries provided a basis for constitutional challenge to capital punishment. Epstein and Kobylka, *Abortion and the Death Penalty,* 40–41.

35. *Francis v Resweber* 329 U.S. 459 (1947). In *Wilkerson v Utah* 99 U.S. 130 (1878), in which the Court affirmed that death by firing squad was not cruel and unusual, the Court opined that certain methods of execution—drawing and quartering, public dissecting, burning alive, or disemboweling—would be unconstitutional for any crime.

36. *Weems v United States* 217 U.S. 349 (1910); *Robinson v California* 370 US 660 (1962); *Trop v Dulles* 356 U.S. 86 (1958), at 101.

37. In *Fay v Noia* 372 U.S. 391 (1963), the Court enlarged the scope of federal *habeas corpus.*

38. The memo was published in 1986. See Justice Abraham Goldberg, "Memorandum to the Conference Re: Capital Punishment: October Term, 1963," *South Texas Law Review* 27 (1986): 493–506.

39. For details, see Meltsner, *Cruel and Unusual.*

40. The LDF was formally incorporated in 1940 with Thurgood Marshall as its first director and chief counsel. Later, in 1957, it became an independent organization under the title NAACP Legal Defense and Educational Fund Inc.

41. Kenneth Janken, *White: The Biography of Walter White, Mr. NAACP* (New York: New Press, 2003).

42. On the history of the LDF campaign and the cases, see Epstein and Kobylka, *Supreme Court and Legal Change;* Meltsner, *Cruel and Unusual;* Jack Greenberg, *Crusaders in the Courts: How a Dedicated Band of Lawyers Fought for the Civil Rights Revolution* (New York: Basic Books, 1994); Bernard Schwartz, *Super Chief: Earl Warren and His Supreme Court—A Judicial Biography* (New York: New York University Press, 1983); and Gottschalk, *Prison and Gallows,* 206–210.

43. Robert Burt, "Disorder in the Court: The Death Penalty and the Constitution," *Michigan Law Review* 85 (1987): 1795.

44. Oshinsky, *Capital Punishment on Trial,* 10. See also Jack Greenberg, "Capital Punishment as a System," *Yale Law Journal* 91 (1981–1982): 912.

45. According to Epstein and Kobylka, the LDF shifted its strategy in 1967. The subsequent litigation campaign was supported by a $1 million grant made by the Ford Foundation to improve the legal system's treatment of the poor. Ep-

stein and Kobylka, *Supreme Court and Legal Change,* 53. See also Meltsner, *Cruel and Unusual,* 109; and Greenberg, "Capital Punishment," 912. Anthony Amsterdam's recollection is that this shift in LDF strategy occurred earlier, in the fall of 1966 (personal communication).

46. The displacement phrase is from Thomas Laqueur, "Festivals of Punishment," *London Review of Books,* October 5, 2000, 17–24.

47. Meltsner, *Cruel and Unusual,* 107. On this, see also Bowers, *Legal Homicide,* 16; and Epstein and Kobylka, *Abortion and the Death Penalty.* Anthony Lewis wrote in the *New York Times:* "If the Court does reject those arguments [in *McGautha* and *Crampton*] and upholds the two death sentences before it, the immediate legal barrier to all the other executions will be removed. At least in theory, then, the United States will face the appalling prospect of what must seem a mass slaughter." Anthony Lewis, "Legal Nightmare," *New York Times,* March 22, 1971, 33.

48. Cheever says the number was 589. Cheever, *Back from the Dead.* Powell and the others assumed it was approximately 600. Of the 589, 2 were women; 505 had been convicted of murder, 80 of capital rape, and 4 of armed robbery.

49. The main LDF cases were *Witherspoon v Illinois* (1968); *Boykin v Alabama* 395 U.S. 238 (1969); *Maxwell v Bishop* (1970); *McGautha v California* 402 U.S. 183 (1971); *Crampton v Ohio* 402 U.S. 183 (1971); *Furman v Georgia* (1972); *Jackson v Georgia* (1972); *Branch v Texas* (1972); and *Aikens v California* (dismissed as moot in 1972). See Chapter 10 for more details.

50. Justice Brennan would make the same point in *Furman* when he noted that "the outstanding characteristic of punishing criminals by death is the infrequency with which we resort to it." *Furman* 408 US at 291.

51. Amsterdam, the *Furman* brief, quoted in Roger Schwed, *Abolition and Capital Punishment* (New York: AMS Press, 1983), 134.

52. J. Stewart in *Furman* 408 US at 309.

53. Liebman gives a description of the sentencing process before *Furman.* Liebman, "Slow Dancing With Death," 7. Sentencing discretion in noncapital cases would become a major focus of reform efforts from the mid 1970s onward: see Garland, *Culture of Control.*

54. The American Law Institute Model Penal Code—the codified reform proposals of the nation's legal elite—had earlier suggested that capital trials be bifurcated and that juries be advised on weighing mitigation and aggravation.

55. Transcript of Oral Argument in *Aikens v California* 406 U.S. 813 (1972), quoted in William Brennan, "Constitutional Adjudication and the Death Penalty: A View from the Court," 100 *Harvard Law Review* (December 1986): 313–331, at 322.

56. The Fifth Amendment (adopted in 1791) refers explicitly to capital punishment and impliedly recognizes its validity: "No person shall be held to answer for a capital or otherwise infamous crime, unless on a presentment or indictment of a Grand Jury . . . nor be deprived of life, liberty or property, without due process of law." The Fourteenth Amendment (adopted in 1868) obliges the states not to "deprive any person of life, liberty, or property without due process of law."

57. Burger, in *Furman* 408 U.S. at 381. In April 1972, the California Supreme Court in *People v Anderson* struck down the California law. Before that time, no American court had ever rendered a decision striking down the death penalty.

58. *Wilkerson v Utah* (1879); *In re Kemmler* (1889); and *Francis v Resweber* (1947).

59. Fred Graham, "Warren Defends Johnson's Naming of a Successor," *New York Times,* July 6, 1968, 42; Oshinsky, *Capital Punishment on Trial.*

60. As Earl Warren remarked in the *Maxwell* case conference in 1968, "Death seems to be reserved for the poor and the underprivileged. No person of any affluence is ever executed. Death falls unequally on the poor and the unpopular." Del Dickson, *The Supreme Court in Conference (1940–1985): The Private Discussions Behind Nearly 300 Supreme Court Decisions* (New York: Oxford University Press, 2001), 610.

61. See Banner, *The Death Penalty,* 239. At one time or another, Justices Jackson, Frankfurter, Goldberg, Warren, Brennan, Marshall, Blackmun, Powell, O'Connor, and Stevens have all expressed misgivings.

62. At the *Maxwell v Bishop* conference: see Dickson, *The Supreme Court in Conference.*

63. Blackmun in *Furman* 408 U.S. at 413; Burger in *Furman* 408 U.S. at 377. Rehnquist is reported to have remarked in conference, "As a legislator I would keep it." Dickson, *The Supreme Court in Conference,* 619.

64. William Brennan, "Constitutional Adjudication and the Death Penalty: A View from the Court," *Harvard Law Review* 100 (1986–1987): 313–331.

65. Dickson, *The Supreme Court in Conference.* See also Brennan, "Constitutional Adjudication and the Death Penalty."

66. Quoted in Epstein and Kobylka, *Abortion and the Death Penalty,* 70.

67. *People of the State of California v Anderson* 493 P.2d 880, 6 Cal. 3d 628 (Cal. 1972).

68. *Furman v Georgia,* per curiam.

69. *Furman v Georgia* 408 U.S. 238 (1972); Liebman, "Slow Dancing With Death"; Carol Steiker and Jordan Steiker, "The Seduction of Innocence: The Attraction and Limitations of the Focus on Innocence in Capital Punishment Law and Advocacy," *Journal of Criminal Law and Criminology* 95 (2005): 101–138.

70. *Furman v Georgia* 408 U.S. 238 (1972), at 310. Justice Douglas says much the same thing: "We cannot say from facts disclosed in these records that these defendants were sentenced to death because they were black. Yet . . ." *Furman v Georgia* 408 U.S. 238 (1972), at 254.

71. Douglas begins a paragraph with a reference to Furman's race: "Furman, a black, killed a householder." *Furman v Georgia* 408 U.S. 238 (1972), at 252.

72. *Furman v Georgia* 408 U.S. 238 (1972), at 242, 246.

73. *Furman v Georgia* 408 U.S. 238 (1972), at 312. In his dissent, C. J. Burger responded that this problem could be cured by increasing the use of the death penalty.

74. *Furman v Georgia* 408 U.S. 238 (1972), at 312.

75. *Furman v Georgia* 408 U.S. 238 (1972), at 299, 270. Brennan lists five indicia of evolving standards: "a world-wide trend toward disuse of the death penalty," scholarly literature turning against it, fewer executions in the last forty years, fewer death sentences, and increased public abhorrence (as reflected in the ending of public executions).

76. *Furman v Georgia* 408 U.S. 238 (1972), at 360, 315, 371.

77. *Furman v Georgia* 408 U.S. 238 (1972), at 375.

78. *Furman v Georgia* 408 U.S. 238 (1972), at 418.

79. *Furman v Georgia* 408 U.S. 238 (1972), at 470.

80. *Furman v Georgia* 408 U.S. 238 (1972), at 383, 397, 400.

81. Dieter Reicher, "Bureaucracy, 'Domesticated' Elites, and the Abolition of Capital Punishment: Processes of State-Formation and Numbers of Executions in England and Habsburg Austria between 1700 and 1914," *Crime, Law and Social Change* (forthcoming).

82. William Henry Furman was released from prison on parole in 1984. For a time he worked in construction but subsequently became homeless and went on welfare. In 2004 he was arrested for burglary of a dwelling house and sentenced to twenty years. Cheever reports that of the 322 inmates reprieved by *Furman* and subsequently released on parole, 5 killed again. Of the 164 inmates reprieved but never released, 9 killed guards or fellow inmates. Cheever, *Back from the Dead*, 206.

83. Banner, *The Death Penalty*, 266: "In Arkansas the electric chair would be unplugged and used for giving inmates haircuts. In Pennsylvania the room in which executions were held would be partitioned into offices. In New Hampshire the execution chamber would be used to store vegetables. In Idaho it would hold medical equipment."

84. See Brennan, "Constitutional Adjudication and the Death Penalty," 323. *Dred Scott v Sandford* in 1857 was 109,163 words. There has been a longer one since 1972 as well—*McConnell v Federal Election Commission* in 2003 was 89,694 words.

85. Justice Rehnquist would later call it "glossolalial," that is, speaking in tongues rather than in legal language. Rehnquist in *Woodson* 428 U.S. 280 (1976), at 317.

86. Quoted in Epstein and Kobylka, *Abortion and the Death Penalty*, 80.

87. Bob Woodward and Scott Armstrong, *The Brethren: Inside the Supreme Court* (New York: Simon and Schuster, 1979), 219; Liebman, "Slow Dancing With Death," 27.

88. Charles Black, *Capital Punishment: The Inevitability of Caprice and Mistake* (New York: Norton, 1981), 65.

89. Margaret Jane Radin, "Cruel Punishment and Respect for Persons: Super Due Process for Death," *California Law Review* 53 (1979–1980): 1143–1185.

9. New Political and Cultural Meanings

1. Morton Mintz, "Joy on Death Row; Praise, Scorn on Hill," *Washington Post*, June 30, 1972, A13; "Court Spares 600: 4 Justices Named by Nixon All Dis-

sent in Historic Decision," *New York Times,* June 30, 1972, 1; Martin Waldron, "Ruling Cheered on Florida Death Row," *New York Times,* June 30, 1972, 14; "Death Sentences Voided," *Chicago Tribune,* June 30, 1972, 1; "Ruling Hits Survivors," *Chicago Tribune,* June 30, 1972, C16; "Nixon Hopes Federal Death Penalty Stands," *Chicago Tribune,* June 30, 1972, C16; "Pall Lifts on Death Row," *Los Angeles Times,* June 30, 1972, A20; "Supreme Court Overturns Death Penalty in Nation," *Atlanta Daily World,* July 6, 1972.

2. Quoted in Mintz, "Joy on Death Row."
3. "Calls for U.S. Crime Reforms," *Chicago Daily Defender,* July 13, 1972, 17.
4. Quoted in Richard West, "Calif. Initiative in Doubt," *Los Angeles Times,* June 30, 1972, A1.
5. Douglas Watson, "Guards at Prisons Air Gripes," *Washington Post,* July 24, 1972, C1.
6. Quoted in Mintz, "Joy on Death Row."
7. William Robbins, "Nixon Backs Death Penalty for Kidnapping, Hijacking," *New York Times,* June 30, 1972, 1. Earlier in 1972 the California Supreme Court had ruled the California death penalty unconstitutional. Governor Reagan immediately proposed a public initiative, Proposition 17, to reinstate it. In November 1972 the initiative was passed by a two-to-one margin. Lee Epstein and Joseph Kobylka, *The Supreme Court and Legal Change: Abortion and the Death Penalty* (Chapel Hill: University of North Carolina Press, 1992), 85.
8. Lesley Oelsner, "Banned—But for How Long?" *New York Times,* July 2, 1972, E1.
9. "Around the Nation," *Washington Post,* July 6, 1972, A24.
10. *Los Angeles Times,* June 30, 1972, at A1, reported that Los Angeles Police Chief Edward M. Davis would lead a campaign of the Association of Chiefs of Police to restore the death penalty throughout the country. Epstein and Kobylka write, "In December 1972, the National Association of Attorneys General approved by a 32–1 margin a resolution approving capital punishment." Epstein and Kobylka, *Supreme Court and Legal Change,* 341. See also Thomas Edsall and Mary Edsall, *Chain Reaction: The Impact of Race, Rights and Taxes on American Politics* (New York: Norton, 1992), 46.
11. Christopher Mooney and Mei-Hsein Lee, "Morality Policy Reinvention: State Death Penalties," *Annals, AAPSS* 566 (1999): 80–92; Epstein and Kobylka, *Supreme Court and Legal Change,* 74; Marie Gottschalk, *The Prison and the Gallows* (New York: Cambridge University Press, 2006).
12. Savelsberg reports that approval of the death penalty for persons convicted of murder increased from 42 percent in 1966 to 53 percent in 1972 to 66 percent in 1978. The proportion of Americans believing that "courts do not deal harshly enough with criminals" increased from 48 percent in 1965 to 66 percent in 1972 to 85 percent in 1978. Joachim Savelsberg, "Knowledge, Domination, and Criminal Punishment," *American Journal of Sociology* 99 (1994): 929–930.
13. Epstein and Kobylka, *Abortion and the Death Penalty,* 131; Christopher Mooney and Mei-Hsein Lee, "The Temporal Diffusion of Morality Policy:

The Case of the Death Penalty Legislation in the American States," *Policy Studies Journal* 27 (1999): 766–780.

14. For details of the statutes and their various procedural schemes, see James Liebman and Lawrence Marshall, "Less Is Better: Justice Stevens and the Narrowed Death Penalty," *Fordham Law Review* 74 (2006): 1607–1682.

15. Laura Langer and Paul Brace, "The Preemptive Power of State Supreme Courts: Adoption of Abortion and Death Penalty Legislation," *Policy Studies Journal* 33 (2005): 317–340; Epstein and Kobylka, *Supreme Court and Legal Change*, 85.

16. Epstein and Kobylka, *Supreme Court and Legal Change*, 89.

17. Robert Burt, "Disorder in the Court: The Death Penalty and the Constitution," *Michigan Law Review* 85 (1987): 1741–1819.

18. Reported in Robert Semple, "In the Tight Races, the Backlash Vote May Mean Victory," *New York Times*, October 17, 1966, 1.

19. Dan Carter, *The Politics of Rage: George Wallace, the Origins of the New Conservatism, and the Transformation of American Politics* (New York: Simon and Schuster, 1995), 349.

20. Semple, "Tight Races," 1. See also Rick Perlstein, *Nixonland: The Rise of a President and the Fracturing of America* (New York: Scribner, 2008), 164.

21. Quoted in Michael Flamm, *Law and Order: Street Crime, Civil Unrest, and the Crisis of Liberalism in the 1960s* (New York: Columbia University Press, 2005), 1.

22. See Albert Hirschman, *The Rhetoric of Reaction: Futility, Perversity, Jeopardy* (Cambridge, MA: Harvard University Press, 1991).

23. Flamm, *Law and Order.*

24. Thomas Sugrue, *The Origins of the Urban Crisis: Race and Inequality in Postwar Detroit* (Princeton, NJ: Princeton University Press, 2005).

25. Edsall and Edsall, *Chain Reaction.*

26. Flamm, *Law and Order,* 5.

27. Ibid., 58.

28. Ibid., 146; Douglas Massey and Nancy Denton, *American Apartheid: Segregation and the Making of the Underclass* (Cambridge, MA: Harvard University Press, 1993); Edsall and Edsall, *Chain Reaction.*

29. Edsall and Edsall, *Chain Reaction,* 7, 35.

30. Sundquist, quoted in Edsall and Edsall, *Chain Reaction,* 52.

31. Nixon quoted in Perlstein, *Nixonland,* 334.

32. Flamm reports a Harris poll of August 1967 as finding that "Blacks typically (by a 2–1 margin) cited police brutality as a major factor. Whites overwhelmingly (by an 8–1 margin) rejected it." Flamm, *Law and Order,* 84.

33. Ibid., 1–2.

34. Quoted in Edsall and Edsall, *Chain Reaction,* 72.

35. Perlstein citing a Gallup poll from February 1968. Perlstein, *Nixonland,* 238. The 1972 poll showed anxiety about crime continuing at historically high levels. Edsall and Edsall, *Chain Reaction,* 111.

36. Flamm, *Law and Order;* Edsall and Edsall, *Chain Reaction,* 224.

37. Perlstein, *Nixonland,* 284, 300.

38. Interview with Atwater, in Alexander Lamis, *The Two Party South* (New York: Oxford University Press, 1990), 26.
39. Ibid.
40. Edsall and Edsall, *Chain Reaction,* 131.
41. Flamm, *Law and Order.*
42. Sundquist quoted in Edsall and Edsall, *Chain Reaction,* 71.
43. Carter, *Politics of Rage,* 378.
44. Flamm, *Law and Order.*
45. Nixon quoted in Flamm, *Law and Order,* 173.
46. Wallace quoted in Perlstein, *Nixonland,* 224.
47. Flamm, *Law and Order,* 178.
48. Edsall and Edsall, *Chain Reaction,* 215–216.
49. Gottschalk, *Prison and Gallows.* In 1975, an influential neoconservative policy expert argued that the evidence on the deterrent effects of capital punishment was inconclusive and that capital punishment ought to be viewed as a question of justice rather than of utility. James Q. Wilson, *Thinking about Crime* (New York: Basic Books, 1975).
50. Quoted in Roger Schwed, *Abolition and Capital Punishment* (New York: AMS Press, 1983), 103.
51. Keeler McCartney, "Capital Crime up 235 Pct Here," *Atlanta Constitution,* March 31, 1972, A1.
52. "Liberals and Crime," *Atlanta Constitution,* January 29, 1973, A4. Governor Ronald Reagan had responded to the California Supreme Court's 1972 decision that the state's death penalty was unconstitutional by calling it "one more step toward totally disarming society in its fight against violence and crime." Quoted in Gottschalk, *Prison and Gallows,* 219.
53. The percentage of those who answered "yes" when asked if they supported capital punishment in 1972 was 57 percent. The annual figures were: November 1972, 57 percent; March 1972, 50 percent; 1971, 49 percent; 1969, 51 percent; 1966, 42 percent; 1965, 45 percent; 1960, 51 percent; 1953, 68 percent. In 1966, more people (47 percent) had said "no" than said "yes" (42 percent).
54. As a congressional political aide remarked, "The death penalty becomes part of a complex web of issues. People think, if you agree with me on the death penalty, you probably agree with me on . . . a number of other issues." Quoted in Beth Donovan, "Congress Could Focus the Debate: Death Penalty is Re-emerging as a Presidential-Level Issue," *CQ Weekly,* June 18, 1988, 1657.
55. David Anderson, *Crime and the Politics of Hysteria: How the Willie Horton Story Changed American Justice* (New York: Crown, 1995). Ellsworth and Gross note polls that report that the death penalty was a significant factor in voter choice in the 1988 election. Phoebe Ellsworth and Samuel Gross, "Hardening of Attitudes: Americans' Views on the Death Penalty," in Hugo Bedau, ed., *The Death Penalty in America: Current Controversies* (New York: Oxford University Press, 1994), 90–115.
56. Robert Singh, *Governing America: The Politics of a Divided Democracy* (New York: Oxford University Press, 2003), 385.

57. In 1972, the Democratic national platform called for "abolishing capital punishment" on the grounds that it was "recognized as an ineffective deterrent to crime, unequally applied and cruel and excessive." By 1996, the party's platform was claiming credit for adding "the death penalty to nearly 60 violent crimes" and for signing "a law to limit appeals." Naomi Murakawa, "Electing to Punish: Congress, Race and the American Criminal Justice State" (Ph.D. dissertation, Yale University, 2005), 129.

58. Maddox is reported to have shouted these remarks when a death penalty bill failed to pass the Georgia legislature. See Milo Dakin, "Angry as Death Bill Fails: Need More Hangings—Maddox," *Atlanta Constitution,* February 10, 1973, A1.

59. Celestine Sibley, "House Passes Bill to Reinstate the Death Penalty," *Atlanta Constitution,* February 14, 1973, A2. Another article in the same newspaper reports that a law-maker in the Georgia House "called for a return to public hangings 'in the courthouse square.'" This probably referred to the same incident.

60. Sibley, "House Passes Bill," 2A.

61. Another article, two years later, notes that some rural Georgians advocated "public executions in the courthouse square." Sam Hopkins, "Rural Georgians Urge Return to Public Executions," *Atlanta Constitution,* January 28, 1975, D8.

62. William Craze, "Death Penalty Stalks South," *Atlanta Constitution,* March 11, 1973, B2.

63. Both quotes from Mintz, "Joy on Death Row."

64. "Ruling Hits Survivors," *Chicago Tribune,* June 30, 1972, C16.

65. Reported in the *Fort Worth Star-Telegram,* February 25, 2000.

66. A similar response greeted federal attempts to end lynching in the 1890s and 1900s. See David Garland, "Penal Excess and Surplus Meaning: Public Torture Lynchings in 20th Century America," *Law & Society Review* 39 (2005): 793–834.

67. See the *Tampa Tribune:* "the people's representatives did not make a decision. Instead, five justices imposed on the nation their moral judgment." "The Troubling Undercurrents of Court's Death Penalty Rule," *Tampa Tribune,* March 2, 2005, 10. Also see the *Baltimore Sun:* "The death penalty is a matter for state legislatures." Gregory Kane, "The Nine Divines—and the Constitution," *Baltimore Sun,* March 5, 2005, B1. The death penalty has a special significance in the context of states' rights because it is one of the few powers associated with sovereignty that the American states ever possessed. Other marks of sovereignty, such as the powers "to make war or peace, to form commercial treaties with other nations, to raise armies or navies, to control the rule of citizenship, to coin money" were never possessed by the American states. See Gary Wills, *A Necessary Evil: A History of American Mistrust of Government* (New York: Simon & Schuster, 1999).

68. Edward Lazarus, "The Supreme Court and the Juvenile Death Penalty," http://www.cnn.com/2005/LAW/03/03/lazarus.death.penalty/index.html (accessed January 27, 2010).

69. *Greenville News,* March 3, 2005, 10A; "Death Ruling Slip-Up: Foreign Views out of Place in Court Opinion Restricting U.S. Executions," *Omaha World Herald,* March 3, 2005, B6.

70. See Judge Tom Parker, "Alabama Justices Surrender to Judicial Activism," *Birmingham News,* January 1, 2006.

71. *Kennedy v Louisiana* 554 U.S. __ (2008). The other states were Georgia, Montana, Oklahoma, South Carolina, and Texas.

72. *Chattanooga Times Free Press,* "Our Busybody Judiciary," January 9, 2008, B7.

73. Quoted in the *Seguin Gazette-Enterprise* (Texas) of June 29, 2008.

74. Press conference reported by *ABC News,* June 25, 2008. See also http://www.wsws.org/articles/2008/jun2008/obam-j26.shtml (last accessed January 31, 2010).

75. Patrick Buchanan, "The (Linda) Greenhouse Effect," *Tulsa World,* April 23, 2008.

76. In a speech to the 1992 Republican Convention, Pat Buchanan invoked this idea: "My friends, this election is about much more than who gets what. It is about what we believe, what we stand for as Americans. There is a religious war going on for the soul of America. It is a culture war, as critical to the kind of nation we will one day be as was the Cold War itself." Paul Galloway, "Divided We Stand: Today's 'Cultural War' Goes Deeper Than the Political Slogans," *Chicago Tribune,* October 29, 1992, C1.

77. Tom Parker, "Alabama Justices Surrender to Judicial Activism," *Birmingham News,* January 1, 2006. Kahan highlights this subterranean status dimension of the death penalty debate. Dan Kahan, "The Secret Ambition of Deterrence," *Harvard Law Review* 113 (1999): 413–500.

78. Jeremy Rabkin, "The Supreme Court in the Culture Wars," *Public Interest* 125 (1996): 8–9.

79. "Court's Ruling Has Not Ended Controversy," *Los Angeles Times,* June 30, 1972, A24.

80. "Letters to the *Times,*" *Los Angeles Times,* July 3, 1972.

81. Banner writes that Solicitor General Robert Bork, who argued the *Gregg* case for the federal government, "viewed opposition to capital punishment as a sign of moral decay." Stuart Banner, *The Death Penalty: An American History* (Cambridge, MA: Harvard University Press, 2002).

82. Death Penalty Information Center, http://www.deathpenaltyinfo.org/number-executions-state-and-region-1976.

83. David Garland, *The Culture of Control: Crime and Social Order in Contemporary Society* (Chicago: University of Chicago Press, 2001).

84. Mark Warr, "Poll Trends: Public Opinion on Crime and Punishment," *Public Opinion Quarterly* 59 (1995): 301; and Frank Newport, "In U.S., Two-Thirds Continue to Support Death Penalty," www.gallup.com, October 13, 2009, http://www.gallup.com/poll/123638/in-u.s.-two-thirds-continue-support-death-penalty.aspx (accessed January 12, 2010), 2. Public support for capital punishment has declined since the mid-1990s and has now settled at or around 65 percent in favor. McVeigh's execution in June 2001 marked the

high point of the punishment's popularity but also the beginning of the displacement of "law and order" politics by new fears and concerns. In the period since, crime has become a less urgent concern as homicide rates have continued to fall and other insecurities have taken crime's place. The narratives in
which the death penalty is framed by the media have shifted to include DNA
doubts, stories about innocents on death row, a growing pressure of international opinion, and high-profile challenges to the protocols of lethal injection.
See Frank Baumgartner, Suzanna De Boef, and Amber Boydstun, *The Decline
of the Death Penalty and the Discovery of Innocence* (New York: Cambridge
University Press, 2008).

10. Reinventing the Death Penalty

1. Robert Cover, "Violence and the Word," *Yale Law Journal* 95 (1986): 1601–
   1629; James Liebman, "Slow Dancing With Death: The Supreme Court and
   Capital Punishment, 1963–2006," *Columbia Law Review* 107 (2007): 1–130.
   Law clerks who assist justices in preparing opinions have described the draining effect of this encounter: see Edward Lazarus, *Closed Chambers: The First
   Eyewitness Account of the Epic Struggles inside the Supreme Court* (New
   York: Time Books, 1998).
2. Justice Scalia describes it as "incoherent" in *Kansas v Marsh,* 548 U.S. 163
   (2006) (Scalia, J. concurring), at p. 1 of slip opinion. Justice Thomas called it
   "Byzantine" in *Knight v Florida,* 528 U.S. 990 (1999), at 991 (Thomas, J.
   concurring in denial of certiorari). Weisberg refers to the "intellectually embarrassing Eighth Amendment jurisprudence." Robert Weisberg, "Cruel and
   Unusual Jurisprudence," *New York Times,* March 4, 2005.
3. For detailed accounts see Robert Weisberg, "Deregulating Death," *The Supreme Court Review* (1983): 305–395; Robert Burt, "Disorder in the Court:
   The Death Penalty and the Constitution," *Michigan Law Review* 85 (1987):
   1741–1819; Carol Steiker and Jordan Steiker, "Sober Second Thoughts: Reflections on Two Decades of Constitutional Regulation of Capital Punishment," *Harvard Law Review* 109 (1995): 355–438; and Liebman, "Slow
   Dancing with Death."
4. *Gregg v Georgia,* 428 U.S. 153 (1976); *Jurek v Texas,* 428 U.S. 262 (1976);
   Profitt v Florida, 428 U.S. 242 (1976); *Woodson v N. Carolina,* 428 U.S. 280
   (1976); and *Roberts v Louisiana,* 428 U.S. 325 (1976). That each of these five
   cases involved a white defendant suggests that the avoidance of race discrimination issues may also have been a factor in their selection.
5. Powell in oral argument in *Gregg v Georgia,* quoted in Lee Epstein and Joseph
   Koblyka, *The Supreme Court and Legal Change: Abortion and the Death
   Penalty* (Chapel Hill: University of North Carolina Press, 1992), 109. See also
   Marie Gottschalk, *The Prison and the Gallows* (New York: Cambridge University Press, 2006) 222 ff.
6. Brief for the United States as *Amicus Curiae* for the respondent in *Gregg v
   Georgia,* quoted in H. L. Pohlman, *Constitutional Debate in Action: Criminal
   Justice* (Lanham, MD: Rowman and Littlefield, 2005), 162.

7. Justice Stewart in *Gregg v Georgia,* 428 U.S. 153 (1976), at 198, 186–187 (Stewart J., plurality opinion).

8. In determining sentence, juries must be allowed to consider "the possibility of compassionate or mitigating factors stemming from the diverse frailties of humankind." *Woodson v North Carolina,* 428 U.S. 280 (1976), at 304.

9. Anthony Amsterdam and Jerome Bruner, *Minding the Law* (Cambridge, MA: Harvard University Press, 2000), 196. For a succinct account of the legislative implications of *Gregg,* see the guide on "how to legislate a death penalty" provided by the Council of States. Howard Schwab, *Legislating a Death Penalty* (Lexington, KY: Council of State Governments, 1977).

10. Del Dickson, *The Supreme Court in Conference (1940–1985): The Private Discussions Behind Nearly 300 Supreme Court Decisions* (New York: Oxford University Press, 2001), 622.

11. *Gregg,* 428 U.S. (1976), at 187.

12. "The penalty of death differs from all other forms of criminal punishment, not in degree, but in kind. It is unique in its total irrevocability. It is unique in its rejection of rehabilitation of the convict as a basic purpose of criminal justice. And it is unique, finally, in its absolute renunciation of all that is embodied in our concept of humanity." *Furman v Georgia,* 408 U.S. 238 (1972), at 306 (Stewart, J., concurring). The argument is articulated again in *Woodson* at 303–304 (Brennan, J.), and *Gregg* (plurality at 188).

13. See Margaret Jane Radin, "Cruel Punishment and Respect for Persons: Super Due Process for Death," *California Law Review* 53 (1979–1980): 1143–1185, on super due process; see Weisberg, "Deregulating Death," and Charles Fried, "Impudence," *The Supreme Court Review* (1992): 183, on the relaxation of regulation and finality. For a sharp critique of the latter, see Anthony Amsterdam, "In Favorem Mortis: The Supreme Court and Capital Punishment," *Human Rights* 14 (1987): 52.

14. See *Booth v Maryland,* 482 U.S. 496 (1987), later reversed by *Payne v Tennessee,* 501 U.S. 808 (1991); *Penry v Lynaugh,* 429 U.S 302 (1989), later reversed by *Atkins v Virginia* (2002); *In Re Stanford,* 537 U.S. (2002), later reversed by *Roper v Simmons.*

15. *State v Makwanyane et al.,* 1995 (3) SA 391 (CC); Decision No. 23/1990 of the Hungarian Constitutional Court (October 24, 1990).

16. *Woodson,* 428 U.S. 280 at 303 (Stewart J., plurality opinion). See also Justice Stevens in *Gardner v Florida,* 430 U.S. 349 at 358.

17. On the various meanings of the term "juridification" in legal theory, see Lars Blichner and Anders Molander, "What Is Juridification?" (Working paper, Centre for European Studies, University of Oslo, 2005).

18. See Justice Blackmun in *Callins v Collins,* 510 U.S. 1141 (1994), at 1145–1146.

19. As Justice Stevens wrote in *Spaziano v Florida* 468 U.S. (1984) 480 at 490: "In the final analysis, capital punishment rests not on a legal but on an ethical judgment . . . And . . . the decision that capital punishment is the appropriate sanction in the extreme cases is justified because it expresses the community's moral sensibility—its demand that a given affront to humanity requires retri-

bution." Later, in *Baze v Rees*, 553 U.S. 35 (2008), Justice Stevens in effect renounced capital punishment.

20. "To identify before the fact those characteristics of criminal homicides and their perpetrators which call for the death penalty, and to express these characteristics in language which can be fairly understood and applied by the sentencing authority, appear to be tasks which are beyond present human ability." Justice Harlan in *McGautha v California*, 402 U.S. 183 (1971), at 204.

21. *McGautha v California*, 402 U.S. 183 (1971), at 249 (Brennan J., dissenting).

22. Blackmun in *Callins v Collins*, 510 U.S. 1141 at 1145.

23. On the effect of the Court's jurisprudence on the flow of executions, see Weisberg, "Deregulating Death."

24. *Woodson*, 428 U.S. 280 at 303 (Stewart J., plurality opinion).

25. *Witherspoon v Illinois*, 391 U.S. 510 (1968); *Furman v Georgia*, 408 U.S. 238 (1972).

26. *Gardner v Florida*, 430 U.S. 349 (1977); and *Green v Georgia*, 442 U.S. 95 (1979).

27. *Lockett v Ohio*, 438 U.S. 586 (1978); *Godfrey v Georgia*, 446 U.S. 420 (1980); *Ford v Wainwright*, 477 U.S. (1986); *Enmund v Florida*, 458 U.S. 782 (1982). Five years later in *Tison v Arizona*, 481 U.S. 137 (1987), the Court modified *Enmund* by holding that a felony murder accomplice may receive a death sentence if his participation is major and his conduct evidences reckless indifference to human life (at 152).

28. Weisberg, "Deregulating Death," 305.

29. Justice Blackmun, in *Callins v Collins*, 510 U.S. 1141 at 1145.

30. Rehnquist in *Coleman v Balkcom*, 451 U.S. 949 (1981), at 956 and 958. My emphasis.

31. Linda Greenhouse, "Justice Powell Assails Delay in Carrying Out Executions," *New York Times*, May 10, 1983, A16.

32. *Zant v Stevens*, 462 U.S. 862 (1983), *Ramos v California*, 463 U.S. 992 (1983), *Barefoot v Estelle*, 463 U.S. 880 (1983), *and Barclay v Florida*, 463 U.S. 939 (1983).

33. See *McCleskey v Kemp*, 481 U.S. 279 (1987) where the Court declined to find for the defendant despite evidence of racially disparate outcomes, and *Teague v Lane* 489 U.S. 288 (1989) which limited the retrospective impact of new Court holdings.

34. See, for instance, the *Anti-Terrorism and Effective Death Penalty Act* of 1996.

35. For details, see Liebman, "Slow Dancing With Death"; Anthony Amsterdam, "Remarks at the Southern Center for Human Rights Frederick Douglass Awards Dinner," October 2, 2008; and Carol Steiker and Jordan Steiker, "The Seduction of Innocence: The Attraction and Limitations of the Focus on Innocence in Capital Punishment Law and Advocacy," *Journal of Criminal Law and Criminology* 95 (2005): 101–138.

36. *Wiggins v. Smith*, 539 U.S. 510 (2003); *Williams v. Taylor*, 529 U.S. 362 (2000).

37. For the view that these rulings inhibit state power, see Justice Scalia's dissent in

Atkins v Virginia (2002). For the view that super due process claims are demonstrably false, see Amsterdam, "Remarks."

38. The Court's Eighth Amendment jurisprudence involves a peculiar and contradictory form of reasoning. As a constitutional protection, the prohibition on cruel and unusual punishments would normally be understood as a restraint on the power of the people and their representatives to impose excessive punishments. As Justice Brennan points out in *Furman* at 268: "The right to be free of cruel and unusual punishment, like the other guarantees of the Bill of Rights, 'may not be submitted to vote; [it] depends on the outcome of no elections.'" Yet the Court has repeatedly sought to determine the meaning of "cruel" and "unusual" by reference to the changing sensibilities of the majority of the people, as indicated by the conduct of juries, legislatures, and public opinion polls. A supposed protection *against* the majority will is thereby activated only if the majority wills that it ought to be so activated.

39. *Woodson v North Carolina,* 428 U.S. 280 (1976), at 288.

40. The two Eighth Amendment cases that are usually cited in "civilizing" opinions are: *In Re Kemmler,* 136 U.S. 436 (1890): "Punishments are cruel when they involve torture or a lingering death; but the punishment of death is not cruel, within the meaning of that word as used in the Constitution. It implies there something inhuman and barbarous, something more than the mere extinguishment of life" (Justice Fuller at 447); and *Louisiana v Resweber,* 329 U.S. 459 (1947): "The cruelty against which the Constitution protects a convicted man is cruelty inherent in the method of punishment, not the necessary suffering involved in any method employed to extinguish life humanely" (at 463).

41. Brennan, *Furman v Georgia,* 408 U.S. 183 at 270 and 288.

42. Justice Brennan, dissenting, in *McGautha v California,* 402 U.S. 183 (1971), at 311

43. Justice Brennan in *Glass v Louisiana,* 471 U.S. 1080 (1985), at 1085.

44. *Furman v Georgia,* 408 U.S. 183 (1972), at 272; *Gregg v Georgia,* 428 U.S. 153 (1976), at 230.

45. "The North Carolina statute impermissibly treats all persons convicted of a designated offense not as uniquely individual human beings, but as members of a faceless, undifferentiated mass." *Woodson v North Carolina,* 428 U.S. 280 (1976), at 304.

46. *In re Stanford,* 537 U.S. 968, 972 (2002).

47. *Furman v Georgia,* 408 U.S. 238 (1972), at 371 (Marshall J., concurring).

48. *Coker v Georgia,* 433 U.S. 584 (1977); *Enmund v Florida,* 458 U.S. 782 (1982); *Ford v Wainwright,* 477 U.S. 399 (1986); *Atkins v Virginia,* 536 U.S. 304 (2002); *Roper v Simmons,* 543 U.S. 551 (2005); *Kennedy v Louisiana,* 554 U.S. ___ (2008).

49. In *Roper v Simmons,* 543 U.S. (2005), at 575, Justice Kennedy notes "the stark reality that the United States is the only country in the world that continues to give official sanction to the juvenile death penalty . . . 'the civilized nations of the world are in virtual unanimity.'"

50. The Nebraska Supreme Court in *State v Raymond Mata* (2003) ruled that the

electric chair amounted to cruel and unusual punishment under the state constitution. And in 1994, the Ninth Circuit upheld a federal district court ruling
that the California gas chamber was unconstitutional: see *Fierro v Gomez,* 77
F 3rd 301 (9th Cir. 1996). It is often state legislators, acting in anticipation of
a court ruling, who adapt execution technology to civilized norms: see Laura
Langer and Paul Brace, "The Preemptive Power of State Supreme Courts:
Adoption of Abortion and Death Penalty Legislation," *Policy Studies Journal*
33, 3 (2005): 317–340. In January 2000, the Florida legislature passed a law
replacing the electric chair with the lethal injection, thereby mooting a Supreme Court case—*Bryan v Moore,* 99–6723—that was expected to declare
Florida's electrocution protocol unlawful.

51. Chief Justice Fuller, *In Re Kemmler,* 136 U.S. (1890) 436 at 446; *Campbell v
Wood* (1994) 18 F.3d 662 at para. 256. The U.S. Court of Appeals for the
Ninth Circuit decided in *Rupe v Wood,* 863 F. Supp. 1307 (W. D. Wash.
1994), that Washington state could not hang Michael Rupe because his excessive weight might result in decapitation.

52. *Dawson v Georgia,* 274 Ga 327 (2001). The graphic language used by the
Georgia court is characteristic of "civilizing" arguments. See Justice Brennan
in *Glass v Louisiana,* 471 U.S. 1080 (1985), at 1086–1088.

53. *Baze v Rees,* 553 U.S. 35 (2008).

54. The quotation is from *In re Kemmler,* 136 U.S. 436 (1890), at 447.

55. *Woodson v North Carolina,* 428 U.S. 280 (1976), at 313 (Rehnquist J., dissenting); *Atkins v Virginia,* 536 U.S. 304 (2002), at 348 (Scalia J., dissenting).

56. *Furman v Georgia* at 408 U.S. 238 (1972), at 383 (Burger J., dissenting). See
also Justice White's dissent in *Witherspoon v Illinois,* 391 U.S. 541 (1968), at
542; and Justice Rehnquist, in his dissent in *Atkins v Virginia,* 536 U.S. 304
(2002), at 324.

57. Rehnquist in *Furman v Georgia,* 508 U.S. 238 (1972), at 468 (Rehnquist J.,
dissenting).

58. Scalia, in *Callins v Collins,* 510 U.S. 1141 (1994), at 1128.

59. *Godfrey v Georgia,* 466 U.S. 420 (1980), at 450.

60. Powell in *McCleskey v Kemp,* 481 U.S. 279 (1987), at 319. Internal quotation
marks omitted.

61. Liebman, "Slow Dancing With Death."

62. *Kelly v South Carolina,* 534 U.S. 246 (2002); *Roper v Simmons,* 543 U.S. 551
(2005), at 21 of slip opinion.

63. *Coleman v Thompson,* 501 U.S. 722 (1991), at 726.

64. For a carefully controlled study of prosecutorial decision-making in capital
cases, see Leigh Bienen et al., "The Reimposition of Capital Punishment in
New Jersey: The Role of Prosecutorial Discretion," 41 *Rutgers Law Review*
27 (1988).

65. Liebman, "Slow Dancing With Death," 122–126, 4. The Court's decisions in
Atkins v Virginia and *Roper v Simmons,* which prohibited capital punishment
for the mentally deficient and juvenile offenders, are important exceptions to
this pattern.

66. *Lockett v Ohio,* 438 U.S. 586 (1978), at 587.

67. Liebman, "Slow Dancing With Death," 40; Weisberg, "Deregulating Death."

68. Harlan in *McGautha v California*, 402 U.S. 183 (1971), at 202. The jury is important not just in capital cases but in the U.S. constitutional structure more generally. The right to a jury trial is guaranteed by the Sixth Amendment.

69. *Spaziano v Florida*, 468 U.S. 447 (1984).

70. *Ring v Arizona*, 536 U.S. 584 (2002). *Ring* applied the holdings of *Apprendi v New Jersey*, 530 U.S. 466 (2002), to the capital context.

71. Breyer in *Ring v Arizona*, 536 U.S. 584 (2002), at 614 (Breyer J., concurring in judgment).

72. Justice Stewart, writing for the Court in *Gregg*, said: "capital punishment is an expression of society's moral outrage at particularly offensive conduct." *Gregg v Georgia*, 428 U.S. 153 (1976), at 182.

73. Stevens in *Spaziano v Florida*, 468 U.S. (1984) at 481; Breyer in *Ring v Arizona*. 536 U.S. 584 (2002).

74. *Wainwright* at 458, 459, and 460.

75. *Harris v Alabama*, 513 U.S. 504 (1995).

76. Breyer in *Ring v Arizona*, 536 U.S. (2002), at 619.

77. *Booth v Maryland*, 482 U.S. 496 (1987), at 508 (Powell J., majority opinion).

78. On the rise of the victims' movement, see Jonathan Simon, *Governing Through Crime* (New York: Oxford University Press, 2007).

79. *Payne v Tennessee*, 501 U.S. 808 (1991). Justice Rehnquist's opinion for the Court in *Payne* also justified the decision by reference to the need to "balance" the mitigating evidence of the defendant's character witnesses.

80. *Maxwell v Bishop* (1970) was a capital rape case involving a black man in Arkansas. So were the cases decided with *Furman*—*Branch v Texas* and *Jackson v Georgia* (1972).

81. Steiker and Steiker, "Sober Second Thoughts," 360.

82. "*Furman* aspired to eliminate the vestiges of racism and the effects of poverty in capital sentencing." Justice Blackmun in *Callins v Collins* at 775.

83. See the remarks of Justice Stewart in *Furman* (at 308) and also those of Justice Marshall. This concern continues—when excluding certain forms of victim testimony in the 1997 capital trial of Timothy McVeigh, the judge remarked that a "penalty-phase hearing cannot be turned into some kind of lynching." Quoted in Robert Lifton and Greg Mitchell, *Who Owns Death: Capital Punishment, the American Conscience and the End of Executions* (New York: Perennial, 2000), 146.

84. *McCleskey v Kemp*, 481 U.S. 279 (1987). See Liebman, "Slow Dancing With Death," 82–83.

85. My discussion of *McCleskey* draws on Anthony Amsterdam and Jerome Bruner, *Minding the Law* (Cambridge, MA: Harvard University Press, 2000), chapter 7.

86. *Amicus curiae* brief of Dr. Franklin Fisher et al. in support of the petitioner Warren McCleskey, quoted in Amsterdam and Bruner, *Minding the Law*, at 394.

87. Amsterdam and Bruner, *Minding the Law*, at 200.

88. *McCleskey v Kemp*, 481 U.S. (1987), at 292.

384 Notes to Pages 283–285

89. John Jeffries, *Justice Lewis F. Powell Jr.* (New York: Scribner, 1994).

90. After *Furman*, the New Jersey Supreme Court engaged in rigorous proportionality review to ensure that like cases were treated alike and that the death penalty was implemented without racial disparities. The result was that no death sentences were ever executed in the state, and in 2007 the state legislature repealed its capital statutes. See George Conk, "Herald of Change?: New Jersey's Repeal of the Death Penalty," 33 *Seton Hall Legislative Journal* 21 (2008). See also the Racial Justice Act enacted by North Carolina in 2009.

91. In his dissent in *McCleskey*, Justice Brennan wrote, "The Court next states that its unwillingness to regard petitioner's evidence as sufficient is based in part on the fear that recognition of McCleskey's claim would open the door to widespread challenges to all aspects of criminal sentencing . . . Taken on its face, such a statement seems to suggest a fear of too much justice" (at 339).

92. David Baldus, Charles Pulaski, and George Woodworth, "Reflections on 'Modern' Death Sentencing Systems," *Criminal Law Forum* 1 (1989): 185–197.

11. Death and Its Uses

1. "Whatever purposes the death penalty is said to serve—deterrence, retribution, assuaging the pain suffered by victims' families—these purposes are not served by the system as it now operates." Alex Kozinski and Sean Gallagher, "Death: The Ultimate Run-On Sentence," *Case Western Reserve Law Review* 46 (1995): 4; "In all its inconstancy, vacillation, and ungainliness, the system not only looks irrational but serves no purpose." Jack Greenberg, "Capital Punishment as a System," *Yale Law Journal* 91 (1981–1982): 927; "What we have makes no sense and accomplishes nothing." Ronald Tabak, Remarks at a capital punishment conference (Albany University, 2006); "Capital punishment has . . . become a commodity dispensed without any redeeming social or communal purpose." Robert Johnson, *Death Work: A Study of the Modern Execution Process* (Belmont, CA: Wadsworth, 1998), 9; "[C]apital punishment in the United States is little more than a tragic and painful penal symbol: rarely enforced, applied in an unacceptably arbitrary way . . . for no gain in the diminution of murder." Roger Hood, "Capital Punishment: A Global Perspective," *Punishment & Society* 3 (2001): 344. Justice Stevens, "The imposition of the death penalty 'represents the pointless and needless extinction of life with only marginal contributions to any discernible social or public purposes.'" *Baze v Rees*, 553 U.S. 35, 85 (2008).

2. Peter Wynarczyk, "The Political Economy of Capital Punishment," *Economic Affairs* 19 (1999): 43. Economists who claim to find a deterrent effect are an exception to this generalization. For examples, see Hashem Dezhbakhsh, Paul Rubin, and Joanna Shepherd, "Does Capital Punishment Have a Deterrent Effect?" *American Law and Economic Review* 5 (2003): 344–376; Hashem Dezhbakhsh and Joanna Shepherd, "The Deterrent Effect of Capital Punishment: Evidence from a Judicial Experiment," *Economic Inquiry* 44 (2006): 512–535; Cass Sunstein and Adrian Vermuele, "Is Capital Punishment

Morally Required? Acts, Omissions and Life-Life Trade-Offs," *Stanford Law Review* 58 (2006): 703–750. For a critique of their methods and claims, see John Donahue and Justin Wolfers, "Uses and Abuses of Empirical Evidence in the Death Penalty Debate," *Stanford Law Review* 58 (2006): 791–845; and Franklin Zimring, "Criminology and Its Discontents," *Criminology* 46 (2008): 255–266.

3. Michel Foucault, *Discipline and Punish: The Birth of the Prison* (New York: Allen Lane, 1977), 23.

4. The claim that the death penalty has absolutely no efficacy as a means of deterrence, incapacitation, and retribution is certainly an exaggeration. But in the United States today each of these purposes is undercut by the forms through which it is enacted. Does it deter? Perhaps. But uncertainty, infrequency, and delay undermine its deterrent effect. Does it incapacitate? Yes, certainly. And murderers sentenced instead to life imprisonment sometimes go on to commit further murders. But the fact is that America's current death penalty is, in effect, a system of death row imprisonment, so its current incapacitation effects are little greater than those of its alternative. What of retribution and denunciation? Arguments from moral proportion and moral communication provide the most powerful case for capital punishment today, though these, too, can be contested, resting as they do on conventions and intuitions. And these retributive and denunciatory effects are greatly diluted by a postconviction process in which the murderer often comes to be perceived as the victim of unfairness or mistreatment.

5. On the fascination with murder, see Wendy Lesser, *Pictures at an Execution: An Inquiry into the Subject of Murder* (Cambridge, MA: Harvard University Press, 1998); and V. A. C. Gatrell, *The Hanging Tree: Executions and the English People, 1770–1868* (Oxford, England: Oxford University Press, 1994), 243.

6. Bronfen describes the strange pleasure many people feel when viewing depictions of death. These depictions "delight because we are confronted by death, yet it is the death of the other. We experience death by proxy. In the aesthetic enactment we have a situation impossible in life, namely that we die with another and return to the living. Even as we are forced to acknowledge the ubiquitous presence of death in life, our belief in our own immortality is confirmed. There is death but it is not my own." Elizabeth Bronfen, *Over Her Dead Body: Death, Femininity and the Aesthetic* (Manchester: Manchester University Press, 1992), x–xi.

7. Liebman discusses the "psychic, political and professional rewards" obtained by trial-level actors in capital cases. James Liebman, "The Overproduction of Death," *Columbia Law Review* 100 (2000): 2032.

8. Federal Bureau of Prisons Director Norman Carlson told a Senate hearing in 1983, "When assailants are already serving multiple life sentences, they can act with impunity . . . One more life sentence means absolutely nothing to these individuals." Quoted in Hugo Bedau, *The Death Penalty in America: Current Controversies* (New York: Oxford University Press, 1997), 176. In Canada in 1975, federal prison guards threatened a nationwide strike in sup-

port of the death penalty for the murder of prison guards and police officers. "Prison Guards Support Death Penalty," CBC Digital Archives, http://archives .cbc.ca/society/crime_justice/clips/3340/ (accessed January 28, 2010).

9. R. W. Fagan, "Police Attitudes toward Capital Punishment," *Journal of Police Science and Administration* 14 (1986): 193–201. Police chiefs, many of whom, as we saw, protested the *Furman* decision, now appear less supportive of the death penalty than they were thirty years ago, and less supportive than rank-and-file officers. See Richard Dieter, "On the Front Line: Law Enforcement Views on the Death Penalty" (Washington, DC: Death Penalty Information Center, 1995). Nevertheless, in a 2009 survey of police chiefs, 27 percent described more frequent death penalties as a "highly efficient" use of taxpayers' money in combating crime.

10. *Los Angeles Times,* October 21, 1988.

11. *Newsday,* July 31, 2004.

12. *New York Times,* November 27, 2006.

13. Gene Johnson, "Strategy Changing on Death Penalty," *Associated Press,* July 30, 2007. See also Welsh White, *The Death Penalty in the Nineties: An Examination of the Modern System of Capital Punishment* (Ann Arbor: University of Michigan Press, 1991), 68; and Andrew Welsh-Huggins, *No Winners Here Tonight: Race, Politics, and Geography in One of the Country's Busiest Death Penalty States* (Athens: Ohio University Press, 2009).

14. Liebman, "The Overproduction of Death."

15. Tony Amsterdam stated in comments to a Capital Punishment History Workshop at NYU in May 2007, "Capital litigation serves as a contact sport for . . . star-class legal athletes. The contest between the champions of the DA's office and of the defense bar is partly a personal duel . . . and partly a status-grasping and status-ratifying competition." And former assistant district attorney Ron Sievert describes convincing a jury "to make the supreme decision, the decision to take someone's life" as the ultimate highlight of a prosecutor's career. Quoted in Robert Lifton and Greg Mitchell, *Who Owns Death? Capital Punishment, the American Conscience and the End of Executions* (New York: Perennial, 2000), 114. Reports of celebrations in prosecutors' offices following death penalty verdicts and the occasional sighting of commemorative ties and plaques tend to confirm these claims. See Brent Newton, "A Case Study in Systemic Unfairness: The Texas Death Penalty: 1973–1994," *Texas Forum on Civil Liberties & Civil Rights* 2 (1993–1994): 18; *New York Times,* January 5, 2003, Section 1, page 14, col. 1; and Molly Ivins, "The Big Fry-Off," *Mother Jones,* June 1990, 9–10.

16. Stephen Bright and Patrick Keenan, "Judges and the Politics of Death: Deciding Between the Bill of Rights and the Next Election in Capital Cases," *Boston University Law Review* 75 (1995): 781; Lifton and Mitchell, *Who Owns Death?*

17. *Houston Chronicle,* February 4, 2001. Philadelphia District Attorney Lynne Abraham, who sought the death penalty more often, per homicide, than any other prosecutor in the nation, said that she did so because the death penalty was demanded by the voters who elect her to office. Liebman, "The Overproduction of Death," 2080.

18. See Tom Parker, "Alabama Justices Surrender to Judicial Activism," *Birmingham News,* January 1, 2006; Paul Brace and Brent Boyea, "State Public Opinion, the Death Penalty and the Practice of Electing Judges," *American Journal of Political Science* 52, 2 (2008) 360–372.

19. David Dow, "How the Death Penalty Really Works," in David Dow and Mark Dow, eds., *Machinery of Death: The Reality of America's Death Penalty Regime* (New York: Routledge, 2002), 11–36, at 24.

20. Robin Maher, "Volunteer Lawyers and Their Extraordinary Role in the Delivery of Justice to Death Row Prisoners," *University of Toledo Law Review* 35 (2004), at 585. According to Scheingold and Sarat, lawyers "approach their pro bono work as a cherished break from the routines of corporate practice as well as an opportunity to do good . . . [They] welcome the humanizing impact of intense engagement with marginalized clients—like those on death row." Stuart Scheingold and Austin Sarat, *Something to Believe In: Politics, Professionalism and Cause Lawyering* (Stanford: Stanford University Press, 2004), 79. Oregon prosecutor Joshua Marquis is more cynical: "The strange legal glamour that accompanies some capital cases has convinced dozens of silk-stocking law firms in major cities to assign platoons of lawyers pro bono, all seeking the elusive prize: the innocent man on death row." Joshua Marquis, "Truth and Consequences: The Penalty of Death," in Hugo Bedau and Paul Cassell, eds., *Debating the Death Penalty: Should America Have Capital Punishment?* (New York: Oxford University Press, 2004), 117–151, at 143.

21. Maher writes, "Without exception, [lawyers who have done *pro bono* death penalty work] describe their experience as among the most rewarding and fulfilling of their career." Maher, "Volunteer Lawyers."

22. American prison sentences are, on average, much higher than those of European nations, and sentences of life imprisonment without parole are regularly imposed in some states for repeat felony offending. In such a context, to sentence a murderer to life imprisonment without parole can seem unduly lenient. In Europe, by contrast, a sentence of life without the possibility of parole would likely violate Article 3 of the European Convention on Human Rights. Dirk van Zyl Smit, "Life Imprisonment: Recent Issues in National and International Law," *International Journal of Law and Psychiatry* 29/5 (2006): 405–421. See also Michael Tonry and David Farrington, "Introduction" to *Crime and Punishment in Western Countries, 1980–1999* (Chicago: University of Chicago Press, 2005).

23. Scott Turow, *Ultimate Punishment: A Lawyer's Reflections on Dealing With the Death Penalty* (New York: Picador, 2003), 64.

24. Paul Rock, *After Homicide: Practical and Political Responses to Homicide* (Oxford, England: Oxford University Press, 1998).

25. Samuel Gross and Daniel Matheson, "What They Say at the End: Capital Victims' Families and the Press," *Cornell Law Review* 88 (2002–2003): 486–516.

26. Dr. William A. Petit, Jr., quoted in William Glaberson, "Reliving Horror in a Test for the Death Penalty," *New York Times,* January 18, 2010, A1.

27. During the New York State Assembly debate on capital punishment, Assemblyman Crawley declared, "I voted for the death penalty because I, like many . . . of the people in the state of New York . . . believe we are at war, a war on

drugs, a war on murder, a war on crime." Official transcript, New York State Assembly debate, March 1995, at 374. And Assemblyman Hikind: The death penalty is "not an answer to our problems but . . . an additional tool for the police officers, for the criminal justice system, in their war on crime. It is a war." Official transcript, New York State Assembly debate, March 1995, at 144.

28. Gara LaMarche, "Ending Executions," *American Prospect,* June 3, 2001; Richard Dieter, *Killing for Votes: The Dangers of Politicizing the Death Penalty Process* (Washington, DC: Death Penalty Information Center, 1996); Dwight Conquergood, "Lethal Theatre: Performance, Punishment and the Death Penalty," *Theatre Journal* 54 (2002): 358.

29. Conquergood writes, "The death penalty . . . is a gendered symbol, a mantle of 'political macho' that female politicians, like Diane Feinstein and Jeanne Shaheen, the first woman governor of New Hampshire who vetoed the legislation to abolish the state's death penalty, can wear to masculinize themselves in the public sphere." Conquergood, "Lethal Theatre," 358.

30. In the United States, the power to impose death penalties is the local state power that most powerfully suggests sovereign authority. As Wills points out, none of the other powers usually associated with sovereignty—"powers to make war or peace, to form commercial treaties with other nations, to raise armies or navies, to control the rules of citizenship, to coin money" were ever possessed by the American states. Gary Wills, *A Necessary Evil: A History of American Mistrust of Government* (New York: Simon & Schuster, 1999), 68.

31. See the *Austin American-Statesman,* February 4, 1998; and Ivins, "The Big Fry-Off," 9. Arkansas Governor Bill Clinton made a similar show of support for capital punishment when he interrupted his 1992 presidential election campaign to return to Arkansas and preside over the execution of Ricky Ray Rector. Clinton had learned that political lesson the hard way: "In his first term as governor of Arkansas he was regarded as anti–capital punishment and in more than twenty murder cases declined to set an execution date. He lost the 1980 election and came back in 1982 with a promise that he would not commute any more life-without-parole sentences and set execution dates promptly. He kept his word and never again granted clemency or failed to sign an execution warrant promptly." Thomas Laqueur, "Festivals of Punishment," *London Review of Books,* October 5, 2000, 19.

32. The exchange occurred during the Second Bush-Dukakis Presidential Debate, October 13, 1988. See http://www.youtube.com/watch?v=DF9gSyku-fc (accessed January 28, 2010).

33. Assemblywoman Mayersohn, New York Assembly, March 6, 1995, 287. The phrase "tokens of esteem" is from Jonathan Simon and Christine Spaulding, "Tokens of Our Esteem," in Austin Sarat, ed, *The Killing State* (New York: Oxford University Press, 1999).

34. Douglas Hay, "Property, Authority and the Criminal Law," in Douglas Hay et al., eds., *Albion's Fatal Tree: Crime and Society in Eighteenth Century England* (New York: Pantheon Books, 1975), 17–64, at 49.

35. News coverage varies, of course. Some cases are primarily of local interest and

little noticed outside the county where the trial or execution takes place. In other instances—because of the notoriety of the defendant, the celebrity of the victim, the news value of the story, or the rarity of the event—the story makes the national or international news. See Christopher Kudlac, *Public Executions: The Death Penalty and the Media* (New York: Praeger, 2007); Craig Haney, *Death by Design: Capital Punishment as a Social Psychological System* (New York: Oxford University Press, 2005); Jeremy Lipschultz and Michael Hilt, "Mass Media and the Death Penalty: Social Construction of Three Nebraska Executions," *Journal of Broadcasting and Electronic Media* 43 (1999): 236–253; Marlin Shipman, *"The Penalty is Death": US Newspaper Coverage of Women's Executions* (Columbia: University of Missouri Press, 2002); and Susan Bandes, "Fear Factor: The Role of Media in Covering and Shaping the Death Penalty," *Ohio State Journal of Criminal Law* 1 (2004): 585–598.

36. Stephen Greenblatt, *Will in the World: How Shakespeare Became Shakespeare* (New York: Norton, 1994), 176.

37. James Christoph, *Capital Punishment and British Politics: The British Movement to Abolish the Death Penalty, 1945–57* (Chicago: University of Chicago Press, 1962), 96.

38. Stephanie Cohen, "Fry Baby," *New York Post,* January 31, 2007, available at http://www.nypost.com/p/news/regional/fry_baby_E6155J5hHLUmhJzdav MIDK (accessed January 12, 2010); Michael Brick, "Jury Agrees on Death Sentence for the Killer of Two Detectives," *New York Times,* January 31, 2007, A1.

39. See, for example, the *New York Post,* November 27, 2002, at 4: "A jury sentenced a dry-eyed and emotionless John Taylor to death yesterday . . . Taylor . . . sat dry-eyed and motionless as his fate was announced." Or the *Staten Island Advance:* "Wilson's face appeared drained and empty as the jury foreman handed down the capital sentence in a forceful voice. . . . On the other side of the courtroom, the victims' family members greeted the death sentence with shouts of 'yes!'" Jeff Harrell, "He Gets Death," *Staten Island Advance,* January 31, 2007.

40. William Miller, "Clint Eastwood and Equity: Popular Culture's Theory of Revenge," in Austin Sarat and Thomas Kearns, eds., *Law in the Domains of Culture* (Ann Arbor: University of Michigan Press, 1998).

41. Leigh Bienen, "What We Write About When We Write About the Death Penalty," *Journal of Criminal Law and Criminology* 89 (1999): 757.

42. Rock interviewed relatives of homicide victims and found that "[s]urvivors resented the more general transformation of homicide into entertainment of others." He quotes a letter of complaint sent by one survivor to a newspaper: "Modern society treats murder as entertainment, both in the world of the novel and the film, and also the closely reported real-life drama of a murder trial. The real tragedy, as shown by the devastation caused to the lives of loved ones left behind, does not make good reading and is therefore seldom explored." Rock, *After Homicide.*

43. See Lesser, *Pictures at an Execution.* Even the most public of recent execu-

tions, that of Timothy McVeigh, was an anticlimax from the media's point of view. Paul Farhi, "Networks' Quiet Coverage: Commercials Only Jarring Note in Reports on McVeigh," *Washington Post,* June 12, 2001, C1.

44. Quoted in Brian Lacy, "Man Repentant Before Execution for 1987 Beaumont Killing," *Huntsville Item,* January 21, 2004; and Amy Roberts, "Tyler Man Executed for 1995 Killing of Two Teenage Girls," *Huntsville Item,* August 25, 2004. A survey by the present author of execution reports carried by five local newspapers in death penalty states—*Huntsville Item, Houston Chronicle, Richmond Times-Dispatch, Tulsa World,* and *St. Louis Times-Dispatch*—between 1999 and 2004 showed some variation among newspapers, but the following items appeared in more than 70 percent of reports: final statement of the condemned, time of death, victim's age, whether the condemned expressed remorse or maintained innocence, witnesses to the execution, number of executions in the state, preceding and upcoming executions, description of death, and failed appeals.

45. David von Drehle, *Among the Lowest of the Dead: The Culture of Capital Punishment* (New York: Times Books, 1995), 393–395. See also Kudlac, *Public Executions.* John Wayne Gacy's execution provoked similar celebrations: "in downtown Chicago, hundreds of singing, laughing people, some wearing party hats, others dressed as clowns, marched through downtown in celebration of the impending execution." John Kifner, "Man Who Killed 33 Is Executed in Illinois," *New York Times,* May 10, 1994, A12. Jacoby and Bronson find that local (state) newspapers carry reports of all in-state executions; national newspapers carry a sizeable proportion; and TV news, a small proportion. Coverage by national TV and newspapers decreases as execution rates increase. The prominence and length of reports within states also diminish as executions become routine, though the local papers continue to carry reports on all events. Joseph Jacoby and Eric Bronson, "More Executions, Less News, Little Public Knowledge: News Coverage and Public Awareness of Executions in the U.S., 1977–2003" (Paper presented at the ASC meetings, Nashville, November 17–20, 2004). Anthony Parades and Elizabeth Purdum, "'Bye-bye Ted . . .': Community Responses in Florida to the Execution of Theodore Bundy," *Anthropology Today* 6 (April 1990): 9.

46. See, for instance, the following films: *In Cold Blood, Dead Man Walking, The Green Mile, Last Dance, The Executioner's Song,* and *The Chamber.* For discussions, see Austin Sarat, *When the State Kills: Capital Punishment and the American Condition* (Princeton, NJ: Princeton University Press, 2001); Richard Broughton, "Every Day More Wicked: Reflections on Culture, Politics and Punishment by Death," *Journal of Law and Politics* 22 (2006): 113–134; Philip Smith, *Punishment and Culture* (Chicago: University of Chicago Press, 2008). Most academic work focuses on a few high-profile movies that feature the death penalty very prominently, such as *Dead Man Walking* (1995); *Last Dance* (1996); *The Green Mile* (1999); *Monster's Ball* (2001); and *The Life of David Gale* (2003). But a much larger number of recent films and television movies feature the death penalty or death row inmates as a major part of the storyline. In a search of Internet Movie Database, Allmovie.com, and

Fancast.com, the author found that in every year between 1970 and 2008 there have been at least two (and usually many more) American movies that touch on the death penalty. Between 2000 and 2007 there were at least six movies each year, and in the 1990s, at least three such films each year. In 1995 and 1996 alone, eighteen different films per year featured or referenced the death penalty. Data on file with the author.

47. Stuart Banner, *The Death Penalty: An American History* (Cambridge, MA: Harvard University Press, 2002); Herbert Haines, *Against Capital Punishment: The Anti–Death Penalty Movement in America, 1872–1994* (New York: Oxford University Press, 1996).

48. For a different view, see Lynn Chancer, *Sadomasochism in Everyday Life* (New Brunswick, NJ: Rutgers University Press, 1992).

49. Samuel Gross and Phoebe Ellsworth, "Second Thoughts: American's Views on the Death Penalty at the Turn of the Century," Stephen Garvey, ed., *Beyond Repair? America's Death Penalty* (Durham, NC: Duke University Press, 2003), 7–57.

50. John McManners, *Death and the Enlightenment: Changing Attitudes to Death among Christians and Unbelievers in Eighteenth Century France* (New York: Oxford University Press, 1981). Rose describes "the peculiar pleasure images of execution always seem to release." Jacqueline Rose, "Getting Away With Murder," *New Statesman & Society* 1 (July 22, 1988): 36. It is notable, too, that videos of executions are a popular genre on YouTube. See http://www.youtube.com/results?search_query=execution+videos&search_type=&aq=0&oq=execution+ (last accessed Janury 30, 2010).

51. See the evidence provided in Chapter 2 above.

52. Miller, "Clint Eastwood and Equity."

53. Elias Canetti, *Crowds and Power* (Harmondsworth: Penguin, 1973), 56.

54. Several newspaper articles report on the public's fascination with "gallows trivia": see Kim Bell, "Prisoners Choices for Last Meals Become a Source of Fascination," *St. Louis Post-Dispatch,* June 20, 1999, A11; Andrea Weigl, "Prisoners' Last Meals Fascinate the Public," *Houston Chronicle,* January 22, 2006, A12; and Michael Graczyk, "Question of Taste: Ex-Prisoner Chef Book Details Last Meals He Cooked for Condemned," *Associated Press State and Local Wire,* February 13, 2004. A Texas Dept. of Corrections webpage that listed details of last meals was the department's most visited webpage.

55. "Condemned Man's Mask Bursts into Flame during Execution," *New York Times,* March 26, 1997, B9.

56. Personal communication from Allen Ault, former corrections commissioner for the state of Georgia, November 2007. The *New York Times* reports that the Georgia attorney general expressed "extreme disappointment" when the state's Supreme Court found the electric chair unconstitutional. Kevin Sack, "Supreme Court of Georgia Voids Use of Electrocution," *New York Times,* October 6, 2001, A8.

57. Cohen, "Fry Baby."

58. See Allen on how citizens engaged the question of capital punishment in ancient Greece. Danielle Allen, *The World of Prometheus: The Politics of*

Punishing in Democratic Athens (Princeton, NJ: Princeton University Press, 2000). By contrast, Huntsville, Texas, the national capital of executions, advertises itself to tourists as "Home of Ol' Sparky" and has a museum that features an electric chair. See *Fort Worth Star-Telegram,* July 20, 2006.

59. Dubber writes, "The only people who express a desire to inflict capital punishment personally are those who . . . will never be in a position to inflict it . . . By contrast, virtually everyone who actually participates in the system of capital punishment . . . struggles with the fundamental inhibition against inflicting the always physical violence of execution." Markus Dubber, "The Pain of Punishment," *Buffalo Law Review* 44 (1996): 580. For an analysis of statements to the press made by relatives of murder victims in the aftermath of the murderer's execution, see Samuel Gross and Daniel Matheson, "What They Say at the End: Capital Victims' Families and the Press," *Cornell Law Review* 88 (2002–2003): 486–516.

60. Canetti, *Crowds and Power.*

61. I borrow this phrase from Tom Laqueur.

62. This section draws on Gatrell, *The Hanging Tree.* The quotations from Dickens, Farge, and Bronfen are taken from Gatrell, *The Hanging Tree,* 243.

63. Gatrell, *The Hanging Tree,* 243.

64. Bronfen, *Over Her Dead Body,* x–xi.

65. Claudio Lomnitz, *Death and the Idea of Mexico* (New York: Zone Books, 2005), 15–17.

66. See Kearl for a discussion of America's "death-denying orientation" and its differences from cultures that are "death-affirming" or "death-defying." Michael Kearl, *Endings: A Sociology of Death and Dying* (New York: Oxford University Press, 1989), 6. James McPherson, "Dark Victories," *New York Review of Books,* April 17, 2008, at 78, writes that "modern America is, as many critics have noted, 'a death-denying culture' that tries to hide the inconvenient fact of dying." For a different account, see Thomas Laqueur's forthcoming study of the cultural history of death.

67. For an account of some very different cultural attitudes toward death, see Claudio Lomnitz, *Death and the Idea of Mexico* (New York: Zone Books, 2005).

68. On the historical and social conditions that produced this culture, see Philippe Aries, *Western Attitudes toward Death from the Middle Ages to the Present* (Baltimore, MD: Johns Hopkins University Press, 1974); Kearl, *Endings;* Geoffrey Gorer, "The Pornography of Death," *Encounter* 4 (1955): 49–52; and Norbert Elias, *The Loneliness of the Dying* (New York: Continuum, 2001).

69. Kearl, *Endings,* 438; Philippe Aries, "The Reversal of Death: Changes in Attitudes Toward Death in Western Societies," *American Quarterly* 26 (1974): 544.

70. Gorer, "The Pornography of Death," 51. See also Aries, "The Reversal of Death," 537.

71. I am grateful to Jonathan Gradess, New York State Defenders Association,

his assistant, Andy Davies, and Deborah Denno for information about the Gallego case.

72. See Robert Badinter, *Abolition: One Man's Battle against the Death Penalty* (Boston, MA: Northeastern University Press, 2008), 11 and 71, for a description of similar phenomena in France in the 1970s.

73. Scott Phillips, "Status Disparities in the Capital of Capital Punishment," *Law & Society Review* 4, 3 (2009): 807–837.

Acknowledgments

When I moved from Scotland to the United States just over a decade ago I had little familiarity with capital punishment. At the University of Edinburgh, I had taught courses on crime and punishment, but these seldom included lectures on the death penalty for the same reason that they neglected transportation, or banishment, or imprisonment with hard labor: in Britain, as in Europe more generally, capital punishment had little contemporary relevance. Living and working in the United States changed all that.

Like many sociologists, I was already interested in explaining why the United States is such an outlier in the severity of its criminal sentencing, and a study of the death penalty seemed like a way to get at that problem. After reviewing some thought-provoking books on the subject—by Austin Sarat, Stuart Banner, Franklin Zimring, and James Q. Whitman—I decided to investigate American capital punishment for myself. Embarking on death penalty research for the first time, I was soon overwhelmed with the bewildering complexity of the subject, its law, its procedure, its variable practice, its convoluted politics, and its extensive cultural resonance. That I was able to develop the expertise needed to carry out this work is entirely due to the generosity and patience of friends and colleagues here in the United States, and especially at New York University. Whatever is useful in this book is their doing and redounds to their credit.

My greatest debt is to my NYU Law School colleagues Bryan Stevenson and Tony Amsterdam, who took the time to answer my questions about the intricacies of capital punishment law and practice and to share their incomparable knowledge and experience. Other capital punishment experts from whom I also learned much (though they might say not enough) include Frank Zimring, Austin Sarat, Stuart Banner, Roger Hood, David Baldus, Carol Steiker, Jordan Steiker, Jeff Fagan, David Greenberg, and Valerie West. My historian friends Michael Meranze, Randall McGowen, Doug Hay, Dieter Reicher, Dan Hulsebosch, Tom Laqueur, and William Novak pointed me to sources, assisted me with drafts, and engaged me in constructive debate. Steve Bright and the staff at the Southern Center for Human Rights, Atlanta, Georgia, were generous hosts when I made a research visit to the center, particularly William Montross, who prompted me to read more about the morality play as a literary genre. Allen Ault, former commissioner of corrections for the state of Georgia, arranged for me to visit Georgia's execution facility and death row, and shared with me his recollections of death penalty politics in that state. Jonathan Gradess and Andy Davies of the New York State Defenders Association also came to my aid. I was helped by scholars in Europe, Australia, New Zealand, and South America who took the time to supply me with information about various aspects of capital punishment history, especially Jose Diez-Ripolles, John Pratt, Martin Killias, Mark Finanne, Claudio Giusti, Raquel Vaz-Pinto, Thomas Weigend, Pieter Spierenburg, and Tom Daems. I am grateful to them all.

NYU Law School Dean Ricky Revesz has been tremendously supportive in every way. So too have Dick Foley, in his capacity as dean of Arts and Social Sciences, and Dalton Conley, the then head of the Sociology Department. Thanks to them and to a fellowship from the J. S. Guggenheim Foundation, I was able to undertake full-time research for an eighteen-month period between 2006 and 2008. I am grateful, too, for funding from the D'Agostino and Greenberg Research Fund, which has, among other things, provided me with research assistance from a series of talented young lawyers and sociologists. Mitzi Dorland and Lisa Kerr were especially important in advancing my work, as were Owen Whooley, Gail Abbey, Allison McKim, David Fonseca, Stephen Milligan, Craig Heeren, Erin Braatz, Anthony Badaracco, and Robert Anselmi. I have been fortunate to have the assistance of Gretchen Feltes, an incomparable research librarian whose daily support has been invaluable. Larry Fleischer was also helpful in many ways, as was my law school assistant, Janelle Pitterson.

Once the initial draft was written, a number of friends and colleagues took take time away from their own work to help me with mine. Their criticism and advice have made this a better book. I owe a special debt of thanks to my close friend and colleague James B. Jacobs, who organized an all-day workshop on the manuscript, and to Philip Smith, Jeff Manza, Jerome Skolnick, Debby Denno, Stephen Morse, Bryan Stevenson, Rachel Barkow, and Stephen Schulhofer—as well as Jim himself—who took part in that workshop and provided me with comments that were extraordinarily insightful and constructive. Stephen Holmes, Barry Friedman, Jack B. Mackenzie, and Tom Daems also provided critical advice, as did four anonymous publisher's referees. I also learned much from conversations with Rick Pildes, Moshe Halberthal, Eva Cantarella, Laurent Muchielli, Wolf Heydebrand, and Issa Kohler-Hausmann, as well as from various seminar participants and lecture audiences in the United States and Europe.

At Harvard University Press, Joyce Seltzer and Christine Thorsteinsson edited the book with the intelligence and incisiveness for which they are renowned. It was a pleasure to work with them.

Finally, it is with love that I dedicate this book to my wife, Anne Jowett, and our daughters, Kasia and Amy—my fiercest, fondest critics.

Index

Pacification, of population *(continued)*
stages of, 132–133; state formation and, 131; in Western territories, 190
Page, Reginald, 140
Paine, Thomas, 136
Paley, William, 95
Pardon system, 81, 91, 293
Parker, Tom, 251
Parks, Rosa, 239
Parole, 88, 89, 355n35; life imprisonment without, 64, 98, 339n15; parole boards, 204
Pataki, Gov. George, 48, 63
Patton v Mississippi, 215, 218
Paules, Tracy, 2, 4
Payne v Tennessee, 50, 278, 279, 383n79
Peel, Robert, 345n16
Peine forte et dure (pressing to death), 70, 102
Penn, William, 115
Pennsylvania, 41, 42, 43, 87, 115, 372n83; capital defense bar, 203; death row inmates, 201; as former leading execution state, 200; hanging in, 117; prisons, 114; state constitution, 155
"People, the": criminal justice system and, 26; decision whether to retain death penalty, 263; democracy and, 142; democratizing jurisprudence and, 273, 279; jury selection and, 50; lynching and, 31, 33; metaphor of people's will, 61, 67–68
People v Anderson, 371n57
Philippines, 141, 348n54
Pierrepoint, Albert, 110
Pillory, 87, 145
Piracy with violence, 105
Poland, 141
Police forces, 76, 78, 89; attitudes toward death penalty, 289, 386n9; civil rights and, 210; police as murder victims, 282, 289, 293, 386n8; expenditures on, 197; local autonomy and, 159–160; private police powers, 123, 155, 161, 172, 190; professionalization of, 97, 133, 161; reaction to *Furman v Georgia,* 232; reduction in capital punishment and, 133–134, 345n16; violence of, 172
Popular justice, 13, 31, 32, 33, 125
Popular sovereignty, 36
Populism, 175, 181, 184; culture wars and, 251; democratizing jurisprudence and, 273; processes of representation and, 187; Supreme Court and, 191

Portugal, 21, 96, 99, 102, 112, 318n22
Postconviction process, 13, 44
Poverty, 10, 160, 167, 170, 383n82; blackness and, 242; Great Society programs against, 210
Powell, Christina, 1, 4
Powell, Justice Lewis, 225, 227–228, 259, 282–283; democratizing jurisprudence and, 274; juridification and, 267
Powell v Alabama, 215
Prison systems, 76, 104, 130, 133; American state power and, 153; local autonomy and, 160; mass imprisonment in United States, 10, 165, 182, 254, 291; in Northern and Southern states, 196–197; reformatory prisons, 88; threat of death sentences and, 289, 385n8; wardens, 57
Profitt v Florida, 258, 260, 378n4
Progressive period, 120, 158, 164, 183, 254n31, 355n35
Property crimes, 81, 91, 105
Proportionality, in sentencing, 216, 217
Protestantism, 179, 198, 359n75, 364n52; churches as critics of capital punishment, 212; humanitarianism and, 190. *See also* Christianity
Prussia, 77, 87, 102, 105, 129, 137. *See also* Germany
Psychiatry, 96
Psychology, abnormal, 96
Public opinion, death penalty and, 37, 230, 246, 329n68, 373n12, 375n53; abolition against majority, 130; annual number of executions and, 200; communal fears and, 132; death penalty as entertainment and, 301; declining support for death penalty, 211; in Democratic "blue" states, 204; *Furman v Georgia* and, 230, 233, 254; "law and order" politics and, 377n84; varieties of expression, 298–299; "victim-impact" statements and, 273. *See also* Opinion polls
Public sphere, 80, 175, 388n29
Public works projects, forced labor on, 76, 88, 103–104
Punishment: American Exceptionalism theory and, 23; collective, 136; corporal, 103, 104, 131; Islamic justice and, 50; substitutes for death penalty, 21

Quakenbass, Daniel, 36–37
Quakers, 147, 212

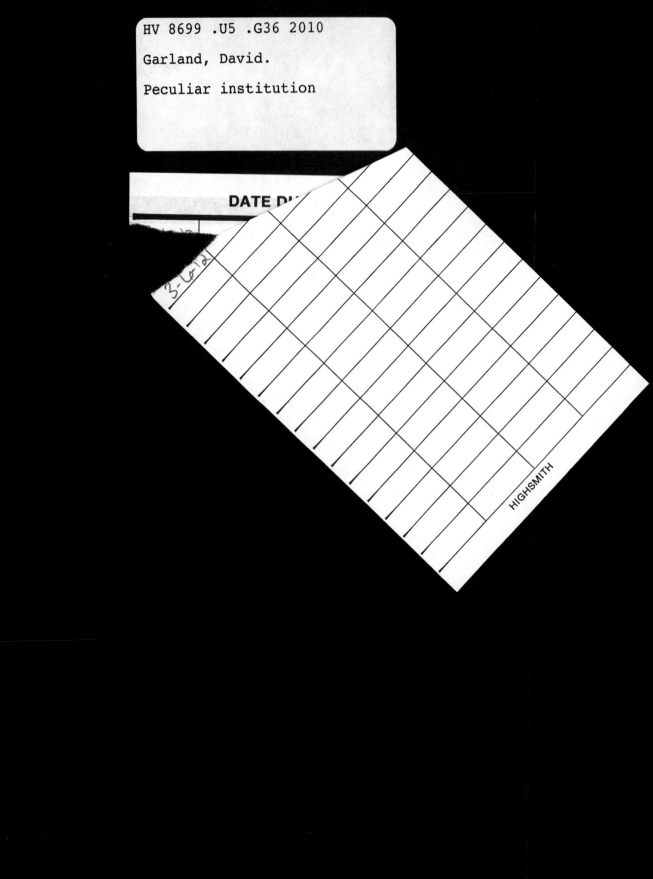